Religion in Chinese Society

A Study of
Contemporary Social Functions of Religion
and Some of Their Historical Factors

BY C. K. YANG

WAVELAND
PRESS, INC.

Prospect Heights, Illinois

For information about this book, write or call:

    Waveland Press, Inc.
    P.O. Box 400
    Prospect Heights, Illinois 60070
    (708) 634-0081

ISBN 0-88133-621-1

Printed in the United States of America

7 6 5 4 3 2 1

PREFACE

FOR MANY YEARS I have been perplexed by the problem of the place of religion in traditional Chinese society, especially the functional basis for the development of religious life and the organizational system by which the religious element in traditional living was propagated and perpetuated. The present volume is a modest attempt at analyzing this problem from the sociological approach. Among the sociological concepts, that of diffuseness and specificity (Talcott Parsons) has provided the interpretive key to the structural aspect of the problem.

In preparing the work for publication I am indebted to the following: to the Rockefeller Foundation, the Social Science Research Council, and the Trustees of Lingnan University for their generous financial assistance; to the administrators and my colleagues at the University of Pittsburgh for partial relief from teaching and for providing a hospitable environment; to the late Robert Redfield for his stimulation and support of my work and his incisive suggestions on this manuscript; to John K. Fairbank for his encouragement and help; to W. T. Chan and Arthur F. Wright for suggesting sources of information; to Howard Linton of Columbia University Library for generous assistance with library resources; to Robert and Aili Chin for their critical comments and suggestions; to Joyce Langford for help in typing the manuscript. Special thanks are due my wife, Louise Chin Yang, who contributed to the improvement of the manuscript, and my two sons, Wallace and Wesley, who once more endured the curtailment of family life in the course of my preparation of this volume.

C. K. Yang

University of Pittsburgh

CONTENTS

I   INTRODUCTION   1

II   RELIGION IN THE INTEGRATION OF THE FAMILY   28

III   RELIGION IN SOCIAL AND ECONOMIC GROUPS   58

IV   COMMUNAL ASPECTS OF POPULAR CULTS   81

V   POLITICAL ROLE OF CHINESE RELIGION IN HISTORICAL
PERSPECTIVE   104

VI   OPERATION OF THE MANDATE OF HEAVEN   127

VII   ETHICOPOLITICAL CULTS: "GUIDANCE BY THE WAY
OF THE GODS"   144

VIII   STATE CONTROL OF RELIGION   180

IX   RELIGION AND POLITICAL REBELLION   218

X   RELIGIOUS ASPECTS OF CONFUCIANISM IN ITS DOCTRINE
AND PRACTICE   244

XI   RELIGION AND THE TRADITIONAL MORAL ORDER   278

XII   DIFFUSED AND INSTITUTIONAL RELIGION IN CHINESE
SOCIETY   294

XIII   THE CHANGING ROLE OF RELIGION IN PRE-COMMUNIST
CHINESE SOCIETY   341

XIV   COMMUNISM AS A NEW FAITH   378

NOTES   405

BIBLIOGRAPHY   423

Contents

APPENDIX 1 *Functional Classification of Major Temples in Eight Localities*   436

APPENDIX 2 *Alphabetical List of Temple Names in Transliteration and in Chinese from Appendix 1*   452

APPENDIX 3 *Terms, Phrases, and Proper Names in Transliteration and in Chinese*   455

INDEX   459

I

INTRODUCTION

THIS STUDY is an attempt to answer the question: What functions did religion perform in Chinese social life and organization so as to provide a basis for its existence and development, and through what structural forms were these functions carried out? Hence, the basic purpose here is functional interpretation of critical facts in order to reveal a pattern of relationship between religion and the social order; no attempt is made to achieve a systematic and exhaustive presentation of data on Chinese religion.

For the purpose of this study, the structural viewpoint of Joachim Wach has been combined with the functional viewpoint of Paul Tillich in defining religion as the system of beliefs, ritualistic practices, and organizational relationships designed to deal with ultimate matters of human life such as the tragedy of death, unjustifiable sufferings, unaccountable frustrations, uncontrollable hostilities that threaten to shatter human social ties, and the vindication of dogmas against contradictory evidences from realistic experience. Such matters transcend the conditional, finite world of empirical, rational knowledge, and to cope with them as an inherent part of life man is impelled to seek strength from faith in such nonempirical realms as spiritual power inspired by man's conceptions of the supernatural.

The supernatural factor is an important component in our definition of religion here because of its prominence in Chinese religious life, the object of this study. This does not mean to ignore religious phenomena without supernatural expressions. But to lay emphasis on nonsupernatural religious forces as a factor in the social order would require extensive examination of the entire ontology and value system of a culture, as any dominant and enduring system of thought or values would inevitably be compelled to face the

ultimate problems of life and, because of the limitations of empirical rational knowledge, would develop in varying degrees concepts
of the ultimate, the unconditioned, the infinite, the eternal, and
lasting validity. Any elaborate consideration of this aspect of religion
lies outside the scope of this study. As the supernatural element has
been an outstanding mark of Chinese religious life, this study treats
the supernatural as a central component of Chinese religion, instrumental to traditional Chinese social organization; nonsupernatural aspects of religion will be discussed only where they are relevant.

The above conception is in close agreement with the traditional
Chinese notion of religion. In the traditional Chinese language,
several terms have been used in connection with religion. The word
chiao (guiding doctrine) is the closest equivalent to the Western
term "religion." Thus, there is *fo chiao,* or the religion of Buddha,
and there is *pai-yang chiao,* or the religion of the White Sun. Another Chinese term with the connotation of religion is *tao,* as used
in *hsien-t'ien* (pre-birth) *tao.* Tao means the Way, the great cosmological principle that governs the operation of the universe, including the human world; used in connection with religious beliefs
and organizations, it means a sect. There is the word *tsung,* meaning piety, devotion, or faith, and the word *men,* meaning door,
the door leading to enlightenment and salvation; in practical application both denote a religious sect. In the modern Chinese language, the term for religion is *tsung chiao* or a doctrine of faith.

The common denominator in all these terms is the concept of
the guidance of man,[1] and the idea of the supernatural is not etymo-
logically apparent. But in actual practice in Chinese religious life,
religion was built on the foundation of beliefs in gods and spirits
and on ritualistic acts and organizations stemming from such beliefs. Chinese classical discussions on religion took the supernatural
factor as the central subject and as the criterion of differentiation
between religious and nonreligious matters. Popular religious life
revolved around the idea of gods and spirits. The present Communist attack on religion has as its main target the belief in the
supernatural. No definition of religion which omits the supernatural
factor would be descriptive of the objective contents of popular
Chinese religious life.

Related to the supernatural factor is the term "superstition," which has been commonly used, particularly by the West, in characterizing Chinese religious life. Objectively, a superstition is an uncritically accepted belief in supernatural powers and its resultant practice or rite; it may be regarded as a part of magic in the sense that it implies not only nonempirical interpretation of natural and human events but also the human attempt to manipulate supernatural forces by either active control or negative avoidance. But in actual usage superstition is a subjective term, for it is generally employed by nonbelievers to signify disapproval of such beliefs or acts. As a part of magic, what is regarded as superstition will be included in the present study, because of the difficulty of separating magic from religion and because of the pervasion of magic in the religious life of China.

Existing Views on the Religious Character of Chinese Society

Among the three leading centers of civilization, Europe, India, and China, the place of religion in society is the least clearly recognized in the case of China. The place of religion in Chinese society has long been a controversial subject because of a number of seemingly contradictory factors in the situation. Viewing Chinese religious life on the folk level, one is inevitably struck by the vast number of magical practices and beliefs; the average man's mental picture of the universe—in fact, the whole pattern of his life—was heavily colored by a shadowy world of gods, spirits, and specters. Furthermore, a large proportion of such beliefs and practices carried no apparent ethical connotation. Because of this, the Chinese people were generally regarded as a superstitious lot who had yet to experience an ethicoreligious life of a higher order. This view was most familiar to the Western world, as it was popularized for over a century by Western missionaries who found this situation to be wholly incompatible with the Christian faith and took it as the most convincing justification for their evangelical zeal.

In addition to the permeation of magical influence, which the Christian West refused to treat as a part of religion, there were other baffling phenomena. Instead of social and political dominance by a religious doctrine and a powerful priesthood, there was the seemingly agnostic Confucian tradition of secular orthodoxy in which the leading scholar-official class were indoctrinated. There was no strong, centrally organized religion in most periods of Chinese history, and there appeared to be no protracted struggle between the church and the state. Confucian ethics dominated the system of social values, largely replacing the ethical function of religion as found in Christianity.

Great Western Sinologues such as Legge and Giles have emphasized the agnostic character of Confucianism. A later generation of Western scholars, who grew up under the influence of Legge and Giles and who became acquainted with Chinese culture through Chinese classical studies and through association with the Chinese educated class, assigned a relatively unimportant place to religion in Chinese society, leaving unexplained the universal presence of religious influence. Thus wrote Derk Bodde:

> The Chinese have been less concerned with the world of the supernatural than with the worlds of nature and of man. They are not a people for whom religious ideas and activities constitute an all-important and absorbing part of life . . . Before . . . the first century of the Christian era, China produced no thinker who could be classed as a religious leader . . . It is ethics (especially Confucian ethics), and not religion of a formal, organized type, that has provided the spiritual basis of Chinese civilization.[2]

Again, in a footnote, he elaborated:

> This does not mean that there have not been periods of intense religious activity in Chinese history . . . Nor does it mean that the Chinese masses have been free from superstitious beliefs; China is one of the richest storehouses in the world for the folklorist. Nevertheless, religion as such has been taken more lightly in China than in most other countries. It is significant that Confucianism, despite periods of eclipse, has for the last eight hundred years succeeded in retaining its dominance at the expense of both Buddhism and religious Taoism.

Modern Chinese scholars have developed the theme of the unimportance of religion in Chinese society to a much greater extreme.

A pioneer of this view was Liang Ch'i-ch'ao, who declared in the earlier part of this century:

. . . The history of religion consists of the story of theology and the change of religious organizations. Theology goes beyond the realistic world to talk about paradise, about the soul after death . . . From these two points, whether China has any religion or not is a question that merits serious study. Recently, some people who respect Confucius wish to make Confucianism a religion . . . First, for religion to succeed, it must utilize the vague emotions of man, which is incompatible with rationalism . . . Confucius is completely different from this; he confines his attention to realism, and his views are incompatible with religious elements. Secondly, there has been no religious organization by the Confucianists. If there are such organizations now, they are counterfeits . . . Since there is no religion among the indigenous products of China, what makes up the Chinese history of religion are mainly the religions introduced from foreign lands . . . The Zen School of Buddhism is a Chinese product, but it belongs more suitably to philosophy than to religion . . . Taoism is the only religion indigenous to China . . . but to include it in a Chinese history of religion is indeed a great humiliation. Their activities have not benefited the nation at all. Moreover, down through the centuries, they have repeatedly misled the people by their pagan magic and disturbed the peace . . .[3]

Of the cultured elite in China, Hu Shih said, "the educated people in China are indifferent to religion . . ."[4] Of China as a whole, he said, "China is a country without religion and the Chinese are a people who are not bound by religious superstitions. This is the conclusion arrived at by a number of scholars during recent years."[5] This view continued to characterize the attitude of a large section of modern Chinese intellectuals. The sweeping statement of Ch'ien Tuan-sheng, a political scientist, supplies another example:

. . . the Chinese are unreligious. No great religion . . . has captivated the bulk of the Chinese population as has been the case with other peoples. Mohammedanism and Christianity have come nearest to such success. But there are only 5 and 1 per cent, respectively, of the Chinese who are Mohammedans and Christians. At its height, between the fourth and eighth centuries, Buddhism was much more in vogue than Mohammedanism or Christianity at any time. But the influence of

Buddhism in China is more in the realm of thought and fine arts than in that of belief. Since the Chinese are unreligious, they may have superstitions, but rarely taboos ...[6]

The modern Chinese scholars' argument for the insignificance of religion in Chinese society was partly a reflection of the world trend toward secularization. Modern Europe emerged from a violent reaction against the medieval church. Science has given man the most powerful weapon yet known for unlocking the secrets of nature and for providing hitherto undreamed-of tangible benefits. Intellectually, this is an age of rationalistic orientation which waves off religion with defiance and even with contempt. It is quite natural for modern Chinese intellectuals, who have followed the West in exalting science, to catch the spirit of the times and to shun religion. But perhaps an even stronger motivation for the assumption of an "unreligious" or "rationalistic" society for China lies in the Chinese intellectual's necessity of emphasizing the dignity of Chinese civilization in the face of the political and economic superiority of the nationalistically oriented Western world. Liang Ch'i-ch'ao was frank when he regarded magical Taoism as a national humiliation. The only reason why any nation should feel humiliated at having developed a magical religion like Taoism is the contempt for religion in general, and for magical cults in particular, of an age when rationalism enjoys supremacy. Occultism was certainly no monopoly of the Chinese.

GENERAL IMPORTANCE OF RELIGION IN CHINESE SOCIETY

But the underevaluation of the place of religion in Chinese society did not find much support from reality. There was not one corner in the vast land of China where one did not find temples, shrines, altars, and other places of worship. The temples and shrines dotting the entire landscape were a visible indication of the strong and pervasive influence of religion in Chinese society, for they stood as symbols of a social reality.

Number of Temples in Local Samples

There are several local sample studies with statistical figures on temples. In Ting county of Hopei province, there was an average of 7 temples per village in 1882, and 1.9 temples in 1928. In terms of families, there was an average of 24 families per temple in 1882, and 50 families in 1928. In terms of population, there were about 600 persons per village in 1928, giving an average of one temple for approximately every 300 persons.[7] A comparative case is found in Wanchuan county of Chahar, where there were 6.5 temples per village in a study of 86 rural villages in 1947.[8] In Wang-tu county of Hopei province, an earlier picture of 1905 showed an average of 5.7 temples per village of 100 families or 500 persons, giving an average of one temple for every 17.7 families or 88.5 persons.[9]

These counties were all located in north China; for the rest of China there are no comparable data on a county basis presently available for this study. County gazetteers for south China contain records of only major temples, omitting smaller ones, particularly minor shrines, thus rendering the data uncomparable with those of north China. There are, however, a few samples of villages in south China that present a relatively complete record of temples and shrines. A field investigation of the village of Nanching in the vicinity of Canton in 1948 showed that there were eight temples, shrines, and ancestral temples for a total of 233 families, averaging one temple for every 30 families. In the village of Sang-yuan Wei in Shun-te county of Kwangtung province, there were five temples, shrines, and ancestral temples for a total of 161 families, averaging one temple to every 32 families.[10] If we take into consideration the general opinion that the people in the southern provinces had more magical cults than those in the north, the northern figures do not seem to reflect any exaggeration of the number of temples and shrines in proportion to the population when compared with the south.

Social Functions of Temples

The permeation of religion in Chinese society may also be seen in the wide range of functions served by the temples. In a mono-theistic religion people pray to one god for all their spiritual or magical needs, but in the Chinese polytheistic tradition people prayed to different gods for different purposes. Table 1 summarizes the functional classification of 1,786 major temples in eight localities distributed over five major sections of China proper. The first two

TABLE I

Functional Classification of Major Temples in Eight Localities According to the Nature of Main Gods in Each Temple *

FUNCTIONS	Wang-tu	Ch'ing-ho	Ch'uan-sha
	NUMBER OF		
I. Integration and well-being of social organizations	48	86	70
A. Kinship group	20	20	26
1. Marriage			
2. Fertility	19	19	24
3. Kinship values	1	1	2
B. Local community protection	3	8	14
C. The state	25	58	30
1. Figures symbolizing civic and political virtues	21	54	25
a. Civic and political figures	10	2	15
(1) Historic personalities	7	1	15
(2) Legendary figures	3	1	
b. Military personalities	11	52	10
2. Deities of justice	1	1	1
3. Patrons of the scholar-official class and the literary tradition	3	3	4
II. General moral order	26	73	20
A. Heavenly deities	14	61	3
B. Underworld authorities	12	12	17
III. Economic functions	12	10	21
A. Agricultural deities	12	10	17
B. Patrons of crafts and trades			2
C. Commerce and general economic prosperity			2
IV. Health	3	2	2
V. General public and personal welfare	10	13	2
A. Pantheons	2	1	1
B. Devil dispellers	1	1	

TEMPLES

Pao-shan	Lo-ting	Fo-shan	Sui-ning	Ma-ch'eng	Number	Percentage
93	59	78	71	97	602	33.7
29	3	31	9	23	161	—
1					1	—
26	2	30	8	22	150	—
2	1	1	1	1	10	—
26	24	15	12	36	138	—
38	32	32	50	38	303	—
34	26	24	43	31	258	—
22	17	9	28	19	122	—
21	14	4	24	18	104	—
1	3	5	4	1	18	—
12	9	15	15	12	136	—
1			1		5	—
3	6	8	6	7	40	—
28	64	117	37	41	406	22.7
10	11	31	29	25	184	—
18	53	86	8	16	222	—
29	18	17	25	11	143	8.1
17	12	8	24	8	108	—
7	4	7			20	—
5	2	2	1	3	15	—
3	1	8			19	1.1
16	4	20	3		68	3.8
1					5	—
		12			14	—

Table 1 (*Continued*)

Functions	Wang-tu	Ch'ing-ho	Number of Ch'uan-sha
C. Blessing deities	7	7	
D. Temples with unspecified gods		4	1
VI. Monasteries and nunneries	25	5	29
A. Buddhist	25	5	20
B. Taoist			9
Total	124	189	144

* For detailed data see Appendix 1.

counties, Wang-tu and Ch'ing-ho, are in north China. The next two, Ch'uan-sha and Pao-shan, are on the east China coast. Lo-ting county and Fo-shan district of Nan-hai county are situated in Kwangtung province of south China. Sui-ning county is in Szechwan province of west China. Ma-ch'eng county is a part of the central China province of Hupeh. The distribution of the eight localities over five sections of China is designed to show the common functional pattern of leading cults among major temples in these localities; the data of each place are not intended to present a systematic model of local religious life. The particular localities in each section of the country were selected on the basis of relative completeness of temple data in the local gazetteers which provide the sources for this table. Among the eight localities, Fo-shan district contains the urban center of Fo-shan, and Ch'uan-sha and Pao-shan both border upon Shanghai and are therefore subjected to urban influence, but the other localities are predominately rural in character.

The classification of temples according to function in Table 1 is relative, not absolute, due to the multifunctional nature of many, if not most, of the cults. But emphasis on certain functions is discernible in most of the cults. The reader should be aware that variations of temple cults reflect geographical and subcultural differences in diverse sections of the vast continental country. Common features among these localities lie in the generalized functional

TEMPLES

Pao-shan	Lo-ting	Fo-shan	Sui-ning	Ma-ch'eng	Number	Percentage
5		5	1		25	—
10	4	3	2		24	—
49	24	28	166	222	548	30.6
48	22	26	146	202	494	—
1	2	2	20	20	54	—
218	170	268	302	371	1,786	100.0

pattern, and not so much in the concrete cults. Even for certain national cults, the names and at times the functions of the same god vary from place to place.

Under the category of social organizations, temples concerning the family were mainly those of fertility cults such as the goddess of mercy (Kuan-yin) in the south and of the child-giving goddesses (Nai-nai or Niang-niang) in the north (Kuan-yin assumed the function of a general blessing goddess in the north without particular emphasis on fertility). Among the cults related to the family were those dedicated to exemplary deceased personalities who symbolized kinship values such as filial piety and chastity. Not only in the localities in this table but everywhere in pre-Communist China were found temples dedicated to fertility cults and to the unusually filial sons and chaste women of the community, a clear reflection of the core importance of the family in the social structure. But ancestor worship, the nucleus of religion devoted to consolidation of the family organization, is not indicated in the table because ancestral temples were not recorded in the gazetteers used for sources of information.

Temples devoted to protection and welfare of the local community include such common cults as *huo-shen* for the prevention of fire. But because of the generalized or comprehensive nature of community welfare, many other categories of temple cults also had significance for community organization. Thus, under the category of moral order, the national cults of *ch'eng-huang* (city god) and *t'u-ti* (earth god) also performed the function of protecting the community against hazards such as drought and fire, and mass worship of these gods either in crisis or at festivals during normal times served as rallying occasions to heighten the community consciousness of the local population. Many cults in the category of economic functions, such as those of the dragon god in the peasant communities and of trade patrons in urban localities, had similar implication for community interest. As to the cults having a distinct emphasis on community protection, wide divergences in concrete local expressions were due to the obvious influence of geographic and economic factors on cultic developments. Hence, the *hai-shen* (sea god) is peculiar to the coastal counties of Pao-shan and Ch'uan-sha, where tidal waves posed a major threat to the local community, and Fo-shan had eleven temples devoted to the fire god because of the fire hazard from the firecracker industry for which the community was well known. But these particular local religious expressions do not alter the functional pattern of cultic development on the generalized basis of community welfare and protection.

Temple cults that emphasized the operation of the state or political order included mainly deified personalities as symbols of civic, political, and military values. Such deities ranged from the legendary ruler Yao and the illustrious historical soldier Kuan Yü to contemporary meritorious officials and community leaders to whom either the state or the local elite attached importance as symbols of political values. Further consideration of this subject will be given in a later chapter on ethicopolitical cults. The cult of Confucius and the patron gods of the literary tradition lent support to the moral and structural position of the scholar-official group as a ruling class. The state cult of Heaven is not found in this table because of its confinement to the national capital of Peking, which is outside the eight localities in this table.

Temple cults devoted to the support of the general moral order of society included heavenly deities and underworld authorities. Many functional interpretations can be rendered for these two types of cults, but in the religious life of the common people the predominant idea of heaven and the underworld was the moral note of reward for good by the higher deities in heaven and punishment for evil by the fearful authorities of the underworld. By offering hope for the good and deterrent for the bad, and by supernatural explanations for ethically undeserved success and morally unjustified misfortune, the cults of heavenly powers and underworld authorities performed the important function of upholding society's moral order.

Temples related to economic life were dedicated to agricultural deities, who controlled the elemental forces and contributed to the cohesion of peasant communities; to patron gods and spirits of crafts and trades, who gave magical blessing for the success of occupational activities and served as spiritual nuclei for integration of occupational groups; and to gods of wealth, who helped individuals overcome the hazards of chance in the general struggle for prosperity. For a society based on irrigational agriculture, we would expect to find certain national cults common to all sections of the country, such as *hsien-nung t'an* (altar for the creator of agriculture, *shen-nung*) and a variety of water-controlling gods, especially the dragon gods under a variety of local designations. But special economic and geographical influences were reflected in such local cults as the insect gods worshiped in localities north of the Yangtze River, where such insect pests as locusts caused repeated extensive damage, and the tree gods in the mountainous county of Sui-ning, where forestry was an important industry. Craft and trade cults developed in close relation to local occupations. While the cult of *ts'ai-shen* (god of wealth) was a national one, the particular gods worshiped for the purpose of general economic prosperity by the common people, especially the merchants, varied in different localities. Very often, Kuan Yü, the god of righteousness and war, was worshiped for this purpose.

In the category of health, there were temples dedicated to deities specializing in medicine or in dispelling epidemics. But people also prayed to other gods to heal sicknesses, for almost any spiritual being was potentially a magical healer. Gods in the health category were only those who were especially noted for their healing function.

Finally, there was the category of temples with deities who did not emphasize any specific function but gave general blessings to individuals and groups who offered supplications of any nature in personal and public life, especially in times of crisis.

Buddhist and Taoist monasteries and nunneries as a separate category of religious establishments need an explanation. Some monasteries and nunneries were open to the public for worship, but many were accessible only to a clientele of lay worshipers. In either case, they may be regarded as temples for the general welfare of the people. But another aspect of monasteries and nunneries was that they served as relatively secluded residences for monks and nuns who tried to lead a life completely dedicated to the teachings of the gods in the hope of salvation of their souls. Thus, inside the walls, each monastery or nunnery represented a miniature sacred order of life different from the secular social order, presumed to be perfect, capable of correcting all the imperfections of the material world and designed for saving men from everlasting suffering. Monasteries and nunneries provided a place for a dedicated spiritual life for the religiously devout, presenting a concrete picture of a sacred order of life as a model for the salvation of a suffering world, and supplying a center for the training and ordaining of priests and clerics who performed religious services for the laymen. As such, monasteries and nunneries may be regarded as the integrating centers of Chinese religious life.

The proportion of temples in each category to the total number of temples does not always measure the relative importance of religion in each aspect of social life. This is partly due to the multifunctional nature of deities. For example, temples of the health category ranked among the lowest in number among the functional categories, and yet L. Newton Hayes' study disclosed that 96.6 per cent of 500 prayer slips in the temples were related to the healing of disease. This is apparently the result of the belief in the omnipotency of all deities; the appeal to almost any god or spirit was believed to be efficacious for good health. The priest of a temple for the fire god in the village of Nanching in Kwangtung province told the writer that some 80 per cent of the worshipers who visited the temple in 1948 prayed for the return of health. Hayes' analysis of the social functions of prayer slips presented in Table 2 shows the multifunctional nature of the popular cults.[11]

TABLE 2

Distribution of Social Functions in 500 Prayer Slips

FUNCTIONS	NUMBER OF PRAYER SLIPS CARRYING EACH FUNCTION	PERCENTAGE TO TOTAL OF 500
Healing of diseases	484	96.8
Marriage	459	90.2
Traveling mercies	440	88.0
Wealth	424	85.0
Lawsuits	391	78.2
Progeny	348	70.0
Family problems	348	70.0
Lost articles	346	69.2
Moving (household)	308	60.2
Business affairs	290	58.0
Crops	273	54.6
Domestic animals	266	53.2
Official position	246	50.0

In spite of this limitation, it is interesting to note the high proportion of temples having some bearing upon the functioning of social relations, ranging from the welfare of the family, protection of the community, and operation of the state to the maintenance of moral order in society. Under the economic category, patron gods of trade guilds as well as general gods of wealth were also related to the integration of social groups and successful human relations. Monasteries and nunneries were designed for the reform of social relations in an imperfect world. All these structures tend to show the important role of religion in the operation of traditional Chinese society. Hayes' study shows a similar emphasis on social relations in the prayer slips.

In Chinese villages, the largest and most impressive buildings were generally religious structures. Even in towns and cities, only government office buildings sometimes surpassed the temples in size and impressiveness. In fact, some of the largest and most artistic buildings in China were religious structures. The gigantic timbers and extremely heavy stones used in the construction of many temples were often hauled from great distances at huge expense. Inasmuch as each temple represented the collective effort of social groups and frequently a whole community, the temple and the religion it symbolized must have loomed very large in the people's mind to command allocation of such huge financial and human resources for its construction.

The importance of temples in the collective life of local communities can be shown in one example. In the above-mentioned village of Nanching, the villagers in the summer of 1949 unstintingly spent the equivalent of about $500 in United States currency for the temple festival celebrating the birthday of the earth god, the community patron deity, while they failed to raise a similar amount for an irrigation reservoir for the village, or to raise one-third of that sum for a literacy class for underprivileged children. No "unreligious" people long under the ordeal of economic hardship would allocate such heavy financial support for a religious occasion at the sacrifice of an irrigation or an educational project.

Other Expressions of Religious Influence in Chinese Social Life

Temples and shrines as places of public worship were only one of the many expressions of religious life of the people. Numerous religious activities did not take place in public. In a sense, every traditional Chinese home was a religious shrine, for it contained spirit tablets of the ancestors, and pictures and idols of many household deities. Not included as a part of public worship were the myriad religious observances centering about food, clothing, shelter, travel, marriage, birth, death, and many other crises in the life of an individual. Not comprehensively expressed in the statistics of temples were the ideas of the world of gods and spirits implanted in the minds of the people by the rich store of mythological lore. The images of gods and spirits came to vivid life in stories told among adults as well as in nursery tales for children, so that in the popular mind the world of spirits intermingled intimately with the world of man. Even many agnostic modern Chinese intellectuals retain a childhood memory of sensing the realistic presence of the ancestors' spirits in front of the shadowy ancestral altar on a dark night. And many a southern boy, before urinating in a dark street corner at night, would announce in a low voice, "I am going to urinate. Please stand aside," so that some carelessly wandering spirit would not be splashed unawares. Among the untutored populace—children and adults alike—a day scarcely ever passed without some thought being devoted to the supernatural meaning of one's daily activities. In the traditional days, it was not the Confucian classics that enjoyed the widest sale, but the *li shu,* the almanac, that gave not only climatological information for agriculture but also magical guidance for activities in daily life.

Religion also permeated the wider cultural setting. Chinese historiography and philosophy were under the influence of theological interpretations. It is a familiar fact that neither of the two dominant strands of Chinese thought, Confucianism or Taoism, escaped the tinge of religion. The mysticism in Taoism was seized by the magical cults and developed into the Taoist religion. In Confucianism, Buddhist influence is plainly visible not only in neo-Confucian theories of cosmology and of problems of "mind and nature," but also in the adoption of the Buddhist technique of meditation by large numbers of Confucians. The theology of Yin-yang (negative and positive) and the Five Elements (metal, wood, water, fire, and earth) penetrated both Taoism and Confucianism.

In literature, no traditional fiction that at all reflected Chinese realism would omit the religious element in depicting human crises. Even the secular novel *Dream of the Red Chamber* climaxed its plot by using Buddhist conversion as an escape for its romance-tortured hero. Above all, mythological fiction was immensely popular among common readers and professional storytellers who spun tales to the illiterate populace. The following example indicates the realistic effect of such mythological tales: In 1953, the Chinese Communist government issued a directive against the reading of mythological fiction, citing its "evil influence" in the case of a handicraft apprentice who, in the same year, escaped from home and tried to go to the Szechwan mountains in search of Taoist magicians who might teach him the secret of immortality.[12]

In the field of poetry and prose, a distinguished and refreshing note found in many masterpieces was the emancipation of man from his mundane struggle and the lifting of his spirit to the loftier plane of a greater universal destiny. An instance is the well-known passage in the prose *Huang-chou chu-lou chih* (The Bamboo Chamber of Huang-chou), written by Wang Yü-ch'ing, a harassed official of the Sung period who was banished to the Yangtze frontier district of Huang-chou (Hupeh province), which was then nearly covered by bamboo forests. Describing the life and the surroundings of the "bamboo chamber" he had built for himself, he said,

After the official duties of the day, . . . I would hold a volume of the *Chou I* [a book of cosmology and divination], burn some incense, sit in meditation, and dismiss worldly thoughts. Besides the river and the mountains, all that meets one's eyes are sails before the wind, birds on the sand beaches, haze and clouds and the bamboo forests.

In this passage, there was of course the obvious echo from the Taoist philosophy of man returning to nature. But the religious influence was also unmistakable in the mention of the mystic book of *Chou I* and the Buddhist practice of meditation as a means of dismissing "worldly thoughts," elevating man's spirit above ephemeral mundane drives, seeking communion with the eternal truth of the universe. That such a world-forsaking note became pronounced in poetry and prose after the period of disunion (A.D. 221–589) was apparently connected with the rooting of Buddhism in Chinese culture.

It is well recognized that religion has contributed much to the basic motifs in Chinese art, particularly decorative art.[13] The lotus motif from Buddhist influence is a prominent example. Few pieces of elaborate traditional decoration omitted the religiously inspired patterns of the cloud, the dragon, the phoenix, or the Taoist fairies. And quite often, religious symbols in art and architecture remained as the only visible trace of many foreign groups who once played potent roles in Chinese history. It was their religious expression in art, not the once mighty structure of their secular power, that successfully withstood the corrosion of time. Thus, the impressive religious art of the Tatung grottoes in northern Shansi are among the few reminders of the historical presence of the once powerful To-pa people of Northern Wei (A.D. 386–534) and the Khitan people of the Liao dynasty (A.D. 907–1125).[14]

As will be seen in later chapters, the concept and structure of all major Chinese social institutions contained religious elements. In this connection, a point that has been subjected to much discussion is the political institution of the Chinese state. The lack of a protracted struggle between organized religion and the state has often been used to suggest freedom of the state from religious influence. Actually, the concept of the Chinese state from the dawn of history down to the Ch'ing period (1644–1911) was inseparable from theological myths. Bloody suppression of religious movements was an outstanding characteristic of nineteenth-century China.[15] As late as 1959, the Communist government was still carrying on a relentless campaign against certain religious societies as counter-revolutionary groups.[16] The lack of sufficient organized strength in religion to oppose the state does not indicate an absence of struggle between the two. It is apparent that a "rationalistic" society or an "unreligious" people could hardly have developed such powerful religious forces as the White Lotus sect that helped found the great Ming dynasty, the Taiping T'ien-kuo that shook the foundations of the Ch'ing dynasty, and the many sectarian movements that still give the present Communist authorities cause for worry. It will not help the understanding of the nature of Chinese society to simply dismiss these movements as products of mere superstitions of an ignorant populace.

Much of the underestimation of religion in China stems from the rationalistic features of Confucianism. But the rationalistic qualities of Confucianism alone did not appear adequate to meet the challenge from the vast domain of the unknown, to explain convincingly the extraordinary phenomena of society and nature, to deal with frustration and shock from tragedies in the crises of life, including death, to lift man's spirit above the level of selfish and utilitarian involvement in the mundane world so as to give man a higher cause for unity and harmony with his fellow man, or to justify the enduring soundness of the moral order in the face of morally unaccountable success and failure. These and other associated questions of life and society led to the inevitable development of religion in China, as in other cultures.

APPROACH, SCOPE, AND DATA OF THIS STUDY

The existing controversial viewpoints and the vast volume of literature on Chinese religion, together with the undoubted omnipresence of religious influence in Chinese life, leave the place of religion in Chinese society obscure. An important reason for the obscurity is the lack of structural prominence of a formally organized religious system in the institutional framework of Chinese society, which leads to the frequent interpretation that the numerous popular cults are unorganized and are of little importance in the Chinese social and moral order. Even Max Weber, who attached great importance to religion, characterized the cultic situation in China as "a chaotic mass of functional gods." This interpretation is largely the result of viewing the religious situation in Chinese culture from the pattern of the Christian world, where religion has a formal organizational system and has occupied a prominent structural position in the organizational scheme of Western society.

Applying the structure-function approach to Chinese society, we can discern two structural forms of religion. One is institutional religion, which has a system of theology, rituals, and organization of its own, independent of other secular social institutions. It is a social institution by itself, having its own basic concepts and its own structural system. The other is diffused religion, with its theology, rituals, and organization intimately merged with the concepts and structure of secular institutions and other aspects of the social order. The beliefs and rituals of diffused religion develop their organizational system as an integral part of the organized social pattern. In the diffused form, religion performs a pervasive function in an organized manner in every major aspect of Chinese social life. Thus, the weakness of formally organized religion in China does not mean the lack of functional importance or of a structural system of religion in Chinese culture.

Employing this approach, we will first demonstrate the place of religion in the Chinese kinship system, in extrafamilial social and economic groups, in the Chinese community, in the Chinese state, in Confucianism as an institutionalized orthodoxy, and in the general moral order. Then we will evaluate the relative positions of institutional and diffused religions in traditional Chinese society. Finally, we will summarize the recent trends of development of the functional role of religion in contemporary Chinese society. In this scheme of treatment, the functional position of religion in Chinese society is emphasized.

This study is confined mainly to the religious systems that have become firmly integrated parts of the Chinese culture. These include Buddhism, Taoism, and the numerous cults of the classical religion. Buddhism is of foreign origin, but it has been so assimilated into Chinese culture that the untutored common man in China is no longer aware that it was introduced from India. Both Christianity and Mohammedanism remain outside this treatment, because they have not attained a similar degree of acculturation; their theology and ethics are not reflected in the life of the common people, and their converts constitute only a small percentage of the population.

In terms of time, the present study is primarily concerned with the recent periods of Ch'ing and the Republic, especially the nineteenth and twentieth centuries. But the roots of Chinese cultural traits extend deep into the past, and an understanding of their present structural and functional position often requires probing into their historical origin and development. Therefore, historical data and discussion will be used in this study to the extent needed to clarify the modern structure and function of religion in Chinese society. Such treatment is of course neither complete nor adequate in the historical sense, but the systematic treatment of the historical development of Chinese religion is properly another task.

An associated methodological device is the use of quotations from the classics. The value of classical quotations for this study lies in their popular acceptance as authoritative statements in guiding thought and behavior in modern life. We are, therefore, not concerned with the age of such statements, nor with their textual authenticity and attributed authorship. Classical statements will be employed wherever they remain effective guiding concepts in a modern social situation involving the role of religion.

The shortage of factual data on Chinese religion, particularly concerning its function and structure, has confronted this study as it has plagued other scholars interested in the functional role of religion in Chinese society.[17] A relatively unexplored source of data is the vast number of Chinese local gazetteers. Thus, said E. R. Hughes, ". . . any study of a county gazetteer . . . will reveal enough material for a large size book on the local ancestral fanes, local deity shrines and Taoist and Buddhist temples, all there in addition to the temple in honor of Confucius. So far these gazetteers have been almost entirely neglected by Western scholars . . ."[18] For the present study, an explorative effort has been made to utilize about a dozen local gazetteers selected to cover five major regions of China proper. From this source, information has been obtained on the types of temples and the popular cults in different localities. Table 1 on the functional groupings of temples is an outcome of this material. The high frequency of certain types of temples indicates the existence of a national system of many of the popular cults. Extensive use has also been made of the inscriptions on temple steles, for they tell of the hagiography and functions of the gods and spirits to whom the temples were dedicated, and thus afford insight into the relation between the cults and social life.

Limited use has been made of an additional source, the mythology and lore contained in fictional literature. These were an outstanding source of religious knowledge for the Chinese people, who either read them directly or heard them from others who had read them. From these stories, and not from sermons, the Chinese learned about the magical powers of the gods, about the fearfulness of evil spirits, about peace and abundance in Heaven, and about the hideous terror of Hell. While most of these mythological stories were written by Chinese scholars, they were not purely the products of imagination entirely divorced from the context of social life. Many of these stories were popular lore for some time before they were written down with modifications and embellishments. Hu Shih showed that that great mythological fiction, *The Journey to the West* (translated by Arthur Waley under the title *The Monkey*) had had a long historical growth from folklore before it assumed its present written form.[19] And mythological heroes in these stories, such as the Monkey in *The Journey to the West,* the Chen-wu (True Military) god in the *Pei-yu Chih* (Journey to the North), and Erh-lang (Second Son) in *Feng Shen* (The Investiture of the Gods), had been deified into popular cults, with many temples built for them in different parts of the country. Mythological lore thus became a part of the development of popular cults in China. As to the influence of such lore, the foregoing story (pp. 17–18) of the apprentice who went to the mountains in search of immortality in 1953 attests to the spell they still hold in the popular mind.

The emphasis of this study is on the analysis and interpretation of the structural and functional role of religion in Chinese society, leaving the systematic description of Chinese religious systems to other works, of which there are already a large number. But there are several points about Chinese religious systems that deserve brief mention here.

While Taoism and Buddhism enjoyed general recognition as formal systems of religion, the original indigenous religion of China has frequently been neglected in historical accounts.[20] We may call this the classical religion because it attained full development in the classical periods of Chou (1122–221 B.C.) and early Han before the foreign influence of Buddhism and the rise of Taoism as a religion. Any general survey of modern Chinese religious life would reveal the widespread influence of classical beliefs and their deities. The core of classical religion was the worship of Heaven and its pantheon of subordinate deities, and the worship of ancestors. It was premised upon the classical statement in *Li Chi* (Book of Rites), "All things stem from Heaven, and man originates from ancestors." Heaven was the supreme anthropomorphic power of the universe directing the operation of the spiritual world. There was a general dichotomy in this spiritual world. At the top was the grand pantheon of gods (*shen*), each of whom was assigned definite functions in the governing of both men and spirits. Below the gods were the multitudes of spirits or ghosts (*kuei*), who constituted the common subjects of the spiritual world.

This system of belief was already well developed by the classical time of Confucius. Later, it was further formulated into the theological system of Yin-yang and the Five Elements as operational principles of the universe and the human world. Cultic symbols were developed to objectify spiritual beings in the form of tablets, images, pictures, and associated sacred objects. Rituals were devised for man to seek communion with the spiritual realm, by sacrifice, divination, and a large variety of magical practices. Thus, classical religion had its theology and its system of rituals.

The importance of classical religion was demonstrated in Grootaers' study of the temple cults in Wanchuan county of Chahar province.[21] Table 3 gives the distribution of the cults. What Groo-

TABLE 3

Distribution of Cults in Wanchuan County
According to Major Religions

RELIGIOUS IDENTIFICATION	NUMBER OF CULTIC UNITS	PERCENTAGE
Buddhism	169	19.7
Taoism	78	9.1
Popular religion	604	71.2
Total	851	100.0

taers called popular religion corresponds generally to classical religion. The predominance of this religious system was further expressed by Grootaers: "In the reality of everyday life, the proportion [of popular religion] is even greater; except half a dozen temples which are managed by monks (Buddhist or Taoist), all temples (or 99 per cent of 569 temples) are a grand common pantheon."

The fact that Buddhism and Taoism, rather than the classical religion, have claimed the main attention of students of Chinese religion is due to several factors. Both Buddhism and Taoism had an articulate religious elite to propound their views by producing a voluminous literature, which frequently appropriated classical theological ideas, deities, and cultic traditions for their own. In the second place, the once influential classical priesthood had long been reduced to the status of professional magicians who operated mainly as unorganized individuals. Thirdly, the theology, rituals, and organization of the classical religion had long been diffused into major secular institutions, particularly the political institution of the state. When Confucian scholars propounded the classical theology, they often treated it as a part of the basic concepts of the secular institutions. Existing mainly in a diffused form, classical religion as a separate system became relatively obscure.

A relevant point here is the highly eclectic nature of Chinese religion. In popular religious life it was the moral and magical functions of the cults, and not the delineation of the boundary of religious faiths, that dominated the people's consciousness. Even priests in some country temples were unable to reveal the identity of the religion to which they belonged. Centuries of mixing gods from different faiths into a common pantheon had produced a functionally oriented religious view that relegated the question of religious identity to a secondary place. An example is the Ch'eng-huang Miao, the temple of the city god, which was found practically in every major locality in China. Ch'eng-huang, the city god, was claimed to be of Taoist creation, but this deity was mentioned in classical Chou times, long before Taoism became a religion. In every temple of the city god there were the inevitable frescoes depicting the Buddhist conception of the Ten Courts of Hell, scenes of subterranean punishment of the dead for misdeeds during their lifetime. Identification of each of these cults with certain religions might interest the savants but hardly occurred to the common worshiper who entered the temple to make supplication. Hence, in this study, we are not concerned with religious identification but only with the functional significance of the cults. The functional orientation of the popular religious tradition, involving a division of labor among the cults, probably reconciled some of the theological contradictions between cults of different faiths and introduced a feeling of consistency in the mixing of gods into one pantheon.

In the preceding discussion Confucianism was not included as one of the major religious systems. Is Confucianism a religion? The answer to this familiar question clearly must vary with one's definition of religion. In a broad sense, religion may be viewed as a continuum ranging from nontheistic belief systems with an emotional intensity that borders upon ultimacy, to theistic belief systems with ultimate values fully symbolized in supernatural entities and supported by patterns of worship and organization. Many nontheistic systems of thought or action, such as Communism, may have the qualities of a religion and may perform some of the basic psychosocial functions of full-fledged theistic religions. Nontheistic belief systems are what J. Milton Yinger regards as functional alternatives to theistic religion.[22] As stated previously, this present study lays emphasis on theistic religion, with the supernatural as a prominent factor. Viewed in this light, Confucianism is not treated here as a full-fledged religion in the theistic sense, but as a sociopolitical doctrine having religious qualities. Confucianism set up no god as the premise of its teachings, and its basic principles were developed mainly from pragmatic considerations. Even the infusion of Buddhist ideas into neo-Confucianism did not alter its basic this-worldly orientation. Confucianism did address itself to the ultimate meaning of life and death, but only in terms of moral responsibility to man, not to any supernatural power. The religious nature of Confucianism as a system of thought lies in its furtive treatment of the ideas of Heaven and fate as an answer to human problems unaccountable for by knowledge or in moral terms. And Confucianism as a practiced doctrine received support from the cult of Confucian worship and from many supernatural ideas and cults associated with the functioning of the Confucian tradition.

The frequent treatment of Confucianism as a religion in Western literature came partly from the influence of the Christian tradition, in which the formulation and enforcement of moral values was a dominant function of religion, for the moral values of Confucianism had long held undisputed dominance and acceptance in Chinese society. Confucianism was at times considered a religion by Western scholars adopting the functional approach, which gave a recognized religious quality to nontheistic belief systems dealing with the ultimate meanings of life, for Confucianism did develop a system of ultimate moral meaning. The treatment of Confucianism as a religion is quite defensible from either of the two views. But for this study we are interested only in analyzing the religious factors in the development of Confucianism as an effective sociopolitical tradition, whether such factors existed as an inherent part of the doctrine or developed outside it as associated cults. Hence we regard Confucianism as a sociopolitical doctrine having religious qualities. Chapters x and xi will deal with the religious nature of Confucianism and the function of religion in the traditional moral order.

II

RELIGION IN THE
INTEGRATION OF THE FAMILY

THE CHINESE COMMON PEOPLE have always felt that, even with the utmost exertion, human abilities and efforts alone were not sufficient to guarantee physical well-being, economic success, or family harmony. There was always the profound feeling that success or failure in these respects was not entirely within human control, but needed the blessing of spiritual forces.

The influence of religion on traditional Chinese family life was everywhere visible. Upon entering any house, one saw paper door gods either painted in colorful portraits or written in Chinese characters, posted on the doors for protection of the house and its family members against possible invasion by evil spirits. Near the door and on the floor was an altar to T'u-ti, the earth god, who protected the family against destructive influences, and who saw that the members of the family behaved themselves with religious and social propriety. T'ien-kuan, the Heavenly Official, was in the courtyard, and the wealth gods, who brought well-being and prosperity to the family, were in the hall or the main room of the house. There was the inevitable Tsao-shen, the kitchen god, on or near the cooking stove, who at the end of the year made an annual report to the Jade Emperor, the supreme god in Heaven, regarding the conduct and behavior of the family and its members, a report that would result in reward or punishment. Religiously devout families would also have an altar for the goddess of mercy or another preferred deity as special patron of the family's well-being. In times of crises or special events such as birth, marriage, or death, or on traditional festival days, there was generally an outburst of religious activity in front of the altars of the many deities in a residential house. At such times, an atmosphere of sacredness and reverence pervaded every aspect of traditional Chinese family life, and the home became a complex center of religious worship.

While household deities were regarded as important for the protection of the property and health of the family and for the promotion of prosperity and harmony in the home, by far the most vital religious element in family life was the worship of ancestors, a cult that contributed substantially to the integration and perpetuation of the family as a basic unit of Chinese society.

The importance of this cult in Chinese family life was indicated by the ancestral altar in the main hall or room in every house, the altar that held a number of wooden spirit tablets, each of them representing a dead ancestor.[1] The presence of the tablets, the ever-burning lamp in front of them that radiated a dim glow, the incense and candles that were periodically offered to them, the religious ceremonies that were performed for them, all suggested that the symbols of the dead continued to occupy a place in the family activities of the living, that the dead in the shadowy world continued to oversee the conduct of the existing members of the family and took part in an invisible way in their struggle for happiness and prosperity. The struggle of the living generation for success and happiness was, in fact, regarded as a continuation of the ancestor's struggle and, through this, the cult of ancestor worship gave the departed predecessors a continuing role among the living generation. The traditional-minded Chinese, to whom this cult was supremely important, greatly feared that an irredeemable calamity might befall the young modern generation who refused to continue the ancestral sacrifices.

The cult of ancestor worship was basically a device to cope with the emotionally shattering and socially disintegrating event of the death of an intimate member in the family group. The living developed a deep emotional, social, and economic dependence on the dead, particularly if the deceased were a mature person who had raised a family. The sudden and irretrievable severance of such a person from the living engendered not merely emotional grief threatening the psychic integrity of the intimate living members of the family, but it also stunned them with dismay and indecision as to how to proceed with life. To whom could the living now turn for comfort, companionship, and economic support? And how could the living face the feeling of emptiness and futility that suddenly descended upon family activities, as characterized by the familiar Chinese poetic line, "Grief is futile as the person is gone, leaving but an empty chamber"?

Obviously, the event of death could not be treated with the cynical attitude expressed by Yang Chu over two thousand years ago and frequently heard in contemporary conversations about death: "[When I die] they may burn my body, or cast it into deep water, or bury it, or leave it unburied, or throw it wrapped in a mat into a ditch." [2] This might be acceptable to the dead or to extremely individualistic thinkers like Yang Chu. But not so to the living, to whom death was not an individual matter but a social tragedy involving the permanent removal of a member from the group. If death was final to the dead, it lingered on among the living who dreaded it, who emotionally refused to accept it, and who faced the task of carrying on life in spite of it.

One alternative to the tragic situation was to assume the continued existence of the deceased and use this assumption to mitigate emotional grief and demoralization, and for the family group to rally their efforts and carry on the business of the living. One expression of this assumption was the belief in the existence of the soul, and another was the perpetuation of the memory of the departed. The elaborate cult of ancestor worship developed from this assumption. In the Confucian tradition emphasis was laid upon perpetuation of the memory of the dead, a point that will be elaborated on later. But it was the belief in the continued existence of the dead in the form of the soul and the further assumption of mutual dependence between the soul and the living that gave rise to much of the cultic behavior in ancestor worship.

Technically, the cult may be viewed as being composed of two major parts, namely mortuary rites which immediately followed death, and sacrificial rites which maintained the long-term relationship between the dead and the living.

BASIC COMPONENTS OF MORTUARY RITES

Mortuary rites, *sang li,* were a complex group of cultic practices that varied considerably in details in different localities, but with basic similarities throughout China. From an already rich descriptive literature in both Western and Chinese languages, we can discern the following fundamental types of cultic behavior.

For the Benefit and Salvation of the Soul

From the refusal to accept the finality of death, there developed a group of religious acts which aimed at the comfort and happiness of the dead in the other world. The very elaborateness of such acts and their symbolic meaning served to confirm to the living kinsmen the reality of the continued existence of the soul.

A typical act, universal in China, was the immediate reporting of the death to the proper governing authority in the underworld, which might be T'u-ti (the earth god), Ch'eng-huang (the city god), or Wu-tao (the god of Five Roads), depending on local tradition. This facilitated admittance of the soul into the spirit world under the belief that one of the functions of such gods was to guard the underworld portals. This practice offers a possible answer to the question raised by many students of Chinese religion as to why northern Chinese reported the death of a kinsman to Wu-tao, the guard of all entrances to the underworld represented by the Five Roads (north, south, east, west, and central); this god had the function of an admittance officer controlling the successful entry of the spirit of the dead into the "sphere of the shadows" and its subsequent journey on to Heaven.

Other religious acts aimed at providing means for a safe and speedy journey of the spirit to Heaven and for comfort at its destination. These included the typical practices of dressing the corpse in the best garments available, putting into the corpse's mouth gold, silver, pearls, or other objects symbolic of great value, and placing in the coffin personal effects that the dead was most attached to while living. Serving the same function was the scattering of paper money at the head of the funeral procession to clear the road of any interference from evil spirits, and, at different stages of mourning, the burning of a large variety of objects that included personal belongings of the dead such as clothing, paper money, paper horses and boats, paper houses that were at times miniature mansions complete with halls, rooms, gardens, furniture, and a retinue of servants. The burning of such objects implied that death was not the final severance of the dead from the living, but that the dead had merely passed on to another existence.

Then, particularly with the well-to-do families, there were religious services every seventh day for seven weeks after a death. Economic means permitting, scripture-chanting services were performed by hired Taoist and Buddhist priests. These services were designed primarily to aid the spirit in traveling successfully through the necessary stages in the journey to the happy land of West Heaven. Such services included helping the soul to pass through Nai-ho ch'iao, the Bridge of Sighs or the Bridge of the Only Alternative. The bridge separated the world of the living from that of the dead, and it was believed that the spirit of the dead could take a last look at the world of the living from this bridge, hence the name, the Bridge of Sighs. In some localities, varying from three to seven days after a death, an elaborate rite was performed which included placing a large paper bridge in the courtyard or in front of the house, with the chief mourner (usually the eldest son of the deceased) taking the spirit tablet of the dead up and down the bridge step by step as the priests chanted their salvational scriptures, and finally the burning of the bridge. Participation of the mourners in such acts strengthened their belief in the continued existence of the soul of the loved one in spite of the termination of his physical existence.

If the family could afford it, there would be a service to aid the dead to pass through the ten courts of judgment in the underworld so that the spirit might not suffer severe punishment for sins committed while living. Sometimes the service consisted only of chanting, but in some cases the Ten Courts of Hell were represented by ten miniature buildings of tiles arranged in a row on a long table in front of the mourning altar, and, while the scripture was being chanted, priests would take the spirit tablet or other symbol of the soul from court to court until it emerged from the tenth court. After that, it was assumed that the spirit had traversed the most tortuous part of the journey through the underworld and was on its way to the happy destination of West Heaven. These and similar religious acts constituted an impressive effort to implant the idea that the dead still lived on, though in an invisible form, and that the living could do much to help them in the other world.

For Protection of the Living from the Dead

While the religious acts mentioned above were primarily expressions of affection of the living who tried to reject the reality of the death of an intimate relative, they also represented efforts to please the spirit of the dead so that it would use its superhuman power to bring blessings to and ward off evil influences from the living. If the spirit relied upon the living for proper mourning rites and religious services to pass safely through Hell and ascend to Heaven, the living depended upon the spirit for protection and blessing.

But, aside from this reliance upon the spirit for protection, there was abhorrence of the dead because of the dreadfulness of death itself. Death was considered evil, and a person possessed by death became nonhuman and unpredictable and might do evil even to his own intimate kin. The entire set of mortuary rites was regarded as unclean and unlucky, contaminated by evil. The living had to adopt precautions against evil influence from their own dead and other associated spirits. Herein lay the significance of another group of mortuary rites that mixed dread with love for the dead and hope for their continued existence.

Before being put into the coffin, the corpse was always placed with its feet facing the door, so that should it rise as a vampire, it would walk straight out the door instead of doing harm in the house. Mourners were tabooed from entering other people's houses for fear of the magical contagion of death. The evil character of the whole event of mourning made it necessary to choose a propitious day and hour by consulting the Chinese almanac or by divination for practically every ritual act so that evil spirits might not be aroused into action, good spirits might not be offended, and favorable influences might be called into play. Hence the meticulous care that went into the choice of the hour and date for placing the corpse into the coffin, for starting the funeral procession, and for lowering the coffin into the grave. Even the cult of *feng-shui* (wind and water, or geomancy), involving the selection of the most propitious location for the grave, was partly a means of averting possible evil influence from the dead upon the progeny as well as being a means of inducing the supernatural influence of blessing. Similar significance could be seen in such rites as chasing from the house the evil spirits that might have congregated there during the event, the final burning of the mourning garments, and, in some localities, the eating of sweetened rice by the mourners. All these symbolized the riddance of an evil affair so that the living could resume normal life with the feeling that there should be no more fear, and that there should once again be confidence and hope.

For the Expression of Grief

Another means of mitigating the emotional shock of a kinsman's death was found in the universal expression of grief at such event, which was carefully prescribed in Chinese mourning rites. Such expression included loud wailing which could be heard out in the street, eating coarse food, using crude utensils, changing into mourning garments made of the cheapest rough cloth, and prohibiting the wearing of clothing or decorations of gay colors or fine materials like silk. During the mourning period, there was also the suppression of events of happiness and gaiety such as weddings or the celebration of birthdays.

These and similar expressions of grief have been noted by all observers of Chinese mourning. What needs be stressed here is that, aside from the function of treating the emotional shock of the death of an intimate kinsman, the expression of grief also had the significance of reaffirming the cohesion and solidarity of the family group, as has been pointed out by both Durkheim and Malinowski in their studies of primitive religion.

Family cohesion could readily be recognized in many Chinese mourning acts, but particularly in the matter of ritualistic weeping.

The loud wailing by the nearest kin—the deceased's children or spouse—was usually a genuine expression of grief. But even with the nearest of kin, acts such as the chief mourners' having to be supported while walking in the funeral procession [3] as though weakened by grief were apparently pretensions. Much of the wailing on numerous occasions during the long period of mourning (often extending to 49 days), especially wailing by persons not intimately related to the dead, was not spontaneous. Periodically during mourning, weeping was done collectively by the entire family group gathering in front of the mourning altar, and in such group weeping, which sounded like a chorus, one could by careful listening pick out those who were really weeping. Above all, as in certain Hebrew tradition, there was the professional weeper hired by well-to-do families to weep at the sacrificial breakfast, lunch, and supper every day during the mourning period.

Ritual weeping is common in many cultures. It is a ritual demonstration of group cohesion and solidarity, whether the weeping is spontaneous or not, and an expression of concern over the loss of a member of the group. Whoever did not weep was regarded by the family as being disloyal not merely to the dead but also to the group. A bride newly married into a family was a frequent victim of such criticism. Without any considerable period of time to cultivate sentimental ties with the deceased, particularly if this should be a disagreeable mother-in-law, a young bride might have failed to weep in accordance with ritualistic prescriptions, and this failure was taken as a sign of disloyalty to the family and might even cause her alienation from the family. Death was not only a private act on the part of the deceased but was also a critical event in the family as a social group, and weeping regardless of spontaneity was a ritualistic token of concern and loyalty toward the family. Hiring a professional weeper was a further expression of the same sentiment of group concern and solidarity.

In ritual weeping, besides sobs and sighs, there were also speeches expressing affection for the dead, hope that his soul would ascend to Heaven, and glorification of his past deeds, the last being particularly prominent in the weeping speeches by professional weepers. In some localities, as in the southern province of Kwangtung, weeping by poor families at sacrificial meals during mourning also included naming imaginary tempting dishes which they were unable to offer the deceased either while alive or after death. The offering of imaginary delicacies was a sentimental expression of affection for the dead. All the highly conventionalized weeping speeches reaffirmed the social sentiments and ties between the dead and the living. The stimulation of such social sentiments and ties at the time of a family crisis had the effect of strengthening the cohesive values for the family group as a whole.

Another notable fact was the gradation of the expression of grief for different types of kinship relations. The closer the kinship with the dead, the greater the degree of grief required by convention. Children of the deceased were expected to weep in the most heart-rending manner, eat the coarsest food, wear the roughest mourning garments, and observe mourning rules for the longest period, which was generally three years. But, for nephews or grandchildren of the dead, merely token weeping was acceptable, the mourning food and garments were not as coarse, and the mourning period after the mortuary rites extended from only three months to a year in accordance with local practice. Looking at a person's mourning garments and gestures in a funeral procession, one could tell the general type of kinship relation each had with the dead.

Mourning rites amounted to a public rehearsing of the formal family status and relations by all the family members, as defined by recognized ritualistic principles governing the organization of a family. Such a demonstrative rehearsal once again had the effect of helping to reaffirm the ties of the family organization at a time when the death of a member, particularly the head of a household, tended to disintegrate family relations. Thus, besides demonstrating affection for the dead and helping the mourners to mitigate the emotional shock of death, the expression of grief in various forms was also a demonstration of group solidarity.

For Reassembling the Family Group and
Reasserting Family Status

The family group was consolidated not only by the mourners' demonstrative behavior but also by reaffirming relations with the wider social circle beyond the immediate family and by reasserting the status of the family in the community. This was an effort to reinforce the social and economic position of the bereaved family.

Acts to fulfill this function began with the sending of obituaries to relatives and friends not merely to inform them of the tragic event but also to invite them to participate in the funeral procession and mourning feast. This was an attempt to assemble the social group of relatives and friends, and the size of the group symbolized the social and economic status of the family. A poor and insignificant family would have only a handful of mourners at the funeral procession and perhaps hold no mourning feast. On the other hand, a family of wealth and influence would attract thousands to the procession and the feast. Recipients of the obituary note who valued or could not afford to ignore the invitation came with condolence gifts, which might be in the form of condolence scrolls containing words of comfort for the living or glorification of the dead, or in the form of condolence money to help defray the heavy expenses of mourning, especially for poor families. Whether in the form of scrolls or money, condolence gifts represented emotional and material assistance from the wider social group to the bereaved family, and symbolized the social ties the family had with relatives and friends. In fact, the size of the social group assembled at a funeral was larger than that assembled at other critical events for the family, such as birth or marriage. The large number of friends and relatives who came bolstered the courage and confidence of the family members who now had to face life without the help of the deceased.

Another effort to reinforce the organizational foundation of a family weakened by death was the various means of reasserting the status of the family in the eyes of the community by demonstrating its wealth and influence. This function underlay the impressive mourning arches built for the occasion in front of the house, elaborate mourning decorations in the halls and particularly around the mourning altar, the lavishness of the mourning feast, and above all, spectacular displays at the funeral procession, including thundering vanguard drums, elaborate banners, signs of honorific titles bestowed by the imperial government (during the days of the

Ch'ing dynasty), glorifying praises written on banners and scrolls sent by individuals and organizations, bands playing funeral music, troupes of Taoist and Buddhist monks in full, colorful religious costumes, long marching lines of mourners from relatives to friends and representatives of civic organizations, the massive decorated sedan chair for the spirit tablet, and finally the coffin, the quality and cost of which frequently served as a measurement of the wealth of the mourning family. This of course was the way of the rich. The poor could only envy this as a dream to be realized. But less well-to-do families often sank into debt to have an elaborate funeral which might require years to repay.

Glorification and praise of the dead and impressive displays at various points of the mortuary rites presented to the public the impression that the deceased had lived up to the classical Chinese ideal of *sheng jung ssu ai,* "Glorious while alive and evoking grief when departed." What was the motivation for this expression of glorification of and grief for the dead? It might be attributed partly to the belief in the continued existence of the soul and its capability of bringing reward or punishment to the progeny or kinsmen. But a traditional Confucian scholar, half-hearted in his belief in the soul, would have given a classic answer: mourning rites were to express the sentiment of filial piety by children toward a deceased parent, or other socially prescribed sentiment by the living toward the dead. As social institutions were not molded by a single motivation, the expression of affection and attachment by the living for the dead, like belief in the soul, might enter into the picture, and the traditional Confucian interpretation might be sound. But both explanations point toward meeting the social need for reassertion of family status and prestige by showing its ability to muster the support of a wider social group at a time when death had diminished the strength and cohesion of that family.

Sacrificial Rites

At the end of the mortuary rites, the spirit tablet symbolizing the deceased was installed in the family altar among other tablets of departed ancestors. The dead member was now considered fully settled in the world of spirits, and would be worshiped periodically by living kinsmen and their progenies. Such worship was done by *chi,* sacrificial rites. The elaborateness, impressiveness, and drama of the lengthy mortuary rites were means of branding into memory the significance of the dead for the living. This having been done, the next step was to stabilize the relationship between the dead and the living by periodical sacrifices so that this memory would not be effaced by time.

Family Sacrifices

As an act of making an offering to the spirits, sacrifice in its simplest form might consist of daily burning of incense, morning and night, and reverential bowing in front of a symbol of the spirit, which was usually a wooden tablet or a portrait. The fragrant smoke spiraling from the burning incense was a means of contacting the invisible spirits of the ancestors and, in the belief of some people, constituted the daily ration for their sustenance. This means of communication with the dead, together with the visible symbol of the ancestral tablets and reverential bowing, served as a reminder of the existence of the role of the dead among the living.

Sacrificial rites were more elaborate on such family occasions as the anniversary death date of each deceased member, festival days, the first and fifteenth days of each Chinese month, and special events such as weddings or births. There would be kowtow (kneeling with the head bent low to touch the ground from three to nine times) and praying. The head of the family performed the rites first, and the other members followed in the order of their status in the family. In the case of sacrifice on the death anniversary of a departed member, full rites were not performed by a senior member to the spirit of a junior member, such as a living father to a dead child. As in the mortuary rites, the enactment of the status of each family member during a sacrifice was a rehearsal of the family organization. The family as a well-patterned unit of collective life was thus periodically impressed upon the members.

Besides incense, there was the burning of candles and paper money as a means of communicating with and providing sustenance for the spirits. Above all, there was the offering of food and drink, always a central item on sacrificial occasions. In well-to-do families there were tempting dishes, and even with the poor the family purse was strained to provide good food for sacrificial offerings. Food and drink were displayed in front of the altar, and were later consumed by the family.

As in many other cultures,[4] the offering of food and drink to the dead and later the sharing of them by the entire family group had serious social implications. Food was the supreme factor in the sustenance of life, and man's struggle for it had always involved the social group. By offering it at the sacrifice, an effort was made to share it between the living and the dead, thus maintaining contact between the two. All formal Chinese written prayers ended with the words *shang hsiang,* meaning "may you enjoy this."

In sharing the sacrificial food in the presence of the ancestral spirits who had returned for the occasion, the family group reinforced the ties of loyalty and solidarity among its members in a sacred atmosphere. In the sacred name of the ancestral spirits, the sacrificial meal was held to share good food, the symbol of the family's good fortune and abundance, and all members must be present at this family reunion. Those making a living elsewhere must return if the distance was not too great. Should some members be unable to attend because of great distance, they remembered such sacrificial occasions as a time of family reunion. This was especially true of such occasions as death anniversaries of parents and annual sacrifices at the graves, which took place in the spring and autumn.

Sacrifices at the Ancestral Temple

The clan constituted an important unit in Chinese social structure. Just as the family relied heavily on ancestral spirits as an integrating factor, the clan also depended upon the worship of ancestors for the maintenance of unity and continuity.

The center of ancestor worship for the clan was the ancestral temple, usually located in the midst of the clan's village. It was usually the largest and most impressive building of the whole clan. Its many halls and courtyards, its clusters of spirit tablets, and its imposing pillars and architectural decorations stood as a lofty symbol of the religious devotion of the clan to the spiritual values of the departed ancestors. In south China, where the clan was more developed than elsewhere in China, the size and elaborateness of the ancestral temple represented the wealth, influence, and distinction of the clan.

The heart of the ancestral temple lay in the ancestral altar in the main hall. The altar consisted of one or more elevated, open cases built of intricately carved wood decorated with gold leaf or gold paint. Inside each case were tiers of ascending wooden steps, and on these steps were rows of spirit tablets, each representing a departed ancestor. The center of the highest tier was occupied by the tablet of the founder or originator of the clan. On the sides and on the lower tiers were the tablets of his descendants, arranged according to the seniority of their generational order. In one ancestral temple, for example, one end of the lowest tier was occupied by the tablets of members of the thirty-eighth generation from the originator of the clan. As one case was filled, another would be built to house new tablets. On the altar the hundreds of spirit tablets (sometimes over a thousand) constituted a visible representation of the long continuity of the clan and stood as a tangible reminder that not living members alone, but the roles of the living and dead together, made up the clan organization.

The spirit tablets were not mere mute blocks of wood, for the members' accomplishments and aspirations were inscribed in wood and stone to resurrect their past. Standing along the walls, hanging under the eaves and on the pillars were carved wooden plaques bearing official ranks, imperial academic degrees, public honors, and citations bestowed upon the clan's illustrious sons by the imperial and Republican governments and public organizations. Other plaques carried mottoes and exhortations left by the forefathers to inspire ambition and moral quality among their posterity. Looking at the mass of spirit tablets and then turning to the plaques of honorific titles and moral admonitions, one could almost hear the voices of the dead speak out from the altar, recounting their exploits, urging the living to respect the foundations built by the predecessors and to achieve even greater glories. The whole environment symbolized a group tradition and a moral atmosphere permeated with the sacred character of the ancestral spirits.

In this sacred environment many sacrifices took place every year. There was the sacrifice during the Chinese New Year, there were the sacrifices when sons of the clan were born or married, and there were minor sacrifices on important festival days. But the most important and solemn occasions were the spring and autumn sacrifices. The importance of these two sacrifices to an agricultural people seems obvious because of their close relation to the natural cycle of the seasons. Spring marked the beginning of life and growth after the frigid winter, and autumn symbolized fruition and abundance. Offering sacrifices to the ancestors in the spring and autumn invoked their spiritual power for the successful operation of the seasonal cycle. The autumn sacrifice also carried the meaning of thanksgiving to the ancestral spirits at the time when the harvest was gathered.

If the ancestral temple was a rather dusty and deserted place during ordinary times, it took on a new look on such major occasions as the spring and autumn sacrifices, when the whole place was scrubbed clean, when the golden paint gleamed again on the ornaments and honorific plaques, when lanterns and decorations of paper and silk added color and pomp to the halls, and when all the males of the clan gathered for the grand ceremony.

The sacrificial offerings consisted of the standard items of incense, candles, paper money, food, and drink, and, for this special occasion, the raw carcasses of a pig and a sheep, and sometimes also an ox. Besides these, there was a dish of blood and hair from the pig and the sheep, which was offered to the spirits by spilling it on the ground. This part of the ritual was called *ju mao hsüeh*, "eating hair and blood." While all the sacrificial offerings were means of communion with the ancestral spirits, as were the family sacrifices, the offering of raw carcasses of animals and their blood and hair presents an enigma. Classical sources such as the *Li Chi* (Book of Rites) refer to *ju-mao yin-hsüeh*, "eating hair and drinking blood," as a primitive tradition before the use of fire was known. It is therefore possible that the raw flesh and blood were offered to the most ancient forefathers, thus inspiring the idea of the long continuity of the kinship group, which constituted a major value in the Chinese consanguinary system. Or, it might have been part of a magical requirement not to alter an ancient formula of sacrifice, though its meaning might no longer be understood.

The sacrificial procedure was carefully guided by a master of ceremonies, who called out each ritual act to be performed. The sacrificial items were usually offered by the head of the clan, who officiated at the occasion. After the offerings were made, other members of the clan performed the kowtow in successive order of their generational seniority. As in the family sacrifice, this ordered performance of the rites served as a demonstration of the status of the members in the organization of the clan. An added importance here was that the large size of the clan and the comparative lack of intimate contact among the members made it necessary to depend on occasions such as this to rehearse the status structure of the extensive organization.

Following the sacrificial rites was the big feast that gathered the clansmen around scores and at times hundreds of tables. This was one of the few occasions when the entire membership of hundreds and sometimes thousands of members were gathered at one place and the group tie was renewed. The sight of the large number of kinsmen and the act of sharing a bountiful meal together impressed those present with a deep sense of group consciousness. After the feast, the carcasses of the sacrificial animals were cut up and divided among all the male members. In the southern province of Kwangtung, one's share of sacrificial meat represented evidence of his membership in the clan, and being denied the sacrificial meat was a sign of excommunication from the group because of offense against its rules.

The whole series of sacrificial rites helped to perpetuate the memory of the traditions and historical sentiments of the group, sustain its moral beliefs, and revivify group consciousness. Through these rites and the presence of the group in its full numerical strength, the clan periodically renewed its sentiments of pride, loyalty, and unity.

CLASSICAL INTERPRETATIONS OF MORTUARY
AND SACRIFICIAL RITES

Mortuary and sacrificial rites played a basic part in Chinese culture, and many opinions have been expressed on them by Chinese thinkers over the centuries. It is interesting to consider their views briefly so as to further understanding of the social functions of the cult of ancestor worship.

During the three hundred years between the sixth and the third centuries B.C., early Chinese culture underwent extensive transition, and the ancient cult of ancestor worship was re-examined in the many new lights of the so-called hundred schools of philosophy. The well-known argument over the matter of simple versus elaborate funeral rites is illustrative of the effort to re-evaluate the ancient institutions at that time. In the end, it was the Confucian view that succeeded in establishing itself as the classical tradition for the subsequent centuries down to the modern times.

According to the Confucian tradition, which upheld the cult of ancestor worship, the most basic reason for practicing the mortuary and sacrificial rites was to "express gratitude toward the originators and recall the beginnings." [5] The long-continued acceptance of this view down to the modern period could be seen in the interpretation given in the local gazetteer of the town of Yüeh-p'u Li of Pao-shan county in Kiangsu province, which was published in 1933:

> The local customs emphasize the worship of spirits and gods and the exaltation of ancestors . . . There is the ancestral temple for the clan and the private altar for the family to settle the souls of the forefathers. Besides the periodic offerings, there is the emphasis on sacrifices to the graves. This is based on the principle of *the fountain of the water and the root of the tree.*[6]

The principle of the fountain and the root was a paraphrasing of the idea of "expressing gratitude toward the originators and recalling the beginnings."

But, for the Confucianists who declined to elaborate on the supernatural problem of the soul, what was the purpose of "recall-

ing the beginnings" and "expressing gratitude toward the originators," who were long dead and would not be conscious of the
gratitude expressed? The answer lay not in benefit to the dead, but
in what the living obtained from performing such rites. The Confucian interpretation was that such rites helped to cultivate moral
values, especially filial piety, and to foster the refinement of human
sentiments that supported these values. This was plainly stated in
many familiar classical quotations. Thus said Tseng Tzu, Confucius' favorite disciple: "Solicitude on the decease of parents, and
the pursuit of them (with sacrifices) for long after, would cause an
abundant restoration of the people's morals." [7] What these morals
were could be found in the statement in the *Ta-tai li chi* (Book
of Rites of the elder Tai):

Funeral and sacrificial rities serve to inculcate benevolence and love.
By attaining to a feeling of love one can perform the rites of mourning
and sacrifice, while the perpetuation of the sacrifices of spring and autumn serves to express the longing of the mind. Now sacrifice consists in
making offerings. When there is a longing and a making of offerings to
the dead, how much more will there be so to the living! Therefore it is
said that when the mourning and sacrificial rites are clearly understood,
the people are filial.[8]

This idea was more explicit in a statement in Hsün Tzu:

The *li* [rites] consist in being careful about the treatment of life and
death. Life is the beginning of man. Death is the end of man. When
the end and beginning are both good, the way of humanity is complete
. . . Funeral rites are for the living to give beautified ceremonial to
the dead; to send off the dead as if they were living; to render the same
service to the dead as to the living; to the absent as to the present; and
to make the end be the same as the beginning . . . Hence the funeral
rites are for no other purpose than to make clear the meaning of death
and life, to send off the dead with sorrow and reverence, . . . Service to
the living is beautifying their beginning; sending off the dead is beautifying their end. When the end and the beginning are both attended to,
the service of the filial son is ended and the way of the Sage is completed.[9]

Underlying this interpretation was the classical concept of *yang-
sheng sung-ssu,* "supporting the living and bidding farewell to the

dead," a concept that has been effective down to the present in summarizing the essence of filial piety. The filial son not only rendered service to his parents while they were living but also performed elaborate funeral and sacrificial rites upon their death in order to express the genuine and lasting quality of filial sentiments. This was the purpose of rendering "the same service to the dead as to the living; to the absent as to the present." From the point of view of the individual, the satisfying feeling that one had done his best for his parents from the beginning to the end served to mitigate the psychological shock of the death of the parents. From the point of view of society, the inspiring of filial sentiments through funeral and sacrificial rites was a means of maintaining filial piety as a basic value in the operation of the kinship system.

In the routine existence of the individual, his social contacts were not very broad, but rather limited to a small circle. Meanwhile, as the members multiplied over several generations, the kinship group grew fairly large, contact between the members became infrequent, and the strength of relationship between them was reduced in reverse proportion to the size of the group. On the other hand, there were occasions that demanded effective relationship among the members in the larger kinship group. In the traditional Chinese social order, where the individual relied heavily upon the size of the family and clan for social and economic assistance, such occasions were very frequent. One way to keep the larger group alive in the consciousness of the individual, even in his socially restricted routine existence, was by constantly reminding him of the common origin of the group and the resultant biological relatedness of all the descendants of the same ancestors, and by keeping alive the social obligations imposed by such relatedness.

It is interesting to note in this connection that the size of the kinship groups within which certain types of effective social obligations were imposed was defined by the degree of remoteness of the ancestors worshiped in the mortuary and sacrificial rites. The more remote an ancestor, the larger the group of descendants and the less binding would be the social obligations between the members. The gradation of mourning obligation according to the closeness of the kinship relation with the deceased, as pointed out above, was an expression of the different degrees of social obligations effective in the concentric circles of kinship relations. A *fang* or subdivision of a clan was composed of the male descendants within five generations tracing down from a male ancestor. Within this group, the number of descendants was not too large, and effective social relations could be maintained without much difficulty. Beyond the *fang* was the large and more loosely integrated group, the clan, with a distant ancestor of several scores of preceding generations as the mark of common origin and the symbol of social ties. The kinship system was structurally composed of the family and the wider family circle, each identified by the different degrees of mourning obligations; the *fang* or subdivision; and finally the clan. The latter two bore no mourning but only sacrificial obligations. Each of these concentric kinship groups was integrated around the generational relationship between the living descendants and the ancestors.

The group integrational function of ancestor worship is further seen in other aspects of the mortuary and sacrificial rites. For instance, the degree of elaborateness of mortuary rites was based upon the importance of the status of the deceased in the family. Those who died at an advanced age received more elaborate rites than those who died younger; a deceased male member of the family was mourned with more elaborate rites than a female, and the rites for the head of the family were more elaborate than for other members. This differential treatment lent religious support to the stratification of the family organization based on the factors of age and sex. Those who died unmarried or under the age of twelve received simple rites or none at all. The latter were not even marked with a spirit tablet in the family altar. The only explanation for this was that the unmarried and the young occupied a relatively less important position in the family organization. As the major purpose of ancestor worship was to strengthen and perpetuate the kinship organization, family members occupying unimportant organizational positions such as those remaining unmarried and those under the age of twelve at the time of death were comparatively ignored. Here is where the classical Confucian interpretation based on the affectional sentiments failed, for affectional sentiments for the young and unmarried were never as weak as indicated in the difference in the elaborateness of the rites. Thus, the basic function of ancestor worship was still the integration and perpetuation of the kinship group. Even the cultivation of social values such as affection and filial piety, as maintained by the classical interpretation, contributed directly to this end.

CONFUCIANIST RATIONALIZATION OF ANCESTOR WORSHIP

There is the remaining question of the religious nature of ancestor worship, a question repeatedly raised in the past both by Chinese and by Westerners. Many Confucianists maintained a nontheistic view of the cult, and there is no doubt that the cult could be interpreted this way. Thus, the mourning rites might be rationalized as expressions of grief at the loss of an intimate member of the family, as symbolistic gestures of reluctance to let the dead go, and as representations of hope that death marked not the end but the beginning of another existence of the deceased, not as souls, but in the memory of the living. *Li Chi* summarized the interpretation by saying that "it is simply the expression of human feelings." [10] That this view is quite sound has been pointed out in the foregoing analysis of the function of mortuary rites in helping to mitigate the emotional shock of the death of intimate members of the family. Confucian rationalists such as Wang Ch'ung and Hsün Tzu insisted that mortuary rites be performed without introducing the supernatural element of the soul. All the ritual behavior and offerings made to the spirits were to be interpreted as an expression of longing for the continued existence of the dead without belief in the actual existence of the soul. Thus, Hsün Tzu said:

Sacrificial rites are the expression of man's affectionate longings. They represent the height of altruism, faithfulness, love and reverence. They represent the completion of propriety and refinement. If there were no Sages, no one could understand this. The Sage plainly understands it; the scholar and Superior Man accordingly perform it; the official observes it; and among the people it becomes an established custom. Among Superior Men it is considered to be *a human practice;* among the common people it is considered to be *a serving of the spirits* [italics added] . . . Divination to find the lucky days, fasting, cleaning the temple, spreading out tables and mats, offering animals and grain, praying for blessings (from the deceased) as if the deceased enjoyed the sacrifice; selecting the offerings and sacrificing them as if the deceased tasted them; . . . With such sorrow and reverence one serves the dead as one serves the living, and serves the departed as one serves those who are present. What is served has neither substance nor shadow, yet this is the completion of refinement.[11]

Again Hsün Tzu said of the sacrificial rite in general: "The Superior Man looks upon it as a fine gloss put over the matter, while the common people consider it supernatural. He who thinks it is a gloss is fortunate; he who thinks it is supernatural is unfortunate." [12]

These and similar quotations from other prominent Confucian thinkers may be regarded as elaborations of Confucius' statement: "He sacrificed to the dead as if they were present. He sacrificed to the spirits as if the spirits were present" (*Lun yü,* Book III, chap. 12). There is little doubt that this interpretation has influenced profoundly the Confucian mind of subsequent generations from the time of Confucius and Hsün Tzu down to the present period. Its influence is seen in the wide use of these and similar quotations in contemporary Chinese literature on the question of religion in general, and on the cultic practices of ancestor worship in particular. This view of sacrifice as an expression of "human feelings" might indeed be predominant in the mind of many Confucianists and among the vast majority of modern Chinese intellectuals. But the supernatural notion was by no means completely dismissed from the thoughts of a large section of traditional Confucianists (see chap. x), with whom the rationalized interpretation gained only partial acceptance.

As Hsün Tzu himself put it, it takes the Sage to understand it plainly. It is a question of how many of the scholars and Superior Men who accordingly perform it can see through the mystery as a "human practice," with the same "plain understanding" as the Sage's. As to the "common people," even the great rationalist Hsün Tzu had to be content that the cult was a "serving of the spirits" and a "supernatural" matter. While the expression of affection for the dead and the hope for their continued existence remained as the basic motivation for the mortuary and sacrificial rites with the "common people," the cult maintained its influence with the common people through their belief in the supernatural element of the soul, the symbol of the affectional sentiments. As a major factor in the integration of the kinship system in Chinese society, ancestor worship developed its effectiveness not from its philosophical but from its religious implications because of the common people's ability to comprehend readily the religious but not the philosophical.

In fact, even with the Superior Men, the mystic experience of communion with the spirit was present in the sacrificial rites if they faithfully followed the procedure as prescribed in the *Li Chi,* the classical authority on rites:

The severest vigil and purification is maintained and practised in the inner self, while a looser vigil is maintained externally. During the days of such vigil, the mourner thinks of the departed, how and where he sat, how he smiled and spoke, what were his aims and views, what he delighted in, and what he desired and enjoyed. By the third day he will perceive the meaning of such exercise.

On the day of sacrifice, when he enters the apartment (of the temple), he will seem to see (the deceased) in the place (where his spirit-tablet is). After he has moved about (to perform his operations), and is leaving the door, he will be arrested by seeming to hear the sound of his movements, and will sigh as he seems to hear the sound of his sighing . . . Still and grave, absorbed in what he is doing, he will seem to be unable to sustain the burden, and in danger of letting it fall . . . In this his heart reaches the height of filial piety and reverence . . . Thus he manifests his mind and thought, and in his dreamy state of mind seeks to commune with the dead in their spiritual state, if peradventure they could enjoy his offerings, if peradventure they could indeed do so.[13]

The three days of vigil and concentrated meditation focused upon the lifetime image of the dead, and the resultant "dreamy state of mind" is typical of the procedure used by visionaries in many cultures to induce the mystical experience of communion with spiritual forces.[14] The use of liquor in Chinese sacrifices, first spilling it on the floor for the spirits and later having it drunk by the living at the sacrificial feast, is likely to be associated with the effort to induce the "dreamy state of mind" and to obtain communion with the spirits, for this is commonly found in the religious experience of many other cultures.[15]

If the sole aim of the cult of ancestor worship was to cultivate the moral sentiments, particularly filial piety, one may ask why the Confucianists chose an ancient religious cult and not some secular means to obtain the same end. Though strongly rationalistic in their views, Confucius and Confucianists saw in the cult a powerful emotional root to strengthen the kinship values and family ties. By reinterpreting the religious rites, by substituting human sentiments for supernatural belief, they hoped to retain the ancient cult and transform it into an enlightened, nontheistic ritual for the purpose of stabilizing and perpetuating the kinship system as the basic unit of social organization.

But the effort to divest the supernatural implications from an ancient religious cult was not altogether successful. One evidence is the classical procedure of sacrificial vigil and meditation to induce the religious experience of communion with the spirits. But the critical proof was the retaining of the supernatural notions of the cult by the vast majority of the people, including a good portion of the traditional Confucianists. In interpreting the secular or religious nature of the cult, Hsün Tzu had to distinguish between the Superior Men and the common people, with supernatural belief causing a gap between the two. Neither Hsün Tzu nor subsequent generations of Confucian rationalists put forth any suggestions as to how to close the gap so that both the Superior Men and common people would take the same nontheistic, enlightened view.

In recent decades the Confucianist head of a family might take the nontheistic views during the mortuary or sacrificial rites, but he seldom interfered with the supernatural beliefs and religious activities carried on by the members of the family, particularly the women, though he had the practical authority to do so. His condoning of the religious beliefs and rituals in the cult showed a lack of interest in closing the gap. Theoretically, universal education as envisaged by Confucius (*yu chiao wu lei,* "with education, there will be no more class distinction") could close the gap, but universal literacy was not a general practical need in a nonindustrial and authoritarian society. Obviously, for Hsün Tzu as well as the contemporary Confucian rationalists, the choice lay between seriously weakening the effect of the cult by forcing out its supernatural elements, or retaining its influence among the common people by keeping its supernatural content. The Confucians seemed to have realized vaguely the modern psychological and sociological views that symbolization of certain moral values by such cultic representations as belief in the soul is instrumental in the perpetuation of these values as a stable popular tradition.

The integrating and stabilizing function of ancestor worship for an extensive kinship system will become more apparent by contrasting the traditional Chinese family, which observes ancestor worship, with a modern, Western-style Chinese family which has largely discontinued the cult—a family type increasingly common in Chinese urban centers. In the modern small family, the care and support of elderly parents still remains a serious duty of the children so long as the parents are living, and brings together the brothers and to a lesser extent the sisters to maintain the family bond. But as the children grow up, marry, have children, and develop diverse individual centers of interest, their common bond becomes progressively weakened. When the parents die, the last focus of common devotion is gone. From this point on, without ancestor worship as a symbolic cult to keep alive the memory of the departed parents and the more distant ancestors and to serve to strengthen the living generation's identification with the kinship group, the grown-up and married children tend to drift apart with little consolidating influence to inspire them to remain together as an organized unit.

The sociological significance of this situation lies in the limitation of biological relatedness as an effective social bond for a relatively small kinship group of probably two or three generations, if such a bond were confined to the relationship among the living members. Continuity of the lineage beyond the living generations and extension of the kinship group beyond the intimate circles of two or three generations would, in the case of the Chinese culture, have to rely on the integrating influence of the ancestor cult, where the psychosocial role assigned to the dead translated biological relatedness into a social bond free from the limitation of time and space, which would restrict effective kinship ties to a small circle of intimate contacts. Hence the ability of the ancestor cult to cement an extensive membership into a well-organized kinship structure. The size of the membership within which biological relatedness remained an effective social bond would be in proportion to the generations traceable back to a common ancestor regularly worshiped by the group.

Thus ancestor worship as a theistic cult, operating with elaborate mortuary and sacrificial rites, performed the critical function of consolidating and stabilizing the Chinese kinship organization. The Chinese family system owed much to this cult for its stability.

However one regards the supernatural element in it, there is little disagreement about the frequent observation that ancestor worship was the "essential religion" in the Chinese culture. The very central importance of the kinship system in Chinese social organization gave the cult its universal importance in China. If there were social class differences among the Chinese people in the matter of religious belief and practice, the cult of ancestor worship, with all its religious rites, transcended class barriers. While Confucianism always turned against religious heresy, it promoted this cult and adopted it as a part of the Confucian orthodoxy, which governed the political and social order of traditional China. Although the dynastic governments were always unfavorably disposed toward unapproved organized religious activities, ancestor worship not merely gained full acceptance with the ruling powers of the past centuries but became a legal requirement to be conformed to. Under the Ch'ing code, even the kinship-renouncing Buddhist monks were required to observe mourning rites for their parents.[16] A basic motivation for state support of the cult lay in the fact that it helped strengthen the kinship system which was instrumental in the maintenance of the orthodox sociopolitical order.

OTHER RELIGIOUS ASPECTS OF CHINESE FAMILY LIFE

Vital as it was, ancestor worship was but one of the many religious elements that contributed to the integration of family organization and the operation of family life. As was pointed out at the beginning of this chapter, practically no aspect of traditional Chinese family life escaped the touch of religion. If ancestor worship was a religious device to face the momentous event of death, other crises of family life, such as birth and marriage, likewise involved religious beliefs and activities.

Marriage and birth were links in the chain of continuity of the family lineage, and, very naturally, ancestor worship also played an important part in both events. The rites of ancestor worship attending the events of both marriage and birth were clearly interpreted in the classical statement in *Li Chi* that marriage (and birth) were "to secure the services in the ancestral temple for the predecessors, and to secure the continuance of the family line for posterity." [17]

But, aside from ancestor worship, the classical religious element of predetermination was also important. The hour, day, month, and year of birth were viewed as connected with certain supernatural forces of either benevolent or evil nature that would affect the future life of the baby. In case of a birth at an unlucky time, there would be a host of magical activities to suppress the evil influences. Whom one should marry and whether a marriage would be a happy one were similarly thought to be affected by the supernatural forces present at the time of one's birth. Forming a part of this basic theme was the popular folklore about the old man in the moon whose function was to tie together the legs of the two intended partners with an invisible red silk string representing the predetermined marital bond. Also a part of the pattern was the lore of the Cow Boy and Weaving Girl, stars that crossed the Milky Way in the sky to meet each other on the night of the seventh day of the seventh month in the Chinese calendar. Girls gazed at the stars on that festival night, and if they saw the two romantic stars crossing the Milky Way, they could soon expect marriage to a predetermined partner. The Niu-lang miao, temple of the Cow Boy and Weaving Girl stars, frequently found in the countryside, was built for marriageable girls to pray for a good partner.

The magical beliefs and activities concerning the predetermination of fate at birth performed many important functions, one of them being the cushioning of the emotional shock from possible premature death or the disappointing development of the child. A

Chinese mother, who usually rested her entire hopes upon a son for the improvement of her family and social status and for support of her old age, would be emotionally shattered if she finally bore a son only to see him die prematurely or grow up to be a wayward character, bringing her trouble instead of the traditional benefits from a filial child. She might even lose faith in the traditional ideal of family life, which valued the bearing of sons. In marriage, she might try her utmost to be a good marital partner and a pleasant and contributing member of the husband's family, and yet she might fail to bear a son, her partner might unfortunately die early, her relatives might be inhumanly oppressive, and what was a romantic dream about a happy marriage might turn out to be a living nightmare, ending in haunting sadness, in humiliation, and even in mental derangement or suicide. After all the rules of traditional ethics and propriety had been faithfully observed, the promised result might not materialize. Such disappointment might shake people's faith in the traditional values undergirding the structure of the family institution.

All these emotional impacts and social difficulties might be mitigated by introducing into the situation the concept of supernatural predeterminism, thereby preserving the individual's credit for honest effort which, given more favorable supernatural circumstances, might have brought success. If something else could be held responsible for the failure, one might not lose all confidence in one's own efforts or in the soundness of the social institution. One's dissatisfaction and despair were directed at fate, not at the family system and its traditionally treasured values. And the overpowering notion of fate tended to breed the attitude of resignation even under adverse circumstance, which was characteristic of the Chinese, instead of inspiring the people to challenge the social institution.

Furthermore, the idea that fate was predetermined by invisible anthropomorphic powers raised the hope that, with continued effort and correct moral and religious behavior, supernatural beings might intercede to alter the course of one's fate. Hope inspired confidence not merely in oneself but also in the social institution in which one struggled for happiness and success. Hence the need for belief in marriage gods like the Cow Boy and Weaving Girl stars, and the host of fertility gods like the goddess of mercy and the flower spirits in the south and the goddesses of motherhood in the north.

But when religious piety and supplications failed, and when objective situations precluded the possibility of success in this life, hope was directed toward the other life in Heaven or the next life on earth through the transmigration of the soul so that faith in the family institution could be preserved in spite of its failure to meet the aspirations of certain unfortunate individuals. Thus, when a widow in Shanghai tried to remarry in 1951 under the Communist new Marriage Law, her mother-in-law told her: "Widowhood is your fate, and the best thing for you is to observe the moral rules of widowhood [not to remarry] and be pious to the spirits and gods so that you will be reborn into a beautiful life in your next existence."[18] The mother-in-law was offering the young widow the explanation of fate for her misfortune and the hope of a better life in the next existence by following the moral rules of the traditional family institution. The numerous sanctuaries in all parts of China dedicated to filial sons and to chaste widows who refused to remarry served a similar function in supporting the moral values that upheld the traditional kinship system. Even those who disbelieved in the soul would cherish the ideal of having posterity remember their names after their death, and for this they were willing to forego improvement of an unfortunate situation.

A further illustration of the adaptation of religious beliefs to social needs is found in a unique type of Chinese ghost story. Ghosts and spirits in Chinese folklore are not all evil-dealing and mischief-making shadowy beings to be feared. Numerous stories are told of attractive female ghosts and incarnations of such animals as foxes, which assume the forms of bewitchingly beautiful women and involve men in romantic situations. There were many stories of a lonesome and poverty-stricken bachelor scholar, poring over his books by dim light at night, who would look up in surprise to see an alluring temptress entering his studio, and the two might live together for years before the romance ended either with the scholar's discovery of the ghostly identity of the lady, or with the lady's taking her exit into the invisible world on account of jealousy or other circumstance. During the whole affair, the ghost or spirit incarnate would display the physical and mental attributes and all the goodness and defects of a human female. The romance, surprise, and thrill made this a most popular type of love story for the traditional-minded Chinese.

A vital factor in the authoritarian structure of the traditional Chinese family lay in its system of arranged marriage, a system that precluded romantic love as a basis for wedlock.[19] But the romantic appetite was difficult to eliminate even in the rigid discipline of the traditional culture, and the tacit approval of prostitution and the system of concubinage was partial compensation for the denial of romantic love in the formal marriage. Under the social convention dictated by the Confucian doctrine, no romantic love should end in formal marriage, and romantic love was discouraged even as a theme in literature, for it could not lead to an ethically approved climax. Here, the supernatural elements of ghosts and incarnations introduced a new twist to the situation. Such stories could be written in full compliance with the Confucian tradition, for, after all, the object of the romance was not a human being subjected fully to the discipline of conventional ethics but a ghost or spirit which could claim exemption from moral judgment. And the story did not have to and could not end in permanent wedlock in the convention-abiding human world. At the climax of the story, the woman evaporated into thin air. Thus a love story with ghosts and spirits provided all the romantic thrill forbidden by the Confucian tradition of marriage and yet violated none of the basic social conventions.

Supernatural folklore and stories did not constitute a cult, but they were a basic source of information about the supernatural world for the Chinese common people. Few Chinese read Buddhist or Taoist sacred scriptures, yet few missed reading or hearing ghost stories.

Another type of supernatural folklore concerned spiritual reward or punishment of those who either observed or violated the conventional code of kinship ethics. This type of ghost story exerted a tangible influence on the Chinese and became a strong sanctioning factor for the moral values of traditional family life.

III

RELIGION IN SOCIAL
AND ECONOMIC GROUPS

IN THE ORGANIZATION of traditional Chinese society, besides the family and clan, there were a number of associations performing social and economic functions that lay beyond the kinship system. The number of such associations was not large, owing to the agrarian nature of Chinese society and the predominance of the kinship system.[1] They nevertheless occupied a functional position in Chinese society by meeting the needs of certain portions of the population that the kinship system failed to fulfill adequately.

While the kinship system enjoyed the advantage of having a strong natural bond of biological relatedness as a cohesive factor, it nevertheless needed ancestor worship and all of its religious implications to give the natural bond a sacred character in order to enhance its influence, to command loyalty, and to generate solidarity among the members. Extrafamilial associations differed from the kinship group in that they were consciously organized for certain definite interests, and were not the result of the process of biological reproduction. Lacking a strong natural bond, the cohesive factor lay in specific common interests together with a body of implemental rules and regulations and associated values and practices. In a preindustrial particularistic society this type of integrating force might not have been sufficiently strong, and so there was the additional need of religious sanction of secular interests in order to strengthen the unity and loyalty of the group. The introduction of the religious element into the situation tended to reduce friction resulting from the members' individualistic, utilitarian interests and to lift their spirits to a collective level by focusing attention on a sacred symbol of the group. This need for an added source of strength for group unity and stability resulted in the widespread presence of the religious element in social and economic associations.

THE RELIGIOUS BOND IN SOCIAL GROUPS

Among the limited number of social associations developed in traditional Chinese society beyond the kinship system, the fraternities and sororities were common types. When several friends felt that their association with each other was unusually close and their social life and interests unusually intimate, it was quite common in the traditional social order for them to organize a fraternity or sorority to consolidate and stabilize their relationship. The process of organizing such a group was called *chieh-pai,* meaning to unite through worship. Although in some cases no religious inauguration rites were performed, the sacred nature of the relationship was fully implied in the term *chieh-pai hsiung-ti* or *chieh-pai tzu-mei,* meaning sworn brothers or sisters, for the members contracted a bond with each other with the sanctification of the deities. But it was common practice to launch an organization, particularly a sorority, with religious rites of burning incense and candles and kowtowing to Heaven and Earth or to certain deities. The favorite deities for fraternities were the triad of Kuan Yü, Liu Pei, and Chang Fei, the three deified sworn brothers who won fame in the third century A.D. by their saga of absolute mutual loyalty.

Besides sanctifying the newly formed social tie, the rites implied the idea of invoking supernatural punishment for possible violators of group loyalty. When such groups were organized for serious and dangerous purposes, such as political struggle, blood was taken from the fingers or arms of the members and either spilled on the ground or sipped by the members, in order to symbolize the formation of a blood tie. Besides the rites performed at the inauguration of the organization and at the initiation of new members, rites were often performed on important occasions such as festival days as a means of re-emphasizing the religious nature of the group.

Once formed, a fraternity or sorority took on the character of a pseudo-kinship group, wherein the members considered it a sacred duty to render mutual assistance in their social and economic life. A survey in 1948 of a village in the vicinity of the southern metropolis of Canton showed the important role of a fraternal group in the social and political life of the village; the group consisted of about a dozen members, all educated and several wealthy or politically important, and the rest shared in their influence. In cities and in multi-surname villages (inhabited by more than one clan), where the kinship system had to face limitations, fraternal groups were likely to play an active role in the social life of a part of the population.

Sororal organizations were common among women who had to make a living outside their homes, particularly in the south. In the silk centers of the southern province of Kwangtung, for example, where sericulture opened up a field of employment for women, celibacy was common among them, and the pseudo-kinship sorority played an important part in their social and economic life. Here, the religious element was more prominent than in the fraternities. Religious rites were inevitable in the installation of the group, in the initiation of new members, and also at gatherings during festivals and similar important occasions.

Many localities in Kwangtung province had a type of sorority for single women, called "old maid houses." Their membership consisted of women who had decided not to marry as well as women who had decided not to return to their husbands. Unlike the common type of sororities, they had as headquarters a house where daily activities such as sewing were carried on, and which also served as a residence for members without a home. Above all, when a member died, her spirit tablet would be placed there for worship by the rest of the members. This was an excellent example of the many types of pseudo-kinship organizations that existed in Chinese society to perform the functions of the family when the latter failed to meet the material and spiritual needs of the individual.

Both the family and the clan were patrilineal organizations for male members and their spouses. Female descendants enjoyed no permanent membership in their own family, for they would sooner or later be married out to another family and clan. Hence, in the theology of ancestor worship, the souls of female descendants who after marriageable age died married or unmarried did not belong to and were not worshiped by the paternal lineage of the family, for they were actual or potential members of other families. The souls of unmarried or divorced women, then, were homeless wandering ghosts without assistance or benefit from sacrifices offered by later generations. To forestall this possibility, "old maid houses" were organized to provide an altar for their spirit tablets and a home for their souls after death, with the living members performing the sacrificial rites of ancestor worship.

Thus it is clear that the religious element of ancestor worship functioned as a spiritual bond to unite the members. Socially, of course, there were important secular functions in such organizations. In Chinese traditional society, where the kinship system was so vital to the social and economic interests of the individual, persons without a well-integrated status in the family and clan found themselves stripped of the advantages of group identification and support. Unmarried and divorced women did not enjoy recognized status in the family of their birth, and this was particularly so with respect to divorced women, against whom traditional society had always discriminated to some degree. The social and economic need for a pseudo-kinship group such as the "old maid houses" is obvious. But secular interests alone might not constitute a sufficiently strong bond to hold the group together, so that the religious element was needed to give a sacred character of respect and awe to the organization and thus strengthen the unity and loyalty of the group.

SECRET SOCIETIES

While it is not necessary to exhaust the list of social groups in Chinese society in which religion functioned as an integrating factor, there remains another example, the secret society, in which religion played an important role. Although it is not intended here to explore the importance of secret societies in Chinese life, it is necessary to mention that many individuals, particularly those without the support of a strong family in their social and economic struggles, found in the secret societies a valuable source of group assistance. This was especially true of the underprivileged classes where the family was small and poor: among poor peasants, urban labor gangs, and the criminal underworld. Politically, secret societies were a perennial factor in rebellions and revolutions. They were undoubtedly among the most strongly organized groups in Chinese society outside the kinship system, and, again, the religious element contributed to their organizational strength.

There were two general types of secret societies. One was of a predominantly religious nature, the religious society, which will be discussed later. The other type had primarily economic or political interests, such as the powerful Ch'ing and Hung societies [2] and similar groups among peasants and urban laborers.

In the second type of secret society, although secular interests were predominant, religion was used as a means of inducing group loyalty and solidarity, which was held more important in this than in other types of social groups, for disloyalty or betrayal might bring ruin to the entire organization. The religious element was particularly outstanding in the initiation rites. While such rites differed in details from society to society, they contained basic similarities. The initiation rites of the Triads, a branch of the Hung society, is illustrative. [3]

The initiation of a new member of the Triad society took place in front of a carefully arranged altar. The deities on the altar included Kuan Yü, god of war and righteousness, the Five Ancestors (founders of the society), and the spirit tablets of prominent deceased members, all arranged according to seniority of generations, similar to the practice in ancestor worship. In front of the deities were the regular items of sacrifice such as food and drink, incense, candles, and lamps. Then there were weapons, such as a sword decorated with seven stars, and spears and clubs, giving an atmosphere of awe, as if the gods and spirits would use the weapons to enforce the purpose and rules of the group. Then there would be a display of symbolic objects that carried magical significance: a red lamp for testing the sincerity or insincerity of the member, a ruler for measuring his conduct, a mirror for reflecting good or evil character, a pair of scissors for cutting the sheet of cloud that darkened the sky (meaning dominance of the country by an adversative political power).

Besides participating in instructional ceremonies, the new member performed full religious rites before the altar. The significance of the rites was clearly expressed in the stereotyped initiation speech by the officiating leader:

> . . . We swear to Heaven that we live and die together . . . We agree to become brothers, and take on the common surname of Hung . . . Tonight, with homage, we take Heaven as our father, Earth as our mother, the sun as our elder brother, the moon as our sister . . . We worship our founding ancestors and the entire family of spirits of our deceased members . . . Kneeling in front of the altar, we cut our fingers and let each other suck the blood . . . As the gods descend to witness [the initiation], everyone must be sincere in taking the thirty-six vows. . . .

The "thirty-six vows" contained solemn promises by the new member to give his life and possessions for the organization and to render mutual assistance. The first vow, for example, stated:

> After joining the Hung family, your parents are the same as my parents; your brothers and sisters, my brothers and sisters; your wives, my sisters-in-law; your sons and nephews, my sons and nephews. Any violation of this rule or any disregard of this sentiment means desecration of this vow, and will bring punishment of death and elimination by thunder.

In the initiation speech and in the first vow an effort was made to weld the members together by simulating the strong natural bond of blood relation. Thus, the organization was referred to as the family, and the relationship between the members assumed the nature of a family relationship. But in order to transfer the center of loyalty of the members from their natural family to the simulated family of the secret organization, Heaven and Earth were taken as new parents, and the common surname of Hung was secretly assumed by all members.

This simulated blood tie was established with religious rites to heighten the respect and awe of the participants, to inculcate the feeling that supernatural powers were behind the entire undertaking, giving support to its purposes and enforcement of its rules. Worship of the founding ancestors and other departed members as a part of the rites was clearly an effort to utilize ancestor worship to provide a spiritual symbol for group unity. Members who performed the rites before the spirit tablets felt tied to the group by a spiritual bond. Joining a secret society was one of the crises in the life of a new member, and the religious element in the initiation ceremonies not only impressed him with the solemnity of the event, increased his respect for the organization and its rules, and inspired in him the feeling of loyalty, but also increased his confidence in this new adventure because of his impression of having approval and support from superhuman powers.

Besides the initiation ceremonies, religious rites in the Hung society were performed before the altar of Kuan Yü and the "ancestors" at every gathering to transact serious business, to punish traitors, and to celebrate special festivals. On such occasions, the rites before the altar renewed the religious beliefs of the members. The dangerous nature of the activities of secret societies led the members to look beyond the limits of available knowledge and experience for assurance of success.

Furthermore, secret societies usually had an extensive organization that encompassed many localities. Frequently, as in the Hung society, they had a nationwide system. The large membership and the variation of local backgrounds implied a divergence of utilitarian interests among the members which might have had a divisive influence in an organization that needed a high degree of loyalty and unity in order to function under the adverse pressure of law and the state. A group tie through secular interests alone might not have been strong enough to harmonize the diversity of individual interests. The religious element, therefore, was helpful in lifting the members' views to a higher plane of spiritual loyalty and devotion transcending immediate materialistic interests.

THE PEASANTS' WORSHIP OF AGRICULTURAL GODS

Among Chinese economic groups, the most predominant numerically are the peasants. If the traditional Chinese, in their effort to develop loyalty and unity for their family and other social groups, looked beyond the limits of available knowledge and secular interests and drew strength from their conception of supernatural power, the peasants in their economic struggle gave religion an even more obvious place. In their efforts to make the soil yield a crop without the aid of modern technology, the peasants faced numerous uncertainties from the forces of nature, against which human abilities and exertion could guarantee only limited success. Few other economic groups had to wrestle with the mighty forces of nature as directly as the peasants. Together with the event of death, the operation of natural forces and their suggestion of animism stood as the earliest cradle of religious ideas. It was no accident that the worship of both agricultural gods and ancestors was a part of the oldest Chinese classical religious tradition, and that temples and shrines for agricultural deities still constitute a prominent part of the landscape in the countryside of China today.

In the imperial days before 1911, in every center of political administration, from national and provincial capitals to county seats, a standard group of altars were dedicated to deities related to agriculture. Few descriptions of Peking omit mentioning the impressive and inspiring architecture of the Temple of Prayer for the Good Year and the associated Altar of Heaven. In provincial capitals and county seats there were the inevitable altars of the creator of agriculture (Hsien-nung t'an), of the earth and grain god (She-chi t'an), of wind, cloud, thunder, and rain gods, and, at times, of the god of drought (Yü t'an). On behalf of the peasants, the emperor, provincial governors, and county magistrates throughout the country plowed ceremonial fields and offered sacrifices to the agricultural deities at these altars in the spring and sometimes also in the fall, praying for assistance from the supernatural forces to bring "harmonious winds and timely rain" for the year.

Aside from the official religious establishments, there were large numbers of shrines and temples dedicated to deities symbolizing man's hope for a beneficial combination of natural elements to bring about successful crops. A statistical list of these temples in eight counties is found in Appendix 1. The main gods of these temples fall into five groups: (1) Deities of atmospheric forces, such as the gods of wind, thunder, and "sweet dew." (2) Deities related to the regulation of water, bringing rain during a drought and harnessing the river in time of flood. They included a variety of dragon gods who governed the rain clouds and rivers, rain gods, river gods, and Yü-wang or Ta Yü, the deified legendary hero of water control in prehistoric China. There was no part of agricultural China without its temples dedicated to some form of water god. (3) Deities of insect control. Temples dedicated to a variety of insect gods were particularly common north of the Yangtze River, where locusts created a constant threat against the crops. (4) Deities of protection for draft animals, such as the horse god who protected not only horses but all domestic animals. (5) Deities for the protection of trees, found commonly in the southern wooded areas, where forestry was an important industry.

In a preindustrial society such as China's, man realized through many bitter experiences the limit of his abilities based on empirical knowledge and tried to invoke superhuman powers to help him face the threat of natural calamities created by intense cold, storms, shortage or overabundance of rain, rampaging floods, swarms of locusts that darkened the sky, epidemics that swept away domestic animals overnight, and other damaging forces that ruined entire crops. Such *t'ien tsai* (calamities from Heaven) constituted an age-old curse on agriculture. As man more frequently failed than succeeded in staying the damage from nature's elements, it was logical that he should entertain the hope that they would not strike again, or at least not so soon again, and that such hope would be translated into religious cults. Should calamity visit again, man would try to remember the times when his prayers had been answered, thus raising his hope and restoring his confidence as he turned from the scene of loss or ruin to face the future, thinking that surely the gods would be with him this time. Otherwise, in the face of overpowering calamities, when man had already done his best and failed, he would have to face the future with little confidence or enthusiasm to carry on.

Some early Confucian rationalists tended to discount the religious element in the worship of agricultural deities. Again quoting Hsün Tzu, who in the third century B.C. set the rationalist tone for subsequent generations of Confucian thinkers:

If people pray for rain and get rain, why is that? I answer: there is no other reason for it. It is simply as if there had been no prayer for rain, and it had nevertheless rained. When people save the sun or moon from being eaten (in an eclipse), or when they pray for rain in a drought, or when they decide an important affair only after divination, this is not because they think in this way they will get what they want, but only to make a fine appearance. Hence the Superior Man looks upon it as a fine gloss put over the matter, while the common people consider it supernatural. He who thinks it is gloss is fortunate; he who thinks it is supernatural is unfortunate.[4]

The meaning of the Chinese word *wen,* which Bodde translated as "fine appearance" or "gloss," is not too clear here. It is a multi-meaning word that holds many possible connotations. In this context, however, should *wen* carry the meaning of an impressive pattern of ritual performances in accordance with the classical tradition,[5] the essence of the paragraph may be interpreted thus: Praying for rain, saving of the sun and the moon from the eclipse, and divination rites for making important decisions are ritualistic performances of fine appearance to impress the public with the solemnity of the matter on hand. Presumably, the creation of a solemn attitude is one way to summon public attention and effort to face a group crisis, and some Confucianists think that this view of public religious rites is acceptable.

But, in the national practice of worshiping agricultural deities, what Hsün Tzu regarded as "unfortunate" prevailed. Reliance upon supernatural forces was plainly expressed in the imperial edict of 1869, bestowing a new honorific title on the river god Golden Dragon, because in that year, "when the dikes of the Yellow River were in imminent danger of collapse, the repeated apparition of the Golden Dragon saved the situation." Again, "last year [1868], on the seventh day of the eleventh month [Chinese calendar], as the Yellow River dikes were in danger, the Golden Dragon suddenly made simultaneous apparitions on the western and eastern dikes. The next day, the force of the river subsided," removing the danger.[6]

Source books on institutions of the Ch'ing period[7] abound with similar imperial edicts in the nineteenth and early twentieth centuries, bestowing honors on river and rain gods because of their presumed saving of the countryside from floods or drought. As expressed in the stele inscription in a temple of the goddess of sailing, "The flood is rampaging. . . . The means of men have come to an end, and upon what except the goddess can we depend?"[8] Many Western observers in the nineteenth century were amazed by the religious rites during a drought in which the county magistrate thrashed Ch'eng-huang, the city god, in order to induce him to give rain. Government officials in the Republican period no longer performed similar religious rites, but, up until the Communist revolution in 1949, it was still a common sight in the interior countryside to see peasants carrying the statue of the water god in a sedan chair in a procession, praying for rain, or holding mass religious services to entreat the dragon god to help curb a raging river.

Illustrative of the large numbers of temples dedicated to a variety of insect gods is the temple to the king of insects in Wanchuan county in the northern province of Chahar. There, the main building of the temple was occupied by a central image, called *Tzu-fang,* the king of insects, and to his left and right are two brothers serving as his assistants. One brother, with a fierce brown face, holds a calabash out of which he releases the insects, and the other, with a benign white face, holds a bottle to gather back the insects.[9]

Prominent among insect gods is the Fierce General Liu, whose temples are widely found in the eastern parts of China. He was a general in the middle of the fourteenth century who later became deified for his magical deed of driving off swarms of locusts with his sword. In the southern county of Ch'uan-sha in the vicinity of Shanghai, his temple was destroyed in the Taiping rebellion in 1861, but was later rebuilt. A paragraph of the inscription on the temple stele tells of the reason for rebuilding the structure:

. . . The temple was burned by the Taiping troops. In 1877, the county was plagued by locusts . . . The county magistrate realized that it was inadequate to meet the situation by merely following the tradition of issuing orders to catch the pests. So he fasted and prayed to General Liu. Later, the natives reported that, after the locusts appeared, droves of crows followed them and chased them eastward into the sea, and the county was spared from their ravage. Is this not clear evidence of protection from the deity so that the people can be succored? . . .[10]

Locusts were always a fearful pest for Chinese peasants because of the difficulty in controlling them. They swarmed like clouds from the sky, and they multiplied miraculously fast, devouring a whole crop in a short time before people could do much about them. The inadequacy of merely "issuing orders to catch" them was a conclusion from tragic experience, and the fasting and praying for supernatural help, or at least for spiritual inspiration for greater human efforts, was forced on the magistrate by a circumstance in which human abilities alone could not assure the chance of success.[11]

This motivation is seen again and again in the numerous official documents dealing with control of the terrible pest. In 1856, people in Hopei and several other northern provinces were so helpless before the rampaging locusts that they came to a point of not daring to kill them, thinking that a pest as overpowering as this must be the incarnation of some supernatural being. The emperor issued edicts to the officials and the people to redouble their efforts to catch the locusts, and meanwhile hastened to bestow an additional honorific title on the insect god General Liu, noting that ". . . in some places, thunder and rain swept the pests clear off the land, thus demonstrating the efficaciousness of the deity in expelling the pests and protecting the people." [12]

These and numerous similar cases show that the cults of the agricultural gods formed a part of the peasants' age-old struggle against the hazards of nature, serving as the rallying points for community consciousness and collective action in the face of common crises.

The Chinese peasant economy centered upon the family farm as a unit of production activities. But beyond the family organization lay many types of economic activities that needed the cooperation of a larger group. Important types of such activities were those symbolized by the agricultural cults. The Chinese state as a large-scale organization had long taken up the economic functions of water control, praying for rain, helping to control insects, and dealing with the elements of nature that affected the agricultural situation of a whole locality. The official religious rites of agricultural worship added prestige and strength to the state by demonstrating its religio-economic function, for they impressed upon the peasants that, besides temporal power, the state was also in command of supernatural forces by acting as the representative of the people in appeals for spiritual assistance to meet the hostile forces of nature. By serving an economic function, the impressive official rites of agricultural worship stood as a symbolic reminder of the collective existence of the state, which as an organization was otherwise distant and intangible to the family-centered peasants.

More immediate and tangible to the peasants was the local community: a village, a group of neighboring villages, or a county. Even more than the state, the local community found its collective symbol in the agricultural cults. In the first place, the shrines and temples were products not of individual but of group efforts, for it was contributions from the community that built most of the temples for the local cults. In the Mulberry Garden Dike Village (Chungshan county of Kwangtung province), after the villagers had rebuilt a main dike broken by the flooding river, they erected a small temple for the flood god (Hung-sheng) on top of the new dike as an appeal to the supernatural power to help protect it, and as an expression of hope and confidence in the renewed efforts of the village to control the raging river.[13] In other localities the building of temples for other agricultural gods was usually the result of community action taken after a major crisis such as a drought or a flood or the threat of locusts. In certain cases, temples were constructed by the state, and only rarely was a temple donated by a single individual. (See chap. xii.)

Thus, when individual peasants prayed in the temple for a good crop or for prevention of epidemics among the farm animals, the opportunity for worship was made possible by community cooperation. But, in addition to individual worship, there were regular annual occasions such as the birthday of the deities; and in times of crisis, the whole community would gather for mass ceremonies. Such religious activities were among the few occasions on which the whole community of family-centered peasants were brought together. Thus, the leading temples dedicated to agricultural gods also performed the function of integrating the peasant community, a subject that will be elaborated on in the following chapter.

RELIGION AMONG THE CRAFTS AND TRADES

Just as agriculture had its numerous protective deities, other economic occupations also had their patron gods. It is true that most occupations and trades depended mainly on empirical knowledge and skill for success, thus being different from farming, which had to combat directly the mighty elements of nature, against which man's abilities often appeared diminutive. But in a prescientific setting in which the technological level was generally low, the success or failure of work and the favorable or unfavorable conditions of the market still contained a pronounced factor of chance which lay beyond dependable control by man.

Thus, most occupations and trades in China, as in many other cultures,[14] had patron gods. Out of the 28 craft guilds surveyed in 1924 in Peking, only four did not worship saints or patrons.[15] The situation was similar in other parts of the country.[16] Patron saints and gods were found among dyers, vintners, tailors, makers of musical instruments, musicians and actors, cooks, barbers, and even professional storytellers. Most illustrative of the religious significance of the patron deities were Lu-pan in the construction trade, Hua-t'o in the medical profession, and T'ien-hou in the occupation of sailing. The popularity of the first two extended beyond trade circles, for even common people knew who they were.

Lu-pan (Kung-shu Tzu), a deified craftsman of great skill who lived in the third century B.C.,[17] was adopted as the patron god by many skilled trades, but it was in the construction trades that the religious significance of the cult was most apparent. At certain critical stages in the building of a house, such as starting the foundation and installing the center rafter of the roof, the workers approached their work with a distinctly religious attitude, shown through their cultic rites. When the center rafter was ready for installation, workers carefully draped a piece of red cloth across it to bring good luck. This action was followed by a simple sacrificial offering of incense and candles and the burning of paper money; sometimes there would also be food and drink. Then the rafter was hoisted into place, and a string of firecrackers was set off to conclude the rites. In a major construction such as a house, a slip made in any one of the critical stages might cause walls to collapse or the roof to cave in, not merely making the work a failure, but possibly causing injury or loss of life. To preclude such possibilities, supernatural power was invoked to enhance the chance for the success of empirical knowledge. A similar situation was found in the boat-building trades, which also worshiped Lu-pan as their protective deity. Religious rites were performed at the laying of the keel and other critical points of the work. Such religious rites were clearly connected with efforts to prevent faulty workmanship that might cause sinking of the boat. At the conclusion of the work project, whether of a house or a boat, a celebration feast was held with religious rites performed to Lu-pan, expressing thanksgiving to the patron deity and providing relief from tension by collective sharing of the abundance which the deity was thought to have helped supply. In these cases, religious rites induced an attitude of reverence, heightened man's alertness, and bolstered his confidence in a piece of work the success of which was not under the complete rational control of man.

Since rational control over sickness and death was always limited before the modern age, the function of supplementing knowledge and skill with supernatural blessing and spiritual inspiration was equally apparent in the worship of such medical gods as Hua-t'o, the famed surgeon of the third century A.D., later deified for his great medical skill. As the patron god of medicine, he became guardian of the practicing tradition of the profession and the sacred integrating symbol of many organized medical groups. Historical records presented Hua-t'o as an empirical surgeon, not a spiritual or magical healer. But his enduring reputation made him not only the patron of the medical profession but also the protective deity of health in general, being worshiped by common people everywhere, as is attested to by the presence of his temples in many localities.

Finally, T'ien-hou as the patron goddess of sailing is interesting because of the highly hazardous nature of the occupation. Among the large variety of accounts given in inscriptions of temple steles found in local gazetteers, there is a basically similar hagiography of this deity.[18] She was born in the tenth century A.D. into an official family living in a coastal village in the southern province of Fukien. While still a young girl, she was able to perform miracles, and she refused to be married. Soon after her death, sailors struggling in storm and other dangers on the high seas frequently claimed to have seen the apparition of her image, which led the ship to safety. In subsequent centuries down to the modern period, stories of the miracles of T'ien-hou continued to be told by sailors returning from dangerous voyages up and down the China coast. As a consequence, there were temples dedicated to this goddess in all coastal provinces as well as in localities along major navigable rivers.

As late as 1951 in Hong Kong, where Chinese religious activities remained unrestricted in contrast to the Communist mainland, the celebration of T'ien-hou's birthday was still one of the most well-attended gatherings in the colony. During the three-day celebration period, the normally quiet surroundings of the T'ien-hou temple were converted into a scene of mass excitement by the numerous temporary stalls selling colorful religious supplies and souvenirs, by the milling crowd of tens of thousands of "boat people" and fishermen who streamed in from the waterfronts of the port city, by the human noise and religious music, and by the pall of dense smoke rising from the temple's gigantic urns for burning incense, candles, and paper money to the goddess. Among the worshipers, there were the poor owners of small sampans, carrying only a piece of chicken as a sacrificial offering, and there were the prosperous proprietors of large sailing vessels, carrying whole roasted pigs and other items of food and drink on red ceremonial trays, all coming to express gratitude for another year of safety on the dangerous seas. For men trying to wrest a livelihood from the risky waters, the goddess of the sea was kept in view not only at the threat of crisis, but also at the end of a safe sailing year marked by a religious celebration which was a reminder of the magical power of the goddess' blessing to supplement human efforts at overcoming the hazards of the waves. Chinese sailors, like those in other cultures, are ranked among the most adventurous and self-confident groups, but they also hold some of the strongest supernatural beliefs, as is attested to by the innumerable magical practices characterizing sailing life.

The occupational cults, besides bolstering man's confidence and optimism toward work and enterprises fraught with danger and uncertainty, also served as an integrating influence for organized occupational groups. This was clearly brought out by Burgess in his study of the guilds of Peking in the 1920's. Even after a period of secularizing influence in major Chinese cities, this group integrational function remained fully discernible in Burgess' investigation.[19]

The annual meeting of a guild was among the few occasions in which the entire guild membership was brought together. At such meetings, religion played a prominent part. Whether the meeting was held in a temple, in a restaurant, in a provincial club or in a guild hall (if the guild possessed one), the dominant structure in the meeting place was not the speaker's platform but a sacred altar on which were placed an image of the guild's patron god and scrolls on either side of this containing names of deceased members, particularly prominent leaders. In front of the image and the scrolls were the standard sacrificial articles: burning incense, candles, food, and drink.

Members arriving for the meeting would first register and pay their dues, and then go straight to the altar either singly or in groups, kneel, and kowtow to the god and the spirits. After most of the members had gathered, a drama was presented honoring the god.

Before or after the play or during intermissions, announcements were made and guild business was discussed. Fines were announced and names of offenders were read, or guildsmen who had transgressed the rules were summoned for trial in the presence of the master (god). The guilty were sometimes required to kneel before the master's picture as a sign of confession of their offences.[20]

The annual feast, held whenever financially possible, was considered a means to honor the guild god. The meeting was finally concluded with the rites of "sending off the god," in which paper money and written prayers were burned.

A similar procedure, in which the transaction of secular business was punctuated by religious rites, was observed in important meetings of social groups such as the well-organized fraternities and secret societies. It was in the name of the gods and spirits that the group was assembled and group business was transacted under their surveillance, so as to add a sacred note to the purely utilitarian activities of the group. Entrance into apprenticehood under a craft master was attended by a religious ceremony in front of the altar of the craft's patron deity. Trial and punishment of guilty members in front of the altar was especially significant, for the procedure clearly represented the group effort to call for the intercession of supernatural powers in an attempt to suppress the aggressive individualistic tendencies of the guilty members which threatened the group's solidarity. This integrating function was especially important to the cohesion of occupational groups which rested on the foundation of the members' materialistic interests. Under the institution of private ownership of property, materialistic interests centered on personal possessions and thus became a leading cause of interpersonal disputes and a dysfunctional factor in group unity. The difficult task of constraining aggressive individualistic tendencies in competitive occupational fields called for the use of sacred symbols of awe and respect for the collective interest of the group as a means of elevating the members' views above the level of immediate individual advantage.

Members of many guilds were conscious of this. Thus the Masons said, "But for the religious bond, the guild might not have lasted so long"; the Awning Makers: "The relation between the religious rites and the solidarity of the guild is very close, for offenders are brought to the master and are fined incense money"; and the Flower Satin Merchants Guild of Nanking: "The religious nature is the vital element of the Association, Masters Chiang and Yün Chin (patron deities) having become the collective symbol of the Association." [21]

This explains why the guild headquarters of the masons and carpenters in Pao-shan and Ch'uan-sha counties in the vicinity of Shanghai were called Lu-pan miao, temples for Lu-pan, the patron god.[22] As late as the 1920's, even in the rapidly modernized city of Canton, among the most colorful annual events of the city were the religious processions held by various prosperous craft guilds in which images of the patron god and related deities were paraded through the streets. The guild temple and the religious pageantry were sacred "collective symbols" of the group which served to enhance the solidarity of the organization and impress upon the community their distinctive group existence, thus strengthening the pride and loyalty of the members toward the group.

The Gods of Wealth

On the role of religion in Chinese economic life, there remains the subject of the ubiquitous presence of wealth gods. The universal desire for wealth, the uncertainty of attaining it by human efforts alone, and the ever-present uncontrollable element of chance and luck, made the worship of wealth gods one of the commonest cults among all Chinese classes, particularly among the merchants, whose special aim was to make money. So, while wealth gods were widely present in private homes and in many temples, they were inevitable in shops and stores.

Many deities served as wealth gods. Some were specialized gods concerned with blessing the acquisition of wealth, while others were general gods which assumed the additional function of imposing social and moral restrictions on the manner of attaining prosperity. Regardless of their iconographic identity, they all shared a common magico-religious function in the economic life of the Chinese people.

The significance of the gods of wealth was nowhere more apparent than in the shops and stores during Chinese New Year festival days, the starting point of the year's economic activities. Clarence B. Day [23] has rendered a significantly vivid description of religious activities in a store in Shanghai on such an occasion— activities which bear a basic similarity to conditions observed elsewhere in China. An elaborate altar was set up on a table at the rear center of the store. A colorful print of a group of wealth gods was placed in the center of the altar. In front of the gods were the usual sacrificial items of food and drink, sweets, burning incense, and candles.

On either side were the symbols of business: an abacus, writing materials, and ruler were balanced by a pile of brand new account books ready to begin the year's business accounts . . . As a final triumphantly finishing touch, on a rack extending three feet above the incense urn, were suspended from dorsal fins in a horizontal manner two live and wriggling fish. Their mouths slowly opened and shut in mute wonderment at thus being called upon to act as symbols for "abundance,"

since the Chinese words for fish and for surplus or abundance are homophones.

In addition to placing the symbols of business prosperity in front of the wealth god, the owner of a store generally had the custom of giving a feast in honor of the wealth gods. Invited to participate in this feast would be

those of his clerks who were to be continued on the payroll during the coming year. Failure to receive such an invitation would be interpreted by any member of the staff as a notice of dismissal. Also, any clerk who wished to resign his position should do so before this event, since voluntary participation in this ceremonial, involving obeisance to the shop's god of prosperity, would constitute an unwritten agreement to remain with the firm another year.[24]

This part of the cult showed a religious function in the integration of the business firm as an economic group, for it was in the name of the wealth gods, in addition to purely materialistic interests, that members were hired to form an organization—the firm—for the new year, and it was again through a religious rite that members were dismissed from the organization. In choosing members for the firm, man did not act alone but with the assistance of supernatural forces to reinforce the loyalty of those who were hired, and to share the blame from those who were dismissed.

Related to the group integration of the business firm were two popularly worshiped wealth gods, the Ho Ho Erh Hsien, Twin Genii of Harmony. According to Chinese folklore, the genii

are said to have been brothers, born of different fathers, who started a large business together and made quite a fortune. Then discord transformed them into open enemies. Seven generations came and went without ending the feud, but at last through the benevolent intervention of some supernatural being the eighth generation saw their descendants friends once more . . . it is clear that these two genii are worshipped by the merchants, who understand the value of union and peaceful harmony in business, and the dependence of wealth upon happy partnership.[25]

Certain religious practices in Chinese shops, though not in the form of a fully developed cult, had distinct significance in fostering group cohesion. An example was the practice of not eating the last piece or pieces of food in a common dish. The practice was most faithfully observed in commercial firms where the personnel traditionally ate together, and less so at the family dining table. The traditional Chinese readily interpreted this as an effort to symbolize surplus, saying that violation of the practice would bring poverty. The interpretation seems consistent with the fact that surplus was most vital to the success of the commercial firm, for surplus means profit. But there was the baffling fact that the practice was confined to food in a common dish shared by a group, and was not applicable to food in the private dish or bowl, which by tradition was to be completely eaten in order to avoid waste, as waste of such food was considered a religious sin inviting punishment of the soul in Hell. Why the differential treatment of food in a common dish and that in a private one? One possible explanation is that the group practice concerned interpersonal relations. In a society characterized by food scarcity, conflict over food was a factor frequently disruptive to group solidarity, and the matter of who was to eat the last piece or pieces in the common dish became a problem to the group, which might be resolved by leaving them alone, to be given away to beggars, to be fed to animals, or to be saved and added to a new dish for the next meal. Thus, the practice might have the double function of symbolizing hope and confidence of surplus and inducing group solidarity.

Another group of wealth gods were concerned with the moral aspect of the acquisition of wealth. Some of these were financially successful men who were deified for their generosity in donating wealth to the needy in times of distress. One of these money-giving figures was Liu Hai, whose image was frequently pictured as a chubby youth with a string of coins hanging around his neck. He was popularly worshiped in shops and stores, and his picture was sometimes pasted on doors as a door god to bring wealth into the house. Kuan Yü, the god of war and the symbol of loyalty, bravery, and righteousness, was often worshiped as the military god of wealth, Wu Ts'ai-shen. In the folkloristic interpretation, he was cast in his role of wealth god not merely by his might to bring wealth (as supernatural magical power could bring anything) but also by his spirit of justice and generosity, which should govern the dispensation of wealth. Worship of these gods not only was considered a favorable influence in one's efforts to acquire wealth but also committed one to the spirit of righteousness and benevolence after prosperity arrived.

While Chinese religion took a hand in trying to mitigate the oppressiveness of the rich by giving supernatural sanction to moral qualities like righteousness and generosity, it did not condemn the acquisition of wealth as such. The prevalence of wealth cults indicates the currency of the belief among merchants that it was supernatural blessings in combination with their own efforts that brought them wealth, and hence they were unlikely to remain entirely unaffected by the moral tenets of the wealth cults. But, save for the renunciation of wealth and all worldly possessions by Buddhists and some Taoist priests, there was no general Chinese religious condemnation of economic acquisitiveness as the sin of avarice, in contrast to what was found in the Christian dogma of medieval Europe,[26] which considered it immoral to earn more income than one's needs.

The fact that Chinese religion produced no prominent cult against avarice or the devious ways of growing rich did not mean that this problem was ignored by Chinese society. Both the Confucian doctrine and the traditional social and political order deprecated the mercantile acquisition of wealth as a profession and merchants as a social class. Growing rich by trade was considered ethically incompatible with virtue and benevolence. The mercantile class was morally despised, socially degraded, and, in many historical periods, politically suppressed or discriminated against. It is possible that the combination of ethical, social, and political condemnations of money-making put such a crippling stigma on this profession that it was unnecessary for theistic religion to add its supernatural censure.

The predominance of particularistic values, especially those pertaining to the kinship group, has been interpreted by Max Weber [27] and others as a cause for China's failure to develop a socioeconomic pattern similar to modern industrialism. Because this present study concentrates on theistic religion, we cannot indulge in speculations on this intriguing problem. But we may point out briefly that Chinese theistic religious tradition placed no discernible constraint on large-scale economic enterprise, for the religious values stressed the supernatural sanctioning of reliability and justice in contractual economic relationships. Such values were essentially universalistic in nature. The ability of traditional-minded Chinese to develop modern commercial and industrial enterprises under another type of social structure in Southeast Asia and Latin America during the nineteenth and twentieth centuries indicates that the answer to the question of China's failure to develop an industrial type of socioeconomic order lies not only in the characteristics of her value system but also in the structural pattern of traditional Chinese society, which favored the sociopolitical dominance of the literary class over the merchants, whose wealth constantly tended to develop into a competitive source of social prestige and political power.

IV

COMMUNAL ASPECTS
OF POPULAR CULTS

IN THE ORGANIZATION of society, beyond the kinship system and the social and economic groups lay the larger social unit of the local community. As in the case of social and economic groups, religion played a prominent part in the life and organization of the traditional Chinese community. Outstanding in the local life of different parts of China were communal events such as temple fairs, mass religious observances during public crises, and collective celebrations of festive occasions; no community in China was without one or more collective representations in the form of patron gods, the cults of which served as centers for communal religious life. These mass observances were among the few types of community-wide activities that developed in the otherwise family-centered social life of the Chinese people.

In such communal events the essential function of religion was to provide a collective symbol that would transcend the divergence of economic interests, class status, and social background, so as to make it possible to coalesce a large multitude into a community. People from all walks of life thus could tread the common ground of popularly accepted cults. Whatever the occasion of the public religious observance, whether it was the holding of a temple fair, praying for rain, or celebrating a popular festival, religion came to serve as a symbol of common devotion in bringing people out of their divergent routines and orienting them toward community activities. The polytheistic nature of leading temples in every locality was probably developed to meet the requirement of community integration as a function of religion. Besides its own main deity, a leading temple usually had supplementary gods of other faiths, often patrons of different occupations, so that people of various religions and occupational backgrounds found the temple a common center of worship. This feature was partly the cause of the enthusiastic throngs at temple events.

TEMPLE FAIRS

Temple fairs stood out as the largest regular community gatherings in which religion played an important role. They were particularly common in the north China countryside, and most of them were held in late winter and early spring, just before spring farm work was in full swing, and at a time that symbolized the beginning of another seasonal cycle of life and growth. They were held generally for three to five days, and each fair attracted thousands of visitors. Usually held in villages and towns centrally located in a district, the temple fair was intended to facilitate rural trade in a countryside where the town and city economy was insufficiently developed. The hundreds of temporary shops and stalls that sprang up on fair days, selling a great variety of commodities, suddenly transformed the serene village or sleepy rural town into a veritable urban center for a short while, packing it with milling crowds who came to buy and sell as well as to engage in social and religious activities.[1]

The temple fair, like the medieval European fairs, displayed a distinctly religious color. With the exception of a few recently instituted ones, the fair was always organized around a temple, and the occasion was a representation of the community's devotion and honor to the temple's principal god (since a temple usually housed many gods). Hence the name temple fair, and the usual practice of holding the fair as an occasion of community celebration of the god's birthday. As to the role of religion in what was essentially a part of the economic institution, a possible answer lies in the power of religious worship to attract crowds from the community regardless of the individuals' economic and social interests. The crowds, once gathered, offered an opportunity for trade and other social activities. Conversely, people who came primarily for trade would also go to the temple to worship the fair's patron god.

The fair was usually opened with elaborate sacrificial rites in the temple, and visiting merchants attending the fair generally visited the temple to burn incense and candles and kowtow to the god before commencing their business transactions. The religious and economic aspects of the fair became intertwined, each attracting participants in the other.

This role of religion is clearly seen in a fair organized as recently as 1927. This was the fair of Yao-lu Chuang village in Ting county in the northern province of Hopei, which was organized because

so many people came to worship the spirit of a willow tree that stood at the edge of the village. The village head had wanted to cut the tree down to get some money for the village school, but before it was done, a man came and said that a god had appeared to him in a dream and had told him that the willow tree was about to be deified and that pieces of the tree would cure sickness. The news spread. People came to worship. A man was cured . . . The tree's reputation increased when a man who had never believed in the willow tree god was struck with paralysis as he passed the tree, . . . A sick man on a journey was impressed by the size of the tree. He stopped, kowtowed, and prayed for help. The spirit of the tree cured him.[2]

So many people came that the village organized a four-day fair, which attracted over 4,000 people a day.

Most of the fairs were held in honor of gods of age-old, well-established position in the local religious system, but the power of a god to attract people lay in his reputed efficaciousness in answering prayers and in bringing miraculous benefits to the worshipers. Whatever the age and status of the deity and regardless of the nature of the legend, the essential function of the religious element was its ability to mobilize the members of a community to attend an event based on common belief and common interest.

The ability of the temple fair to assemble the members of a community is seen in the example of the fair in Pei Ch'i village of Ting county in the 1920's. Save for the few caretakers left in each house, the entire village of 326 families together with their visitors from neighboring villages attended the fair. Practically every village within the county had people arriving for the occasion. Other visitors and merchants came from a distance of twenty miles. On each of the four consecutive days there were about 10,000 visitors streaming toward the temple or milling around the fairgrounds packed with stalls selling commodities or offering entertainment. During the four days over 2,000 draft animals changed hands, and people bought and sold huge quantities of food, farm tools, utensils, hardware, cloth, toilet articles, and toys.

But the religious spirit was not forgotten in the midst of business transactions. The evening before the fair began, the villagers and the merchants worshiped in the temple. Some devout worshipers

spent the night in the temple sitting on the floor in front of the altar. The nearer one sat to the altar the better could one receive the god's blessing early in the morning. In the morning a new robe was put on the god, he was fanned, incense was burned, and feasts were offered on the altar. Oil money was offered to the god.[3]

In addition to pious worship and business transactions, the festivities of the temple fair offered relaxation of conventional restrictions and moral rules. Thus a free community play by a hired troupe was an inevitable part of a temple fair; the play was considered an offering to the patron god. Many large temples had a theater built in the front for this purpose, and those without it would have a temporary stage constructed for the occasion.

This expressive function is plainly seen in the temple fairs. Horse carts which had carried the spectators to the fair lined both sides of the open ground before the stage. The women usually sat in the carts. In the open ground between the two rows of carts were other spectators, sitting, squatting, standing, chatting with each other, or absorbed in the acts of the play. The opening act of the play was usually based on a mythological theme, related to the gods and their blessings for the prosperity and well-being of the community. Many observers of Chinese religious life have wondered about the presence of a theatrical stage as a part of the permanent structure of some Chinese temples.[4] While a theological explanation for the combining of the theater with the temple is beyond the scope of this work, it is clear that the theater served the function of assembling the community for religious worship and keeping community recreation under religious influence. In addition there is the well-known intimate association between religious dances and the early development of secular theater arts, an association that might well have been carried down to the present, thus accounting for the incorporation of a theatrical stage in the temple structure.

There were other forms of entertainment at the temple fair: peep shows, puppet shows, magic shows, acrobatic and boxing performances usually connected with the sale of medicine, professional storytellers, and, above all, the gambling stalls. Besides these there were the inevitable fortunetellers, so that, on such a religious occasion, the people could both enjoy the present and try to look into the future.

The mass excitement of the fair led to a brisk social life, with many of the usual moral restrictions lifted. Gambling, frowned upon in ordinary times, was tolerated in most temple fairs as a means of attracting crowds and also as a source of revenue to finance the occasion. Only in a few of the large and well-established fairs could the administrators afford to ban gambling as an attraction.

Sex segregation was relaxed, and the home-confined womenfolk were given an opportunity to talk and mingle with men. Flirtation was often openly carried on, there being little opportunity for it in the morally rigid daily life. Even the business activities were more than just cold cash affairs, for many of the women who took their handicraft to sell at the fair utilized the occasion to socialize with other sellers and buyers in the process of haggling over prices. "The fairs were one of the few occasions during the year when the entire family came out for recreation and entertainment and so were one of the few times that large numbers of women were seen abroad." [5] The relaxation of sex segregation led many well-to-do and morally rigid families to prohibit their women from attending fairs or similar religious occasions.

Thus, in this grand concourse of thousands and tens of thousands of people, religious worship, economic transactions, and recreational activities intertwined to provide an occasion to bring the individuals out of their family-centered routine activities, to enable relatives and friends to meet and renew their social ties; and to break the simple monotony of the peasants' life which followed the fixed organic cycle of nature. The long northern winter deepened the monotony and accounted for the holding of most fairs in late winter and early spring, so that the peasants would be reinvigorated for the busy farming season which was about to begin. Above all, such a gathering of people from their individual niches represented a congregation of the local community, and the farthest boundary—a radius of twenty miles in the case of the Pei Ch'i fair—from which the fair drew its attendants delineated the area of a collective community undertaking. The great multitude of people collected from the area served to remind the individuals of the existence of the larger social group of the community outside their own narrow social and economic groups in the villages and towns.

In north China, temple fairs represented the most important regular community gathering having outstanding religious features. Their widespread presence can be seen in Ting county. There, within the county's area of 480 square miles, there were 36 fairs in the 1920's, averaging one fair to each 13.5 square miles.[6]

NONECONOMIC COMMUNAL RELIGIOUS OBSERVANCES

While the temple fair was a community undertaking with the economic function playing the principal role, there were many other forms of public religious observances that involved no major economic function. These community religious gatherings were of the periodic or the fortuitous type. The periodic type of mass religious services were held annually at regular times, usually on the birthdays of certain gods or on other anniversaries in the spirit world. The second type included religious observances held because of some community crisis, such as a drought or an epidemic.

Aside from the temple fairs described above, the term temple fair also applied to mass religious gatherings for celebrating the birthday or other event in connection with a god. At these gatherings, no business transactions took place except for the sale of religious goods such as incense, candles, paper money, and religious souvenirs and toys. Frequently such a religious gathering took place at a famous temple on a remote, scenic hill, where the isolated location would be unsuitable as a center for economic transactions. But the factor of religious worship alone seemed sufficient to attract throngs from great distances.

An example of this type was the temple fair at Miao-feng Shan, the Wonderful Peak, in the Western Hills northwest of Peking. Before the Communist revolution, nearby residents went to worship and offer sacrifice, and pilgrim groups came from as far as fifty miles away, a great distance without modern transportation. All the approaching roads were lined for miles with people coming and going. The temple grounds were packed with thousands of worshipers milling in the dense smoke emitting from the burning incense, candles, paper money, and other religious paper objects. In front of the darkened altars in the many halls of the temple were rows of kneeling devotees, each mumbling their thanks to the gods for the good things that had happened and praying for the welfare of the family or the village which a pilgrim group might represent. The pilgrim groups were especially interesting. They were generally sent by villages or special pilgrimage organizations within a village at group expense. Dressed in colorful attire and carrying their baggage and sacrificial food, they generally covered the distance by foot in order to show their devotion. Jingling bells, which were sometimes hung on their belts or on their carrying baskets, added a note of festivity. Arriving at their destination, they performed all the usual rites to the gods, burning incense and other religious items, offering food and drink in front of the altar, and performing the devotional acts of *hsü yüan* or *huan yüan* or both.

Hsü yüan was the making of a wish before the god with the vow that, if the wish should come true, one would come again to worship and offer sacrifice. *Huan yüan* was worship and sacrifice to the god as an expression of gratitude after the wish had come true, whether it was recovery from sickness, the bringing of prosperity, or the begetting of a male heir. One might thank the god for the fulfillment of a wish during the past year, and then make a new wish for the coming year.

After all this was done, if it was too late to start the return trip, the worshipers would pass the night at the temple or in nearby sheds erected for the occasion. The next morning before starting on their homeward journey, they would buy big colorful paper flowers to pin on themselves or on their hats as a symbol of good luck and a sign of their presence at the fair. They might buy some toys for the eagerly awaiting children. Then, with reinvigorated spirits and inner satisfaction, they would start their long trek home. Because of the great distance to some of the famous temples, many individuals could aspire to no more than one pilgrimage in a lifetime.

This type of religious gathering was common at famous temples in all parts of China where the prestige of the temple and its god were outstanding enough to attract pilgrims from afar and to draw large attendance from nearby villages and towns. The great temples in the scenic hills of Hangchow city and among the towering peaks in Szechwan and other provinces frequently were the sites for temple fairs of this type. These fairs were among the few occasions when people had an opportunity to be in a crowd gathered from a broad regional basis. The importance to rural communities of this type of temple fair is indicated by the widespread presence of pilgrimage organizations in the villages and towns, especially in north China.

But the holding of noneconomic religious gatherings was not limited to the temples of renown, which usually numbered only a few in each province. Even the more humble temples in the villages and towns had similar gatherings, though they were attended only by people from the local community. These local gatherings were organized around the celebration of some special event, the birthday of a god being particularly important in the southern parts of the country, where rural trading towns were spread densely over the map. Because of this density, it was not so necessary to hold periodic trading fairs as it was in north China, where town economy was less developed. But the general absence of trade did not make such religious events in the south less festive and exciting, nor did it reduce the mass attendance by the local people as compared with that at the temple fairs in the north.

An example was the celebration of the birthday of the deified general Ma Yüan (first century A.D.), one of whose temples was in a middle-class residential neighborhood in the western part of the southern city of Canton. The celebration occurred between the fifteenth and eighteenth day of the second month of the old Chinese calendar. Before it began, a committee of local leaders canvassed every house in the neighborhood for contributions to finance the occasion, and generally every household subscribed according to its ability. This financial contribution is significant, for it shows the participation of the entire neighborhood community in a religious undertaking

As with the temple fairs of the north, the celebration started with a community play to honor the god as well as to attract a crowd. As in the northern temple fairs, this was among the few occasions during the year when a free community play was given. But invariably, the adults first went into the temple to worship before joining the crowds to watch the stage performance.

Stalls lined the streets near the temple selling incense, candles, and other religious goods, and toys for the children. There were scores of gambling stalls with number games and shell games to tempt the wayward and to fascinate the spectators. The relaxation of moral conventions permitted freer association between men and women, though overt sexual behavior was strictly prohibited, as it was in the northern temple fairs.

For three days and nights, the emotional tension and the religious atmosphere, together with the relaxation of certain moral restrictions, performed the psychosocial function of temporarily removing the participants from their preoccupation with small-group, convention-ridden, routinized daily life and placing them into another context of existence—the activities and feelings of the larger community. In this new orientation local inhabitants were impressed with a distinct sense of community consciousness. Frequently, on similar religious occasions, neighborhoods in the city vied with each other in putting on a better show or in building a more elaborately decorated temporary stage if the temple did not have a permanent one. Such emulation served to sharpen community consciousness of the neighborhoods. Besides such neighborhood celebrations, there were a few similar occasions, such as the birthday of Ch'eng-huang, the city god, in which the inhabitants of the whole city participated.

Similar community religious events were also common in rural villages. Clarence Day mentioned such community celebrations in his study of the Chinese peasant cults, though he did not analyze the community aspects in particular.[7] In the villages in the southern province of Kwangtung, the community significance of similar religious events was clearly observable. There, a prominent example was the annual occasion of *shao p'ao*, or the firing off of rockets. Before the Communists took over the province in 1949, every village held such an event in the fall, usually on the birthday of the local patron god.

Thus, in a village five miles from Canton, such an occasion was the outstanding community activity of the year. The village was divided into two sections; in one lived one clan, and in the other lived four clans. In the four-clan section the community patron god was T'u-ti, the earth god, whose birthday came at the end of the second month of the Chinese calendar (early spring). The celebration lasted three days. There was the usual free community play on a temporary stage constructed of wood and bamboo. The hired theatrical troupe decorated the stage with a colorful backdrop and with banners and scrolls given to the troupe by other communities for previous performances. On the banners and scrolls were tributes to the troupe and such endorsements as "uplifting the moral level of the people" (through the lessons in the plays). Residents in this section of the village, together with those from the other section inhabited by a single clan, came to pack the temporary theater day and night for the duration of the celebration.

But the symbolic event of the occasion was the firing off of the rockets, which took place on the first day. In a large open area a tall platform was built, on the top of which a man would ignite a cylinder-like rocket about ten inches long made out of a bamboo tube. As it fell back to earth, the hundreds and at times thousands of people who had gathered on the open ground rushed to pick it up. Three to five rockets were fired, and the person who picked up the first falling rocket was supposed to receive the greatest blessing from the god, such as having a son or financial prosperity, during the coming year; the persons picking up the second and third rockets would be blessed in that order. Aside from the blessing, there were prizes ranging from quantities of rice to expensive pieces of furniture for the lucky ones who succeeded in picking up the rockets. Each winner was expected to contribute a prize of equivalent value to the one he had received, for the same occasion the next year, particularly if he did have a son or attained some measure of financial success during the ensuing year.

Performed before the multitude, the whole rocket ritual represented the community's collective hope for good fortune and its gratitude to the community patron god for his blessings. The opening sacrificial rites, the free play, the rich display of prizes in the freshly decorated temple, the procession that accompanied the rocket winners to their homes where the rocket was enshrined in front of the family altar for the ensuing year—all contributed to an atmosphere of excitement and festivity, with some degree of religious fervor. It was an occasion which convened the entire community regardless of age or sex. This was an occasion when all four of the clans shared in a common event, crossing the usual social boundaries of patrilineal surnames that separated them into four groups during ordinary times. Not merely did all members participate but every household had made a financial contribution to help defray the cost of the community play and the undonated prizes. Even the spring and autumn sacrifices to the ancestors could not match this degree of community participation, for the ancestral sacrifices were limited to the members of a clan, and largely to the males at that.

The other section of the village, inhabited by the one clan, had its counterpart to this occasion. Its patron saint was not T'u-ti, but Hua-kuang, the fire god, whose birthday celebration came in the late fall. Much the same activities took place here as in the four-clan section. A notable fact was the emulation between the two sections in hiring a better theatrical troupe and putting up richer prizes for the winners. Inasmuch as each section constituted a smaller community within the village, the emulation had the same effect as among the urban neighborhoods in stimulating community pride. Such rivalry, of course, also had the divisive effect of deepening lines of demarcation between the communal groups.

Public Observances During Crises

In addition to the periodic annual gatherings, there were the fortuitous type of religious observances held at times of natural calamities, such as droughts, floods, locust devastation, and epidemics, or
man-made disasters, such as looting and destruction by civil war
soldiers. Records of Chinese religious life abound with descriptions
of mass observances of this type.[8]

If there were a persistent drought, many rural communities,
particularly in the dry northern regions, would hold religious services to pray for rain. There would be impressive sacrifices at the
temples of the gods concerned with the control of rain, ranging from
the dragon gods to the city god, one of whose duties was to induce
rain. There would be a mass procession in which the rain gods,
their assistant deities, and all the religious paraphernalia would
be carried through the streets amidst the sound of gongs and religious music played by bands of Buddhist and Taoist priests or
by hired musicians. In the imperial days before the revolution of
1911, the county magistrate often officiated at such ceremonies.
There was the occasional spectacular scene of the magistrate thrashing the city god under the hot sun, demonstrating his assumed
temporal authority to force the god to give rain. Even in the Republican period, it was not uncommon to find the peasant masses
exposing the city god to the scorching sun in order to induce him
to bring on precipitation. Crowds gathered around the altar to
witness the spectacle and lined the streets to watch the procession.
Mass observances for other kinds of crises differed in ritual details,
but the principles were similar.

In his study of West Town in southwest China, Francis Hsü gives
an incisive account of what a community did during a cholera
epidemic.[9] As the epidemic struck, the increasing number of death
and funeral processions and the growing number of families bereft
of their members finally caused a sense of uncontrollable terror
to sweep the entire community. Then, at strategic points of the
town, there appeared prayer platforms built for the priests to perform religious services to halt the march of death which human

hands had failed to restrain. There were days of incantation and supplication, and eerie midnight processions in which the priests and their helpers waved swords and carried firearms and iron chains to banish the evil spirits that had caused the plague. During the procession, all doors were shut tight, not to be opened even to loud knocking, so as to prevent the evil spirits from gaining entrance to buildings in order to avoid being banished or destroyed by the priests.

In all such public religious services, the magical significance is apparent. Modern men, who have developed knowledge on how to sow clouds to induce rain and how to curb epidemics, may smile at the foolishness of such community performances. But the Chinese masses, who did not have scientific knowledge and skill, could, with the aid of their religious observances, face the calamities of hunger and death without complete abandonment of courage and hope. When men failed to control the devastation of droughts, floods, epidemics, and wars in a culture where the intellectual tradition of science was not extensively developed, it seems inevitable that the people would appeal to superhuman forces for assistance in bolstering their courage and hope in the face of overwhelming tragedy. As such misfortune visited not just a few individuals but the entire group, the community moved into collective religious action.

These religious services were mainly performed by priests, community leaders, and their helpers, and, while there were crowds of spectators, there was no universal participation by the members of the local community, as there was in the temple fairs and the annual religious celebrations. There were some exceptions, such as when a local community might hire a troupe to give a free community play to please the dragon gods in order to induce them to give rain. In such cases, there would be participation by the entire community, much like that of a regular religious celebration. But even without universal participation, a disaster did stimulate community consciousness. The solemn religious rites, the processions, the spectators, and even the people who remained behind tightly shut doors when the epidemic procession passed at midnight, reminded the villagers that the entire community was being faced with a common crisis and was taking collective action to obtain relief. There was a unanimity of feeling that suggested to individual minds the existence of the community as an organized group.

COMMUNAL SIGNIFICANCE OF TRADITIONAL FESTIVALS

The celebration of traditional festivals was another major type of religious occasion that had important communal significance. Though such occasions were usually associated with seemingly secular activities of group rejoicing and feasting, their religious nature is unmistakable, for every major traditional festival had its theistic basis, its mythological explanations, its sacrifices to the gods and ancestors. The activities of worship on a festival day tinged the entire community with a sacred atmosphere. Records of traditional Chinese social life, both in English and in Chinese,[10] abound with descriptive information on festivals. The following paragraphs are confined to interpretation of the social functions of traditional festivals, with special reference to community organization.

In traditional social life, almost every month had its festival, with important ones scheduled for the spring and the fall. The annual cycle of life was thus punctuated with festival celebrations, which marked the progress of the year's activities as laid out by tradition. As such, festivals operated as regulators of a community's scheme of life.

The universal observance of the festivals, beginning with the celebration of the New Year and ending with sending off the old year, was motivated by many conscious and unconscious factors, such as providing relief from the monotony of routinized life, renewing the energy and spirit of the hard-working masses, presenting a sense of relative abundance and reward (through the feast and recreational activities) to the toilers' hard struggle for life. Whatever the practical motivation, the festival celebration was always a group activity, and as such served the function of strengthening family and other group ties. In performing this function, the family feast as a part of most festivals was of especial importance. For the well-to-do, the feast table would be laden with meat, fowl, fish, and other delicacies not found in the daily fare, and for the poor, who could not afford meat even at a festival, the supply of staples was nevertheless liberalized to satiate everyone's appetite in contrast to the restricted daily ration. In either case, the feast radiated a feeling of abundance and reward, which bolstered the spirit of optimism and confidence of men whose daily struggle in life was characterized more by frustration than by success. After prolonged and often heartbreaking toil with no certainty of success in sight, these periodic moments of abundance made even a hard life seem worthwhile and fruitful. But the more significant aspect of the feast was its group setting, convened by the order of the gods to give men the taste of Providence as a reward for their collective endeavors. This common sharing of abundance in a sacred atmosphere transcended the exigencies of practical life and firmly implanted in men's minds the idea that the rewarding moments of life were inseparable from the group. This was fully visible in the expressions of relief and abandon on the faces of those sitting down to enjoy a feast after the performance of religious rites in a festival.

Festivals were also reminders of critical social values, and their celebration performed the function of periodically reaffirming the value system of a community. Rituals of the New Year celebration, for instance, strengthened the moral values of optimism, harmony, and good will. *Ch'ing-ming* (third day of the third month) rituals of "sweeping the tombs" recalled for the individual his kinship ties. The *ch'i-hsi* (seventh night of the seventh month, the festival of the Cow Boy and the Weaving Girl) emphasized the idea of fate in a girl's marital happiness. The Feast of the Souls (fifteenth day of the seventh month) symbolized the sense of community responsibility toward the unfortunate. As it was incisively put by Bronislaw Malinowski, "Religion sets its stamp on the culturally valuable attitude and enforces it by public enactment." [11]

Most of the festival celebrations took place in the family or in shops and stores. But these were not isolated actions of individual groups; they were patterned rituals unanimously and piously performed by the entire community as directed by a common religious tradition. At the New Year, for example, the whole community took on a new appearance with the ubiquitous fresh red paper scrolls pasted on the doors of every house, the colorful decorations in every home, the new clothes people put on, and their propitious mutual greetings that filled the streets. At all major festivals, if one walked through a town or a village at eventide, he would see every family burning incense and displaying sacrificial food before the family altars. The vivid existence of the community was expressed in its common tradition. In guiding such unanimous action, religion gave a community's scheme of life and its value system a sacred character which commanded awe and observance by men.

Among the festivals, a few involved collective community action. An example was the southern custom of staging intervillage "dragon boat" races on the fifth day of the fifth month, the day on which the ancient literary genius and political martyr Ch'ü Yüan was supposed to have drowned himself some twenty-two centuries ago. During the Feast of the Souls, leading Buddhist temples in the cities conducted services for all homeless spirits, and families in the whole community would go to these temples to burn incense. Birthdays and special events of many gods were scheduled to coincide with such festival days as the New Year so as to provide the occasion for staging a community play.

TEMPLES AND GODS AS COLLECTIVE SYMBOLS OF COMMUNITIES

Temple fairs and noneconomic religious gatherings of the periodic and fortuitous types were organized around the gods in the public temples. In this role, the temples and their gods acquired the character of being the collective symbols of the interests and even the very existence of the community. As the vast majority of the temples were collective undertakings of local community groups or the larger community of the state, the temple was a visible expression of the community and its collective interests, and public worship in it represented the periodic mustering of the community for the demonstration of common beliefs and common interests.

The Gods of Earth and Grain

The function of community integration was especially apparent in cults of sufficient general importance to stimulate the religious interest of the entire community. Leading among such cults were those dedicated to deities of elements of nature which had always dominated the consciousness of the peasant population.

One of China's oldest cults of this type was the *she chi,* gods of earth and grain. Few other elements could be of greater importance to the peasant community. The cult had become outstanding and well established in the Chou period (*ca.* 1027–256 B.C.). In the first century A.D. the *t'u ti* or god of earth was introduced, sometimes displacing the gods of earth and grain and sometimes being identified with them.[12]

The merging of *she chi* with *t'u ti* after Chou times existed as a puzzle in the literature on Chinese popular cults, but the merging appears logical to the functional viewpoint. *She chi* was the theistic symbol of the feudal state, while the *t'u ti* was the patron of the local community. Elimination of feudal states after the Chou period removed the political significance of the *she chi* cult, but its affinity to earth and grain retained its economic significance for the peasantry and transformed it from a political to a community cult, endowing it with a new function identical with that of the *t'u ti,* namely symbolizing the collective existence of the local territorial community based on agriculture. Neighborhood units in towns and cities worshiped the two cults for their community significance as carried over from the agricultural tradition. The historical distinctions between the two cults were unfamiliar to the common people in the modern period, for they had come to regard *she chi* and *t'u ti* as one and the same deity, though theoretically *she* and *chi* were two distinct gods and once had a separate existence from the *t'u ti.*

In addition, the functional nature of the etymology of the Chinese words *she* and *chi* probably led people into identifying the cult with *t'u ti. T'u ti* as a phrase simply means earth. The word *she* contains two radicals, one signifying deity and the other earth, thus making *she* identical with the god of earth. *Chi* had come to signify grain in general, though specifically it means panicled millet. In terms of functional significance to the peasants, *she* (earth) implied *chi* (grain), for earth, if it is good, must yield grain. The grain part of *she chi* as a cult, therefore, could be dropped or forgotten without altering the basic nature of the worship of earth for a successful crop. Hence the mutual identification in the popular mind between *she chi* (gods of earth and grain) and *t'u ti* (god of earth). The two cults are treated as functionally identical in this study, as they are in actual popular religious life.

The community significance of these two cults was indicated by their prevalence through the historical periods. In Chou times the altar of *she chi* was universally the sacred symbol of the political community of the feudal state, worshiped by the ruling house in every kingdom. In Han times (206 B.C.–A.D. 220), the *she* or the altar of earth was universally found in all counties, villages, towns, and neighborhoods, and it became the ceremonial ground for a large variety of community activities such as the swearing of a local official into office, praying for rain, taking a public vow, or praying for blessing. Until the modern period, the birthday of the earth god was the occasion for community celebrations and feasting. Because of the community-wide activities of the cult, the word *she* became synonymous with local community. Since the T'ang period, the organization of villages or neighborhoods was often called *she*. From Sung times on, the local public granary was called *she ts'ang*, and local community schools were termed *she hsüeh*.[13] The Chinese never had a general traditional term that signified *society*, and the modern term for *society* is *she hui* or "gathering for the worship of the earth god." This is a poor rendering of the term *society*, as borrowed from the Japanese translation, for it implies a territorial organization, but it does accentuate the importance of the earth god as a religious symbol of community.

In the modern period, the god of earth and at times the gods of earth and grain remained a universal cult found in all villages and towns, and having special importance for local neighborhoods. Its significance for the local community was particularly well developed in the south. In the town of Fo-shan of Kwangtung province, the neighborhood units were called *she,* and the organization of each neighborhood was based on the common worship of the gods of earth and grain:

... Every one hundred households constitute a neighborhood (*li*). In each neighborhood is established an altar for the gods of earth and grain, where annual sacrifices are offered in the spring and fall, with the head of the neighborhood officiating. On that occasion, the earth god is seated on the eastern side, and the grain god on the western side, of the altar. Before the feast that follows the sacrifice, one person reads a written oath: "All persons in this neighborhood agree to observe the rituals, and the strong agree to refrain from oppressing the weak. Violators will first be disciplined by the group and then handed over to the court for punishment. Persons with financial means agree to help those who cannot afford to pay for their own weddings and funerals. Those who fail to observe the common agreement, and those committing rape, robbery, falsification, and other misdemeanors will be excluded from this organization." After the oath, members are seated at the table in accordance with seniority of age. All will enjoy themselves to the utmost at the feast before disbanding. Thus, the reading of the law and the elucidation of the agreements become a part of the function of the spring sacrifice in which the people pray for a good year, and the autumn sacrifice in which thanks are given to the gods . . . now, even the women and children are still pious in the worship of the gods of earth and grain. Officials who are skilled in government *use the gods to assemble the people, and use the congregation to demonstrate the rules* [italics added]. This may be a good way to improve the customs and traditions.[14]

While such ceremonial gatherings and feasts had long been discontinued in that town as well as in many other towns in Kwangtung province, local neighborhoods in many southern towns were still called *she,* and the altar of the gods of earth and grain was regarded as the spiritual symbol of neighborhood communities until the 1920's, when increasing secularization weakened the traditional practice. But, in the rural villages around Canton as late as 1948, the altar of these gods could still be found acting as the protective symbol of the neighborhood, and some governing boards were still elected annually under the name of *she li-shih,* administrators of the altar of the gods of earth and grain, who took care not merely of the annual sacrifices but also of scavenging the economically valuable waste materials of the neighborhood such as garbage. This task was usually farmed out to a collector, but the administrators used the income from the waste for neighborhood welfare work. Underlying this community undertaking was the same principle of using the gods "to assemble the people."

Other Cults of Natural Elements

In addition to the cults of earth and grain, there were cults of many other elements of nature that served as religious symbols for the stimulation of community consciousness. The picturesque five-storied temple of *Chen-hai Lou* (the Storied Building for Controlling the Sea) dedicated to the dragon god, was long regarded as a religious symbol for the southern city of Canton. In a subtropical region of heavy precipitation, the city was under frequent threat of devastating floods. Built on top of a hill overlooking the city on the bank of the Pearl River, the temple represented the collective hopes of the people for protection from inundation. The temple was founded in the Han period, almost two thousand years ago. As time went on, people came to regard the structure and the dragon god later installed in it not merely as a magical means to control floods but also as a bulwark against all evil spirits that might curse the city with misfortune. A rich lore of miracles grew up around the god and the building. In the quickening pace of modernization of the city during the 1920's, there was the rumor of a government plan to dismantle the temple. Loud public protests arose, based on the fear that such action would bring calamity upon the city, for with the magical symbols of community protection gone all the evil spirits would be sure to run rampant. The structure was not taken down, and older people in the 1940's still spoke of it as having the power to ward off evil influence.

Many other cults dedicated to the elements of nature served the same function of symbolizing the interests and sentiments of a community. Among such cults found generally in China was that of the Three Officials (*san kuan*). The gazetteer of Wang-tu county of Hopei province has this account:

The village of Tsai Chuang had a temple of the Three Officials. It was situated on top of an earth mound on the western edge of the village. From the temple one commanded a complete panorama of the whole village and its surrounding landscape. The inhabitants of the village had enjoyed sustained prosperity, and a line of successful scholars with imperial degrees had emerged from their midst generation after generation. But, in recent times, the mound was being eroded away, and the temple after a while was moved to a place north of the village. After that, the tradition of scholarship markedly declined, prosperous families became impoverished, and the whole village was no longer the same as before. Popular interpretation attributed this to the deterioration and the moving away of the temple. . . .[15]

Another popular temple in the countryside, with similar function, was the Wu-yo miao, the temple of the Five Peaks. These temples, dedicated to the spirits of the five great mountains in China, were found in widely different parts of the country. One of their supposed functions was the control of earthquakes, floods, droughts, and other natural calamities.[16] The great mountains, with their towering peaks half hidden in fog and clouds and the fierce animals hidden in their caves and ravines, were long regarded as the source of mysterious, superhuman forces that presided over the operation of many natural elements. Hence a temple dedicated to the spirits of the great mountains was thought to have a protective function for the general interests of the community.

Other temples were concerned with the protection of the community against particular hazards. Of the thousand-odd counties in China, almost none was without one or more temples to the god of fire, who appeared under a variety of designations in different localities. The Confucianists who wrote the inscriptions for the steles in these temples usually emphasized the rationalized commemorative function of the creator of fire as a benefactor of mankind. But many Confucianists and certainly popular opinion dwelled upon the importance of the magical power of this god to prevent incendiary destruction by conflagrations that from time to time devoured a whole neighborhood or village, a disaster in the face of which man felt helpless. In Ch'ing-ho county of Hopei province, for example, the magistrate wrote as the reason for renovating the fire god temple in 1743: ". . . It is the god that controls fire. The county seat was visited by a conflagration, turning almost the entire section inside the north city gate into scorched earth. . . ."[17] Statements commonly found on the steles of other temples of the fire god gave similar reasons for the building or renovating of such temples.

In localities where particular hazards were common, there were special types of temples for the general protection of the community. In coastal localities, such as the Kiangsu counties of Ch'uan-sha and Pao-shan (see Appendix 1) and the Chekiang county of Hang-chow, there were temples to the sea god for protecting the communities from tidal waves or the bore. Where rivers, streams, and canals were numerous, there were temples for the ferry god and the bridge god to protect people from falling into the water and drowning. The temples for the ferry god also often served as sheltered waiting stations for ferry passengers—a typical community undertaking.

Temples for Deified Great Men

Another type of temple was dedicated to deified legendary heroes and outstanding historical civic and political leaders. Such temples were among the most ubiquitous religious buildings in China. Some of them were devoted to prominent individuals and some to groups of civic and political importance. These were men, as individuals or in groups, who had accomplished great deeds for the nation, or, more frequently, for the local community, in harnessing rivers, in constructing great systems of dams and dikes, in bringing orderly government to the land, in defending a region or a county against banditry, rebellions, and invaders, or in bringing relief to localities plagued by exorbitant taxation or natural calamities. These deeds symbolized the fulfillment of the ideal civic and political values, a subject which will be elaborated on in Chap. vii. But these deeds were also symbols of community interests, and the importance of these deified men lay in their leadership in collective activities of the national or local community. As such, these temples were often regarded as having a general protective function for the local community, especially when other popular gods were also housed in the same temple.

Thus, in Wang-tu county of Hopei province, there was the Yao-mu miao, the temple for the mother of Yao, a legendary emperor who reputedly introduced orderly government and civilization to the Chinese people. Besides its ethicopolitical function, the temple was regarded as a symbol of community welfare. Among many of the blessings it was thought to have brought to the community was the drying up of a swamp.

The original cause for building the temple was the formation of a big swamp in the lowlands after torrential rains. People in the county piled a mound of earth on the spot, and built the temple on top of it to suppress the evil influences. After that, the water dried up, never to return, and this proved to be a great convenience for local communication. . . .[18]

In Kiangsu and Chekiang provinces, many temples dedicated to local personages were used as centers of local religious worship, since the deified persons were regarded as community patrons. These temples became the site for such communal religious occasions as New Year celebrations.[19] Such was the community function of temples like Shih Hsiang-kung miao (temple of the scholar Shih) or Yang Yeh miao (temple of the Lord Yang) in Ch'uan-sha county of Kiangsu province.

A third type of temple common to all parts of China, particularly in the coastal provinces of Kiangsu and Chekiang, were those bearing the names of localities, such as Hu-ts'un miao (temple for protection of the village), Ta-ch'ang miao (temple of Ta-ch'ang village) and T'an-chia miao (temple of T'an-chia village).[20] These temples were devoted to a variety of gods, sometimes a deified personality and sometimes one of the many popular cults like the god of earth or Buddha. Whatever the deities in them, the fact that these temples bore the names not of the gods, but of villages, towns, and districts, indicated their function in serving as the center of local religious worship, and their role as a symbol of the collective life of the community. An interesting feature of some of these temples was that in the small towns and villages they were the only places where people could rent a large number of chairs, tables, china bowls, and dishes for gatherings, ceremonial occasions, and feasts. These articles were instruments of group life, and it was meaningful that the temples rather than secular organizations supplied them to the public. Other popular temples such as Chen-wu miao or Kuan-ti miao sometimes had the same articles for rent.[21] In larger towns and cities, however, there were commercial firms that specialized in renting out such articles, thus removing this function from the temples.

V

POLITICAL ROLE
OF CHINESE RELIGION
IN HISTORICAL PERSPECTIVE

THE POLITICAL STATE stands as the largest social unit, integrating the numerous local communities into a unified national system. While the role of religion in the family, in social and economic groups, and in the community is relatively apparent, the relationship between religion and the traditional Chinese state has long been an unsettled question among students of Chinese culture. Among the three leading types of contemporary civilizations, the European, the Indian, and the Chinese, it is the Chinese civilization in which the role of religion in political life has been the least systematically studied. The place of religion and the Church in the development of the European state has been clearly delineated. The permeating effect of religion on Indian political life was indicated by the forcefulness of religious divergence in the division of that subcontinent into Pakistan and India. But in China the political role of religion was somewhat obscured by the dominance of Confucian orthodoxy in the function and structure of the state, for Confucianism had very prominent nonreligious, secular features.

In China, as in other cultures, the state was never a purely secular and utilitarian structure or a cold mechanical apparatus operated by empirical knowledge and for materialistic interest alone. The machinery of government was always propelled by value systems intricately interwoven with dogmas and myths and other nonempirical beliefs rooted in religion. Consequently, neither the structure nor functioning of government was independent of religious systems.[1]

Theoretically, religion may be related to the state in three different patterns. Religion may actively ally itself with the state, either dominating it or supporting it as its instrumental force; religion may withdraw into seclusion by renouncing secular political life; or it may actively struggle against the state either to preserve itself or to gain political dominance.[2] In recent Chinese religious life, all these forms were simultaneously present to some degree. Thus we see an intricate system of religious values lending support to the state. We see, as in the case of the Taiping rebellion, religion struggling for political dominance, and the many secret religious societies which continued their clandestine activities of an unmistakably political flavor. But we also see great monasteries standing at peace with the state, carrying on their work of salvation in splendid seclusion from secular life.

This variegated pattern of relationship between religion and the state would be difficult to understand from studying modern facts alone. It represents results of historical developments the once active forces of which have become latent influences in the modern scene. Hence, it is necessary to attempt a brief historical analysis of the roots of these forms of relationship and a review of the critical forces once at work in producing these forms.

In most periods of Chinese history, religion consistently lent support to government by giving supernatural sanction to the ruling groups and by enforcing traditional values instrumental in maintaining the ethicopolitical order. To assure itself of the desired support from religion and at the same time to minimize religious organizations as competitive political forces, the Chinese state exercised elaborate controls over religious belief and organization. But the success of such control was never complete. From time to time, religious beliefs and organizations rose to challenge the ruling power, and religion played an active role in rebellions and in the succession of dynasties and governments. The sanctioning function, the governmental attempt to control religion, and the sporadic outbreak of religious resistance against control as well as the active participation of religion in the struggle for political power characterized the political role of religion in Chinese history. These three leading factors will be the subject matter for this and the following four chapters.

A brief historical survey may well begin by delineating three major periods in the development of Chinese religion with particular reference to its political significance.[3] In the first period, lasting from the dawn of Chinese history in the second millennium B.C. to the end of the Early Han empire (206 B.C.–A.D. 9), classical religion played an intimate role in political life and the organization of the state. The second period, extending from the first to the eleventh century A.D., saw the rise of Taoism and Buddhism as voluntary religions competing for dominance both against the traditional classical religion and against the state. The third period, from the eleventh century to the contemporary times, was characterized by stabilization of government control over religion, which had become an eclectic system by the interpenetration of classical religion, Taoism, and Buddhism.

CLASSICAL RELIGION IN EARLY CHINESE POLITICAL LIFE

The dawn of Chinese history revealed a close structural identification between the religious and the political community. An early historical record, the *Kuo Yü,* pictured pre-Shang religion as a political function conducted by an officially appointed priesthood, the *wu* or magicians, and regarded the subsequent rise of private worship as a sign of deterioration of the early moral and political order.[4] Classical records also showed at least two magicians occupying the post of "prime minister" in the Shang state, which thrived in the second millennium B.C.[5]

The classical religion—the indigenous religious system which developed and matured in relative isolation from outside influence during the classical period of Shang, Chou, and Early Han—contained four leading elements: ancestor worship, the worship of Heaven and its subordinate system of naturalistic deities, divination, and sacrifice. Although Marcel Granet regarded these elements as parts of the feudalistic official religion as distinct from peasant religion,[6] such distinction does not reduce the functional significance of classical religion as an integrative force in the early Chinese political community. The integrative function of ancestor worship for kinship groups among the common people, as indicated in Chap. ii, was an important factor in stabilizing the ancient political structure. Among the nobility, the ancestral temple added significance as a symbol of political power, and the ancestral temple of the ruling house, the *tsung miao,* ranked with *she chi* as collective representations of the feudal state. Herlee C. Creel linked ancestor worship with the origin of the supernatural concept of Heaven among Early Shang rulers, who regarded Heaven as the collective abode of the ancestors' spirits.[7] In subsequent centuries down through the modern Ch'ing period, the imperial temple and the sumptuous sacrificial rites performed in it always had the significance of symbolizing political power. The use of a sacred symbol, the ancestral temple, to represent political power and the state was a means of stabilizing the ancient political order.

Divination became a private religious practice in later periods, but it had notable political functions in classical times. The earliest systematic Chinese writings were inscriptions on oracle bones, bearing records of divination on matters of war and peace of the Shang state (*ca.* 1523–1027 b.c.). It is significant that these early Chinese ideographs were found in association not with secular communication but with the religious purpose of seeking guidance from the gods on public affairs. As a means of peering into the future and as a link between the world of men and the world of gods, divination both in the Shang and in the Chou (*ca.* 1027–256 b.c.) periods was conducted by official priests and the nobles, a fact that may have some bearing on the inclusion of the *I Ching,* the Book of Changes which was used for divination, in the Confucian classics adopted as texts for training in statecraft. The control of divination was apparently one of the early means of political leadership, for it imparted a sacred character to political decisions and facilitated their popular acceptance. Through divination, political decisions became commands of the gods.

Chapter x will take up the question of the relationship between Confucianism and religion, but it may be noted here that, in spite of its rationalistic character, Confucian thought did not drastically reduce the political function of classical religion. In addition to enshrining the mystical *I Ching* among the classics, the Confucians gave support and ethical elaboration to the practice of sacrifice and

ancestor worship. The Mohists derided them for trying to perpetuate the religious practice of sacrifice without concomitantly accepting the belief in spirits. But, above all, the Confucians fully endorsed
the divine character of political power by supporting the concept
of the Mandate of Heaven. Mencius' (*ca.* 372–288 B.c) reinterpretation of the concept of Heaven's Will in terms of the people's interest
and public opinion resulted in a redefinition of the duties of the
ruler, but did not offer a secular theory on the origin of power.

The vigorous development of secular thought in the Ch'un Ch'iu
and the Warring States periods (from the eighth to the third century B.c.) was partly due to the shaken confidence in Heaven's justice and providence at a time when the land was plunged into protracted social and political chaos. When the country finally saw
enduring unification for the first time under the Han empire,
classical religion not merely was revived with full force but also
gained new development, particularly in the political implementa-
tion of the worship of Heaven under the theology of the Yin-yang
(positive and negative forces) and the Five Elements (metal, wood,
water, fire, and earth).[8]

In the pre-Han period, the classical religion was an ill-coördinated
body of religious beliefs and practices containing many local elements, and the concept of the Will of Heaven and the Mandate
of Heaven was but a vaguely conceived idea of a supreme supernatural force. The Yin-yang school in the Han period gave classical
religion its first theological systematization. And its theory of "interaction between Heaven and Man," propounded by Confucianist
Tung Chung-shu (d. 104 B.c.), together with the resultant apocryphal literature, gave an ethicopolitical meaning to the anthropomorphic attributes of Heaven and its relationship to the public conduct of men. Instead of being a "mute and silent" force as in the
Chou period, Heaven according to the new outlook was to give
expression to its approval of good and punishment for evil by causing a variety of extraordinary phenomena to appear in the skies
and on earth. The theory of the succession of political power based
on the five virtues, corresponding to the five natural elements, was
a further extension of the Yin-yang theology into political life.[9]
From the imperial court down to the common people, Han society

breathed in a religious atmosphere of magic, alchemy, and occultism that penetrated deeply into political life.

The concurrent revival of religious influence with the first prolonged unification of the empire was more than historical coincidence. In the Middle and Late Chou period, Chinese culture and politics were rapidly expanding into "barbarian" territories, and Chinese national society was a heterogeneous conglomeration of many local groups, each following its own indigenous traditions and beliefs. To build a lasting unified empire on the foundation of such a society required more than the success of power politics alone. The short-lived Ch'in dynasty, the precursor of the Han empire, was crowned with success in secular power, but it was singularly lacking in religious vitality, suggesting a reason for its early disintegration. The long-lasting unification of the Han empire saw not merely a revival of religious influence in general but also a theological systematization of the classical religion which exerted a universalizing influence on the many local religious traditions. This was accomplished by incorporating local spirits and deities under the belief in the supremacy of Heaven and its system of supernatural forces. The theology of Yin-yang and the Five Elements was to explain the basic principles governing the entire world, Chinese and barbarian. This unifying influence is still to be seen today, where local cults in every community exist as subordinate bodies to the belief in the supreme power of Heaven and Earth. The Taoist theology worked within this framework, and in the popular mind even independent Buddhism did not escape this influence, for the Buddhas and the Boddhisattvas were considered a part of the grand system of deities under the supremacy of Heaven.

The resurgence of classical religion under the basic belief in the supremacy of Heaven and Earth lent direct support to the newly established centralized government. The incorporation of local religious elements into a national system of classical religion, together with the renewed importance of the worship of Heaven and Earth, contributed to the consolidation of the Han ethicopolitical order. It is important to note that Tung Chung-shu, the chief protagonist in the Yin-yang and the Five Elements theology, was the most instrumental figure in the enshrinement of Confucianism as the ethicopolitical orthodoxy not only for the Han but also for all subsequent major dynasties. Herein lay the interplay between religion and the moral order as the foundation of political power.[10]

This unifying influence of religion has been observed in other cultures by students of the history and sociology of religion. Jacob Burckhardt, for instance, pointed to religion as "the most substantial bond of humanity."[11] Religion was a strong factor in holding together a large social group, such as the state, through calamities and crises at times when secular, utilitarian social ties were shattered or too weak to orient individuals toward society. It provided a common ground for men to live in harmony and peace, and a common idealistic social order where differences between individuals and groups could be mitigated. The Han empire arose at a time when many of the local social ties of feudal China had been shattered by previous centuries of social and political transformation, and when local religious traditions could no longer serve the needs of a large and unified imperial society. So it was that a religious system based on the universal concept of Heaven and Earth and its related naturalistic forces came to meet the exigencies of a new era.

POLITICAL IMPLICATIONS OF THE RISE OF TAOISM AND BUDDHISM

This integrating function of religion, which helped to minimize local and individual differences and to bring about social unity, was important for the consolidation of a dynastic sociopolitical order and was also partly responsible for the recurring rise of religious movements in times of chaos when there was a longing for the restoration of peace and order. This is seen in the rise of the Taoist and Buddhist religions during the prolonged period of disunity following the collapse of the Han empire. Since the history of these two great religions in China can be found in standard works, this study will merely point out the political significance of the rise of these two religions.

Communal versus Voluntary Religion

A distinguishing feature of the post-Han religious life was the rise of voluntary religion. Up until the Later Han period, the classical religion possessed a predominantly communal character. The worship of Heaven and the sacrifices to the ancestors and other deities were conducted by officials and civic leaders for the well-being of all the people in the state or community, and the great ideal was to enlist the help of Heaven and the spirits to build a kingdom on earth after the pattern of the celestial order. Every individual was considered a believer by virtue of his membership in the state, the community, or the social group, such as the family or clan. Regardless of his will, he was supposed to be benefited by the religious rites, such as a community prayer for rain, and he was forced by group pressure to take part in ancestral worship. There was no choice in religious beliefs, but neither did it occur to the common man to make any other choice. Religious values were embedded in the traditional moral order, and religion was an integral part of communal existence, inseparable from the individual's existence.

The rise of the Taoist and Buddhist religions changed this picture. For the first time in Chinese history, membership in a consciously organized religion was based not upon one's inherited affiliation with a community, but upon conversion—voluntary choice by the individual believer. Previous to this, the classical religion had also permitted certain private voluntary worship such as the practice of magic, but such activities were unorganized and did not deviate from traditional beliefs. It was the Taoist and Buddhist religions that first introduced organized systems of voluntary religion.

The rise of voluntary religion had political implications. The new religions might sanction and support the existing political order, as both Buddhism and Taoism did in their long history of development in China. But more significant was the inherent nature of moral and at times political deviation in religions which could thrive only by attracting converts. The communal character of classical religion, which grew up as a tradition without a distinct founder, was based on universal acceptance of a system of common belief which, in principle, admitted of no choice. But voluntary religion based on conversion implied departure from the accepted belief of the group.

The very nature of deviation in voluntary religion lent itself to the development of political movements in two ways. First, political groups and leaders struggling against the established ruling power might utilize the deviate nature of voluntary religion to build up their own movement of rebellion. Second, voluntary religion might become a political movement itself because of its deviate character. A great organized religion generally developed out of dissatisfaction with reality, an urge to deliver humanity from suffering, and the conception of a new ideal world to replace the existing social and moral order. Such an organized effort might acquire political character as its reform extended to the political aspect of social life in order either to realize the entire ideal for a new society or to ensure freedom of religious life for its believers. Even when large-scale organized religion chose to or was forced to resign from secular society, its independence as an organized group drew frequent objection and interference from the secular government. This was frequently so in times of peace and order when the secular governing power was in firm and efficient control. But when the centralized government waned in strength, when suffering was widespread and local unrests began to disintegrate the orderly pattern of social and political life, the ideal of a new religion offered fresh hope in the remaking of life from the old order, and there was a strong tendency for voluntary religious movements to become politically involved. All this was clearly demonstrated in the rise and development of the Taoist and Buddhist religions in China.

Rise of Taoist Religion

Typifying this process was the rise of Taoist religion at the close of the second century A.D. and its development into a strong popular movement in the subsequent four centuries of continued sociopolitical disintegration.[12] Toward the end of the second century, the political apparatus of the once-powerful Han empire was torn by the violent struggle for power and wealth between rapacious groups of eunuchs and empresses' clans and the predatory strong families attached to either of the two groups. The intelligentsia, desperately protesting against the widespread corruption and abuses in the government, was decimated by the eunuchs' persecution and massacre. The Confucian ideology, the guiding doctrine for the Han sociopolitical hierarchical order, was losing its hold even among the intellectual elite for its failure to offer either convincing explanations or effective cure for the accelerating disorganization of the once orderly Han society. In the provinces increasing concentration of land ownership in the hands of powerful gentry families rendered a large proportion of freeholding peasants landless and shifted ruinous taxation onto the rest. Floods and droughts periodically dislodged multitudes from their precarious hold on the land and sent them into servitude in the gentry families, into banditry, into public relief where this was available. For the oppressed and uprooted peasantry, the socioeconomic disorganization of Han society was approaching a catastrophic state.

With the plight of the populace unrelieved by an internally divided government and with the Confucian doctrine now rendered vacuous, increasing masses of the peasants drifted into the Taoist religious communities which mushroomed in most of the provinces of the Han empire to offer hope and social stability under a hierarchy of religious leadership which made life once more tolerable and provided an avenue of status advancement for the ambitious and talented. The magical cults of Taoism raised confidence and morale, and their organization reintroduced order to shattered lives. But the spread of the locally autonomous organizations led to inevitable encounters with the Han authority and with the preying forces of the landed families. The accumulation of local conflicts finally ignited two great Taoist rebellions.[13] In 184, the *T'ai-p'ing tao* (Great Peace Taoism) raised a large-scale rebellion in Chu Lu (in present-day Hopei province of north China) which spread rapidly through the eastern part of the empire under the leadership of its founder, Chang Chüeh. Protection of their common vested interests temporarily united the warring factions in the Han government for a concerted attack on the rebels, the Yellow Turbans. A strenuous campaign finally crushed the rebellion, but it also laid waste large sections of the empire, a ruin from which the Han dynastic power never recovered.[14]

In 189, another Taoist rebellion broke out in the western province of Szechwan under the leadership of Chang Tao-ling (or Chang Ling), the founder of the Five-Peck-Rice sect of Taoism, five pecks of rice being the admission fee for a new member. Taking advantage of the disintegration of the Han empire, the rebellion succeeded in setting up a local political rule which Max Weber called a "church state." [15] It held sway for over two decades in Szechwan, Shensi, and neighboring territories, where Taoist priests staffed the political administration, collected taxes, and maintained discipline and peace among the population. When it finally surrendered to the secular power of Ts'ao Ts'ao in 215, it received considerate treatment and was allowed to disseminate its teachings peacefully among the people. The descendants of the Chang family, which founded the sect, became the government-recognized hierarchy of Taoism in China in the subsequent centuries.

While many of the details of the Great Peace Taoist movement have been lost in time, there is significant information about the Five-Peck-Rice sect. Its leaders required converts to read Lao Tzu's mystical *Tao te ching,* which urged a return to the primitive social order of simplicity as a cure for the illnesses of a complex civilization. It taught that the redemption of sin came not only through prayer but also through charity and the building of roads. It established hostels throughout its region and dispensed free meat and rice to travelers. Its teachings and acts indicated that the movement had an ideal pattern of universal brotherhood to substitute for the collapsing social and political order.

Subsequent centuries continued to see Taoist sects stage political rebellions, and many religious societies that caused political upheavals bore the mark of Taoist teachings. But it is not correct to associate Taoism exclusively with political rebellion, for during most of Chinese history after its inception as an organized religion, it lived in peace under government recognition.

The Taoist ascetic tradition and its resignation and seclusion from secular struggle enabled it to adjust its existence to the rule of temporal power, and it made a significant contribution to political peace and order by adding to Chinese classical religion the deification of legendary and historical personalities who symbolized the traditional moral and political ideals, thus lending religious support to the existing ethicopolitical order. Until the Han period, classical religion was limited largely to the worship of Heaven and its subordinate naturalistic deities, and, with the exception of the ancestor cult, the worship of departed secular men did not occupy an important place in the classical system. Theologically, the systematization of the classical beliefs was begun by the Yin-yang school in Han, but it was completed by Taoism in the subsequent centuries, molding diverse classical beliefs into a corporate system and organizing the large number of national and local gods into a hierarchical pantheon.

Taoist magic attracted many converts from the ruling class. In the first half of the fourth century, when the Taoist religion had become a great movement, the devout Taoist Wang Ning-chih was a mighty chieftain under the Eastern Tsin dynasty. When the enemy attacked his territory, he rejected the suggestion that he strengthen the defenses, claiming that he had prayed for and had obtained promise of help from the "ghost armies." Though Wang was finally slain in spite of the promised help, the incident showed that the Taoist claim of magical power had won political patronage for the new religion.[16]

Rise of Buddhism

Because of its renunciatory attitude toward secular society, the political significance in the development of Buddhism was less apparent than in Taoism, but it was not any less real. More than the Taoist religion, Buddhism offered an ideal order to replace the existing world as a means of "ferrying humanity across the sea of suffering."

The social setting during the Later Han period and the period of disunion was certainly conducive to the introduction and development of the salvational role of Buddhism. Buddhism, like religious Taoism, found a fertile soil in which to grow during the troubled years of the decline of Han, when people of all classes were longing for relief from widespread suffering. Buddhism developed into a strong independent force in the four centuries following the collapse of the Han empire, when there was a progessive deepening of the crisis of social and political disintegration.

The end of Han was succeeded by a century of internal struggle by short-lived Chinese kingdoms, and the subsequent two centuries and a half unfolded with further disasters. During the fourth and fifth centuries the entire Yellow River basin, the home of the Chinese civilization, was completely overrun by invading hordes of Huns, Mongols, Tungusic, and Turkic tribes, who continuously preyed on each other and replaced each other in rapid succession in a refeudalized land. The displaced Chinese government led a feeble existence under the Tsin dynasty (265–420) in the Yangtze valley, ever threatened by impending barbarian attacks from the north and torn by dissension and demoralization from within. Life in the newly colonized south was haunted by constant dislocation and uncertainty. From the fall of Tsin in 420 to the reunification of the empire by the Sui dynasty in 590, four Chinese dynasties quickly paraded through the south. Thus, in barbarian north as in the Chinese south, power and political fortunes were ephemeral and life was fraught with unexpected tragedies. The ruling class sank into cynical decadence. The intelligentsia was demoralized and bewildered, now that the Confucian doctrine, which had undergirded the Han order, could no longer offer guidance or enlightenment in the onrushing chaos. But the worst burden of the tragic age was borne by the common people, who as conscripts were pawns on the bloody battlefields and as civilians supplied *corvée* labor and paid exorbitant financial levies both for the endless wars and for the pleasure of the conquerors. In addition to the continuous destruction of life and property, the luckless common men in these anarchical centuries were struck by a greater frequency of floods, droughts, and other forms of natural calamities than in more stable periods of Chinese history. In the two centuries from 220 to 420, history recorded 304 calamities, and between 420 to 589, a period of 169 years, 315 calamities, in each of which thousands and tens of thousands perished.[17] From the second to the sixth century, as the years and decades rolled by, the people saw no relief from the unending procession of disasters, and the dependability and orderliness of life which they had once experienced under Han rule seemed to have gone forever. In those years, a drowning humanity eagerly reached out for anything which suggested mental or material relief from their plight. It was against this background of the structural and ideological breakdown of Chinese society that Buddhism, a foreign faith, made its inroad into China and finally spread like an uncontrollable fire, fed by the people's growing helplessness in an increasingly chaotic era.

OFFICIAL PATRONAGE AND MAGICAL FUNCTION The exact time and manner in which Buddhism made its entry into China remains an unresolved problem. But authenticated information shows two characteristics which were especially important for the early phase of the establishment and growth of Buddhism in China: patronage by the ruling class and emphasis on magical functions.

In contrast to religious Taoism, Buddhism was a foreign faith, and its establishment in an ethnocentric and authoritarian country required approval and sponsorship from the politically controlling group. Thus the earliest historical records of Buddhism in China were connected with the imperial court. Emperor Ming Ti of the Han dynasty sent an emissary to Central Asia in A.D. 65 to obtain Buddhist scripture. In the same year, a community of Buddhist monks was recorded as thriving in the northern part of present Kiangsu province under the patronage of the emperor's brother. A century later, in 166, Buddha was mentioned as a palace god along with the Yellow Emperor and the Taoist saint, Lao Tzu. During the period of disunion, the spread of Buddhism in north China was undoubtedly connected with the dominance of non-Chinese tribes, whose chieftains were favorably disposed toward Buddhism as a non-Chinese faith. In the south, Buddhist conversion of many monarchs and large groups of officials was a part of the process of establishing the new faith in the Chinese cultural milieu. Even in the centuries after Buddhism had fully established itself as an organized religion, the ebb and flow of its influence followed closely its ability to obtain patronage from the ruling power.

In its early phase of development, Buddhism was mainly a magical cult, the claim of magical power for Buddhist deities being a major reason for its ability to attract patronage from the ruling groups and followers from the common people. In a polytheistic culture, people were ever receptive to claims of the efficacy of new gods, particularly in times of widespread insecurity and mass anxiety, such as the decline of Han and the period of disunion, when the

ancient gods seemed to have lost their magical power. But even
after Buddhism had established itself in China, its magical function
of providing supernatural protection for the state and for the worshiper continued to be a leading channel by which the new faith
spread or maintained its influence. This was clearly indicated in
Han Yü's memorial to Emperor Hsien Tsung (reigned 806–820)
against the building of the "Pagoda of the True Body for Protection of the State" to enshrine the relic of a finger bone of Buddha,
Sakyamuni:

My humble opinion regards Buddhism as but a way of the [barbarian]
I, and Ti. Emperors from Huang Ti to Yü, T'ang, Wen, and Wu all
enjoyed long lives and their people were secure and happy. At that time,
there was no Buddha in China, neither was this due to worshiping
Buddha. Buddhism began with Ming Ti of Han. Ming Ti remained on
the throne for only eighteen years, and what followed were internal
strife and the fall of the dynasty. Down from the dynasties of Sung, Ch'i,
Liang, Ch'en, Yuan, and Wei, Buddha was worshiped with increasing
piety, but these dynastic reigns became progressively shorter. Only Wu
Ti of Liang dynasty [reigned 502–550] ruled for forty-eight years,
during which he thrice relinquished the throne to enter the Buddhist
priesthood . . . But at the end he was subjected to Hou Ching's force
and starved to death in T'ai-ch'eng, and his kingdom also perished soon
afterwards. The worship of Buddha was to gain happiness, but actually
it was an invitation to disaster. We know from this that Buddha was
not worth worshiping. . . . If Buddha were really efficacious, capable
of causing misfortune and curse, let any such misfortune fall on my
body, and I would neither complain nor repent, as witnessed by Heaven
above.[18]

Magic as a factor in the rise of Buddhism was enhanced by the
predominance of Hinayana (Smaller Vehicle) sects in its early development in China, for Hinayana Buddhism emphasized attainment of magical power to ward off demonic influences which
wrought misery in the human world.[19] Paul Tillich has interpreted
demonic forms as exaggerated symbols of organs of will power [20]
(bulging eyes or protruding teeth), and certainly the emphasis on
magic and demonology after the tradition of tantrism had special
relevance to the development of Hinayana Buddhism in an age

when general social disintegration removed institutional inhibition and control over aggressiveness and hostile tendencies from the individual, a psychological fact which might have underlaid much of the endless conflicts and the dissolution of social ties in those centuries of disorder. The fear of demonic influences could serve as an unconscious curb of men's own aggressive tendencies during a time when an effort was being made to restore some form of social order so vital to the successful functioning of the state. This tantrist tradition in Hinayana Buddhism had an obvious effect on the Taoist development of demonology, which did not appear to be a feature of religious Taoism before the introduction of Buddhism into China.

BUDDHISM AS A POPULAR MOVEMENT While the early development of Buddhism was characterized by the Hinayana school, which emphasized the salvation of the individual, expansion of the new religion into a major religious movement paralleled closely the growth of Mahayana (Greater Vehicle) Buddhism, which advocated pity for all creatures and salvation for all humanity as the only possible means of achieving personal salvation. This emphasis on world salvation not only lifted Buddhism above the individual and magical levels but also enabled it to serve as the focus of a new spiritual orientation at a time when the Han order was disintegrating, when the people's faith in the celestial power of the classical religion and Confucianism was being shaken, and when a new faith was needed in the face of widespread social and economic misery. The transformation of Buddhism from a magical cult into a large-scale religious movement embracing all social classes depended partly on the development of this faith in its Mahayana form. Intellectuals with a Confucian background were attracted by its metaphysical discourse, its universalism, and many of its moral precepts which were consonant with Confucian ideas.

Although in the second century rudimentary ideas of Mahayana Buddhism were being introduced by monks from India and Central Asia, the intangible and elaborate ideas of this form of Buddhism could develop vigorously only after Chinese pilgrims such as Fa Hsien and famous foreign monks such as Kumarajiva from

India had produced their intelligible Chinese translations of the scriptures toward the end of the fourth and the beginning of the fifth century. Particularly important for the popular dissemination of the new religion was the retranslation of the *Fa Hua Ching* (the Lotus Flower Scripture of the Mysterious Law), a monumental work depicting a world of fantasy in which the gods and demons enacted their dramatized parts in almost limitless stretches of time and space, where the Buddha, Sakyamuni, spoke his words of eternal truth, and where the deities, demons, and kings came forth to acclaim the enlightenment which taught the awakening of the Buddha nature that was in every mortal man as the only means to personal as well as universal salvation. Such a universalized faith, together with belief in the *karma,* the endless revolution of the wheel of causal retribution, had a natural appeal during the four centuries of disunion in China, when the protracted struggle between contending forces seemed to mirror part of the powerful scenes depicted in the *Fa Hua Ching.* And the teaching that life was illusory and transitory found most convincing proof in reality during this turbulent period, when nothing indeed seemed permanent or enduring, either a dynastic fortune or a humble commoner's life and property.

As social and political chaos increased from the third century on, the message of universal salvation and life as an illusion brought Buddhism into favor with a large section of intellectuals and officials, gained acceptance for it among kings and emperors, and disseminated it among the populace until, early in the fifth century, it could be said that "nine out of ten families worshiped the Buddha" in the northern capital of Ch'ang-an.[21] Although this statement was exaggerated, it did reflect the popular character of the movement. By the first half of the sixth century, Emperor Wu of the Southern Liang dynasty was among the three emperors and one prince during the period of disunion who took the vows of Buddhist priesthood. Rulers like Emperor Wu probably were genuine converts to Buddhist enlightenment, while others sought refuge from the fierce struggles of the times in the relatively peaceful monastic life, forsaking power and wealth as an illusion. As for the common people, who were groaning under devastating wars, heavy taxation, and economic hardship, entrance into the Buddhist priesthood was at once a spiritual consolation, a magical protection, and a material relief because they were now exempt from military conscription and public levies.

Such a powerful movement naturally became coveted by dynastic contenders. This accounted for Buddhism's patronage by many contemporaneous rulers, including the mighty Emperor Yang of the Sui dynasty, who restored to unity the long-divided empire.[22] A ruler professing the Buddhist faith would win religious endorsement for his cause and attract sympathetic support from a Buddhist-oriented population.

CHALLENGE OF THE MONASTIC ORDER AGAINST POLITICAL RULE Unlike the classical religion, which diffused into the secular social institutions and became subject to their complete control, Buddhism had its independent organized existence in the form of the monastic order, an existence based upon the renunciation of secular life. Monasticism represented an effort to set up an ideal world, within which operated a self-contained system of authority, discipline, material sustenance, and social life. On the ground that the members of the monastic order had renounced secular life and withdrawn from society, the order claimed freedom from secular political control and exemption from the burden of taxation and military service. Ideally, the final salvation of the world would come when the monastic order had expanded to embrace all mankind, completely replacing secular society, including its government. It is obvious that, short of the conversion of the monarch, the expansion of such a religious movement would eventually bring it into conflict with the secular political power. Historically, such was the case.

By the middle of the third century, Indian missionaries began translating monastic rules into Chinese in response to the need of the Buddhist movement as an organized religion. By the fourth and fifth centuries, Buddhism reached its height as a religious force organized around the monastic order. Not merely huge numbers of helpless commoners sought refuge from conscription and taxation in the monasteries, but also noblemen and powerful officials placed their land and property in the hands of the monasteries and took the vows of priesthood in order to evade taxes and other public responsibilities, thus deeply embroiling the new religion in politics. By the first part of the sixth century, this "state within the state" had developed to such a scale that, even under the devoutly Buddhist Emperor Wu of the Southern Liang kingdom, there was strong protest against this expansion of organized Buddhism at the expense of the secular political power. Influential officials such as Kuo Tsu-shen memorialized the throne:

Over a hundred thousand monks and nuns possess vast wealth and property. In addition, the monks have neophytes and the nuns have adopted daughters. *Nearly one half the population in the whole empire is lost to them. I fear that every building will turn into a monastery, and the people in every family will be ordained into the priesthood, and not one foot of soil will remain to the state* [italics added].

Another official, Hsün Chih, presented a similar memorial complaining that the chief Buddhist priests lived a sumptuous life comparable to that of the emperor, and that retainers served them in the style of court officials.[23]

Such developments made conflict inevitable between the new religion and the secular political power. On the one hand, feeling confident and powerful, Buddhist groups more than once openly challenged the government authority. Between 477 and 535, in less than sixty years, there were eight attempts at armed rebellion by Buddhists in Northern Wei alone, a kingdom where political patronage had enabled Buddhism to develop into a powerful organized force. Even in a period of unity and strong central government such as in the T'ang dynasty (618–906), Buddhist encroachment upon the state prerogative of taxation and conscription was an issue forming one of the central points in the famed memorial of Han Yü (768–824), which demanded, "Restore its people to human living! Burn its books! And convert its buildings to human dwellings!"[24] This conflict between organized Buddhism and the interests of the secular authority was behind the four historic persecutions of Buddhism in 446, 574, 845, and 955.[25] After 955, there were no further major persecutions of the Buddhists, but Buddhism as a nationally organized force intimately linked to political issues also came to an end. From this period on, Buddhism became acculturated to the Chinese social milieu both in its theology and its organizational relationship with the secular authority.

REASSERTION OF THE CLASSICAL RELIGION IN ECLECTIC FORM

The development in China of an originally Indian religion, Buddhism, into a major organized religion with extensive political influence closely paralleled the domination of the Yellow River basin by non-Chinese invaders during the period of disunion. During the early part of the fourth century, for example, Shih Hu, the ruthless monarch of the northern kingdom, the Later Chao, rejected the suggestion of renouncing Buddhism as a non-Chinese religion by saying that he himself was of foreign origin, that Buddha was a foreign god, and therefore should be worshiped. In the T'ang dynasty the continued flourishing of Buddhism on a vast scale was partly due to the cosmopolitan character of the T'ang policy, which tolerated a variety of foreign influences.

But with the rise of the Sung dynasty (960–1279) in the second half of the tenth century, there was a general resurgence of Chinese national culture against foreign influences. Nationalism characterized the religious picture in the thousand years that followed, with the exception of the century of Mongol rule (1260–1368), which was under considerable Buddhist influence.

An expression of this nationalistic tendency was the reassertion of classical religion in political life, centering upon the belief in the supremacy of Heaven and its associated deities and their ability to bring about a united and peaceful empire by giving mankind a "True Son of Heaven." Religious faith in the political order once again rested on the classical blessing of Heaven on the monarch and secular government. Retreating into the background was the once mass fervor for salvation through faith in Buddha, who alone could deliver mankind from its eternal suffering.

The nearly three hundred years of unity and strength during the T'ang dynasty had restored faith in the possibility of a united empire under one supreme government. By the Sung period, the reassertion of Confucianism helped to renew faith in the classical religion as the spiritual support for the imperial political order. This was due partly to the traditional Confucian acceptance of classical cults, and partly to resolute Confucian rejection of a foreign faith such as Buddhism, with its independent monastic order, as the major religious support for the secular authority. Once more, the dominant faith of the land, so far as political life was concerned, was oriented toward the Confucian system of sociopolitical hierarchy supported by classical deities that promised to bring celestial order to earth.

Buddhism had arisen in the wake of the weakening of Han Confucianism as an accepted political ideal, a weakening which stemmed partly from the metaphysical deficiency of that doctrine, from its inability to deal with the questions of an ever-changing reality versus the constancy of eternity and the final fate of mankind, from its inability to inspire confidence and give consolation to man in the face of overpowering adversity and suffering such as existed in the post-Han period. By the Sung period, the neo-Confucian Philosophy of Reason had incorporated enough Mahayana Buddhism into its system to make up much of this deficiency, as Hughes has noted.[26]

Taking up the challenge from Buddhism on the questions of the illusion of life in the ever-changing existential world and the eternal truth of nirvana, neo-Confucianists went back to the study of the *I Ching,* the mystic classical Book of Change that had baffled Confucius, and evolved their theories concerning the objectification of the mind in relation to matter; the physical world as a harmonious system governed by knowable laws (*li* or reason) within a limitless universe; the emergence of tangible forms from intangible ethereal substance (*ch'i*); the alternation between movement and stillness, the two integral aspects of all phenomena; the constant changeability and unlimited variation of life and matter as a contributing part of the immense complexity of the eternal universe and not as a dreamlike illusion. Once more, man's hope for salvation was oriented toward reality rather than toward the eternal dream of nirvana or the Taoist paradise of fairyland.

With the restoration of unity and peace to the empire and with the social order under some degree of control, the revitalized doctrine of Confucianism was able to displace both Buddhism and religious Taoism as the moving spirit of the age.

But neo-Confucianism contained much Buddhist inspiration in its theories on the mind and matter. Much of the hard-headed realism of the neo-Confucian interpretation of the universe as a self-operating mechanism could not develop very far without employing rigid scientific methodolgy, something that was not possible at the time. Consequently, the neo-Confucianists resorted to the Ch'an Buddhist formula of meditative mental concentration and sudden enlightenment as the chief means to knowledge of universal laws. Thus, reflective meditation became an intimate part of the personal life of many Confucians.

The Mahayana Buddhist pity for all creatures and the hope of salvation for all humanity fused into the Confucian concept of universal benevolence and devotion to moral duties regardless of personal consequence. The modern Confucianist K'ang Yu-wei acknowledged this Buddhist influence in his fervor to save the Chinese empire through reformation.[27] The individual's identification with eternal truth helped him disregard present adversities and personal danger in the pursuance of moral duties. In these and many other ways, elements of Buddhism became incorporated into the governing doctrine of China from the eleventh century on.

Among the common people, many basic Buddhist beliefs had become firmly implanted in their moral life. The Buddhist concept of transmigration of the soul and the law of causal retribution had gained universal acceptance among the masses and was instrumental in the enforcement of folkways and mores, and became a powerful support for the operation of the ethicopolitical order. Both Buddhism and religious Taoism had contributed many new deities to popular fiction and folklore as well as many dignified temples that symbolized the moral and political values of the traditional social order. Even that citadel of classical religion, the worship of ancestors, became enriched by the participation of Buddhist and Taoist monks and the adoption of their theology and rites in funeral and sacrificial services. And the strengthening of the family institution through religious influence had apparent political significance in a Confucian state which emphasized the family as a basic unit of the political order.

After repeated persecutions before the eleventh century and under the resurgence of Confucianism as the leading spirit of the times and the emergence of a more enduring political unity and peace in the empire, the once vast Buddhist monastic order became reduced in size and withdrew from active struggle for political influence. Instead of being a center for world salvation bent upon converting kings and officials as well as the common people, the monastic order became mainly a place of refuge and retreat for individuals who had been overwhelmed by social and economic adversities. It stood passively waiting to receive all who had failed to find peace and security in secular society or in Confucianism, which so closely identified itself with social reality. With resignation, the monasteries preserved the identity of Buddhism as an independent religion in spite of government control and the dominance of an eclectic folk religion. This course of resignation also characterized the Taoist religion after the failure of its early insurrections.

But this does not mean that these two religions had become completely submissive to the secular political power. Time and again, down to the present, they jointly contributed to the development of secret religious organizations that become instrumental in fomenting rebellions and dynastic changes.

VI

OPERATION OF
THE MANDATE OF HEAVEN

IN ITS HISTORICAL PERSPECTIVE, as seen in the last chapter, traditional Chinese government was never purely secular, but instead there was always an intimate interplay between religious and political forces. From the twelfth century on, large-scale organized voluntary religion wielding independent political influence retreated into the background, and the reassertion of the Confucian state provided an opportunity for certain classical religious elements to develop once more their function within the framework of the political institution. This function lay mainly in giving religious sanction to the ethicopolitical order of the state. It was in this direction that religion developed its political role in harmony with the Confucian principles which insisted upon secular control of political power.

EFFECTIVENESS OF THE MANDATE IN MODERN TIMES

It is a familiar fact that many of the religious influences in Chinese political life stemmed from the basic concept of Heaven and its subordinate system of deities as a supernatural force that predetermined the course of all events in the universe, including political events. Of central importance to this concept was the idea of the Mandate of Heaven, the symbol of legitimacy claimed by every dynastic power and widely accepted by the common people. The grand imperial sacrifice to Heaven, which struck the Jesuit missionaries in the sixteenth and seventeenth centuries as the most impressive institution in the Middle Kingdom, was continued with all its traditional solemnity and splendor throughout the entire Ch'ing period (1644–1911). Thus stated Hughes:

> There was the solemn rite of the emperor's worship of Heaven, when as the representative of his people he presented himself at the great Altar of Heaven. After due fasting and with his great officials in their gorgeous robes to support him, the greatest monarch on earth prostrated himself before something which was not represented by any image, something which was above him and his people as the blue sky was above the white marble altar, something without whose providence in the ordering of seasons the people could not live, and by whose commission he held his throne.[1]

This one classical religious tradition was neither displaced by foreign beliefs nor tarnished by time through its more than three thousand years of existence and development. The founding of the Ch'ing dynasty in 1644 and the coronation of each successive monarch until 1909 was accompanied by the most sumptuous sacrifice to Heaven and Earth[2] as a symbol of receiving the Mandate of Heaven to rule the empire. Throughout the duration of that dynasty, the administrative district in and around the national capital of Peking was named Shun-t'ien Fu, the Prefect in Accord with Heaven. In 1850, when reviewing the position of the dynasty in the face of the raging Taiping rebellion, Emperor Tao Kuang reiterated that, "We, the Great House of Ch'ing, received the Mandate from Heaven."[3] Four years later, Emperor Hsien Feng tried to justify his dynastic power in the face of that spreading rebellion by reaffirming the same claim: "I rule the people as a representative of Heaven."[4]

Similar pronouncements abounded in the edicts of every monarch in the entire Ch'ing period, particularly when the political power of the dynasty was challenged by dissension or rebellion. The imposing and stately sacrifices to Heaven were meant to be testimony to these pronouncements. In normal as in troubled years, such pronouncements and sacrifices served as tangible reminder to the people that the power to govern was not an affair among men, but an arrangement between Heaven and the ruling group.

Similar significance was embodied in the popular myth that the emperor was the incarnation of the dragon. As the most powerful living creature, the mythological dragon dwelt in the clouds and was intimately associated with the heavenly forces that controlled rain and other climatic elements so essential to agriculture. Hence the use of the dragon and cloud pattern as the basic decorative motif on the embroidered imperial robes, on palace buildings, and on objects used by the imperial household. All these were traditional means of associating Heaven and its forces with the imperial power.

This basic notion of political power as a divine commission from Heaven did not die with the end of the Ch'ing dynasty in 1911, for an impressive sacrifice to Heaven and Earth constituted part of the preparation by which Yüan Shih-k'ai, the Republican renegade, attempted his abortive restoration of the monarchical system in 1915. At that time, the provincial assemblies of the shaken Republic were maneuvred into issuing a declaration urging Yüan to assume the "supreme position in accordance with Heaven's will." [5] The following story continued to circulate in Peking from the time of the restorationist crisis to the 1930's. Yüan's cook served him rice every day in a treasured porcelain bowl in his bedchamber. One day the bowl fell from the cook's hand while he was in the chamber, and broke. To save himself, the cook said to Yüan, "As I was entering your room with the rice bowl, I suddenly saw a huge dragon stretched on your bed. I became frightened and the bowl fell from my hand and broke." Yüan, so the story goes, was very pleased and did not punish the cook. Whether or not there was such an incident is inconsequential. What is significant is that the story circulated among the people in the capital at a time when the restorationist movement needed supernatural justification to help it gain popular support.

SANCTIFYING THE SUPREMACY OF THE CENTRAL POLITICAL POWER

Thus, through impressive sacrifices, official pronouncements, and popular lore, constant effort was made to associate imperial power with Heaven and the heavenly forces. The reasons for such effort are well recognized by students of Chinese culture.[6] The basic factor was the overwhelming power of Heaven and its forces. There was no more readily observable symbol of supremacy above man than the mysterious, limitless heights of Heaven. The regular movements of the heavenly bodies symbolized Heaven's regulative power to keep the universe in stable order. And the power of the heavenly forces to produce the proper succession of seasons was of particular importance to an agricultural people.

Any individual or group that succeeded in convincing the people that they were the earthly representatives of such forces would enjoy in the public mind Heaven's sanction and would share Heaven's superhuman power. Thus, in 1881, in introducing the subject of official sacrifice, the local gazetteer of Ma-ch'eng county of Hupeh province quoted the ancient classical statement: "Just as there are ten planets in Heaven, there are ten classes among men; it is for the low [classes] to serve the high [classes], and it is for the high [classes] to be in communion with the gods." [7]

Investing political power with sanctity is universal with primitive tribes as well as with premodern states.[8] But with the Chinese state, there was an additional factor underlying the constant effort to impart a divine character to imperial political power in order to ensure its supremacy and to inspire awe and respect. This factor was related to the failure of Confucianism as the state orthodoxy to present a theory of the origin of monarchical power, thus leaving this power without an ultimate secular justification.

The Confucian principle of *government by men of merit through selection* (the civil service examination system) was the basis for the authority of the administrative officials, but not for the power of the monarch. Theoretically, the principle of merit was extendible to the head of the state, for Confucian classics abound with discussions of the qualities an ideal head of the state should possess. He should, for example, have sagelike wisdom and perfect self-discipline; he should have a boundless heart for benevolent government; he should devote himself completely to public duties; he should know not only the "Way of Man" (*jen tao*) but also the "Way of Heaven" (*t'ien tao*).[9] Centuries of Confucian literature kept harking back to mythological rulers like Yao and Shun for examples of such ideal heads of state.

Some of these qualities may be considered what Max Weber

called charisma, the gift of grace, and they already carry an element of the divine. In spite of the Confucian theory that through cultivation and effort such qualities are attainable by men, history showed no such examples. Setting up such standards resulted only in lengthy imperial titles given to rulers through the centuries, titles that claimed sagely wisdom, unusual abilities, and perfect virtues, all in order to create an aura of superhuman qualities around the imperial personage. Such titles, often mockeries of the real qualities of their owners, served to inspire awe and respect and to represent post-facto justifications for power. The establishment of such standards also gave a pontifical character to the traditional imperial edicts, which were called "sage will" or "sage instruction." As we will soon see, these titles and standards also formed a part of a Confucian "ideal pattern," designed for moral control of power. But there still remained the question of why a person of falsified merits should be permitted to occupy the seat of supreme power.

In the Confucian orthodoxy, another unanswered question was how an ideal person was to attain the position of monarch, even granting that he could be found. Neither Confucius nor Mencius saw fit to dwell on the mythological "yielding of power" by a sage monarch to a successor chosen purely on the ground of merit, and the formula was glaringly impractical in an actual power struggle (as seen in the yielding of the Han throne to Wang Mang in A.D. 9 under duress). Mencius' theory of revolution by the people was a negative measure for removing tyrants, not a positive formula for selecting a meritorious person and installing him in the position of supreme power, and the theory never was developed into an institutionalized principle. It may be suggested here that the Confucian sense of practical politics and its emphasis on universal harmony prevented the full development of a theory of revolution or the extension of the idea of the civil service examination system to the selection of the head of state.

At any rate, in founding the Confucianist doctrine, both Confucius and Mencius chose not to elaborate on the question of the origin of imperial power, but rather to confine themselves to formulating a body of ethicopolitical principles defining the duties and guiding the actions of a ruler after power was placed in his hands. In subsequent centuries the Confucian tradition offered no objection to—in fact, implicitly accepted—the historical adage, "The one who won [power] became a king; the one who lost [power] became a bandit." It was plainly the familiar expedient formula of accepting power as an accomplished fact and then trying to harness with it the pressure of moral prescriptions.

This accomplished fact represented success in the struggle for dynastic power through the most sanguinary and destructive violence. Post-facto moralization of the situation alone would not be sufficient to wipe away the bloodstain from the winner and build respect and confidence in him and his new position of power so as to stabilize the institution of government. Beyond moralizing, a supernatural explanation was needed to force popular acceptance of the new leader. Such a supernatural explanation was supplied by the Will and Mandate of Heaven, which favored the winner; the outcome of the whole struggle was part of the predetermined course of events, unalterable and unchallengeable by men. And, above all, Heaven as the predeterminer of events stood as the supreme judge of universal morality. It was in this sense that the people accepted the winner as part of an overwhelming fate, assenting to him along with the moral precepts attached to the situation as ordained by Heaven. Thus the awe and respect for the supernatural was a vital factor in putting the coat of morality and honor on a dynastic founder, who was basically a master at the manipulation of force and violence.

In the subsequent events of a dynasty, should the monarch be a charismatic figure capable of exemplary leadership, his effective political performance partly became the justification of his power. But, should he be mediocre or derelict in his duties, some other justification for his power was needed in order to maintain the people's respect and confidence in the institution of government. It was here again that Confucian orthodoxy accepted the arbitrary concept of the divine sanction of political power.

The question has often been raised as to how the rulers received the "Mandate" from Heaven. Such mystery was not explained by Confucianism or by any other doctrine, nor was such explanation necessary. More than anything else, the Mandate of Heaven was invested in the office of the throne, rather than in the person of the ruler. It was the possession of the office, as symbolized by the performance of the sacrificial rites to Heaven and Earth, that imparted a sacred character to the person of the ruler. The divine endorsement of the office, and not the person, enabled Confucian doctrine to justify the change of a ruling house as the situation arose. It was in this way that the administration of the empire was stabilized on an arbitrary center of supreme power which was justified not by the secular consent of men but by the sanctifying power of almighty Heaven.

INSPIRING CONFIDENCE

Besides endorsing the supremacy of the imperial power, divine sanction from Heaven also inspired confidence in the governing authority as a stabilizing factor in the political structure of the empire. If chance and the limitations of empirical knowledge were factors in the development of cultic worship in social and economic activities, the same factors applied to the development of the state cult of Heaven and Earth and its system of subordinate deities. Even the most effective ruler could not assure perfect success in the complex affair of ruling a vast empire, as natural calamities and human upheavals might upset his plans. At times of uncontrollable crises, it was again natural that man would draw confidence and strength by appealing to the supreme power of Heaven.

A prominent example of this was the religious activity of the imperial court during the Taiping rebellion. At the height of the rebellion, edict after edict was issued by the emperor to enlist the help of the gods to suppress the rebels. When at last the rebel capital of Nanking was recaptured in 1864, there was a burst of religious activities, including the impressive imperial sacrifice to Heaven and Earth, the supplication to the spirits of the imperial ancestors, and the numerous sacrifices to local deities by officials in the provincial communities, all offering thanks for divine assistance in the great achievement. Thus, an edict from Emperor T'ung Chih in that year stated that the widespread destruction wrought by the rebels had angered both the gods and men, that the imperial government had launched its campaign in the name of Heaven, and that the success in recapturing the city of Nanking was "due solely to favored protection from Heaven and affection from the spirits of the sage ancestors." [10]

Such religious activities and pronouncements reflected the court's lack of confidence in human abilities alone to restore control over the empire and a tendency to draw inspiration from the supernatural realm. Even if we should doubt the sincerity of the rulers, these edicts and sacrifices neverthless impressed the people with the notion that Heaven and the gods continued their sanction and support for the house of Ch'ing. Still effective as a guiding political principle was Confucius' statement that a state, if forced to, could forego defense and even food, but it could not stand without the people's confidence in the government (*Lun yü,* Book VII, chap. 7). Even in times of peace and order, the imperial government needed religious sanction from Heaven to help maintain the people's confidence. In times when the people's confidence in the government was shaken by its inability to maintain unchallenged supremacy, public belief in supernatural help was so much the more necessary.

The Popular Foundation of the Mandate of Heaven

The question may be raised as to how the common people came to believe in the idea of the Mandate of Heaven and to accept the supremacy of imperial power partly on the ground that it was a predetermined course ordained by the gods. The question is particularly pertinent in view of the relatively tenuous tie between the central imperial power and the intimate life of the common people. As the common people were rather unconcerned over the central government, one questions how religious ideas about the central political power made such a deep impression on the minds of the people.

Many factors were involved. Secular matters, such as the possession of naked force and coercion by the government, the occasional devastation of war, the exaction of taxes and levies, and the intermittent exercise of law and justice, all brought the central political power into the intimate life of the people. But so far as the religious belief connected with political power was concerned, the idea of the Mandate of Heaven rested on the popular acceptance of Heaven as the supreme power which predetermined all events in the universe, from great affairs of state to humble occurrences in the individual's life.

The theology of Yin-yang and the Five Elements provided a mystical explanation for the relationship between the heavenly forces and the affairs of state; the succession of dynastic powers was thought to be predetermined by the rotation of the Five Elements.[11] The same theology also interpreted the predetermination of all personal events by the set of forces of Yin-yang and the Five Elements, which were connected with the movement of the stars in directing the mystical operation of time, which, in turn, determined the nature of personal events.

Hours of the day, for example, were designated by twelve Chinese characters representing the "twelve earthly branches," and the years were designated by the combination of these characters with ten other characters representing the "ten heavenly pillars." Each time unit stood for a certain combination of heavenly and earthly forces at work. The meeting of these forces at a certain hour in combination with a certain day in a certain month in a certain year might be harmonious and lead to good luck, whereas another combination might mean an antagonistic meeting of forces and lead to misfortune. The idea was similar to that of combining Friday and the thirteenth day of the month, which signifies bad luck in the Western tradition. A man born at a certain time, because of the rare combination of harmonious forces at that time, might be destined to mount the throne, while another person born at a time when there was an antagonistic meeting of mystical forces might be fated to die of starvation. The results of human action were similarly predetermined by the particular time such action took place. Thus, a person's whole career and fate depended on the operation of these mystical forces as they affected him. And so the magic-oriented common people would not take any major action, from holding a wedding to opening a store, without consulting the religious almanac for an auspicious time. The same theology of Yin-yang and the Five Elements underlay the theory of *feng-shui* (geomancy), which interpreted the effect of a certain space or the location of a building or a grave upon the luck or misfortune of the affected individuals. Space, no less than time, was involved in the operation of the mystical forces of Yin-yang and the Five Elements. Fuller descriptions of the beliefs in the magical influences of time and space are abundant in other works dealing with Chinese mysticism and superstitions.[12]

Observers have generally regarded these practices of divination and geomancy as a chaotic mass of ignorant superstitions. Actually they represented a well-coördinated system of religious concepts containing the belief in the power of Heaven and Earth to pre-determine the course of all events, large or small, by controlling the time and space within which they occurred. It was because the people believed in Heaven's power to control the fate of their personal lives that they came to embrace the idea of the Mandate of Heaven and the divine character of the supreme political power. Otherwise, the worship of Heaven as a political cult would have been something quite distant from the intimate experience of the people. In this sense, the theology of Yin-yang and the Five Elements served as a link between the supernatural basis of the affairs of state and the intimate life of the people.

UNIVERSALIZING INFLUENCE OF HEAVEN

The universal acceptance of the supreme power of Heaven over all gods and man provided the imperial power with an important religious basis for the political integration of a vast country. The immensity of China, its variegated geographical settings, and the complexity of ethnic backgrounds in the local communities all tended to breed religious and political variations that might have threatened the unity of the empire. But when Heaven was accepted as the supernatural power that governed all the gods regardless of faith or creed, and when Heaven was used as the sanctifying authority for the central political power, the effect was to increase the empire's unity by subordinating to central control a variety of local religious traditions that otherwise might have become sanctioning symbols for local political autonomy. The supremacy of Heaven over all gods created a hierarchical system out of the numerous local deities, which otherwise would have presented a chaotic conglomeration of mutually exclusive religious traditions, a situation that would have inevitably affected the unity of the empire's political life. Heaven thus represented a universalizing influence in the imperial unification of diverse localistic beliefs and traditions. Under this system the peasants in Chekiang or Kwangtung province might be intensely devoted to local gods and spirits stemming from a particular ethnic background, but these deities were a part of the hierarchy of supernatural powers subordinated under Heaven, the formal worship of which was monopolized by the central political power.

ETHICOPOLITICAL SIGNIFICANCE OF HEAVEN—THE "INTERACTION BETWEEN HEAVEN AND MAN"

With the acceptance of social and political life as Heaven-ordained came the development of the popular attitude of "Obey Heaven and adjust to time; be content with oneself, and accept fate," an attitude that was most conducive to the consolidation of the power position of the rulers. But this predetermined course of events, however inevitable it might be, needed an ethical content in order to create a submissive attitude in the populace. The inculcation of moral meaning into political power yielded an ethicopolitical order that was essential to the stability of the political institution. It was in this connection that religion came to play another influential political role.

Religion and the Moralization of Power

It has been previously pointed out that the Confucian orthodoxy extended implicit recognition to the winner of the violent struggle for power as the legitimate ruler, and then imposed on him and his government a body of institutionalized ethicopolitical precepts and rules. Confucianism repeatedly emphasized rule by ethical virtue as against rule by force and law. The principle was symbolized by the

Confucian key term of *cheng chiao,* or government through educational guidance. By this formula the Confucian orthodoxy inculcated moral meaning into imperial power, power that had generally
been acquired through ethically unmotivated channels of violence
and coercion. The moralization of power gave a stability to the
institution of government which could never have been achieved
by force alone.

The moralization of power had added importance for the governing of as vast an area as the Chinese empire with but a simple
political structure and a strikingly small number of officials. In the
nineteenth century there were only about 40,000 official positions for
the management of the central and local government agencies that
ruled over 3,500,000 square miles and an estimated population of
400,000,000.[13] This contrasts with some 1,500,000 officials in Communist China in 1957, in addition to the ruling elite of 12,000,000
members of the Chinese Communist Party and 23,000,000 members
in the Youth League as part of the governing apparatus.[14] The system of formal imperial government stopped at the county level,
with counties averaging about 200,000 population each. Without the
assistance of the Confucian ethicopolitical order that was internalized
into the conscience of the people, a scantily staffed formal government would not have been able to maintain unity and order in the
extensive country.

But the effective operation of the ethicopolitical order depended
partly on religious influence, especially in a traditional society such
as the Chinese. One apparent reason was the ability of religion to
inspire awe, respect, and a sense of overwhelming universal destiny
for the ethicopolitical order that had incorporated the religious element into it. Another reason was that no moral system or ethicopolitical order could be infallible in actual, long-term operation.
History as well as personal experience abounded with cases of
morally undeserved successes and ethically unjustifiable miseries.
Such instances raised doubts on the soundness of the ethicopolitical
order and tended to weaken its hold on the individual's conscience.
It was here that the idea of a superhuman destiny came into operation to remedy the ever-present moral fallibility of the secular political system. This may be seen in two major aspects of Chinese

religion: the theory of "interaction between Heaven and man" (to be discussed immediately below) and the ethicopolitical cults (to be considered in chap. vii).

The Moralization of Heaven

The theory of "interaction between Heaven and man" was a familiar corollary in the state cult of Heaven worship. Developed in Han times (206 B.C. to A.D. 220) by men like Tung Chung-shu, the theory became institutionalized into a guiding political concept and yielded voluminous apocryphal literature. Interpreting this theory with respect to the political life of the land became an official responsibility of the court astronomers down to the end of the nineteenth century, and the common people continued to believe in it up to the present time, as shown by Communist propaganda against it during the eclipse of the sun on Chinese New Year's Day in 1953.

The theory itself was rather simple and unsophisticated. In the ideal state, the world of man and the world of nature operated as a harmonious whole. When man, either the ruler or the people, committed evil acts, he upset the order of universal harmony, and Heaven would respond by either sending warnings before the act was committed or by meting out punishment afterward. The warnings would be in a variety of forms of extraordinary phenomena of nature, such as an eclipse of the sun, especially on an unusual day such as New Year's Day, the appearance of a comet, the falling of a star, or the birth of abnormally formed animals or humans. Examples of Heavenly punishment would be droughts, floods, unseasonable precipitation, earthquakes, fire, and destruction by lightning. When portents appeared or when punishment descended, it was time for man to mend his ways, to redeem his sins, and to try to restore harmony to the universe.

The primary political significance of such an interpretation of nature was obvious. It was the investment of moral meaning into what otherwise would have been morally meaningless forces of nature. It was true that the power of natural forces, as symbolized by Heaven, had been the essence of the cult of Heaven worship which helped to impart an awesome quality to the political institution of the state. But, as popular acceptance of a political institution must be founded on concepts of ethics and justice, the idea of power alone, however superhuman and awe-inspring, would not have been sufficient to enable the worship of Heaven to play its vital role. The operation of natural forces might be morally blind or indifferent, damaging or benefiting good and evil men alike regardless of their ethical quality. This was what Lao Tzu meant when he characterized Heaven and Earth as unkind, treating all things as "grass and dogs," with indifference. And it was the widespread misery devoid of moral meaning in the latter part of the Chou period (sixth to third centuries B.c) that led to a certain degree of loss of faith in Heaven and gave rise to rationalistic thoughts on the subject. In order to become the center of a faith capable of inspiring confidence in a political institution, Heaven and its system of natural forces needed to acquire a moral connotation.

This is what the theory of "interaction between Heaven and man" sought to achieve. Accepted by the rulers and the people alike, Heaven represented not merely a powerful but also a morally meaningful body of forces, operating on ethical principles which were fully binding on man as an integral part of the universe. In all cultures, extraordinary phenomena of nature have always been associated with religious ideas. In China, through this theory, such phenomena were interpreted as manifestations of the ethical motivation of the universe, as symbolized by Heaven. Power and ethical motivation together made Heaven a most suitable sanctioning authority for the political institution.

Down through the centuries since the Han times, this theory was used as a tool of power politics. Political factions blamed each other for misdoings that called forth Heaven's rage in the form of portents,[15] and rebels accused the ruling dynasty of misgovernment as witnessed by the appearance of extraordinary phenomena. But in the modern Ch'ing period, as in many former dynasties, the ethico-political interpretation of extraordinary natural phenomena became the sole monopoly of the state, and the circulation of free interpretations was drastically prohibited by law. Under these circumstances the theory of "interaction between Heaven and man" became a justification for the power position of the ruling dynasty. This role of Heaven was particularly clear at the time when the dynasty faced challenge from rebellions.

In 1814, for example, an edict by Emperor Chia-ch'ing, on the subject of two rebel bands that were disturbing the area near the capital, started with the assertion that ". . . the principle of inter-action between Heaven and man . . . never failed to work." The edict further stated that, since the successful suppression of the rebellion led by Li Wen-ch'eng in Hopei province in the previous year, the area had had seasonable rain and snow and there were abundant crops of wheat and millet, bearing evidence to "Heaven's forgiveness and benevolence." But, the edict continued, the band of rebels led by Lin Ch'ing was still causing disturbance in the area near the capital, thus preventing "seasonable snow in the winter and timely rain in the summer," and this was "punishment from Heaven." Hence the emperor offered sacrifice at the temple of the god of the Black Dragon, pleading for forgiveness from Heaven and for rain from the dragon god.[16]

Again, from 1851 to 1854, as the great Taiping rebellion ran rampant over half the empire, Emperor Hsien-feng offered sacrifice to Heaven nine times in four years, pleading for Heaven's help in suppressing the uprising, and edict after edict blamed the rebellion for all the floods, droughts, and unseasonable weather that caused agricultural damage in different parts of the country. This was echoed in the apocryphal records of the local gazetteers throughout the empire. A typical example may be found in an entry in the Ch'uan-sha county gazetteer for the year 1861:

In the latter part of the sixth month, the Comet appeared with a sparkling tail of several tens of feet [warning of a forthcoming war]; on the nineteenth day and night of the seventh month, howling of ghosts was heard in all directions, and destructive storms and torrential rains followed immediately; on the nineteenth day of the twelfth month, the Taiping rebel forces captured this county, and this was followed by three days and nights of extremely heavy snow starting from the twenty-seventh day of the month; the bitter cold stopped traffic on the roads, and the people were deprived of food. . . .[17]

Thus, the unseasonable precipitation, the comet, the torrential rains, and the unusually bitter cold were all expressions of Heaven's anger at the rebellions, especially the Taiping rebellion, which was interpreted as having disturbed the harmony of the state and hence as having dislocated the proper order of the universe. The ruling dynasty had religious justification for its campaign to restore its power, and had a religious explanation for the failure of the ethico-political order, for all calamities and miseries were attributed to the disturbing acts of the rebellions. Imperial edicts on this subject usually carried self-deprecations by the monarch for dereliction of duty, but these were in conformity with Chinese polite humility, and they in no way interfered with his claim to the status of being the Son of Heaven, nor did they weaken the interpretation of continued divine support for the dynastic power and of Heaven's anger at the rebels for the dislocation of the cosmic order. In any event, Heaven as the supreme authority took final responsibility for meting out calamities and sufferings, and the dynasty was thus theoretically spared from being the direct target of popular discontentment and attack.

The political effectiveness of this cultic theory depended on its popular acceptance. The presence of lengthy apocryphal sections in modern local gazetteers of all counties attested to the wide currency of this belief among the population. Even in the mid-twentieth century, in the towns and villages, the appearance of extraordinary phenomena seldom fails to arouse speculations and comments on their connection with human events as ordained by Heaven.[18]

Whether the educated ruling class sincerely believed in the theory is another matter. From Wang Ch'ung in Han times to many like-minded rationalists through the subsequent centuries, the fallacy of the theory had been more than once pointedly exposed. But such a rationalistic interpretation of nature never gained wide acceptance partly because of the fact that the theory of "interaction between Heaven and man" was founded not on the appeal to empirical truth but rather on the emotional need for superhuman assurance.

The traditional educated class inherited the outlook of Confucian rationalism, and hence it might not be thoroughly and sincerely convinced of apocryphal interpretations. But there was also the profound Confucian sense of destiny based on predetermination by Heaven. Few living Chinese who received a classical education can ever forget the familiar Confucian lines, "When a nation is about to flourish, there are sure to be happy omens; and when it is about to perish, there are sure to be unlucky omens." [19] The frequent quotation of this line in current comments on politics by Chinese critics shows the unconscious influence of supernatural ideas on the Confucian mind. All these induced the traditionally educated man to take a more serious view of the theory in the prescientific age, when man's knowledge about the abnormal phenomena of nature was limited. Even if rationalistic views weighed more heavily on the Confucian mind, it was the Confucians who wrote the apocryphal literature and started many of the superstitious rumors; they understood the function and effectiveness of such a theory as a political tool for harnessing the masses or in struggling for power.

VII

ETHICOPOLITICAL CULTS:
"Guidance by the Way of the Gods"

S<small>UBORDINATE TO THE WORSHIP OF</small> H<small>EAVEN</small>, there developed in the long course of Chinese history a complex body of popular cults that had vital ethicopolitical significance for the functioning of the traditional state. The ritualistic aspect of the cult of Heaven, together with the official interpretation of the theory of "interaction between Heaven and man," was the prerogative of the imperial court, and the ritualistic performances were not shared with the people. (See chap. viii.) While the theology of Yin-yang and the Five Elements brought the idea of the supremacy of Heaven and its subordinate system of deities close to the intimate life of the people, the common people were nevertheless without benefit of the ritualistic practices needed to keep alive this belief in their minds. Hence there was need for the development of popular ethicopolitical cults, subordinate to the supreme power of Heaven, which could be brought nearer to the people through ritualistic participation so that they could be constantly reminded of the supernatural powers in their political and civic life.

In the Chinese religious tradition the supernatural realm was patterned closely after the image of the human world. In temporal life the common people were rigidly excluded from any contact with the monarch, but they were permitted to deal with the lower echelon of officialdom. Following the same principle, while the people were excluded from direct formal worship of Heaven, they were permitted to deal with Heaven's subordinate deities, the objects of worship in the popular cults.

The Confucian tradition had long recognized the need for popular ethicopolitical cults, as numerous classical statements attest. Perhaps the most succinct is found in the Confucian Commentary on the mystic Book of Change: "The sages devised guidance by the way of the gods, and the [people in the] empire became obedient." Whether or not Confucius actually wrote this commentary matters little for the present purpose. The fact is that the statement was widely quoted in traditional discussions on religious matters down to recent times, thus showing its effectiveness. Many further elucidations were given to this statement, such as the one in a 1923 gazetteer of the town of Fo-shan in Kwangtung province: "In the world of light there are rites and music [moral regulations], and in the world of shadows there are spirits and gods. Where rites and music failed to rule [the people], the spirits and gods succeeded without exception." [1]

THE OFFICIAL CULTS AND THE POPULAR CULTS

The basic idea of "guidance by the way of the gods" as implemented through the popular cults became a definite part of the traditional political institution. All comprehensive reference literature for administrative officials, such as the compendia of official documents and the local gazetteers, containing lengthy sections on religious matters, divided all temples into two main categories, those of official sacrifice (*kuan ssu*) and those of people's sacrifice (*min ssu*), a classification based more on sponsorship than on the content of the cults. A cult of official sacrifice was one listed in the registry of official sacrifice (or the sacrificial canon). It became part of the administrative duties of the officials to offer sacrifice to the gods enjoying government recognition at proper times of the year, usually in the spring and autumn. Hence knowledge of sacrifices became part of the intellectual equipment of the traditional official. Nineteenth-century Chinese law stipulated that it was the duty of chief administrators in the prefectures and counties to officiate at the sacrifice to the gods of earth and grain, mountains and rivers, wind, clouds, thunder and rain, and to the spirits of the sage monarchs, brilliant princes, loyal officials, and heroic martyrs whose temples lay within the district. The law further specified a punishment of one hundred lashes for officials who omitted this duty or procrastinated in its performance.[2]

One distinction between an official cult and a people's cult was that the sacrifice for the former took place at the beginning of spring and autumn, while that for the latter was offered at the birthday of the individual god. The offering of sacrifice in official cults in spring and autumn has dual significance. First, it was associated with the vital idea of the cycle of life, so important for an agricultural people, and the suggestion of official control over it. Secondly, the offering of sacrifice in all official cults at a stated time of year had a unifying and universalizing effect for the religious tradition of the extensive empire. Considering the multiplicity of official local cults, offering sacrifice to each god at his birthday or on some other individual occasion might cause the ceremonies to be regarded as purely local events and therefore would have a disorganizing effect on the central political power.

Another contrast between the official and local cults was that official cults received recognition from the government in the form of honorific titles and citations, often bestowed by the emperor, and many of their temples were constructed or renovated at government expense. The ritual of official sacrifice was carefully prescribed in formal regulations. In content, a cult could become an official one if it fitted the classical definition given in the Book of Rites:

> According to the institutes of the Sage-kings about sacrifices, sacrifice should be offered to those who gave laws to the people; to those who have labored unto death in the discharge of their duties; to those who through laborious toil have strengthened the state; to those who have warded off great evil . . . As to the sun and moon, the stars and constellations, the people look up to them. As to mountains, forests, streams, valleys and hills, these supply them with the materials for use which they require. Only men and things of this character are admitted into the sacrificial canon.[3]

This definition singled out two general types of cults for official worship: those related to political leadership and civic virtues, and those symbolizing the vital natural forces and resources. Although set down some two thousand years ago, this definition still governed the development of official cults in the early twentieth century,[4] as indicated by the types of cults falling into the official category in Table 4. A classification of 1,786 major temples distributed over five provinces showed 22.2 per cent of them belonging to those housing official cults. In Gamble's survey of Ting county in the northern province of Hopei for the years 1925–1933, temples of official cults accounted for 26.0 per cent of the total of 855 temples.[5] The presence of official cults in all parts of China attested to their important place in the traditional political order.

The high percentage of official cults in the areas of political leadership and moral order shows the vital role of religion in the system of ethicopolitical values and the consistent attempt of the traditional ruling class to exert direct control over such cults. The significant proportion of official cults among temples dedicated to agricultural deities had ethicopolitical meaning because they concerned the peace and security of the state. The high percentage of official cults among temples of craft and trade deities is due to the official status of the large number of temples along the southern coast dedicated to T'ien-hou, goddess of the sea and sailing. In the category of monasteries and nunneries, an occasional one received official status, but none were found in the eight localities studied in Table 4.

While large numbers of temples in the "people's sacrifice" category emphasized the interests of the individual in health, economic prosperity, and personal welfare, it would be inaccurate to exclude all temples in this category from any ethicopolitical significance. Many temples related to local political leadership and moral order belonged to the "people's sacrifice" category, as did cults designed for integration of the family and the local community, but all had vital meaning for the maintenance of the ethicopolitical system. Although no monastery and nunnery in the eight localities belonged to the "official sacrifice" type, these organizations had ethicopolitical significance in the sense that they strove for mass moral salvation. The pecentages of official cults, however, show the extent to which the government directly operated the people's cults as a religious instrument for the stabilization of the ethicopolitical order.

Table 4

*Temples of Official and People's Cults in Eight Localities
Based on Local Gazetteers Published from 1921 to 1936* *

CLASSIFICATION OF TEMPLES ACCORDING TO FUNCTION OF MAIN GOD IN TEMPLE	TOTAL		TEMPLES OF OFFICIAL CULTS		TEMPLES OF PEOPLE'S CULTS	
	Number	Percentage	Number	Percentage	Number	Percentage
I. Integration and well-being of social organizations	602	100.0	210	35.0	392	65.0
A. Kinship group	161	100.0	0	0	161	100.0
1. Marriage	1	100.0	0	0	1	100.0
2. Fertility	150	100.0	0	0	150	100.0
3. Kinship values	10	100.0	0	0	10	100.0
B. Local community protection	138	100.0	7	9.6	131	90.4
C. The state	303	100.0	203	67.0	100	33.0
1. Figures symbolizing civic and political virtues	258	100.0	172	67.0	86	33.0
a. Civic and political figures	122	100.0	59	48.5	63	51.5
(1) Historic personalities	104	100.0	59	56.7	45	43.3
(2) Legendary figures	18	100.0	0	0	18	100.0
b. Military personalities	136	100.0	113	83.1	23	16.9
2. Deities of justice	5	100.0	2	40.0	3	60.0
3. Patrons of the scholar-official class and the literary tradition	40	100.0	29	72.5	11	27.5
II. General moral order	406	100.0	114	27.6	292	72.4
A. Heavenly deities	184	100.0	56	30.4	128	69.6
B. Underworld authorities	222	100.0	58	26.2	164	73.8

CLASSIFICATION OF TEMPLES ACCORDING TO FUNCTION OF MAIN GOD IN TEMPLE	TOTAL		TEMPLES OF OFFICIAL CULTS		TEMPLES OF PEOPLE'S CULTS	
	Number	Percentage	Number	Percentage	Number	Percentage
III. Economic functions	143	100.0	74	51.7	69	48.3
A. Agricultural deities	108	100.0	63	58.3	45	41.7
B. Patrons of crafts and trades	20	100.0	11	55.0	9	45.0
C. Commerce and general economic prosperity	15	100.0	0	0	15	100.0
IV. Health	19	100.0	0	0	19	100.0
V. General public and personal welfare	68	100.0	0	0	68	100.0
A. Pantheons	5	100.0	0	0	5	100.0
B. Devil dispellers	14	100.0	0	0	14	100.0
C. Blessing deities	25	100.0	0	0	25	100.0
D. Temples with unspecified gods	24	100.0	0	0	24	100.0
VI. Monasteries and nunneries	548	100.0	0	0	548	100.0
A. Buddhist	494	100.0	0	0	494	100.0
B. Taoist	54	100.0	0	0	54	100.0
Total	1,786	100.0	398	22.2	1,388	77.8

* See Appendix 1 for names of localities and sources of data.

To understand the psychosocial mechanism by which the ethicopolitical cults functioned, we may classify them into three groups: cults related to Heaven, Earth, and the underworld; cults of deified personalities; and the cults of Confucius and literary deities. Cults in the first group performed the function of integrating the supernatural world into a hierarchical system of authority for the enforcement of general morality as well as of specific ethicopolitical values, and the major persuasive element was the power of the forces of nature. Cults in the second group supported specific ethicopolitical values by honoring the exemplary performance of distinguished men. Cults in the third group sanctified the Confucian orthodoxy and the scholar-official class as guiding forces in the entire system of ethicopolitical values.

In fulfilling an ethicopolitical function, supernatural power played a dominant role in the cults of the first two groups and a lesser role in those of the third group. The supernatural element was often so prominent that it obscured the ethicopolitical function. But it was through awe and respect for supernatural power that the popular cults reinforced general morality. As T'an Ssu-t'ung (who died a martyr in the Hundred-Day Reform in 1898) stated in his *Jen Hsüeh* (Study of Benevolence), "Should we accost any person with the question why he would not commit arson and murder, his answer would inevitably be, 'Three feet above our heads there are gods and spirits. Even if we were undeterred by the punishment of law, we should be afraid of retributions in the afterlife.'" [6] Herein lay the intricate interplay between the supernatural factor and the ethicopolitical function in the actual operation of the popular cults, to be considered below.

Heaven, Earth, the Underworld, and Karma

For the traditional-minded common man, the dominant religious belief was in Heaven, Earth, and the underworld, which represented a hierarchy of supernatural beings possessing the power to determine the fate of every man on the basis of his moral conduct. Thus, in popular belief, the monarch in Heaven was the Jade Emperor, whose temples were found in most localities in China. His imperial court consisted of gods of the stars as well as high deities of Buddhist and Taoist creation. Subordinate administrators under the heavenly court were the spirits immanent in the natural elements of the earth, such as mountains and rivers, and, above all, the complex system of authorities of the underworld. The organization of these supernatural authorities was patterned after the traditional temporal Chinese government, with the emperor wielding the highest power, with the six boards of central administration, with subdivisions into administrative districts from the province and prefecture down to the county and village, and with the multitude of common souls as subject people, comparable to the inhabitants of the otherworldly "kingdom of shadows." [7] Stories of the vast number of spiritual authorities and their administrative duties abound in the existing volumes on Chinese cults and superstitions. Through punishing the evil and rewarding the good, both in this and in the next life, the hierarchy of supernatural powers functioned in much the same manner as the temporal government.

The patterning of the supernatural hierarchy after the temporal government made the former convincing because such patterning was already familiar and not something totally strange and unrelated to the reality of life. Also, it enhanced the effectiveness of the temporal government, for it impressed upon the people that the same system for the enforcement of morality, justice, and status governed not only this world but also the world beyond. There was no place, not even in the realm of the spirits, to which one's imagination could take flight from the pressure of the moral order as enforced by temporal authorities. This was vividly demonstrated in the cult of the city god, to be considered later.

While this dual system of government grew out of the native classical conception of the supernatural powers of Heaven and Earth, the effectiveness of its operation in utilizing the moral order of society as a foundation for the political order was tremendously strengthened by incorporating Buddhist ideas. Buddhism added elaboration and realism to the idea of Heaven and the underworld, thereby making them more awe-inspiring. Above all, Buddhism introduced the totally new and powerful idea of karma, the endless revolution of the wheel of causal retribution to which the transmigrating soul was eternally tied. One's present existence represented only a minute segment of an eternal existence of the soul, which was reincarnated into other forms of life as one existence succeeded another. In this endless parade of existences of the same soul in different physical forms, reward and punishment for moral conduct were not limited to this life but extended to the next, while the transmigrating soul carried the seed of merit or evil from one life to the next.

Thus, a morally conscientious person might suffer misery not because of what he had done during his present existence, but because of a sin committed by the same soul in a previous life, for which punishment was deferred to the next rebirth. A person might be wicked, violating all moral decency, and yet enjoy success and fortune, but he would get his deserved punishment in the next life by having his soul reborn into a life of misery or even into the form of a beast.

Karma thus reinforced the moral order by putting its innate soundness beyond empirical proof and by introducing a positive interpretation into the many morally unaccountable situations which otherwise might have driven men to act in defiance of the group conscience. The contemporary currency of belief in karma is found in the frequent use of retributory proverbs by morally conscientious men who, in the grip of misfortune, exclaim: "It must be that I have committed sins in my previous life." The acculturation of the Indian idea of karma endowed the classical cults of Heaven and Earth with a new role by extending the power of the supernatural over men beyond their present lifetime for the strengthening of the ethicopolitical order. The following three cults will show the way in which the supernatural element was woven into the fabric of traditional civic morals and political life.

THE CULT OF CHEN-WU   Among the many popular cults associated with the power of Heaven, a prominent one was the national cult of Chen-wu, present in most major districts throughout China (see Appendix 1). Chen-wu was the god of the northern sky, as symbolized by the seven mansions of the zodiac. The Chinese characters Chen-wu mean literally "truly military," conveying the idea of military prowess, for in folklore and mythological literature this god was known for his magical power in suppressing demons and evil spirits,[8] which from time to time were reincarnated into bandits and rebels to disturb peace and order on earth.

The legendary military quality of Chen-wu was mainly responsible for popular belief in his special magical power in protecting local communities from banditry and crimes. It is probable that this protective function of Chen-wu helped to spread the cult to all parts of China. Even into the twentieth century, if local people were asked why there was a Chen-wu temple in the town, the most frequent answer was that the god protected the community from banditry and destruction by war.

Testimony to this function is commonly found in inscriptions on steles in the god's temples. A stele inscription in a Chen-wu temple in Wang-tu county in the province of Hopei gives the reason for founding the temple in the fifteenth century and for the renovation of the temple in subsequent centuries. In the fifteenth century, according to the inscription, the locality was sparsely populated, and it suffered from banditry. The local people "built the Chen-wu temple to suppress this, and banditry was stopped, . . . for Chen-wu was Heaven's supreme god in the suppression of demons. . . ."⁹

Reflecting the god's ethicopolitical role are stele inscriptions in the Chen-wu (also called Hsüan-wu) temple in the town of Fo-shan in the southern province of Kwangtung.¹⁰ Twelve steles were erected in the temple over a period of four and a half centuries, the earliest in 1451 and the latest in 1899. The inscriptions on all twelve are well preserved, and they tell of a series of miracles performed by the god during that period. According to one inscription, bandits had run rampant toward the end of the fourteenth century, and a large fleet of bandit fighting boats launched an attack on the town of Fo-shan. Suddenly columns of black clouds arose in the clear and sunny sky, and a violent storm upset many of the bandit boats, drowning most of the bandits. During the battle, the people saw the god Chen-wu, with long flowing hair, in the clouds. He thus saved the town from plunder.

Another inscription tells of a strong local rebellion that broke out in the middle of the fifteenth century. Led by a "bandit" who had escaped from jail, the rebels captured the surrounding villages and laid siege to the river town with over a thousand fighting boats. Deserted by government troops, the town's militiamen erected a long wooden barricade for defense and prayed in the Chen-wu temple for divine assistance. In the midst of the ensuing battle, clouds of seagulls suddenly appeared from the sky and descended on the rebel boats. A black ball of mosquitoes collected over the top of a tree, arranging themselves into the shape of a fluttering flag. And the people reported seeing the military figure of a god in the dusk, pacing the ground outside the barricade. "The morale of the townsmen rose and the defenses held." Soon afterward, the rebel leader was captured in the provincial capital, the siege was lifted, and the town was spared from plunder and destruction.

In still another inscription, a victim of theft prayed to the god Chen-wu; the burglar became insane, personally returning all the goods to the owner. On another occasion, a businessman made an unfair division of profits with his partner. A prayer to the god resulted in calamity for the dishonest partner.

These and other miracles recorded on the steles formed the body of local lore about the god Chen-wu and his temple. The writers of the inscriptions seemed fully conscious of the moral and political significance of such miracles. An early stele erected in 1529 carried this statement:

> . . . the image of the god is made only of clay and wood. He utters no words for people to hear, and issues no commands to hold them in awe. Yet he can prevent brutal men from bullying others, and can cause the unscrupulous to fail in their plots. The god has indeed lived up to expectations in enforcing law among the people and warding off great calamities and misfortune. The people have good cause to worship him. . . .[11]

A later stele, erected in 1797, presented a similar reason for renovating the temple and maintaining the cult. It stated that the town had grown into a large trading center where strangers gathered from all directions, and where bad elements found a haven, as well as a hunting ground for victims. Besides strict enforcement of law, the inscription went on, there was the need for refurbishing the Chen-wu temple in order to "inspire reverence and awe" for morality and law.[12]

Whether it was serving to inspire the townsmen to defend themselves against hunger-driven mobs labeled bandits or rebels, or to induce awe and reverence for the moral tradition, the popular worship of Chen-wu helped to uphold government and law and maintain the general morality of society. The series of miracles accumulated over the course of four and a half centuries had built up a rich lore which had strengthened the people's faith in the god and in the ethicopolitical values he had come to symbolize. Hence the official status of this cult, the repeated bestowing of honorific titles upon the god, the government subsidy for the periodic refurbishing of the temple, and the local people's protest at the end of the nineteenth century against the absence of the county magistrate at the sacrificial rites in the spring and autumn.[13]

GODS OF MOUNTAINS AND RIVERS Subordinate to the deities of Heaven were the gods and spirits of the earth, notably those of mountains and rivers. Like the heavenly deities, this group of gods and spirits served ethicopolitical functions, as pointed out in the inscription on a stele in the temple of the god of the Five Peaks (*Wu-yo miao*): ". . . Through blessing or condemnation, the gods help the Son of Heaven in the administration of justice, so that good and evil, sincerity and dishonesty, however concealed from view, will not escape [judicious treatment]." [14]

The way in which the gods helped the "Son of Heaven in the administration of justice" was through the popular belief in supernatural control over a person's fate in this world and over the disposal of his soul after death. Thus the mountain god of T'ai-shan (Mount T'ai) was believed to have authority over both the present and after life, as the god was one of the judges in the Ten Courts of Hell where man's soul was tried for his sins. In some localities this god was regarded as the summoner of souls, and in others he was the object of prayer for sons.[15] But in all localities the god of T'ai Shan had the function of protecting the community from distress and bringing peace and order.

This protective function was not limited to the cult of T'ai Shan, but was also granted by the gods and spirits of mountains and rivers in general. In the recapture of the insurgents' capital of Nanking at the end of the great Taiping rebellion, the imperial court bestowed honorific titles upon the gods of mountains and rivers in different parts of the country, and local officials were instructed to offer special sacrifice to them. Thus read an imperial edict, "It was through the assistance and blessing of the gods of mountains and rivers that the campaign against the rebels achieved success." [16]

The fact that mountains and rivers inspired mystical thoughts in men and produced religious cults was explained in the Book of

Rites: "Mountains, forests, rivers and valleys can emit clouds, produce storms and rain; and people see mysterious things in them
. . . There must be gods in all these." This classical statement was
widely quoted in modern writings on religious matters, bearing
witness to its continued efficacy.[17]

THE CULT OF CH'ENG-HUANG, THE CITY GOD   While cults of mountains
and rivers were a ubiquitous sight in China, the worship of deities
of the underworld was equally common in all parts of the country.
The underworld was a rather complex system of spirits. Many
deities associated with earth, like the god of Five Roads (Wu-tao)
and the god of earth (T'u-ti), were also a part of the underworld
system because of their authority in the administration of souls.
Stories of the Ten Courts of Hell and the eighteen purgatories were
well publicized, and their moral significance was obvious. But more
illustrative of the ethicopolitical function of the underworld cults
was the national worship of Ch'eng-huang, the city god. No major
locality in China was without its temple to him. The annual sacrifices, celebrations, and processions for this god were among the
most impressive and the most widely observed public activities in
traditional community life. Much has been written about the
hagiographical development of this cult, which is over two thousand years old.[18] Here, it is necessary only to analyze its moral and
political significance.

The cult of Ch'eng-huang, beginning as that of a protective god
for city walls and moats, subsequently developed into a systematic
authority over the souls of the deceased. In contemporary usage, the
term Ch'eng-huang denoted an office in the underworld instead of
any particular individual deity—a supernatural authority governing
a territory, patterned after the administrative areas of the temporal
government. Hence there was a system of graded Ch'eng-huang,
with the rank of each god dependent upon the size of his administrative territory, which might correspond to the earthly province,
prefecture, or county. The temporal neighborhood was, however,
governed by another subordinate deity, the T'u-ti or local god of
earth. Spirits of deceased officials were appointed to the office of
Ch'eng-huang for a term of three years, the rank of the super-

natural office often depending on the rank of the official in the temporal government during his lifetime. In the traditional days, in each locality the image of Ch'eng-huang was taken out of the temple three times a year and carried in a procession. The first procession was on the third day of the third month of the Chinese calendar, when the god released the spirits; the second, on the first day of the seventh month, when he took a census of the spirits and saw to it that they were properly fed; and the third, the most elaborate, on the first day of the tenth month, when he collected the spirits and gave them clothing and housing for the winter.[19]

By thus governing man's soul after death, the cult of Ch'eng-huang influenced man's conscience through deterrence, just as the temporal government controlled man's conduct through fear of the law. The ethicopolitical significance of this cult was clearly pointed out in stele inscriptions in the numerous Ch'eng-huang temples throughout the land, of which the following is an example. Though the stele was erected in the sixteenth century, its inscription is representative of those found on later steles, which still influence the attitudes of contemporary common man:

. . . Ch'eng-huang temples are universally established, from the national capital to the prefectures and counties. *While it is the magistrates who rule in the world of light, it is the gods who govern in the world of shadows. There is close cooperation between the two authorities* [italics added]. When Emperor T'ai Tsu of the Ming dynasty [in 1370] conferred titles on the gods of Ch'eng-huang throughout the empire, there were ranks of emperors, princes, dukes, lords, and marquises. . . . The gods' power is effective everywhere, rewarding the good with blessing and punishing the evil with calamity, . . . thus extending great benefit to man. Man prays to him for good harvests and for the avoidance of floods, droughts, and pestilence. It is not improper at all to show reverence to him . . . When His Honor Wen-hsi came to govern this district, there was a locust plague. His Honor prayed to Ch'eng-huang, and the locusts dispersed without damaging the crops. A burglar stole some money from the county treasury. His Honor prayed again to the god, and the burglar was caught and all the money was recovered. His Honor was moved by the god's efficacious protection, and became more devoted to his worship than ever. He said, "The temple is for sacrificing to the god. If not decorated and expanded, how can it house the god, show

special reverence, and bring security to the people?" (Hence the renovation of the temple and the erection of the stele to record the event.) [20]

The moral and political significance of the cult is clearly recognized in this inscription. The accumulated body of mythological
lore, including what the local people believed to be the gods' blessings and miracles, was a factor in inspiring faith in the cult.

The system of appointing spirits of deceased officials to the office
of Ch'eng-huang once more points toward the inculcation into the
people's minds of the idea that there was no escape whatsoever
from the ethicopolitical order, for the human officials who had ruled
them in this world were the same ones appointed as Ch'eng-huang
to govern them after death. And the infusion of the Buddhist idea
of the Ten Courts of Hell to judge and punish souls inspired even
more awe for the ethicopolitical order. No child taken to visit a
Ch'eng-huang temple ever came away without being deeply impressed or badly frightened by the terrifying frescoes of the Ten
Courts, where souls were tried by subterranean judges, and the
purgatories, where evil ones were sent through horrible tortures.
These inevitable scenes in the Ch'eng-huang temples lent vividness
and tangibility to the folklore about punishment in Hell for violation of morality in this world.

In the twentieth century, Ch'eng-huang temples still stand as
prominent religious establishments everywhere in China. Even in
the 1940's, the people in an interior town in Yünnan province believed that one of its outstanding citizens had been appointed to
the office of Ch'eng-huang.[21] This bears witness to the contemporary
influence of this cult as a means of enforcing the ethicopolitical
order among the common people.

Cults of Deified Men

If the cults of Heaven, Earth, and the underworld were a combination of gods of naturalistic elements (like stars and mountains
and rivers) with the spirits of departed men, there was another
group of cults made up exclusively of deified spirits of men
who had won moral and political distinction in their lifetime. While
the apotheosis of departed distinguished men is a common phe-

nomenon in many cultures, its very extensive development in China undoubtedly made it a unique characteristic of Chinese religious life.

This tradition has been noticed by some scholars on the subject. John Shryock, for instance, stated:

Probably there has been no country where the cult of heroes has been more fully developed than in China . . . while some heroes are worshiped as gods, many more never received divine rank and are offered sacrifices simply for their deed as men . . . This has been encouraged by the government, since it holds up examples of good men for public emulation and encourages virtue by keeping alive the memory of great deed. Doubtless there is also the feeling that benefit may accrue to the worshipers from the increased power of the hero in the next world.[22]

The cults of deified men fall into two categories: cults of nationally prominent personalities who were worshiped throughout the country, and local cults of figures whose temples were found only in certain localities. Every community in China had temples of both types, with a few dedicated to national personalities and a larger number devoted to deceased local figures. On rare occasions, a temple was dedicated to a prominent man still living. The ethicopolitical significance of these cults will be seen in the following cases.

THE NATIONAL CULT OF KUAN YÜ Among the contemporary national cults of deified men, none was more prominent than that of Kuan Yü, whose temple became an integral part of every major Chinese community. Like the popular cults of Ch'eng-huang, the cult of Kuan Yü performed the function of supporting both general and specific values, despite the fact that this third-century warrior was best known to Western observers as the god of war.[23] He was worshiped by merchants as a god of wealth and of fidelity in business contracts, by common people as a curer of disease, by soldiers as their patron god, and by many local communities as the chief protective deity against calamities and destruction. For many social organizations, such as fraternities and secret societies, he was the overseer of fraternal ties and a blessing spirit for their cause of mutual interest and justice.

There was, however, a more specific ethicopolitical aspect to this cult which caused it to be universally fostered in all parts of China by both the government and the gentry. This was its symbolization of the civic values of loyalty, righteousness, and devoted support for the legitimate political power. Popular literature and folklore dramatized Kuan Yü's heroic exploits in his ill-fated battle to restore the legitimate government of the Han dynasty against usurpers. This basic value of the cult was repeatedly stressed in stele inscriptions in the numerous temples dedicated to the god. An example is the inscription in a Kuan Yü temple in the southern town of Fo-shan. It states that, while the god upheld civilization for all subsequent generations, his greatest specific contribution lay in "glorifying the loyal and rewarding the good" by "clarifying the standards of merit and evil." This is why, states the nineteenth-century inscription, "from large districts and great cities to isolated corners in mountain valleys and seashores, people hold him in awe as if he were intimately overseeing every move of their personal conduct." [24]

That people everywhere held Kuan Yü in awe was partly due to moral glorification of him, and partly to numerous stories of his magical power which circulated in every locality. The apparition of Kuan Yü was among the commonest miracles occurring in local communities throughout China, leading to communal excitement, religious gatherings and processions, and at times mass action toward the people morally involved in an issue, such as an offender against mores or even an unpopular official. The magical aspect of the cult had supreme importance as a substratum for the ethicopolitical values the cult symbolized. The traditional ruling class apparently realized the importance of the cult's magical aspects, for supernatural stories of every description were obviously encouraged by the government.

An imperial edict, for example, told of Kuan Yü's divine assistance in the suppression of a rebellion that broke into the Forbidden City in 1813.[25] Said the edict, "The confession from some of the captured rebels stated that, while they were creating a disturbance in the Forbidden City, in a dizzy state of mind, they saw the image of Kuan Yü. In fright, they immediately broke rank and were routed and captured." As a consequence, the imperial court conferred additional honorific titles upon the god and ordered special sacrifices to him. After the suppression of a series of local uprisings in the southern Pearl River delta in 1826, the official documents made a similar claim of divine assistance by the apparition of the god, which awed the rebels into submission. Two years later, a rebellion in the northern Amur region was claimed to have been suppressed by the aid of the same god, who whipped up a blinding dust storm against the insurgents.[26]

These and numerous similar mythological stories about Kuan Yü, abounding in the official documents and local gazetteers, were the immediate cause for many grand special sacrifices offered to the god, for the showering of additional honorific titles on him, and for the periodic renovation of his temples in various localities of the empire. Mythological lore and the resultant periodic ritualistic activities were important in inspiring people's faith in the god and in keeping the cult alive and effective for more than a thousand years, with its luster undimmed.

Other national cults of deified men, such as the cult of the ancient military hero Ma Yüan of Han times, and of General Yo Fei of the more recent Sung dynasty, had the same ethicopolitical and magical significance.

LOCAL CULTS AND THE TZ'U In addition to the national cults, every Chinese community had a number of cults dedicated to local leaders and officials who in their lifetime had prominently served the public interest, sometimes by sacrificing their lives and fortunes. These were the men (and occasionally women, as pointed out by Shryock) who served as virtuous examples for later generations because of their great deeds, and who acquired a sacred character in the eyes of the public by being enshrined in a temple.

The building which housed such cults was not usually called a temple (*miao*), but a sanctuary (*tz'u*). A *tz'u* is a building housing gods or spirits for periodic group sacrifices, while a *miao* is a building housing one or more deities for the general public to worship at any convenient time. But the cults of some local personalities had acquired extensive magical functions, answering prayers of all sorts offered, and their *tz'u* were not limited to periodic sacrifices, but

were open to daily public worship as well. Thus an ethicopolitical
cult was transformed into a general popular cult, granting divine
assistance for sundry public or personal interests. Some sanctuaries
were dedicated to single individuals, and others were devoted to a
group of personalities.

General observation suggests that every culture, simple or complex, develops some mechanism to perpetuate the memory of illustrious men who exhibit extraordinary moral qualities and perform
public duties unusually well. This is especially true of those whose
death results from the performance of their duty. The function of
such a device is to induce similar virtues in later generations and
to uphold the value system of the culture. Such a device is represented in the public statues and memorial shrines in the town
squares of the Western world. In the Chinese culture, the system
was embodied in the *tz'u*.

The ethicopolitical nature of the vast majority of local cults of
personalities is told in many of their common names: "sanctuary
of the loyal and righteous," "sanctuary for local meritorious personalities," "sanctuary for the adoration of the virtuous," "sanctuary
for tribute to public achievements," "sanctuary for repaying public
gratitude," "sanctuary of famed officials." A stone stele in the
sanctuary or a record in the local gazetteer tells the ethicopolitical
significance behind each of these cults.

The "Sanctuary for the Perpetuation of Fame of the Loyal and
the Righteous" in the town of Fo-shan, for example, was dedicated
collectively to twenty-two local leaders who, at great risk and self-
sacrifice, helped to quell a local uprising in the fifteenth century.
The sanctuary was built for them and was kept in periodic repair
until recent decades, because "as plain common men, . . . with
neither prominent office nor commanding authority," they succeeded
in quieting a rioting mob, thus sparing a whole district from destruction.[27]

Elsewhere, common men who rendered distinguished public
service often received posthumous divine titles from the government
or had a sanctuary built in their memory after death. In Jen-ho
county of the coastal province of Chekiang, for instance, the temple

of Lord Fu-yu (Lord of Assured Assistance) was dedicated to the three Chiang brothers, who in their lifetime were known for unusual generosity in contributing to charitable and just causes. The imperial court conferred divine titles on them and ordered local officials to offer regular seasonal sacrifices to them. A wealthy woman in the same province sacrificed her entire fortune building a dike for a community in the thirteenth century. The grateful local people built a sanctuary in her memory, and subsequent rulers extended her official recognition. She continued to receive divine titles and official sacrifices until the end of the ninteenth century.[28]

But it happened more frequently that the local officials rather than the common men became deified and enjoyed public sacrifice for unusually virtuous deeds that benefited the community. Practically no locality was without one or more temples or sanctuaries dedicated individually or collectively to departed officials. It is apparent that a leading underlying function of these local cults was to encourage civic values and the principle of good government as well as to inspire the people's faith in government and law. This is clearly suggested in the inscription on a stele erected in the nineteenth century on the occasion of the renovation of the temple for the mythological Emperor Yao: "No one who understands the principle (of good government) would not revere its god, and no one who reveres the god would refuse to follow the principle conscientiously." [29]

For similar reasons many localities had a Wen Wu Kung (Palace for Civil and Military Officers) to house the spirits of notable public servants. In Ch'uan-sha county of Kiangsu province, a Yang-te tz'u (Sanctuary for the Adoration of the Virtuous) was dedicated to a magistrate and a garrison commander who had repelled Japanese pirates in the fourteenth and fifteenth centuries, built city walls for the defense of the county seat, and constructed irrigation canals for the improvement of local agriculture. The official prayer for the annual sacrifices to these spirits contained this line: "As the people continue to enjoy the fruits of your ancient virtuous service, let [you] be forever remembered. With utmost sincerity this sacrifice is offered . . . may [your spirits] come to enjoy it." [30] The line was rather typical of sacrificial prayers for cults of this category, which were commemorative, designed to perpetuate civic values and political principles symbolized by exemplary departed officials.

The Cults of Confucianism

From the above, we have seen the role of religion in sanctioning the political power of the state and maintaining the ethicopolitical order. In addition to these two categories of cults, the cult of Confucianism was an important factor in the power of the state and the ethicopolitical order. The essential features of this cult have been presented by John Shryock in *The Development of the State Cult of Confucianism,* and we need not devote space to it here. It will suffice to point out that, while it is true that Confucius was never deified as a god and was revered only as a great man, it is nevertheless unsound to dismiss all religious significance in this cult.

The wooden tablet with the inscription of Confucius' honorific title, even without the formal deification of his soul, had the symbolistic significance of representing a body of social values and inspiring awe and reverence for the teachings of the Master. The sacrificial rituals, with incense and candles, the kowtow, and formal prayer, almost completely resembled those in other cultic rituals having a deified object of worship. Confucian temples that housed the tablet and in which the grand sacrificial rites were performed were the same type of religious buildings as were temples of other fully deified cults. In fact, Confucian temples, found in every administrative center, from the county and the province to the national capital, surpassed most other temples in size and religious dignity. Their general lack of ornateness served to inspire the feeling of sobriety that was characteristic of the teachings of the Master.

Around the Confucian temples developed a group of satellite cults and mythological lore. Examples of these cults, which formed a part of the landscape of every large center of population, were the cult of Wen-ch'ang, the patron god of literature, and the cult of K'uei-sheng, the star of literary success. Cultic worship and mythological lore served the purpose of promoting literary tradition and bolstering scholars' hope of success in the imperial examinations. The cult of Ts'ang-chieh, reputedly the creator of writing, found widely in southern localities, and the lore woven around the magical power of papers written or printed with words and the consequent reverence for writing were part of a religious subsystem designed to inspire awe and respect for literary learning, the heart of Confucianism as a social and political tradition.

Taken together, these satellite cults and beliefs formed part of the broader picture of the cult of Confucianism and gave the Confucian tradition a religious reinforcement. Although the great Master was singularly not deified, the cult of Confucianism may nevertheless be regarded as what Emile Durkheim calls a commemorative cult invested with considerable religious elements. This subject will be further elaborated on in Chap. x. As Confucianism formed the core of the traditional ethicopolitical order, it is important to recognize here that religious influence played its part in making this doctrine a revered institution not only among scholars but also among the vast illiterate population.

Psychosocial Elements in Ethicopolitical Cults

What are the basic elements that go into the making of a cult designed to perpetuate the memory of ethicopolitical values as embodied in the meritorious deeds of men? Analysis of a number of such cults suggests the following. First, the founding of such a cult was generally marked by two inseparable elements: a public crisis and a hero. One function of the hero was to exemplify the operation of certain virtues through unusually meritorious performance of public duties; the critical situation not merely prepared for the rise of the hero but also provided the social setting in which ethicopolitical values played a more prominent role than in normal times. The symbolic value of the hero for this purpose would be especially striking to the public mind if he died in the performance of his duties.

The physical symbols, another component of the cult, consisted of the temple building and an image of the person or a wooden tablet bearing his name and title. As in any cult, rituals constituted an inevitable element. In the case of the *tz'u,* the basic rituals were the semiannual sacrifices, in the spring and the fall, usually around the time of the solstice. The sacrifice, often accompanied by impressive ceremonial acts, was another device to refresh the people's memory of the hero's virtues.

But in time the temple and the image might fall into neglect, the sacrifices become perfunctory and finally be discontinued, and the entire cult might eventually be obliterated, with only ruins to mark the site of communal effort to remember a virtuous man once living in eventful times. If the cult was to last and thrive, a body of mythological lore had to develop to sustain it. Coming into play here was the common belief that a man of unusual virtue or ability would become, after death, a spirit of extraordinary magical prowess, capable of performing a variety of miracles. And the reputation of the prowess of his soul was enhanced by stories of his legendary capabilities in his lifetime, thus transforming him into a divine hero who lived on as an efficacious spirit overseeing the activities of the community.

Through the magical prowess of his soul, the deified hero was able to enter into the common people's daily life and into their memory by receiving their worship and listening to their prayers of mundane affairs—requests for an heir, for cure of sickness, for financial prosperity, for safety on a dangerous trip, for success in work. Occasional realization of success in any of these requests enhanced the fame of the hero as an efficacious god. At this point, the value of the cult to the common people underwent a temporary transformation from ethicopolitical inspiration to magical efficacy.

This development was vital to preserving group memory of the deified man. Social values of a high moral tone might motivate officials or the Confucian elite to establish the cult and to perpetuate the formal sacrifices; such values might even enable the common people in the midst of crisis to recognize the greatness of the hero. But, while great men, great deeds, and great virtues were prominent elements in a crisis, they became dormant in the common people's humble struggles during normal times. As a crisis passed into history, the memory of the prominent men and their great moral lessons gradually disappeared from the uneducated man's consciousness. To be remembered by a community over a long period of normal times, the hero had to become part of the common people's workaday life, serving them with humble values and assisting them with their modest deeds.

But a community was certain to face new crises—wars, famines, mass miseries of one sort or another—crises that confronted men with overpowering forces beyond the control of the individual or even the group. In such critical times, the ethicopolitical values would re-emerge from their dormant state and reassert themselves through miracles, such as an apparition of the hero's spirit or some unnatural phenomenon, which would help the community to weather the storm. Had there been no magical tradition or mythological lore attached to the cult, the hero would have been forgotten and would have failed to reappear in the people's mind as a source of inspiration for moral qualities needed by the community to surmount the new crisis.

One result of the performance of miracles in a new crisis was imperial or public decorations for the god, with honorific titles extolling his magical prowess and moral inspiration. Another result might be the renovation of the old temple, should it have become weatherbeaten or dilapidated. Often the god was honored with both decorations and a renovation of his temple or refurbishing of of its interior. Decorating the god and renovating his temple were grand community occasions that served to add moral glorification and mythological embellishments to the deified hero and strengthened the group memory of him.

Finally, there was the component of the organization of the cult. Organizationally, the cult was diffused in the institutional structure of the community, and did not exist with a priesthood or a congregation separate from the general populace. Ritually, the cult functioned through formal and informal worship. Formal worship was undertaken at the spring and autumn sacrifices, at which local government officials or community leaders or both would officiate and the local population would participate as spectators. Private worship consisted of individual visits to the temple for prayer and sacrificial offerings. When worship, formal or informal, was not being undertaken, the cult operated in people's lives through stories of moral glorification and mythological lore that were told and re-told among adults and by adults to children, all without the formal organization of sermon preaching.

VALUES, MAGIC, AND DEVELOPMENT OF A SAMPLE CULT

Among the components of a cult of deified men, the most vital are ethicopolitical values and magical beliefs, which play mutually sup-porting roles in the development of the cult. This is indicated in numerous records of such cults, some of which have been cited in the previous pages. The most illustrative example is the case of two military commanders who died defending the Chekiang coast against the British invasion during the Opium War in 1841–1842, and who continued to influence the morale of the populace during the French invasion of the same district in 1881–1882, a part of the series of skirmishes leading to the Sino-French conflict in 1884. The following are excerpts from a report to the Chekiang governor by Hsüeh Fu-ch'eng, an intendant for the invaded district of Ning-po and Shao-hsing. The text is quoted at considerable length because of the meaningful details not often available in documents of this nature.

Last year [1881], the French violated the treaty and provoked inci-dents along the coast in the eastern part of Chekiang province. Fighting broke out repeatedly in Ma-chiang and T'ai-pei, and there were frequent alarms. Panic spread among the people. By the first month of this year [1882], the enemy warships launched their attack on the port of Chen-hai, and our fortresses and warships checked them to a stalemate. But tranquillity reigned among the populace in the district of Ning-po and Shao-hsing as if there were no enemy poised at our very threshold.

The tranquillity is due to the repeated rumor that the spirits of gener-als Chu and Ke made their apparition to protect the district, and made known to the people that the locality would be safe, however treacherous the enemy might be. Because of the wide circulation of this story, the town remained calm in the midst of thunderous bombardment, and the morale of the troops soared as the enemy closed in. Each time the situa-tion turned critical, people seemed to see a violent storm and strange clouds arising from the west and drifting eastward to the sea. Some said that numerous spirit soldiers aided in the battle to repel the enemy.

Some reported mysterious lights and flags bearing the characters of Chu and Ke among fortresses on the north and south banks of the harbor during the night. And frequently there was a curtain of fog that cut off the enemy's vision so that their guns failed to find their targets.

. . . Upon investigation, aide-de-camp Tu reported that, while fighting alongside the officers to repel the enemy under a shower of gun shells, practically no one was wounded. While the enemy bombarded our line daily with heavy shells weighing several hundred pounds each, most of them failed to explode. One cannot say that there has been no assistance from the spirits. . . .

It was found on investigation that General Ke was Ke Yün-fei, a deceased garrison commander of Ting-hai district. He (together with two other commanders) defended Ting-hai in bloody combat for six days and nights against the British invasion in [1841]. Ke lost half his face to an enemy's swinging sword and suffered a chest wound the size of a bowl from a shell, and still he slew over ten enemies before he died . . . His native district was Shan-yin [Shao-hsing], where his ancestral temple and graves are located, and it is reasonable that his loyal spirit would extend protection to this and the neighboring territory. This humble intendant [had suggested a petition to the throne] to place the Sanctuary for the Three Loyal Ones in the sacrificial canon for official sacrifices in the spring and autumn so as to satisfy public opinion.

General Chu was . . . Lieutenant General Chu Kuei-fang. When British warships occupied Ning-po, the General led . . . nine hundred troops to defend the Ta-pao hills in the Tz'u-hsi district. As the enemy approached . . . from both land and sea, the General personally held the flag and led the men into battle. From dawn to dusk, a large number of the enemy were killed and wounded. But the troops on his flanks suddenly collapsed, isolating him from any support. The General charged with his horse and slew several tens of the enemy. Two bullets hit his body, and his horse fell. [But he got up and continued fighting] until he also fell from a mortal wound. His son Ch'ao-nan also perished in the battle. But the soldiers held their ranks and continued the fight until they suffered over two hundred dead. Enemy dead also littered the field. And the enemy . . . admitted they suffered their heaviest loss since they launched their invasion. From then on, clouds constantly enveloped the top of the Ta-pao hills, and faint sounds of drums and trumpets could be heard. Some people saw gleaming lights and moving flags. The enemy who occupied the district city was frightened and gradually retreated.

This was in [1842]. [The deceased general] was rewarded by the throne. The gentry and the people in the Tz'u-hsi district contributed money to build a sanctuary to express their gratitude and to offer sacrifices. Now, forty years later, the sanctuary is as well maintained as if it were new, and prayers are known to have been answered efficaciously.

During the late spring and early summer of last year [1881, the year of the French invasion], local residents heard during the night sounds of drums emitting from the sanctuary as if calling troops to arms. This continued for ten nights. A wandering beggar who slept in front of the sanctuary heard sounds of men and horses marching through the thoroughfare. The beggar felt as though he had been stepped on by a horse, and he became ill.

This was a time when the French had become increasingly oppressive. The local people said that the General went to his grave with unpacified patriotism and anger, and that his spirit was helping to defend the coastal border against the invading enemy. As this talk gained wide circulation, the public became calm [despite the crisis of invasion]. Now that . . . the enemy has come under the restriction of a treaty . . . and tranquillity of the border has been restored, meritorious officers have all received recognition and promotion; even this humble intendant shared in the undeserved reward. But how could one dare to usurp the credit of Heaven, thus obscuring the efficacious role of the gods? Hence my request for a petition to the throne for an additional divine title for the Generals, or for imperial honor plaques for each General's sanctuary and the sanctuary of the Three Loyal Ones, and for the inclusion of both temples in the official sacrificial registry. This is for the glorification of utmost loyalty and for expressing gratitude toward divine protection.[31]

This case is quoted despite its length because it furnishes an excellent illustration of the interplay between the magical factor and ethicopolitical values in the popular cults, and because it represents one of the most recently documented cases of this nature. In it one sees the applicability of the general principle that extraordinary qualities and unusual performance in a person's lifetime led to belief in the magical prowess of his soul, especially when his death was directly connected with the extraordinary performance.

For such a personality, death might destroy his body, but his spirit would remain undaunted. As people could not forget his unusual qualities, their memory of his spirit continued and inspired the mythological lore to substantiate and perpetuate the memory. This undaunted spirit was a part of the Chinese concept of *hao-ch'i,* which in Mencius' definition means the immense and indomitable spirit. A traditional condolence gift for the funeral of a prominent man was a cloth or silk banner bearing the line *hao-ch'i ch'ang ts'un,* "the immense and indomitable spirit lives on." This spirit, present in a personality of extraordinary qualities and unusual performance, was associated in the popular mind with magical prowess and inspired the development of a cult.

The present case is interpreted in this light: the unusual performance of the two deified soldiers was related to the ethicopolitical value of exceptional courage and utmost devotion to public duty. The development of this cult through the building of sanctuaries, public sacrifices, bestowing of imperial honors, and a whole set of mythological lore woven around the two military figures was motivated by these ethicopolitical values as expressed in their exceptional performance. Their unusual moral strength and heroic death fit into the classical conception of the "immense and indomitable spirit" and inspired the lore of the magical power of their souls, including their efficaciousness in answering all sorts of prayers during the intervening forty years. And in a time of crisis, when the land was once more subjected to foreign invasion, the widespread belief in the magical power of these two warriors that had kept the cult alive among the common people soon fired the popular imagination again and produced additional mythological lore that revivified the symbolized values of courage, loyalty, and patriotism, generating high morale among the populace and maintaining faith in the ability of the defenders to repel the new invaders.

There is general validity in this case that may shed light on other ethicopolitical cults of departed great men. In overwhelming crises it was natural that men should recall similar crises in the past and exclaim, "If only our hero were with us today, we would once more be successful in riding out the storm under his leadership!" And here he was, as men had come to believe he was, through the psychological mechanism of mythological rumors that arose from the impending calamity, through the cultic symbols of the temple and the hero's image or idol, through the performance of cultic rituals in his honor, and through belief in his magical efficacy.

Heightened group morale and the reported calmness of the local population in the face of crisis showed the practical function of the cults and provided grounds for the district intendant's efforts in keeping the cults alive by attempting to renew their public glorification in the form of imperial honorific titles and plaques. It is possible that, in the intendant's eyes, it was not the credibility of the mythological lore but the ethicopolitical value of courage and patriotism symbolized in mythological form that served to calm the public and raised the morale of the defenders and that provided the basic motivation for his request to the provincial governor for imperial glorification of the cults.

Cults of local heroes which succeeded in surviving for generations appear to have developed in a cyclical pattern of three successive stages. First, the founding of the cult was characterized by a crisis and the dominance of such values as patriotism, courage, and extreme self-sacrifice required to meet the critical situation. Secondly, in its subsequent existence through a long period of normal times, the cult was sustained by common magic and mythological lore. In the third stage, a new crisis would again bring out the ethicopolitical values which by now were deeply interwoven with the magical and mythological aspect of the cult, and the cycle would be repeated.

This pattern applies to surviving cults, but not to cults which declined and eventually disappeared. The countryside was studded with *tz'u* which had fallen into neglect, some with their interiors taken over by layers of dust and cobwebs, and some with only crumbled walls or ruins to mark their former existence. Such temples, after a glorious beginning in a crisis, failed to develop the second phase, magic and mythological lore, to sustain their existence through the long period of normal times when the ethicopolitical values gradually lost their urgency and importance. Sacrifices were offered in decreasing regularity and communal interest in maintenance of the temple waned after several generations, until the cult finally disappeared and its role was replaced by a new cult of another hero in another crisis.

Some popular cults had an ethicopolitical nature to begin with, but survived, sometimes for a thousand years or more, mainly as magical cults, with their original values almost forgotten, possibly because changed historical circumstances had made the ancient heroes unfit to serve the community in new crises having different value requirements. One example was the Chiang-chün miao, widely found in the south. The temple was dedicated to Ma Yüan, the "vanguard general" who spearheaded the imperialist expansion of the Han dynasty some two thousand years ago. Popular worship of the general began as an ethicopolitical cult in the fifth century A.D.[32] among Chinese settlers who needed the spirit of the warrior to symbolize courage and confidence in their struggle with non-Chinese peoples in the newly opened south. But contemporary worshipers of this ancient warrior in the Chiang-chün miao in Canton knew only of his magical efficacy in answering prayers in their daily existence, which had long passed the stage of struggle with aboriginal tribes in a freshly settled land.

But some popular cults, such as that of Kuan Yü, endured for over a thousand years with their ethicopolitical values undimmed by time. Their development followed closely the above-mentioned cyclical pattern. In the case of Kuan Yü the symbolized values of loyalty, justice, and courage transcended time and space, and the wide circulation of the popular work of fiction, *The Romance of the Three Kingdoms,* probably kept alive the memory of the hero.

POPULAR CULTS OF THE DEAD AND THE LIVING

Ethicopolitical cults were characteristically founded upon deified historical personalities instead of upon other types of spiritual beings, because such values could be more realistically symbolized by the qualities and performance of an historical human being than by attaching moral meanings to personified objects such as heavenly bodies or objects of nature on earth.

The fact that such personalities were generally deified after their death rather than during their lifetime may be explained by two factors. First, it was easier to idealize moral qualities and produce a model of perfection from the image of a person already dead rather than from a living figure whose imperfections would be difficult to hide, however great the social distance and however rigid the isolation of and secrecy around that person. Second, magical and mythological lore could more easily be woven around the soul of a departed person.

This, however, does not mean the total absence of anthropolatry of living persons in China, as is sometimes asserted by writers on the subject, as by Max Weber. In different historical periods, and even in modern times, sanctuaries were occasionally built for outstanding living persons to whom the local communities owed public gratitude. These structures were known by the traditional term *sheng tz'u* or "live sanctuaries." The magistrate of Ch'ing-ho district in the northern province of Hopei was an example. He brought about a substantial reduction in taxation and other government levies and thus lightened the financial burden of a hard-pressed people. In 1886, two years after he was transferred to administer another district, the grateful populace of Ch'ing-ho built a sanctuary to commemorate him.[33] As late as the 1920's, a "live sanctuary" was built in Ch'in-chou district in the southern province of Kwangtung for a magistrate who had brought relief during a local famine and had saved many people from starvation. An official in the agricultural ministry of the Nationalist government told this writer that, in the early 1940's, after he had built an irrigation system to bring water to a parched area in the northern part of Szechwan province, grateful local leaders proposed to establish a "live sanctuary" for him. The sanctuary was never built, and the whole proposal might have been his own wishful thinking, but even so it is significant, for it shows that anthropolatry of the living personality was a part of the religious tradition, although practiced very sparingly.

Such "live" cults, like other popular cults, encouraged civic values. For officials who came to rule a district where a "live sanctuary" had been built for one of the preceding administrators, such a sanctuary, and sanctuaries for departed figures as well, served to remind them of their exemplary predecessors and silently suggested that they too might be glorified if they observed similar values and performed similar deeds in the public interest. The cults of exemplary officials, living or dead, also inspired public confidence in government and law, for they proved that, given good men, government could be good, and that bad government by bad officials was no refutation of the basic soundness of government.

RELIGION AS A SUPPORTIVE FACTOR FOR THE POLITICAL INSTITUTION

The foregoing discussion and illustrations show that the religious factor played an important role in justifying political power, in establishing administrative authority, in maintaining peace and order, in upholding civic values, and in inspiring faith in the government and raising popular morale during public crises. The significance of religion in political life will be more clearly pointed out in Chap. ix on the place of religion in political rebellions which in the name of the gods challenged the established political power. As has already been mentioned, the political importance of the religious factor was quite consciously recognized by the Confucian tradition that supplied the basic doctrine for the ruling class. Such recognition was fully implied in the widely quoted classical expression, "Guidance by the way of the gods." An amplification was supplied by the following statement, inscribed on the stele of the temple of the navigation goddess (T'ien-hou miao) in the town of Fo-shan:

Confucius glorified the virtues of spirits and gods. But narrow-minded scholars of subsequent generations might have taken this as something akin to discourse on mystical phenomena, and would have refused to discuss it any further . . . In my humble opinion . . . Heaven and Earth are merely immense lifeless objects, and it is the spirits and gods that help to make them a functioning entity. When administrative orders from the national and local capitals attain their objectives, and when there is the Way of Man to serve as effective principles and discipline [for ruling the people], it is not necessary that spirits and gods play an impressive and prominent role. *But when* [the administrative orders and the Way of Man] *fail to effect justice, spirits and gods will be brought to light . . . As the ancients put it, in the age of perfect government, spirits became inefficacious* [italics added]. It is not that the spirits are inefficacious. When reward and punishment are just and clear, the *Yang* [positive elements of man] functions effectively, and the *Yin* [negative elements of the spirits] retreats into the background . . . so there is no need for the efficaciousness [of spirits and gods].[34]

The italicized statement presents the view that, when the Way of Man falters, when law and the institution of government fail to maintain peace and justice, the Way of the Gods will emerge to assume a political role. Religion here was the bolster for an institution in distress. Given perfect government, there would be no need for the gods. But the millennium of perfect government never arrived, and spirits and gods became a constant part of political realism.

Once again, the fallibility of the human order in achieving universal justice and in successfully solving every critical problem forever subjected the basic ethicopolitical principles to challenge and doubt, which would have undermined their stability. Mobs that rebelled because of hunger could see no justice in a political institution that demanded peace and civil obedience from them. A criminal who rose to political power and became an oppressive tyrant inspired no respect for the soundness of the human order. This situation, which occurred all too often, might cause a general loss of faith in the institution of government.

Here the religious factor came into play. Political calamities were not interpreted as the result of defects of the moral rules, but instead could be explained as expressions of the gods' anger at the misconduct of a certain group of men. Ethically unaccountable success or misfortune could be justified as predetermined fate, or by punishment or reward in the next life through reincarnation of the soul. Tottering faith in the government or sinking popular morale could be restored by popular belief in divine assistance during a crisis. When human means failed to appease popular disappointment at the public authority for its inability to administer justice or to avert calamities, the gods and spirits that had formed part of the ethicopolitical order stepped in to share the responsibility. Thus, when sacrifices and prayers failed to halt a prolonged drought, the governor or magistrate at times might thrash the Ch'eng-huang image or expose him under the scorching sun to induce rain, something that never ceased to amaze nineteenth-century observers from the West. In all cases, whatever the religious interpretation of human failures and however exotic the cultic acts, the net result was to spare the ethicopolitical order from direct blame, thus helping to preserve faith in its basic soundness in spite of its fallibility in many circumstances.

Significant to the ethicopolitical function of Chinese religion was the communal nature of the popular cults and the acquisition of communal character by many gods and spirits of voluntary religions such as Buddhism and Taoism. The cult of Ch'eng-huang, for instance, was originally that of a classical deity which later assimilated both Buddhist and Taoist elements. Explaining the communal nature of miracles performed by the god in giving rain and in helping to catch a burglar, a stele inscription in a Ch'eng-huang temple said,

In answering the prayers for rain and for catching the burglar, the god was not granting a private favor in return for man's flattery and coaxing. The prayers for rain and for catching the burglar were offered in public on behalf of the people, and the god's efficacious answers to the prayers were a response to this public spirit . . .; gods and men thus cooperated to bring security to all the people in the empire. . . .[35]

Prayers in all official sacrifices also contained only praise for the gods' efficacy in supporting public causes and in strengthening moral and political traditions; there was no request for personal salvation or private favors. This communal nature equipped the popular cults for their ethicopolitical role.

CEREMONIAL FORMALITY VERSUS THE ACTUAL FUNCTION OF THE CULTS

Comments have been offered by prominent scholars of Chinese culture that official sacrifices to the public cults were merely ceremonial formalities bearing little realistic significance in Chinese social life. As keen a thinker as Max Weber made this observation:

The great spirits of nature were increasingly depersonalized. Their cult was reduced to official ritual, the ritual was gradually emptied of all emotional elements and finally became equated with mere social convention. This was the work of the cultured stratum of intellectuals who left entirely aside the typical religious needs of the masses.[36]

This view is not limited to Western observers. Hu Shih, for example, remarked to an inquiring American missionary: "The sacrifices are mere formalistic ceremonies without serious realistic significance."

If the case of the two deified generals is taken as an example, Weber and other protagonists of this view will have to explain why the sanctuaries were established, whether there was any actual influence on the popular mind from the lore that grew up around the cults, whether there was any functional relation of the cults' development to the bestowing of imperial titles upon the deified generals and the continuation of official sacrifices to them. In the case of the two generals, it is obvious that official sacrifices formed an integral part of the cults. Unless the entire existence of the cults, including the mythological lore, was an empty formality, the official sacrifices cannot be lightly dismissed.

The "ceremonial formality" view of the ethicopolitical cults, above all, has to face the task of explaining why the matter of sacrifice and sacrificial rites received such great emphasis from early Chinese classics down to the modern records of government. Thus the *Li Chi* says: "Of all the ways for keeping men in good order, there is none more important than *li*. The *li* are of five kinds, and none of these is more important than sacrifice." [37] If this passage in *Li Chi* is regarded as mere dead letters in an antiquated Confucian classic, an explanation is needed for the fact that every compendium of government documents and every local gazetteer in the modern period contained carefully edited sections on official and unofficial cults and their sacrifices, and that new cults continued to rise.

Even if the emphasis on sacrifices in contemporary official documents may be regarded as literary formality, one would have to explain the existence of the hundreds of thousands of temples that housed the cults, the regular sacrificial activities undertaken by the government and community leadership, and the social and religious motivations that lay behind such sacrificial activities. The large number of temples and the elaborate sacrificial activities cannot be explained as mere formalities, not even by the theory of cultural vestige. Temples ranked among the largest and most elaborate architectural structures in any community, and sacrificial rites similarly were among the most elaborate of traditional group activities. Temples and sacrifices represented a heavy item of public expenditure. In a preindustrial society, where the general level of economic surplus was generally low, these heavy items of public economic investment cannot be convincingly dismissed as either empty formalities or as cultural vestiges.

Finally, the "ceremonial formality" or "cultural vestige" view implies this assumption: Chinese ethicopolitical life might have been carried on without such cults and their sacrifices. What would have happened if this religious factor were eliminated from the development of the Chinese ethicopolitical order is of course something subjected to every speculative turn of the imagination. But the important fact remains that such a situation never occurred and that the ethicopolitical cults, with their temples, their sacrifices, and their mythological lore, were an integral part of political life up until the Communist regime. This historical fact can be intelligently interpreted on one ground: the cults were significant socioreligious realities founded on their active ethicopolitical functions. It is in this light that we can clarify the social implications of this type of popular cult and many of the penetrating interpretations given in the quoted Chinese documents.

VIII

STATE CONTROL OF RELIGION

THE DISCUSSION OF THE WORSHIP OF HEAVEN and the ethicopolitical cults has demonstrated the potency of the idea of the supernatural in establishing popular acceptance of the ruling power and the institution of government. Fully conscious of this vital function of religion, the ruling group, particularly the Confucians, tried to exert a systematic control over religious forces so that they would serve exclusively the ends of the established power structure. History had suggested to the ruling class that, without political control, the vital religious forces might be utilized by other groups, such as an independent priesthood, or worse still by a rebel force, to develop competitive centers of power.

This chapter deals with the questions of how the traditional government tried to demonstrate its mastery over supernatural forces, how the government imposed a monopoly over certain rituals and interpretations of religious matters, how it exerted administrative control over religious organizations and the priesthood, and, above all, how the traditional authorities tried to prevent and suppress the development of heterodox religious movements.

In tracing some of the answers to these questions, quotations are used from the *Ta-ch'ing lü li* (Fundamental and Supplementary Laws of the Ch'ing Dynasty). This raises the question of the extent to which the official rules and regulations reflected the actual situations in the Ch'ing period, in view of the perfunctory character of many traditional Chinese laws and regulations. As will be pointed out later in this chapter, the effectiveness of enforcement of the laws and regulations on religious matters varied partly according to the historical situation. Even when they were not seriously enforced, they reflected the persistent attitude of the government, and this was an important factor in a society in which institutionalized attitudes had a greater function than formal law in the guidance of human behavior. Historical records show that, given a critical situation, many of the laws would be enforced, whereas in normal times they were tacitly ignored.

TEMPORAL CONTROL OF SUBORDINATE SUPERNATURAL FORCES

In order to make the belief in supernatural forces instrumental to the exercise of power, the traditional government developed a number of devices to demonstrate its superiority and mastery over some of these forces. As was pointed out in the last chapter, the hierarchy of supernatural powers was closely patterned after the structure of the temporal government, and the two systems were considered to be in intimate coöperation in the maintenance of the ethicopolitical order. On this basis, it was believed that a living official had superior power over the gods and spirits of a rank lower than his. So, under certain circumstances, an official could treat a god or spirit as his subordinate, giving reward or punishment or administrative orders as the situation required.

A familiar illustration of this was the granting of honorific divine titles to deserving gods and spirits by the monarch who, at the top of the power hierarchy, assumed superiority over all but the highest of the supernatural beings. The universal sight of plaques and tablets bearing imperial honors and titles adorning the numerous temples throughout the land gave the unmistakable impression that the monarch's superior power extended not only over men but also over many of the gods and spirits.

Such an impression was in fact fully intended. In granting an honorific divine title to the river god for facilitating the transportation of revenue grain over the Grand Canal, Emperor Chia-ch'ing stated in his edict, "The sage Son of Heaven grants favors to a hundred gods. . . ."[1] Whenever the people or the officials believed that the miracle of a god had helped in a major public crisis, the emperor would bestow a title upon the deity as a reward, until no district of the empire was without such titles in some of its temples.

The city god in the county seat of Pao-shan in Kiangsu province was an example. The god was the spirit of Han Ch'eng, an officer who died in 1558 fighting Japanese pirates. He was deified as Ch'eng-huang (city god) in 1728, when Pao-shan was established as a regular county. During the Taiping rebellion, it was believed that his assistance aided the government forces to recapture the city from the rebels in 1853, and the emperor granted him an additional title of "Divine Manifestation." In 1860 and 1863, rebels twice failed to break the defenses of the city, and the repeated rumor of miracles worked by the god led the imperial court to add the honorific adjectives "Divine Manifest Protective" to the previous title. In 1883 and 1885, the god was believed to have contributed to the preservation of the sea wall during a devastating storm, and the emperor bestowed on him another plaque bearing the line "Eternal Assistance with Timely Precipitation." [2] In the same district, for repeated miracles in dispelling locusts in the years 1854 to 1887, the insect god General Liu-meng consecutively received six divine titles from the emperor: "Protection of Abundance, Universal Blessing, Divine Manifestation, Efficacious Benevolence, Charitable Succor, Assistance to Transformation (of the crisis), and Efficacious Assurance." [3] Similar instances could be multiplied indefinitely.

By the same principle, the monarch, as the ruler of both the temporal and celestial orders, could promote or demote the divine ranks of the gods and spirits or punish them for dereliction of duty. Thus stated Parker, who observed Chinese life in the early years of the twentieth century, "They [Chinese officials] even thrash their gods if no result comes of persistent prayers. The emperor rewards the gods frequently if their succor comes sharply; and in one instance, I remember reading a decree instructing the governor to admonish a lazy deity." [4] Such unusual action was generally taken against Ch'eng-huang, the city god, when he failed to answer prayers for rain. While many interpretations could be given to the somewhat shocking ritual, one effect was the demonstration of the ability of the political rulers to command the service of the gods, thus increasing the awe-inspiring quality of their temporal power in the eyes of a superstitious public.

GOVERNMENT MONOPOLY OF THE WORSHIP OF HEAVEN AND
THE INTERPRETATION OF CELESTIAL PORTENTS

Temporal superiority over the supernatural was limited to deities lower in rank than the governing official. There was one group of supernatural forces over which even the emperor claimed no superior power. That was Heaven and some of the heavenly deities. Even the monarch prostrated himself in the sacrifice to Heaven, the highest of all powers. As the temporal power could not command the service of Heaven by hierarchical rank, but could only claim identification with Heaven's will and plead for assistance through rituals, it was necessary to prevent other groups from pleading to Heaven by performing the same rituals and thus claiming Heaven's blessing and sanction in their struggle for power against the established rulers. Parenthetically, the acknowledgment by the highest temporal power, the monarch, of the supremacy of Heaven, mitigated somewhat the shock to the monotheistic Christian mind of seeing Chinese officials thrashing their gods.

A traditional imperial device was to declare a strict monopoly over the performance of rituals in the worship of Heaven, thus keeping others from sharing the same privilege. Thus stipulated the laws of the Ch'ing dynasty:

Those who make private appeal to Heaven and worship the Seven Mansions [of Ursa Major], burning incense at night, lighting the Heavenly Lamp and the Seven-Star Lamp, shall be punished with eighty strokes of the stick. The head of the family shall be held responsible for violation of this law by female members of the family. Buddhist monks and Taoist priests setting up religious services with written appeals to Heaven shall be administered the same punishment, to be followed by reversion to secular status.

The official commentary to this rule stated:

The sacrificial rules are based on the status of the performers of the sacrifice. In addition to ancestor worship, private citizens are permitted only to offer five sacrifices to the five local gods. Should they reach upward to offer sacrifice to the gods of Heaven, this would be usurpation of status. Hence eighty strokes of the stick. Usurpation is sacrilege.[5]

Many students of Chinese religion doubted the effectiveness of the legal prohibition against the worship of Heaven and the major heavenly deities by private citizens. It was obvious that many traditional cults openly conducted by private citizens were connected with Heaven and the heavenly deities. In the courtyard of many traditional homes, particularly in the south, there was a little shrine dedicated to the T'ien-kuan, the Official of Heaven. Traditional wedding rituals in many localities included a sacrifice to Heaven and Earth. The cult of Chen-wu, the star god belonging to the zodiac group, and the cult of Wen-ch'ang, the star god of literary success, were worshiped by the common people. Many similar examples have been used to show the possible ineffectiveness of this law.

But proponents of this view seemed to have missed the main point of the law, which was to prevent persons other than government authorities from performing collective rituals in the worship of Heaven and the heavenly deities for political purposes. The letter of Chinese traditional law was characteristically general and ill-defined, and the spirit of the law was not clearly expressed, but the implication was unmistakable, especially if it is studied in connection with the associated rules to be considered below. Taken in this light, the popular cults connected with Heaven and the heavenly deities were sanctioning agents for the ethicopolitical order, and were not used as rallying points for political struggle. One may consider the prohibition against the worship of Heaven to have served its purpose rather effectively, for so long as government authority reigned there was no openly organized mass worship of Heaven and heavenly deities, conducted with the intention of associating a political group with the supernatural power of Heaven. To be sure, private worship of Heaven might acquire political character, and secret religious movements frequently used the worship of Heaven and the heavenly deities for a political purpose. In such cases, persecution generally followed.

As it was, the ritual of the worship of Heaven was strictly the prerogative of the monarch. The imperial sacrifice to Heaven not only excluded all common people from participation but also prohibited officials of lesser rank from entering the grounds of the Altar of Heaven as spectators. In 1823 an imperial edict reiterated this prohibition, and in 1853 imperial armed guards were posted around the altar grounds at the time of the grand sacrifice to keep the curious mob from obtaining a glimpse of the unfathomable mystery of the worship of the mightiest of gods, Heaven, by the mightiest of men, the monarch.[6] Thus, through rigid control of the sacrificial ritual, the monarch became the only intermediary between Heaven and man. Even the sacrifice to many of the popular cults became a graded privilege based on official status, though such ritual performance was brought closer to the people by permitting the presence of spectators.

A much more politically sensitive matter was the interpretation of heavenly portents. As has been pointed out, according to the theory of interaction between Heaven and man, any unusual phenomenon of nature could be interpreted as Heaven's anger at the misconduct of some individual or group, and could thus become divine sanction for political action to rectify the misconduct or to redress the injustice. The authority of such interpretation was the prerogative of the government in order that the phenomenon would not be interpreted by dissenting groups. The government monopoly on such interpretations thus formed a major aspect in the political control over religious affairs.

In this respect, violation was threatened with the most severe punishment under the Ch'ing law: "Those who make up heretic apocryphal literature, and circulate heretic talk to deceive the public, shall be punished by decapitation. Those who conceal heretic literature without surrendering it to the officials shall be punished by one hundred strokes of the stick and three years imprisonment." The attached official commentary stated that apocryphal literature was prophecy of good fortune or misfortune for the country.

Any heretic apocryphal writing that organizes past strange occurrences as grounds for predicting the coming rise and fall of the state, or any misrepresentation of the gods and spirits in heretic and rebellious talk, . . . these are all falsifying discussions of good fortune or calamity of the state and the flourishing or decline of the nation, with intention to mislead the public and to hatch a political plot. Hence decapitation for both the founder and the followers.

The commentary continued with citations of several cases of execution or banishment of violators in the nineteenth century, reminding readers of the earnestness of the law.[7]

The Ch'ing laws contained another significant stipulation: "Sorcerers of the Yin-yang school are not permitted to enter the homes of civil and military officers of any rank and make disorderly talk on the good fortune or calamity of the state. Violators are punishable by one hundred strokes with the long stick. . . ." An attached commentary explained: "Disorderly talk on the good fortune or calamity of the state is tantamount to misleading the people and interfering in the affairs of the state." [8]

Civil and military officers were the most strategic part of the political machinery, and the prohibition against subversive propaganda among them was naturally considered vital to the security of the state. During the nineteenth century, the issue of heretic proselytism among civil and military officers came up repeatedly. In 1815, for example, there was the case of Wang Shu-hsün, a Buddhist sectarian monk, who succeeded in converting several examination degree holders (candidates for official positions) in Peking and in establishing social relations with officials in the provinces. As a consequence, he was prosecuted, convicted, exposed in the cangue, beaten with the long stick, and forced to return to secular status. More cases of this type appeared in the years when religious rebellions greatly increased in number. In 1840 many Manchu officers and men in Ching-chou (Hupeh province) were persecuted for holding religious meetings. In 1845 a member of the Manchu garrison of Hukuang was persecuted for possessing heretic religious literature and for making common cause with heretics among the Chinese population.[9] The imperial government became so sensitive about the disaffection of military officers and men that it required them to obtain official permission before sorcerers could visit them for curing sickness.

One effect of these laws was the general absence of proselytizing and group preaching of any kind, as people came to fear being regarded as participants in heresy.

ADMINISTRATIVE CONTROL OF TEMPLES AND THE PRIESTHOOD

Control of the Erection of New Temples and Monasteries

In addition to demonstrating the rulers' power to command the services of the gods and spirits, there was the traditional political control of the erection of temples, the ordination to the priesthood, and the conduct of the priests. Such administrative control was applied to the major legally recognized religions of Buddhism and Taoism but usually did not apply to sectarian cults and their priests, both of which were treated as heretical and therefore objects of suppression. Taoism and Buddhism had won the legal right to exist in spite of their heterodox nature, but a system of administrative control was designed to keep them in line with the policy of the state and to prevent them from threatening the sociopolitical order.

Until the end of the Ch'ing dynasty, religious administration was a part of the function of the *li pu,* the Board of Rites, which was one of the six boards of the central administration in the national government. One of the Board's administrative functions was to approve the erection of new temples, sanctuaries, monasteries and convents or cloisters. Thus stated the Ch'ing law: "Private erection of temples and convents is prohibited; violation of this law by Buddhist and Taoist priests is punishable by one hundred strokes of the stick, to be followed by reversion to secular status and banishment to borderland garrisons, and violation by nuns is punishable by slavery in official families." "People wishing to build a monastery or temple must petition the provincial governor, who in turn will forward the matter to the court; building may proceed only upon approval by imperial decree. . . ." "Officials who fail to prohibit the private building of a temple by the ignorant people, and who furthermore grant an official proclamation for a new establishment, are to be fined one year's salary." [10]

The relative effectiveness of these legal stipulations is a pertinent question, for it reflects the degree of actual government control over an important aspect of the religious life of the people. At the beginning of the Ch'ing dynasty in the seventeenth century, there were 12,482 monasteries and temples founded with imperial permission as against 67,140 erected without official approval.[11] In other words, about 84 per cent of all the listed temples and convents were built without the government's official permission. Apparently a very large number of small temples and shrines that dotted the countryside were listed in the official statistics, and from general observation the overwhelming majority of these were likely to be privately built. There are no comparable statistics for subsequent periods. But the stipulated punishment for officials who failed to prohibit private building of temples and monasteries seems to indicate the frequency of breakdown in the enforcement of the law. The fact that some officials would issue a formal proclamation for the opening of a privately built temple suggests that the rule was largely ignored even by the officials themselves. In their listings of places of public worship, the local gazetteers, which were an important source of information for the government administrators, made no distinction between temples and monasteries built with and those built without imperial permission. This may be another indication that the rule had been generally disregarded.

The reasons for requiring official permission for the building of temples and monasteries were twofold. It was a means of control of heretic sects, and it was a way of limiting the size of the clergy by granting only a minimum number of permits for new temples and monasteries. Although the rule does not seem to have been effective, it did express the consistent policy of the traditional government toward control over religion.

Licensing of the Priesthood and Restriction of Its Size

Whether or not a temple or monastery was built with imperial approval, its priests (if any) came under another set of controlling stipulations. First was the licensing of the priesthood by the Board of Rites, a practice stemming from the tenth century and continued until the Republican period. Thus stated the Ch'ing law: "Surreptitious receiving of ordination by the Buddhist and Taoist priesthood without an official ordination certificate shall be punished with eighty strokes of the stick; the master priest administering the surreptitious ordination is punishable by the same, to be followed by reversion to secular status." [12] An official commentary followed: "Once a person becomes a Buddhist or Taoist priest, he is exempt from military conscription, conscript labor, and police surveillance. Therefore, ordination should not be given without government approval." In view of the fact that before the Republican period a traveling monk or priest generally carried along his ordination certificate to show possible accosting authorities, this rule seems to have been seriously enforced.

Clearly implied in this law was the intention of the traditional government to keep down the size of the priestly population so as to reduce the hazard of dissension and financial loss to the state. This intention is unmistakable in another stipulation of the Ch'ing law:

Buddhist and Taoist priests must be over forty years of age before giving apprenticeship to a neophyte, and each ordained priest is permitted to train only one neophyte. The training of neophytes by a priest who has not reached the age of forty, or the training of more than one neophyte by a priest, is punishable by forty strokes of the long stick; the case is to be treated as rape or burglary; and the neophytes involved are to be returned to secular status. [13]

Another rule stipulated that when a priest died his ordination certificate was to be surrendered to the government. [14] The purpose was obviously to prevent the certificate from being passed on to a new priest without clearing through official channels.

By limiting a priest to the training of one neophyte and by preventing the ordination certificate of a deceased priest from being passed on unofficially to another neophyte, the priesthood would be kept at the self-replacing level at best, assuming that every priest trained one neophyte before his death. The age stipulation in this law probably embodied the same purpose. In view of the relatively short life expectancy, a priest after the age of forty could not teach many neophytes with the limited number of years remaining to him. Another possible factor would be that a man over forty is likely to become conservative in his attitudes and outlook, and thus less inclined to embark on the adventure of trying to gather a mass following and organizing a political rebellion.

How effectively this law was enforced is an important question. Unfortunately, there are no available statistical data on the subject. We can only say from general observation that two leading facts were probably partly connected with the operation of this law. One was the small size of the priesthood in proportion to the total population. Another was the absence of mass training of neophytes by one master priest in the Ch'ing period; the collective training of Buddhists in special schools or academies was a development of the Republican period, and such schools were none too successful in producing large numbers of priests. The numerical restriction on the priesthood and the political motivation for it will receive further consideration later in this chapter.

Control of the Conduct of the Clergy

After a man attained priesthood in spite of all the legal restrictions, his activities and conduct came under the control of a special authority. If he were a practitioner of the Yin-yang theology (a combination of geomancy, astrology, and divination), he came under the control of a special officer in his locality. Within each province each department, prefecture, and county had an officer (appointed from the accomplished Yin-yang theologists) whose function was "to control the Yin-yang theologists, to prevent them from misleading the populace with imaginary and false talk, and to use them properly for major public ceremonies, for selecting locations for major construction works, and for divining propitious days and hours." [15] The statement "to prevent them from misleading the populace with imaginary and false talk" recalls the threat against the ruling power by the Yin-yang theologists' interpretation of natural portents in relation to politics.

Buddhist and Taoist priests were under a different system of offices, whose officials were selected and appointed from the priesthood by the Board of Rites. For the control of Buddhists, there were the following: in the national capital of Peking, there was the *Tseng lu ssu,* or the Administration of the Records of the Buddhist Priests; in the *fu* or department in a province, there was the *Tseng kang ssu,* or the Administration of Discipline among the Buddhist

Priests; in the *chou* or prefecture, there was the *Tseng cheng ssu,* or Administration of Rectification of Buddhist Priests; and in the *hsien* or county, there was the *Tseng hui ssu,* or the Administration of Assembly of the Buddhist Priests. A counterpart to this system was set up for the governing of the Taoist priests.[16] Priests of numerically minor religions like the Moslem had no special administrators, but came under the general control of the Board of Rites when cases had to be dealt with.

When Buddhist or Taoist priests violated religious canons and rules, their cases were to be settled by the administrators in their respective system. As the administrators were appointed from the priests of each faith, the administrative system constituted self-government in a limited sense, subject to the secular courts; if convicted, the priests would be forced to return to secular status.[17] Thus, control of the priesthood was part of the function of the secular government, and no religious group was ever left completely free and ungoverned. The only exceptions were the Christians, who gained their independence from political control by military force of the Western powers in the latter part of the nineteenth century. But this independence was repealed under the Republic.

In addition to the above administrative systems set up by the government, there was the special function assigned to the so-called pope of the Taoists, Chang T'ien-shih (Chang the Heavenly Teacher), whose headquarters were in the Dragon and Tiger Mountain in Kiangsi province. He was directed by the Ch'ing government to aid in preventing heretic religious influences from affecting the people's faith in the government and its orthodoxy. The duty of the Taoist pope, as ordered by the founder of the Ch'ing dynasty in the seventeenth century, remained the traditional government policy toward the highest Taoist office until recent decades: ". . . You are ordered to inherit your ancestors' post in administrating the Taoist scripture and in leading your clan and subordinates, so that heterodoxies and sorcery do not deceive and incite the ignorant populace."[18] For the performance of this function, the Board of Rites appointed for the Taoist pope a staff of twenty-six priests, divided into different ranks.[19] Thus the Taoist pope was a functionary of the temporal power, showing once more the supremacy of the traditional imperial authority over all religious organizations.

THE REJECTION AND PERSECUTION OF HETERODOXY

The entire system of administrative control over religion was based on the general purpose of guarding the interests of the ruling power and the state against the possible subversive influence of heterodoxy. Many Western scholars, notably J. J. M. De Groot, emphasized the long Chinese tradition of firm rejection and at times ruthless persecution of heterodoxy. But these scholars have not sufficiently recognized the relation of this tradition to the power structure and the ethicopolitical order of the state. Suppression and persecution were a part of the traditional authoritarian system of social and political life which contributed much to the rise of rebellions in the past and to the chain of revolutions in the modern period. Nevertheless, it is important to study the basic political motivation of such a tradition in order to advance our understanding of the vital role of religion in the traditional political life of China, a role that is by no means entirely negligible even in the present Chinese political situation.

Political Motivation for Persecution

Analysis of this subject may best begin by considering what the traditional government regarded as heterodoxy—a theoretically simple procedure. Any religious belief and activity divergent from the state orthodoxy of Confucianism might be regarded as heterodoxy. Hence, the stamp of heterodoxy might be set on any ethicoreligious belief that was not founded on Confucian classics, and on the worship of any god or spirit that was not a part of the official registry of sacrifice. Ceaseless tirades against heterodoxy were made by outstanding Confucians through the centuries, from Mencius in the Chou period to T'an Ssu-t'ung (who died as one of the six martyrs in the Hundred-Day Reform in 1898) in modern times. All true Confucians turned from any belief or activities associated with the term *i-tuan* or heterodoxy, which was fully defined in the Ch'ing laws and imperial decrees. Thus, in the suppression of a sectarian movement, Emperor Chia-ch'ing declared in 1813:

No so-called religion exists beyond the *three basic relations* [between sovereign and minister, father and son, husband and wife] and the *five constant virtues* [benevolence, righteousness, rites, knowledge, and trustworthiness]; and there is no quarter from which happiness may be sought after, other than from the way of Heaven and the laws of the monarch.[20]

Why was heterodoxy such an object of vehement rejection by Confucians and an object of intolerance by authority and law? During the Late Chou period, Confucians such as Mencius and Hsün Tzu attacked competing schools of thought on philosophical grounds. But in subsequent times, Confucianism having been enshrined as the supreme orthodoxy of the state, the basic ground of discrimination against heterodoxy shifted from theoretical incompatibility to the practical political consideration of safeguarding the Confucian state. The assumption of Confucian magical superiority over heterodoxy, as represented by the popular belief that a copy of a classical book could ward off evil spirits, might be a factor in reinforcing the superior position of Confucianism in the traditional social attitudes. But contrary to the belief of scholars such as De Groot,[21] the magical power of the Confucian doctrine played at best a negligible part in the political rejection and persecution of heterodoxy.

There is an abundance of empirical facts to show that it was not philosophical or theological objection but practical political consideration that was the leading motivation for the traditional antagonism toward heterodoxy. One may say that purely religious arguments between Confucianism and other doctrines or faiths did not exist in Chinese classical literature. Confucius himself repeatedly refused to discuss supernatural subjects. In subsequent times, although both Buddhism and Taoism were heterodoxies by the classical definition, the essence of their teachings was both formally and informally blended into Confucianism, with little objection from political authorities. Mere theological difference was no ground for political antagonism. Thus decreed Emperor Chia-ch'ing in 1812:

Other doctrines, such as Buddhism and Taoism, although not esteemed by Confucianists, can be reckoned to belong to what the Book of Yü [in the *Shu Ching,* or Book of History] has in view in speaking of happiness obtained by following the Tao, and misfortune by opposing it, since they also encourage what is good and reprove what is evil. Hence [Taoist] gods and Buddhas and their temples are alloted a place in the Sacrificial Canon, and the law does not prohibit performing rituals in veneration of them, or praying to them.[22]

Moreover, the most frequent objects of political persecution, namely the religious societies, were generally the result of blending Buddhist theology, Taoist rituals, and Confucian ethics into an organized system. In many of these societies, such as the Lung Hua sect, Confucian ethics played a dominant role. Yet the Confucian element in them did not spare them from political persecution, and the suppression of the Lung Hua sect was among the most bloody episodes in the nineteenth century.[23]

Practical political interests rather than purely philosophical and religious considerations as the basic ground for the rejection and persecution of heterodoxy were clearly expressed in many outstanding imperial pronouncements on the subject. One example was the decree of 1724, which served as the guiding spirit for government policy and laws on the control of heresy throughout the Ch'ing period. The Ch'ing government made it a policy to keep this document in wide distribution in the schools in all the provinces.[24] Its importance justifies its quotation at length:

. . . The accomplishments of the sages and the principles of the sovereign are all founded upon orthodox learning. As to the writings that are not those of the sages, and those unclassical (*pu ching*) books which arouse mankind and alarm the populace, causing disorder and confusion of views and gnawing at the people and their wealth as corroding insects—these are all heterodoxy (*i-tuan*) and ought to be absolutely excluded.

. . . From ancient times, three religions have continued in propagation, viz., the school of Ju (Confucianism) and besides this, those of

Taoism and Buddhism. The philosopher Chu Hsi says that Buddhism does not bother with the material universe but considers only the subject of the mind, and that Taoism merely aims at the preservation of the spiritual essence of man. This fair statement from Chu Hsi clarifies the fundamental objects of Buddhism and Taoism.

But a class of loafers, with neither a livelihood nor an abode, have since come forth to usurp the name of these religions and corrupt the practical use of the same. The majority of them use (their doctrine about) calamities and felicity, misfortune and happiness to sell their foolish magic and baseless talk. They begin by cheating on goods and money to fatten themselves. Then they proceed to hold meetings for the burning of incense, in places where males and females mingle promiscuously. Farmers and craftsmen forsake their business and trades, and engage themselves in talking about miracles. Worst of all, rebellious and subversive individuals and heretical miscreants glide in among them, establish parties and form leagues by taking membership oaths. They assemble at night and disperse in the daytime. They thus transgress their proper status and sin against their duty, mislead mankind and deceive the people. Then, one day the matter is discovered by the authorities, the culprits are arrested, affecting all those who are connected with it; they are cast into prison, and their wives and children become involved. The chiefs of the sects are treated as principal culprits; so these men who passed as givers of felicity and bliss have become the very source of misfortune. Sects such as those of the White Lotus and of Smelling Incense are instances of this. . . .

Indeed, the misleading of the people by heresy is not pardonable by law (on Heresy); against heretic leaders and priests and against heretic practices the realm has regular punishment. The object of the Court in creating laws is none other than to guide the people toward virtuousness, excluding heresy and elevating orthodoxy, thus removing dangers and realizing security for the people. You soldiers and people, you have been born of the bodies of your parents in trouble-free days of universal peace; so you are assured of raiment and food and you are free from worry about the support for your wives and children and for your parents. If, nevertheless, you choose to obscure your firmness of characters so much as to form connections with rebellious parties, thus violating the principles of the government and transgressing the laws of the empire, do you then not show yourselves the biggest of fools?

. . . In its original condition the heart contains orthodoxy, and not heresy. So, if you remain master of it, it cannot go astray of itself, and if you walk in every respect the straight and correct road, no heresies can possibly conquer orthodoxy. Concord and obedience will then reign in your homes, and when trouble comes, they will convert these into felicity. To serve one's parents with filial piety and one's ruler with fidelity, and to attend to human affairs to the best of one's ability, will suffice to accumulate heavenly bliss. By not seeking things that lie beyond one's proper status, by abstaining from wrong doing, and by devoting oneself to one's own occupation, all felicities which the gods bestow may be received. (Ye people), devote yourselves to your ploughs; (ye soldiers), talk together of military matters; keep quietly to your constant duties with respect to (the production of) woven stuffs, pulse and rice, and yield to the teachings which bring general peace and orthodox correctness; the heresies will not wait to be driven away, but of themselves will cease to exist.[25]

This important decree contained four major points. First, there was a conciliatory tone toward the basic philosophies of the two leading heresies, namely Buddhism and Taoism, and neither philosophical nor political objection to them. Second, political objection began with the tendency of heterodoxy to create "disorder and confusion" in the public mind and to "arouse mankind and alarm the populace." This objection was based on the danger of heterodox influence in undermining the people's faith in the Confucian orthodoxy which undergirded the entire moral and political order of the state. Third, political rage and persecution fell on those who not only accepted heretical beliefs but who "came forth to usurp the name" of heretic religions and made "corrupt" use of them in organizing a mass following which might become a force for rebellious activities, directly threatening the state. Fourth, the decree reiterated the familiar Confucian admonition that man's happiness and security lay in faithful devotion to the orthodox moral, economic, and political order and that heretical religion would lead not to salvation but to punishment and misfortune.

The first point needs no further elaboration. The remaining three points are reflected in the consistent effort by the government throughout the Ch'ing dynasty to preserve the supremacy of the Confucian orthodoxy, to safeguard the Confucian social and moral order, and to eliminate any actual or potential danger from organized religious groups in rebellion against the state. These are the main topics of the following discussion.

The traditional state was founded upon Confucianism as the supreme orthodoxy, which laid down the basic principles of the power structure and the ethicopolitical order of the empire.

The policy of keeping the Confucian orthodoxy in the supreme position was ever-present in over a thousand years of continuous struggle against the influence from religions, particularly Buddhism. The assertion of Confucian supremacy over religion gained national attention from the famous tirades uttered by the rulers during the four most disastrous persecutions of Buddhism in Chinese history, in 446, 574, 845, and 955. Confucian supremacy was popularized among Chinese intellectuals by Han Yü's essay *Yüan Tao* (Origin of the Tao) and his renowned memorial against his emperor's intention to welcome a finger bone of the Buddha, Sakyamuni.

With the full reconsolidation of the Confucian state in the Sung dynasty (960–1279), constant vigilance was maintained against any popular religious movement that might have threatened the dominance of the orthodoxy. Thus, in 1106, Emperor Hui Tsung ordered a correction of the popular practice in which many temples and monasteries placed the founders of Buddhism, Confucianism, and Taoism on the same altar, with Buddha at the center, Lao Tzu on the left, and Confucius on the right.[26] The image of Confucius was ordered to be moved to the academy halls and the other two to be taken to the temples or monasteries of their respective faiths. The imperial objection was against associating Confucianism with the other two religions in a common place of worship, for this might lead to contamination of the purity of the orthodoxy. Above all, the court objected to an arrangement of the three images in which Buddha occupied the dominant central position, with Confucius and Lao Tzu in secondary places.

Six centuries later, an almost exact repetition of this incident occurred under the illustrious ruler Ch'ien Lung of the Ch'ing dynasty. The emperor's decree in 1744 shows that there was a strong popular movement of the Three Religions in Honan province. No less than 590 Halls of Three Religions were counted in several districts in that province. In each of these halls, the image of Buddha occupied the principal center seat, that of Lao Tzu was on the left, and that of Confucius on the right or the lowest place. Furthermore, the images of Lao Tzu and Confucius were smaller than that of Buddha. The monarch's order was almost the same as in 1106. Each image was to be taken to the place of worship of the respective faith. But the governing officials were given the alternative of converting the Hall of Three Religions into a Confucian school.[27] To make the image of Confucius smaller than that of Buddha in addition to placing him in the lowest seat was of course offensive to a monarch who well knew that his very throne and the sociopolitical order of his empire depended on the effective functioning of the Confucian doctrine.

Available sources offer no further instances of government action against the demotion of Confucianism in a syncretic faith, but such blending was common in popular religious societies, with Buddhist deities and ideas playing a more dominant part than Confucianism. What was absent was only the visible symbol of the arrangement of the three images. The Ch'ing government's historic policy of maintaining the dominance of the Confucian orthodoxy was certainly a factor in its consistent antagonism to popular religious societies. Above all, in the case of political rebellion by religious movements, the replacement of the Confucian orthodoxy by heterodox doctrines was always a central issue. In the familiar example of the Taiping rebellion, the deposing of Confucianism not only was stressed by all imperial proclamations against the uprising but also was one of the main reasons why the educated class, the Confucians, refused coöperation with the rebels—a major cause of the failure of the movement. This proposed deposition nullified some of the nationalistic appeal of the rebellion and motivated Tseng Kuo-fan, who more than any other leader helped in saving the tottering Manchu dynasty, to proclaim that the struggle against the Taiping was a struggle to save Confucian civilization. In the Republican period, the continued suppression of some religious societies came partly from the fact that many of the officials were consciously or unconsciously Confucians in their political outlook and thus were intolerant of heterodoxy.

Preservation of the Established Socioeconomic Order

But why was the dominance of the Confucian orthodoxy so jealously guarded? Again, the basic motivation in this long historical tradition was not the theological or even philosophical difference between Confucianism and the heterodoxies. It was, instead, the practical consideration of maintaining the established socioeconomic order. In this consideration, two issues stood out prominently. One was the preservation of the basic ruler-subject and parent-son relationships. It is now well recognized that the authoritarian pattern of Chinese family organization, with filial piety as its central factor, was basic training for the people's submission and loyalty to the traditional authoritarian state. The safeguarding of these two relationships, therefore, was of prime importance to the state. The second issue was political antagonism against the rise of an economically nonproductive class of priests who would cause a loss in the nation's productivity and in government revenue. The fact must be kept in mind that the orthodox classical religion was diffused into the major social institutions and had no extensive independent priesthood. These two issues applied particularly to the political antagonism against Buddhism, which advocated the renunciation of all worldly ties, including the ruler-subject and the parent-son relationships, as well as the renunciation of active economic pursuits.

These socioeconomic motivations were clearly spelled out in the historic root of the long anti-heterodox tradition. For example, in the first major persecution against Buddhism, in 446, Emperor Shih Tsu of the Wei dynasty charged that historical precedents had shown that the Buddhist faith had caused failure in the operation of the government, corroded the standards of social conduct, blinded the people with the religion of spirits, and led them to disregard the laws of the government.[28]

But how did the Buddhist religion cause failure in the operation of government and corrode standards of social conduct? There was much confusion among contemporaneous disputants on this issue. But, by the time of the rise of the T'ang dynasty, when the Confucian orthodoxy had begun to regain its dominant position after some four centuries of eclipse, the Confucian stand on the issue became clarified and in subsequent centuries attained the status of a classical tradition. Thus, in 624, the powerful minister Fu I summarized the political objection to Buddhism: in teaching the renunciation of all worldly ties, it led people to become disloyal to the ruler and unfilial toward parents, and it turned converts into idlers and wandering mendicants who, by donning the priestly garb, also dodged the payment of taxes. He proposed forcing the more than one hundred thousand monks and nuns existing at that time to return to secular status by each taking a spouse. The state, Fu I continued, would then gain over one hundred thousand families, which would give birth to a new generation of economic producers for society and soldiers for the state.[29]

The famed Confucian Han Yü built his case against Buddhism and Taoism on basically the same grounds. His memorial of 819 against the welcoming of Buddha's finger bone rested on his charge of Buddha's ignorance of "the duties of the ministers toward the sovereign, and the sentiments of the child toward the parents." In his widely read essay *Yüan Tao,* he upbraided both the Taoists and the Buddhists for the rise of a clerical class that impoverished society by living off the labor of farmers and artisans, that dodged payment of revenue to the state, that abandoned the ruler-subject and parent-son relationships, and that through celibacy inhibited procreation and the rearing of new generations. This, he pointed out, was a disruption of the fundamental fabric of social relations and the basic Confucian system of education. By his clear forceful style, Han Yü summarized the views of his predecessors for Confucian statesmen in subsequent centuries in their fight against heterodoxy.

The basic political objection to the development of religion as an independent organized force was clearly indicated in the indictment against Buddhism in a memorial by Li Te-yü in the latter part of the T'ang dynasty:

In the district of Szu-chou [Kiangsu province], altars are set up for the ordination of Buddhist monks and nuns. In the area between the Yangtze and Huai rivers, when a family has three males, there will be one taking the tonsure, with the intention of dodging labor conscription and escaping payment of taxes for the family property. I inquired at the ferry dock in Suan-shan, and counted over one hundred persons crossing every day to receive ordination. I inquired at the ordination altars in Szu-chou, and found that the neophytes who came would pay only two strings of cash and receive their ordination certificates, without any other religious procedure. Should this be permitted to continue, when the time of the religious festival comes, the area of the Yangtze and Huai rivers will have lost six hundred thousand male adults. This is not a small matter.[30]

It was but a reiteration of these same points when Emperor Wu Tsung issued his famous indictment in 845, at the time of one of the most disastrous persecutions against Buddhism; he stressed the displacement of the people's respect for the ruler and the parents by the relationship between the religious teacher and the student, the abandonment of one's spouse for the observation of religious commandments, and the economic wastefulness of a large non-productive priesthood.[31] Fan Chung-yen (A.D. 989–1052), who ranked high among the founders of the modern Confucian tradition, had no new particulars to add when he proposed once again to impose control over the Buddhist and Taoist priests in order to strengthen the kinship foundation of society and to assure economic prosperity for the nation.[32]

Here it may be added that the economic objection to the clergy included the practice by which many wealthy families tried to escape taxation by having a part of their extensive holdings, mainly agricultural land, listed as temple or monastery property. The result was not only loss of revenue to the state but also political disturbance created by the coalition of wealthy families and an influential clerical group, forming a powerful alliance in local politics that at times defied the central authority. This situation was quite common during times when the Buddhist organization was socially and politically influential, as in the Northern Wei and the Liao periods.[33]

In the modern period, up until the early years of the Republic, this means of hiding a part of extensive property from taxation was by no means unknown in many localities in China where large temples or monasteries and convents existed, although the political aspect of the situation had long ceased to be a factor because of the waning of the clergy as an organized force.

These then, were the major political motivations in the historical tradition which guided the authorities of the Ch'ing dynasty when they wrote their laws and ordinances for the control not only of Buddhism and Taoism but also of all other heterodoxies. The traditional economic objection to a large priesthood was elucidated in the official commentary on the law requiring official permission for the building of new temples and monasteries:

The Buddhist and Taoist clergy are exempted from taxation, conscription, and the *corvée*. When the clergy increase, the [secular] population decreases. These creatures do not plow and have no trades, but dress and eat at the expense of the people. So they cannot be permitted to build temples freely and to receive ordination without restriction.[34]

There was substantial ground for the complaint against Buddhists (and some Taoists) for their subversive influence on the kinship system. A Buddhist priest was traditionally called a *ch'u-chia jen*, "a person who has left the family." Among the ritualistic acts of Buddhist ordination was to designate for the neophyte a *fa ming* or *fa hao*, a name of the dharma or a religious name, with the kinship surname omitted, so that the new priest carried no mark of family identification and its suggested social ties. The tonsure, another ritual in ordination, was to symbolize the severing of the "ten thousand strands" of vexing ties with the secular world. Thus each ordained Buddhist and each *ch'u-chia* (family-forsaking) Taoist was a loss to the kinship organization, undermining its integrity.

The historical tradition of safeguarding the kinship system from subversive religious influence was fully written into the Ch'ing law:

A secular male who, coming from a family having less than three males, leaves home to become a priest is punishable by one month under the cangue; priests and abbots who have knowledge of the situation but fail to report it to the authorities are punishable by dismissal from their respective positions and reversion to secular status.[35]

Both Taoist and Buddhist priests, in spite of the latter's renunciation of kinship relations, were required by law to participate in ancestor worship and to observe mourning for their kin in the same manner as required for the secular population.[36] Another rule of similar significance was the prohibition against keeping any young pupils (boys or girls) in the monasteries or cloisters unless they had no parents or homes to support them. In fact, in the modern period, most Buddhist and Taoist priests and nuns had been orphaned or widowed or were from families too poor to support them. A family of satisfactory economic and social conditions seldom yielded a member to the clergy.

Confucian antagonism to Buddhism was based, at least in part, on Buddhist renunciation of kinship relations, thus threatening the kinship system and indirectly the social and political order. The Catholic prohibition of ancestor worship by Chinese Christians was but a part of an age-old issue, and the conflict of power between the Chinese monarch and the pope was only one aspect of the historical situation.

In common with many religious organizations in other cultures, Chinese religious sects often countenanced a relaxation of conventional restrictions on sex segregation and even on promiscuity. Some Taoist sects approved of sexual intercourse for their members. Many syncretic sects allowed mingling of the two sexes in their membership and ritual activities, resulting in actual or rumored irregularities in sexual behavior. Many imperial decrees against heterodoxy in the Ch'ing period mentioned the violation of sex segregation as one of the undesirable features of heretic organizations. There was a law against permitting women to worship in temples and monasteries where they might come into contact with male priests or male worshipers.[37] This rule was never enforced or enforceable, for women were always in the majority among worshipers in temples, and temple grounds were familiar places for romance, but it nonetheless indicated one of the basic reasons for political antagonism to heterodoxy. In persecutions of religious organizations, immorality often became one of the major points of indictment. Such cases of persecution were innumerable during the Ch'ing dynasty. In 1839, for example, the sectarian society of Kun Tan Hui was persecuted for sexual promiscuity and for selling official ranks to its members.[38] The name of the society, meaning Rolling of Single Persons, suggests some similarity to the Holy Rollers and the revival meetings of an earlier America. Members were required to join the organization in pairs, a man and a woman, and the government alleged that meetings were held at night in complete darkness, thus allowing irregular sexual conduct. Again, in 1887, the persecution of the Lung Hua Hui was partly based on the indictment that the society lured young women into its membership, leading to surreptitious sexual affairs, thus corrupting social morality.[39]

The seclusion of women through sex segregation was a major means by which the traditional Chinese family maintained its solidarity and authoritarian structure. The relaxation of sex segregation had long been recognized in Chinese literature as a serious threat to the cohesion of the family system, so vital to the traditional sociopolitical order.

Suppression of Competitive Centers of Power

With the allure of escape from worldly sufferings through a different social order, with religious fervor and loyalty that might be generated for the sacred cause, and with leadership and organization, a heterodox movement could easily turn into a formidable contender for political power. Such, indeed, was often the case in Chinese history, and Chinese political thinkers had long taken notice of it. The early classic, *Chou li* (the Chou Book of Rites), had laid down the rule: "For disturbing the affairs of government with heresy, capital punishment." [40] From Han times on, political disturbance from religious movements in every historical period had resulted in legal control over organized religious groups that might produce a mass following for political struggle.

In the Ch'ing period, such control was expressed in severe legal provisions against any organized religious movements. Thus stated the most basic article of the anti-heresy law:

Religious instructors and priests who pretend to invoke heretic gods, write charms or pronounce them over water [to cure sickness], or carry around palanquins with idols in them, or invoke saints, calling themselves true leaders, chief patrons, or female leaders; further, all societies calling themselves at random White Lotus societies of the Buddha Maitreya, or the Ming-tsun religion, or the school of the White Cloud, and so on, together with all that answer to practices of heresy; finally, they who in secret places have portraits and images, and offer incense to them, or hold meetings which take place at night and break up by day, whereby the people are stirred up and misled under the pretext of cultivating virtue shall be sentenced, the principal perpetrators to strangulation, and their accomplices each to a hundred blows with the long stick, followed by banishment to the distance of three thousand *li* [about 900 miles].

If any solider or civilian dress or decorate himself like the image of a god, and receive that god with the clang of cymbals and the beating of drums, and hold sacrificial meetings in his honor, one hundred blows with the long stick shall be inflicted, but only to the principals. . . . Services of prayer in the spring and thanksgiving in the summer [for the harvest] in honor of the communal gods of the soil do not fall under these restrictions.[41]

In the Ch'ing law against rebellion, severe punishment was stipulated for those who set up heretic sects, gathered a following through proselytism, and thereby "misled the multitude and disturbed the peace." [42] Thus stated a rescript which was not consistently enforced but nevertheless expressed the policy of the traditional government toward religious organizations: "The Buddhist and Taoist clergy shall not hold sutra readings in market places, nor go about with alms bowls, nor explain the fruits of salvation, nor collect moneys; and they who infringe upon this rescript shall be punished." [43]

These laws and rescripts and many other related ones contained one central theme, namely the government's fear of the rise of organized forces driven by religious fanaticism, integrated by a system of leadership, supported by a mass following, and strengthened by contributions from the members. The rise of such a force clearly spelled the possibility of a competitive center of power should its leaders acquire political ambition. From this fear stemmed the prohibition against the holding of heretic services at night and dispersing in the daytime. The sounding of cymbals and drums in a religious procession or service was always meant to summon a crowd or gather a following, and hence the legal stipulation against it. The same held for the preaching of the sutra in the market place and proselytizing by Buddhist and Taoist priests, which might lay the foundation for an organized congregation.

The matter of organized leadership was always emphasized in the anti-heresy law. The finger of persecution pointed especially at those who "acknowledge a religious teacher or transmit their religion to proselytes." The significance of this stipulation lay in the fact that the teacher-student relationship was one of the firmest and most lasting bonds in traditional Chinese society. The introduction of this social tie into a religious movement meant cementing a following into a strongly organized group.

The whole matter of government vigilance against the rise of organized forces among the populace can be more fully understood by studying some of the stipulations of the anti-rebellion law in the Ch'ing period. A prominent example was the threat of punishment by death for those who formed a sworn brotherhood by the initiation ritual of letting a few drops of the members' blood and burning to the gods a written oath with a list of names of the members. Should such a sworn brotherhood have a membership of more than twenty persons, the death sentence for the leaders was to be carried out immediately without the necessity of obtaining approval from the imperial authority. Even the formation of a sworn brotherhood without the ritual of letting blood and burning a written oath and a membership list would incur death for the leaders should such an organization have more than forty members; if the membership should be less than forty persons, there was still the severe punishment of one hundred blows with the long stick and banishment to a distance of three thousand *li* for the leaders.[44]

The religious bond formed by the ritual of letting blood and burning a written oath and a membership list added strength to an organization by invoking the witness and sanction of the supernatural, and the law took full cognizance of this. The widespread existence of brotherhood organizations in traditional Chinese society pointed to the ineffectiveneess of the law. Nonetheless, the law expressed the constant vigilance of an authoritarian political tradition against any suspicious organization among the people, particularly when it possessed the strength of a religious bond among the members.

The basically political motivation of these anti-heresy laws is found in their actual operation in suppressing organized religious movements. As will be seen in the following chapter, throughout the Ch'ing dynasty down to the Republican period, all major persecutions against organized religious movements were connected with political rebellion or the government's fear of it. In the Ch'ing period, most of the political rebellions were related to one or more of the blacklisted sectarian organizations such as the White Lotus sect, the White Sun religion, the Red Sun religion, the Eight Diagrams religion, the T'ien Li (Celestial Principle) religion, the Lung Hua (Dragon Flower) society, the Hsien T'ien (Prebirth) Tao, the Heaven and Earth society, the Triads of the Taiping movement, and the Boxers' association so familiar to the West. The Triads, the Heaven and Earth society, and the Hung society, all of which had a religious sectarian base, were all to some degree participants in the Republican revolution that overthrew the Ch'ing dynasty in 1911. In the Republican period, religious rebellions continued to emerge.

The political motivation in religious persecutions can also be seen in the ways in which the imperial authorities dealt with sectarian troubles in the nineteenth century. In the bloody suppression of the Eight Diagrams society in 1813, for example, imperial decrees time and again instructed the officials to discriminate between those who joined the sect for personal salvation and those who actually took part in the revolt.[45] In the effort to adjudicate the struggle between the orthodox and reform sects of the Moslem religion in Chinese Turkistan, the imperial court ruled that the criteria for heterodoxy was whether the members of a sect had participated in political rebellion against the government, completely ignoring the theological controversy in the situation. In the suppression of the Lung Hua sect in Fukien province, the Ch'ing officials asked why it was necessary for the members to wear white garments and to employ other means of identification if the sole purpose of the sect was, as it was claimed to be, nothing more than the worship of its own gods and the practice of its own moral creeds. Insignia of membership meant the building up of organizational strength, which always aroused the fear of rebellion in the minds of the rulers.

The gnawing fear of rebellion not only brought persecution upon religious organizations that actually plotted or precipitated revolts but also placed other heterodox groups under suspicion, thus subjecting many purely religious bodies to persecution. The gathering of large numbers of people for a heterodox cause always spelled political danger to the traditional authorities, who were not tutored in the principle of freedom of assembly.

The demolition of so-called heretic temples constituted a familiar type of persecution against nonpolitical religious groups. Such persecutions occurred from time to time throughout the entire Ch'ing period. For example, in 1824 the temple of Five Gods in the vicinity of Soochow city in Kiangsu province was ordered demolished so as not to permit "the ignorant people to form associations" for the worship of heretic spirits. In 1838 the temple of Fork-Branch Mountain and the temple of White Cloud Mountain in Shantung province were ordered dismantled "for fear that bad elements might mix with the large crowds gathered at the temple fairs" and threaten peace and order. The sectarians were saved from serious persecution when the official found that religious gatherings at these temples were a matter of long local tradition, without permanent leadership and without proselytism. The next year, 1839, Emperor Tao Kuang warned that "in different provinces there are temples bearing heretic labels, collecting crowds for religious services, thus easily lending themselves to inciting and deceiving the public." Temples dedicated to gods that had been associated with rebellious sects were likely to be demolished. An example was the Wu-sheng Lao-mu (the Unbegotten Mother, a goddess who transcended the cycle of birth and death). The deity was worshiped by many leading politically rebellious sects after the latter part of the Ming dynasty. In 1839, ninety-three of its temples in Honan province were torn down, and many priests connected with the temples were punished by the authorities, in spite of the absence of any concrete evidence of rebellious acts.[46] In the 1860's, immediately following the great Taiping rebellion, orders were issued forbidding the rebuilding of heretic temples destroyed during the uprising.[47]

In short, the entire record of the Chinese government's attitude toward heterodoxy, as exemplified by events in the nineteenth century, was one of persecution of religious sects because of actual or possible political rebellion. It was not until the Republic that government control over religious activities relaxed and persecution of purely religious groups based on fear of rebellion was largely discontinued.

Under the constant effort to weed out organized heterodox groups as possible competitive centers of political power, it was logical that the traditional Chinese government would not give temples and monasteries the right of sanctuary to shield violators of the law from the hands of the authorities. The temporal power of the government extended to all corporate religious bodies. Decrees and laws were issued to prevent violators of laws from taking refuge openly or secretly in temples and monasteries. In the extensive persecution of Buddhism in 955, for example, an imperial decree specifically forbade ordaining into the clergy any unfilial sons who had deserted their parents, any slaves who had escaped from their masters, any lawbreakers, any gangsters, or any persons who hid from the law in the woods and hills.[48] Imperial decrees at other times also prohibited deserters from the armed forces from taking refuge by having themselves ordained into the priesthood, a situation that led Confucian scholars to characterize the clergy as a reservoir of unclean elements. In some periods, such as during the Later Chou in the tenth century, neophytes were required to take an examination before ordination to make sure that they knew the sacred scripture in order to exclude those who entered the clergy as a mere expedient.[49]

The Ch'ing law retained this tradition and permitted no extra-legal status whatsoever to the clergy and their temples or monasteries. The chief priest of a temple or monastery and the ecclesiastical authorities in the administrative system were fully responsible to the government for the good conduct of the clergy. Authorities in the ecclesiastical administrative position were allowed to adjudicate matters concerning the violation of religious rules, but the secular court handled all cases involving priests accused of violating secular laws or concerning difficulties between priests and secular society. No one with a criminal record was allowed to receive the ordination certificate. The chief of a monastery was required to report to the government anyone staying under his roof who had no ordination certificate.[50] Under the Republic, the priesthood was held responsible to the secular authorities for the proper conduct of its members.

Even in conducting purely religious affairs, religious organizations were not independent of secular control. This applied particularly to their collection of dues or revenues from members. Throughout the Ch'ing period, practically no major indictment against religious sects was without the standard charge of "cheating through proselytism." With some of the religious sects, the charge of defrauding superstitious believers perhaps had factual grounds. Even in the British colony of Hong Kong, such charges led to the imposition of certain government controls over the activities of religious organizations.[51] But, aside from the government's wish to maintain law and justice, there was its fear that a religious organization would gain strength by collecting dues and contributions, particularly when the following was an extensive one. An example is a case in Shantung province in 1837. The government charge was that a religious sect led by Ma Kang collected dues from the members, thus providing economic sustenance for the leaders, who then could devote their full time to developing the organization.[52]

POLITICAL DOMINANCE OF RELIGION

As the government imposed an administrative system on legally approved temples and the priesthood and laid down severe controls over all organized heterodox activities, the situation pointed toward complete political dominance of religion. In the case of the classical religion, the worship of Heaven and Earth and the system of functional gods was largely diffused into the major social institutions, giving the latter the support of sanction, and the question of dominance of the political institution over religion did not arise. (See chap. xii on diffused and institutional religion.) But political control of the voluntary types of religion was a consistent pattern in Chinese history. Institutional religion developed extensively in China only under political approval or sponsorship, and persecution and loss of organized strength followed deterioration in its politically favored position. This was clearly represented in the waxing and waning of Buddhism as an institutional religion in close relation to the interests and attitudes of the ruling class in various historical periods (see chap. v and pp. 187–192).

The tradition of political dominance over organized religion was so persistent that even under the Republic, when most of the effective legal control over religion was relaxed, the development of a religious movement still depended much on the patronage of prominent political figures. The sudden growth of the Buddhist movement in Hunan province in the mid-1920's, for example, owed much to the patronage of the provincial governor, T'ang Sheng-chih, who was known to be a devout Buddhist. Under his sponsorship, the Hunan Buddhist Conversion Association (Hunan Fo-hua Hui) gave birth to a host of Buddhist training and worshiping organizations throughout the territory. But when T'ang was deposed, the whole movement evaporated as rapidly as it had arisen.[53]

Historical facts belie the common assertion that there was no protracted conflict between the state and religion. But from the fifth to the tenth century, a period of sharp conflict between Buddhism and the state, the story was consistently a one-sided persecution by the state and not a struggle between two equal forces. At no time did the state lose its dominant position.

Why the state was so strong in comparison to religion is too complex a problem to be thoroughly explored here. One factor was the early diffuse pattern in which religion developed, combining itself with the major social institutions instead of being an independent organized institution with separate functions and structure. When voluntary religion was developed, it faced a well-entrenched political institution that had long assumed a controlling position over religious matters.

But a more interesting fact was the overwhelming strength of the government of a united continental empire as against the divided strength of religions in a land where polytheism and the coexistence of many faiths weakened the organized force of religion as a whole. This situation is the reverse of that found in Europe, where, before the Reformation led to the rise of sectarianism, religion enjoyed the advantage of united strength on a continental basis, whereas secular government was divided into small feudal and later national units. The strength of Christianity was its continental unity, and the weakness of temporal government was its division. In Europe, the international church could play the sovereign of one state against that of another, frequently forcing a temporal government to its knees. But in China, where the tradition of a continental empire was maintained, religion was faced with one monolithic opponent. On the other hand, the conflicting religions often betrayed each other in order to gain favor with the ruler, as shown by Taoist attacks on Buddhism which brought persecution upon the latter, and vice versa. And the imperial authorities often exploited the interreligional conflict to control religious movements or to exterminate certain religious sects. This situation continued through the Ch'ing period. There was only one imperial government, but there were many religions and numerous sectarian societies. And the Ch'ing government, as already mentioned, made use of the Taoist pope to help control other heretic sects.

RELIGIOUS DEVELOPMENT UNDER POLITICAL DOMINANCE

With the temporal government having an overwhelming superiority, with rigid legal control, and with bloody persecutions from time to time during more than fifteen hundred years, none of the organized religions developed a lasting national system of ecclesiastical organization. As will be elaborated on later, even Buddhism, having the strongest religious structure, was reduced to disconnected units of scattered temples and monasteries. The so-called Taoist pope had only a title, without organizational authority over the individual Taoist sects, temples, and convents.

The *Ta-ch'ing hui-tien shih-li* (1900 edition, chüan 390, p. 4) gave a national total of about 140,000 Buddhist and Taoist clergy for the year 1667. De Groot concluded from this that, since the T'ang dynasty fixed the total quota for Buddhist and Taoist priests at 126,000, there had been little progress for these two religions for a thousand years. Almost three hundred years later, under the Republic, the total number of priests for the country was estimated to be between 500,000 and 1,000,000.[54] The increase was not great, in view of the fact that the population of the country had probably grown three- to fourfold since the seventeenth century. This fairly static ratio is probably a reflection of government control over religion, especially the legal limitations on the construction of new temples and the size of the clergy. Undoubtedly, political control and antagonism had vastly reduced the number of temples and monasteries that contained sizeable colonies of Buddhist or Taoist clergy. Furthermore, constant warnings against and frequent persecutions of heterodoxy had created the popular attitude that membership in the clergy or religious societies was not merely questionable but might even bring destruction. Few people of respectable status and with a satisfactory livelihood would undertake such an adventure. This attitude served to reduce both the numerical size and social position of the clergy.

In the modern period, the severest political blow was aimed at the heterodox religious societies which, unlike the temples, monasteries, and the Buddhist and Taoist priests, were not registered and approved by the government, thus remaining outside routine administrative control. By legal threats and by actual persecution, popular religious organizations and movements were driven underground. To this day, these organizations carry a certain degree of secrecy, regarding legal authorities as a natural enemy. As repeatedly demonstrated above, the government was rather indifferent toward theological problems of heresy, and an individual had a large measure of freedom in choosing his own belief without being molested by the law. But as soon as he tried to create or join an organized religious movement, the law would take punitive action. The suppressive measure turned the later Chinese empire into a land of numerous secret religious organizations and movements.

These, then, were some of the tangible results of the long political dominance and control over religion. But government restriction did not exterminate religious developments in China. Severe and rigid as the legal stipulations were, their effectiveness remained a question. The vastness of the country, the primitive state of the transportation and communication system, the scanty number of officials in the system of formal government, all combined to make it well-nigh impossible to enforce the law effectively in the modern sense. Basically, traditional China was a huge conglomeration of numerous folk communities, each operating largely on local folkways and mores, and superimposed over them all was a national system of law which came into full operation only on critical occasions. So long as a religious movement did not grossly violate local traditions, it was tolerated by the community or even by local officials. Usually, only when it committed politically dangerous acts or when it had grown to sizeable proportions would local authorities set the anti-heretic law into motion. By that time it often happened that the movement had become entrenched and widespread and proved difficult to uproot even by bloody persecution. Evidence of this is found in the imperial decrees of the nineteenth century, with their repeated reprimands of local officials for negligence in nipping sectarian organizations in the bud and permitting a movement to affect extensive areas, often several provinces, before the sword of persecution fell. Thus heterodox organizations and movements continued to rise and develop despite the dominance of national political power and rigid legal restrictions.

The resulting picture of traditional China was one throbbing with religious life everywhere, even though many of the heterodox activities were on a furtive or at times secret basis. Despite official efforts to limit the number of temples and partial success in reducing the number of large ones containing colonies of priests, the density of temples remained high throughout the country, and a large proportion of their gods were heterodox in nature. As mentioned previously, some 84 per cent of the temples in China in the seventeenth century were built without official permission, and this figure obviously did not include the numerous small shrines privately built.

Political domination by Confucian orthodoxy did not result in a one-religion empire. Instead, China was known as the land of three religions, which is a misnomer as it ignores the numerous syncretic sects which from time to time won many adherents. New gods and new doctrines continued to emerge, giving birth to new religious groups and movements. As one organization was suppressed by persecution, it either re-emerged under another name or made room for another movement.

Many of the sects remained unmolested for a long time, mainly because of ineffectiveness in the enforcement of the anti-heretic law. The Huang-t'ien Tao (Yellow Heaven doctrine) in Wanchuan county in Chahar province, for example, originated as a movement in the middle sixteenth century and was revitalized in the 1870's with the construction of an impressive temple consisting of six main halls and many smaller temples in the area. These temples stood intact and the sect continued to exist down to the 1940's.[55] Even under successive persecutions, many of the heterodox movements showed astonishing vitality over a long period of time. The White Lotus sect had a fully organized existence for over 600 years, and the Buddha Maitreya religion, for 1,200 years, surviving persecution after persecution under different dynastic governments, changing only their names and altering their tactics from time to time.[56] The military and political organization of the Taiping rebels was crushed a century ago, yet its associated Triads and the Hung society continue to this day.

It appears that governmental emphasis on orthodoxy neither prevented the rise of a large variety of heterodox movements nor reduced the life span of the major heterodox systems. The relative ineffectiveness of the anti-heretic laws was only one of the causal factors. Beyond this, there was the polytheistic and syncretic tradition that tended to tolerate religious differences and accept the coexistence of varying faiths. Consequently, no one religion dominated. As pointed out, the government's antagonism to heterodoxy was based largely on practical political grounds, not on theological reasons. In addition, the Confucian orthodoxy was not a religion in the theistic sense, and the classical religion which was sponsored by the orthodoxy had developed into a broad polytheistic river receiving influence from many religious tributaries. Furthermore, the classical religion in its actual operation was largely diffused into the social institutions, and thus it was not an independent institutional religion competing against other religions. Historically, when an institutional religion gained court favor and acquired political influence, other institutional religions suffered. Thus, when Buddhism was in favor during the Yuan dynasty, Taoism came upon difficult days, and vice versa in other periods. The fact that no single institutional religion gained protracted hold on the imperial government and thereby dictated its dogma gave other religions a chance to develop. In spite of the dominance of and restrictions by the Confucian orthodoxy, traditional China was far from being a religiously sterile land.

Despite political antagonism the reason for the singular success of Buddhism among the many foreign faiths in China has been a problem often posed by students of Chinese religion. Many familiar explanations have been given: the spiritual void of the earthly Confucianism which needed to be filled to meet the needs of the population; the Buddhist concept of the soul being fitted into the Confucian cult of ancestor worship; Buddhism's hope of universal salvation; and the syncretic nature of Mahayanism, which helped its acculturation in the native polytheistic setting. We have mentioned in the foregoing chapters the function of the karma in remedying the fallibility of the moral rules and in thus upholding the moral tradition of Chinese society. But, politically, Buddhism had a flexible creed of renunciation of worldly ties, which aimed at advancing to engulf the world and finally to transform it by expanding the monastic order to envelop the entire population when the time was favorable; the case of the Buddhist theocracy of Tibet is an example. But, in times of political hostility, the creed enabled the religion to withdraw from the world and to use this withdrawal to argue for its own preservation, since it was no longer a part of secular political life, and thus should be left alone to pursue its own form of life. This was essentially the argument advanced by the Buddhists during the crisis of persecution in the T'o-pa Wei period.[57] In subsequent periods down to modern times, the partial acceptance of this argument by the government was one of the reasons for the continued existence and development of Buddhism. The creed gave Buddhism a tool by which to adapt itself to both favorable and hostile political climates.

IX

RELIGION AND
POLITICAL REBELLION

In the present science-oriented age, religion is often regarded as a conservative or even reactionary agency bent upon protecting the social and political status quo. In China, facts show that religion was indeed a strong undergirding force for the established institution of government. But, on the other hand, the rejection and persecution of heresy indicated a clear threat to the ruling political power by religion in its heterodox forms. Max Weber has already pointed out the revolutionary role of religion, and other scholars in the sociology of religion have also noticed that religion could uphold as well as tear down a political structure.[1] The purpose of the present chapter is to consider the role of religion in political revolts and some of the ways by which religion contributed to the development of rebellious political movements in modern China.

Religious Societies in Political Rebellion

History shows ample evidence of the persistent role of religion in political struggles against ruling dynasties. The Taoist Yellow Turban rebellion in the Han period; the scattered uprisings of Buddhist groups in the period of disunion; the sporadic nationalistic resistance led by the Taoist sect Ch'üan-chen Chiao (Complete Truth religion) against the Chin and Yüan rulers; the White Lotus rebellion that helped topple the Mongol rule and gave the succeeding dynasty its name, Ming, through its messianic figures of Big and Little Ming Wang (Brilliant Kings), who were thought to have been sent by Buddha Maitreya to the world to restore peace and order; these are only prominent instances in an endless chain of religious rebellions that spread across the pages of Chinese history for two thousand years.[2]

In the Ch'ing period, religious rebellions crowded the records of every decade after the middle of the eighteenth century. Military operations of that dynasty were marked by two major types of campaigns, one the expeditions to the borderlands against non-Chinese peoples in the earlier part of the dynasty, and the other the suppression of religious revolts during the latter half of the dynasty. Except for several uprisings such as that of the twice-renegade, Wu San-kuei, when the dynasty was still struggling to establish itself, very few political rebellions of any appreciable proportion were totally unconnected with some religious element or organization. This broad historical outline is significant, for it indicates the intimate relation between religious forces and political movements, arising from the domestic population, which seriously weakened the dynastic rule and finally helped to bring about its collapse.

The vast complexity of the religious rebellions in the Ch'ing period defies summary here, and it must suffice to consider a few prominent examples. The reign of Emperor Ch'ien Lung, the climax of the dynasty's power and glory, was marred by repeated religious rebellions, such as the uprisings of the White Lotus (also known as the Incense Smelling and the White Yang) sect in 1774, the Eight Diagrams and the Nine Mansions sects in 1786-1788, the Heaven and Earth society in 1786-1789, and the re-emergence of the White Lotus forces in 1794, which spread over nine provinces and took eight years to suppress, seriously sapping the government's strength and marking the beginning of the dynasty's decline.[3]

The nineteenth century was marked by three major domestic events, all dealing heavy blows at the dynastic power. The century started with the great rebellion of the Eight Diagrams or T'ien Li (Celestial Principle) sect in 1813, which followed closely upon the heels of the temporary pacification of the White Lotus revolt. The middle of the century saw the dynasty shaken to its foundations by the great explosion of the Taiping rebellion, the first major religious uprising to derive its inspiration from a European religion. The century ended with the development of the Boxers' association, which began as a domestic opposition movement but was diverted by the Dowager Empress against foreign powers in the Boxer Rebellion of 1900. In between these three leading events were a continuous series of local revolts by religious societies in every part of the empire.

The political nature of these religious revolts, large or small, can hardly be denied. An imperial decree gave what seemed to be an accurate analysis of the Eight Diagrams rebellion of 1813: "In normal times, the [Eight Diagrams or Celestial Principle] Society was engaged in daily worship of the sun and reciting scripture, claiming thereby to make its members invulnerable to weapons, fire, or drowning; and, in times of famine and disorder, they might plot for the 'great enterprise.' " [4] This appears to characterize the course of development of many religious societies in China. In times of peace and order, the organizations would gather a following through their salvational activities, and in times of widespread suffering and disorder, they would emerge to try their hand at the "great enterprise." The "great enterprise" (*ta shih*) referred to the founding of a new dynasty. The Eight Diagrams insurrectionists broke into the Forbidden City in Peking, aiming at nothing less than capturing the throne. Further back, in the early seventeenth century, the White Lotus sect leader, Hsü Hung-ju, assumed for himself the title of Chung-hsing Fu-lieh Ti, or the Renaissance Great-Blessedness Emperor, at the height of his bid for power, which ended in his execution.

Other religious rebellions were more modest in their attempts, but were nonetheless involved in unmistakable political action. In 1834, the persecution of the T'ien-chu Chiao (Celestial Bamboo) religion in Honan province was based mainly on the discovery of weapons, gunpowder, and some rebellious-sounding documents in the house of the leader of the sect. In 1835, the persecution against the Hsien T'ien (Prebirth) sect was prompted by the discovery of an alleged plot of rebellion, and one branch of the sect in Shansi province did briefly occupy the county city of Chao-ch'eng, burn the government office buildings, liberate all the prisoners from the county jail, attack a post station near the city, and take the postal horses. In 1837, in the eastern part of Shantung province, a re-

ligious leader, Ma Kang, and a large number of his fellow sectarians met death at the hands of the law partly because they had
attacked the county city of Wei Hsien, killed the magistrate, and
liberated prisoners from the county jail.

From here, as the tide of rebellion rolled on toward the great
Taiping explosion, local religious uprisings became more numerous.
These local revolts repeated a classic pattern: killing the local
magistrate, burning government buildings, and freeing prisoners
from the county jail as a symbol of rectifying the injustices of
misgovernment. At times even some Chinese local police and
Manchu soldiers would cast their lot with the rebels. Religious
sects were rife in the 1840's in the mountainous territory bordering
upon the southern provinces of Hunan, Kweichow, Kwangsi and
Kwangtung, a territory long troubled by armed local bands that
defied the authorities, and an area destined to become the home
base of the powerful Taiping rebels. By 1850, leaders of religious
sects counted among them such colorful titles as the "Great King
of Red Heaven" in Honan, the "Great King of Red Earth" in
Szechwan, and the "Great King of Red Mankind" in Kwangtung.[5]
The Taiping revolt, therefore, was but the climax of a half-century
of widespread political action by religious societies that blanketed
every part of the Ch'ing empire at a time when dynastic strength
was on the decline.

After the Taiping revolt there was a respite of two or three decades when religious uprisings tapered off in frequency. But toward the end of the nineteenth century, politically rebellious religious sects were again on the march. The Boxer movement raged
in the north, while in the south, smoldering elements of the Triad
society and the Heaven and Earth society, once among the basic
forces of the Taipings, were rekindling political resistance and contributing their underground systems to the revolutionary movement that brought the end of the Ch'ing dynasty.

Under the Republic, the chaotic 1920's saw the rise of the Red
Spear and the Big Sword societies in north China, offering their
members magical invulnerability to firearms and resisting the provincial authorities. In Shantung province, Ma Shih-wei led the
I-hsin T'ien-tao Lung-hua Sheng-chiao Hui (the Single-Hearted

Celestial Principle Dragon-Flower Sacred Religion society), and set himself up as emperor until the local warlord Han Fu-ch'ü finally crushed his organization in 1930 and drove him off to the then Japanese-occupied city of Dairen in Liaoning province.[6] In the long Japanese occupation of China during World War II, one of the many White Lotus ramifications, the I-kuan Tao (Unity sect), re-emerged, becoming a nationwide movement that has had varied political implications. The Communist regime started its rule with a series of persecutions against religious societies, the I-kuan Tao being one of the main objects for elimination. As late as 1956, the Communist government was still pursuing an active campaign against a host of religious sects operating around the central theme of *pien t'ien* or "changing Heaven," that is, changing the ruling power.[7]

The persistent association of religious movements with political rebellions in the Ch'ing period resulted in a popular attitude which regarded all heterodox religious organizations as politically dangerous. This traditional attitude partly accounts for the Communist government's crusade against all sectarian societies. As pointed out, many sectarian groups were nonpolitical in nature, and the government's persecution of them was based not on finding rebellious intention or action but on the age-old fear that, given a politically ambitious leadership in troubled times, such groups could easily become instrumental in rebellion. Whatever the motivation, constant government suppression reinforced the popular attitude concerning the political nature of sectarian organizations.

The opposition between institutional religion and the government grew out of an inherent conflict between the two parties in an authoritarian political tradition. As indicated in the last chapter, the government considered that the established social and political order was threatened by heterodox movements with dissenting social and political orientations. The Buddhist organization before the tenth century clearly presented such a threat, though it never resorted to large-scale armed resistance. Through the expansion of its monastic orders and its creed of universal salvation, it hoped eventually to replace the existing world order. Buddhist undermining of the Confucian social and economic order reached appreciable proportions during its periods of successful organized development, such as between the third and the tenth centuries and during the Liao rule in north China. Confucian statesmen, for whom the study of historical lessons always constituted an important part of their intellectual orientation, were wary of a repetition of the same situation if they countenanced a similar organized growth of other heterodox movements.

Under the traditional authoritarian control and repeated persecutions, heterodox religious movements which did not win a legally recognized position like that of Buddhism and Taoism were forced to seek cover, and frequently were ready to offer armed resistance to the ever-present threat of suppression in order to develop their own forms of religious life. Secrecy and readiness to resist suppression were particularly necessary for religious sects that aimed at universal salvation, as their doctrine usually claimed superior power for their deities over the world order—a dogma that was obviously offensive to the authoritarian temporal power, which would tolerate no superior doctrine other than the accepted orthodoxy.

The assumption of spiritual superiority over the temporal power is clearly illustrated in the reason given by the modern I-kuan Tao (Unity sect) in its refusal to register with the government as required by Republican law in the 1930's and 1940's. An instruction to its membership stated:

. . . we all are [Unbegotten] Mother's children, and the officials in the government are also her children. How can there be any reason for the Mother to register with her children? Ch'u Min-i [an important Nationalist figure] is already converted, and all the other prominent officials are also fated to be converted sooner or later. . . .[8]

Under the Ch'ing dynasty, such a document would undoubtedly have been regarded as an expression of rebellious intentions, thus bringing persecution and possible armed resistance. The claim of the superior power of certain deities to control the world order was made by most of the leading sects in the Ch'ing period, as will be considered in the following discussion on salvation and prophecy.

But not all religious rebellions were the result of political oppression and the necessity to defend a chosen way of religious life.

Political cause or ambition was clearly an integral part of many sectarian movements, as is shown by the repeated efforts of the White Lotus sect to overthrow the Ch'ing dynasty and to restore the Ming house. Other sects began as purely religious movements but turned into open rebellion when troubled times presented favorable opportunities for political struggle. The Taiping rebellion seems to fall into this category. Still other sects exhibited a dominant political character at the very beginning, as shown by the many sects in which the leaders assumed the titles of emperors and kings, distributed official ranks among their followers, used official government seals, and included military tactical books in their religious literature.

Whatever the basic cause of rebellion, the important fact remains that at least during the Ch'ing period most of the leading political opposition movements were linked with religious societies.

SOCIAL SETTING OF RELIGIOUS REBELLION

In what social settings were religious rebellions most likely to rise? One obvious setting was persecution by the authoritarian government. Persecution could provoke many a purely religious organization into armed resistance. And, under an authoritarian government, many otherwise purely political movements were forced to operate in disguise as religious enterprises, ending in the form of religious rebellion. The Eight Diagrams rebellion at the beginning of the nineteenth century represented the former, and rebellions led by the Great Kings of Red Heaven, Red Earth, and Red Mankind in the 1840's were illustrations of the latter. During the Republican period, heterodox religious movements thrived in many parts of the country, but the removal of the anti-heretic law and the relaxation of government control of religion resulted in a far smaller number of religious rebellions than during a similar length of time in the latter part of the Ch'ing rule.

In addition to the authoritarian setting, there was the important factor of social crisis arising from the inadequacy of the existing institutions to meet the needs of the people. A religious rebellion was basically a collective effort by a group to introduce or to force a change in the existing social or political order. In this respect, religious rebellions might resemble other movements of social reform or revolution; when the established social and political order failed to provide a solution for a critical situation, and when the people were at a loss as to what to do, religious movements rose to improvise an answer which would cause a situation of conflict with the government.

In other cases, a public crisis which the government had failed to cope with would provide a politically dormant religious organization with the opportune moment to develop its political ambitions through open rebellion. The official Ch'ing comment on the Eight Diagrams rebellion (cited previously) made an accurate observation when it remarked that the sect was engaged in religious activities in normal times, but plotted for great political enterprise in times of famine and disorder.

Economic hardship and disaster constituted a frequent type of crisis that bred religious movements and rebellions. Famine due to crop failure was a recurrent crisis typical of an agricultural society, leading to many forms of mass action. We may say that no major politicoreligious upheaval in Chinese history was without some form of extensive agricultural crisis as a backdrop.[9]

Instances of this kind were too frequent to enumerate, but we may name a few examples. The area adjoining the three northern provinces of Honan, Shantung, and Hopei was traditionally a hotbed of sectarian movements in modern times, and it was also an area of recurrent famines because of its geographical location, which subjected it to frequent rain failure and flood damage. Famine was never out of sight in the areas affected by the series of rebellions of the White Lotus and the T'ien Li sects in the closing years of the eighteenth and the early years of the nineteenth century. The rebellion of the Hsien T'ien (Prebirth) sect in the northern part of Hopei came in 1835, a year described in an official document as one when "not a drop of rain had fallen there, and all the people were in a state of agitation, anguish, and dismay, thus prepared at any moment to be stirred up by evil-brewers."[10] The Taiping uprising arose in a mountainous southern region where tillable land was limited and the struggle for a livelihood always hard, and came at a time when famines due to drought had struck frequently.[11]

In the hilly districts of Hunan province, where a host of rebellious groups arose in 1851 to join the sweeping Taiping uprising, the sectarian organizations bore such descriptive names as the Straw Plaiters' sect, the Grass Cutters' sect, and the Firewood Gatherers' sect. These were among the poorest occupations, and the rise of religious sects among them indicated critical economic difficulty for the lowest stratum of the population in that troubled province. Similar situations occurred even in recent decades. In the 1920's, for instance, the Red Spear society in Honan and Shantung provinces emerged from the background of a series of famines.

In addition to economic crises, there were political crises of disorder, excessive oppression, and extortion by corrupt officials, making a normal life extremely difficult. In the face of destruction by war and banditry at times when the weakened and corrupt government could no longer maintain peace and order, religious societies often turned into armed groups to help make a semblance of normal life possible. Such political crises were frequently the derivative effect of serious economic difficulties, which then led to the rise of banditry and religious sects, and these in turn offered an opportunity for the corrupt government to extort money and labor from the people, thus deepening the crisis.

This was the background of the White Lotus rebellion in the early years of the nineteenth century, as was pointed out in the well-known Memorial on the Suppression of Heretic Sects (Cheng Hsieh-chiao Su) by Hung Liang-chi. "After the bandits left, the officials came. After the burning and pillaging by the bandits, there was oppression from the officials." [12] Even a decree from Emperor Tao Kuang admitted "it was extortion by local officials that goaded the people into rebellion." Using the arrest of sectarian members as a threat, local officials and police extorted money from the people. "Whether or not an arrest was to be made depended only on the willingness or refusal to pay, and not on actual participation in sectarian worship." In different localities of Hupeh and Szechwan provinces, where the White Lotus rebellion originated, "thousands of innocent people were implicated." [13]

A similar picture lay behind the Taiping rebellion half a century later.

. . . The government grew increasingly degenerate, and corrupt officials infested the land . . . The provinces of Kwangtung, Kwangsi, Yünnan and Kweichow [home territory of the rebellion] were struck frequently by famine due to drought, and the people lacked food and clothing. Yet the officials kept oppressing and extorting them. Adventurous elements were thus forced to turn to banditry. Innocent people suffered from corrupt officials above them and from the bandits around them; they could not maintain their livelihood and became homeless drifting migrants . . . Thus rose the Pao-liang Kung-fei Hui [Society for Protecting the Innocent and Attacking the Bandits, the forerunner of the Taiping movement] to answer the need of the time.[14]

ORTHODOXY, "DEVIATING ORIENTATION," AND THE SALVATION MOVEMENTS

From widespread suffering in overwhelming crises arose the eagerness for salvation in this and in the next life. Two courses appeared to be open: following the beaten path of the orthodox sociopolitical order, or contriving a divergent plan. In which direction lay salvation for the tortured populace? The government, fearing the rise of heterodox movements as a result of the crises, firmly admonished the people that their salvation lay not in incredible magic and visionary talk but in observing the established law and order and continuing their faith in orthodoxy.

The imperial decree of 1724 (pp. 194–196) set the tone for many edicts during the Ch'ing period. In suppressing the Eight Diagrams rebellion in 1813, Emperor Chia-ch'ing pontificated: beyond the Confucian social and moral principles, "no so-called religion exists, and outside the principles of nature and the laws of the ruler, happiness may not be sought after; happiness proceeds from complying with orthodoxy, and misfortune from following heresy." Again in 1835, an imperial edict forbidding the forming of pilgrim organiza-

tions ordered the officials to explain to the people that it was ignorance to assume that the worshiping of [heretic] gods would bring
blessing and protection but that, through contentment with one's
own occupation, blessing would be obtained.[15]

Amid economic and political crises that condemned millions of
people to starvation and misery, such admonitions were hollow,
impractical, unrealistic. What people in a crisis were facing was the
exact opposite of the enjoyment of "trouble-free days of universal
peace." The practice of filial piety to parents and fidelity to the ruler,
and the exertion of the utmost effort—all these, which brought
blessing in normal times, were of no avail to a people gripped by
an overpowering crisis. And even as the people knew well that
blessing might be obtained by following one's own occupation with
diligence and contentment, the chaos and destruction in a crisis
made it impossible for a large number of people to pursue this
course.

The sociopolitical order based on the Confucian orthodoxy had
proven its efficacy in periods of established peace and tranquillity,
but during an economic and political crisis the call of heresy gained
an immediate audience. When the orthodox path led nowhere, it
was logical and natural that the people would look in a different
direction for deliverance. Herein lay the magical appeal of heresy.
In Chinese, heresy or heterodoxy was expressed by two characters,
i-tuan, meaning *deviating orientation.* Hence, "deviating orientation" as a salvational path may be regarded as a normal product of
an extensive social crisis. With the traditional antagonism to heterodoxy, this deviating path led to collision with the authorities and
often to armed rebellion.

The rise of heterodox religious movements was often attributed
to the "earthly character" of the Confucian orthodoxy, which left
a spiritual void. While there is truth in this interpretation, there
are also decided limitations in its application to the rise of religious
movements, particularly of the politically rebellious type. It is important to note that times of extensive crises saw the greatest development of religion in Chinese history. Aside from the modern
period mentioned above, there was the classic example of the four
centuries of continuous economic and political chaos from the third

to the sixth centuries, which saw the greatest organized development of new religions in China. In both modern and ancient periods of great crisis, the Confucian orthodoxy failed to meet not
only the spiritual need but also the basic material need of security
and sustenance.

RELIGIOUS SALVATION, UNIVERSAL AND PERSONAL

It is interesting to ponder why it was religion, instead of the
"earthly" Confucianism, that often contributed toward a new salvation for an "earthly" crisis. Perhaps the answer lies largely in the
familiar fact of the extreme conservatism of the Confucian orthodoxy. Constantly oriented toward past precedents, it always discouraged the blazing of a drastically new path despite the pressing
needs of a crisis. Being predominantly this-worldly, Confucian
thoughts were restricted in imagination because of the confinement
to realism. The highest native form of religious imagination was
immortality, which was merely an extension of the concrete existence.

On the other hand, from earliest times, religion has universally
performed the unique function of producing a picture of life different from that in concrete existence, and hence the morally uplifting effect of religion in changing the world to conform to the
imaginary or ideal pattern as conceived by the founders. Religion
thus has always sought to differ from and not to conform to reality,
in contrast to the tradition-confined and reality-bound Confucian
orthodoxy. Either as the discovery or as the product of man's power
of imagination, religion contains a seed of revolution except when
it is thoroughly diffused or merged into the established moral and
political institutions, as the Chinese classical religion was. This
partly explains why it was religion more often than the Confucian
orthodoxy which advanced a new path of salvation for a crisis.

Some of the salvational propositions were comprehensive and
sophisticated, and others simple and naïve. Buddhism as an example
of the former developed a complete system of life. The voluminous
Buddhist Tripitaka contained such varied concepts as a cosmological
explanation of the universe, an ethical interpretation of the world,

a total solution for all human frailties and social illnesses, and re-fined rules and regulations for every practical detail in monastic life, designed to transform tortured humanity into an angelic race and bring the "Western Paradise" to earth. An ideological system of such comprehensiveness could take over the operation of a state, as did many Buddhist theocracies. Buddhist monastic orders were organized as miniature model worlds, and their message of universal salvation contained such broad appeals to all humanity, from kings to beggars, that its ambition to transform the world was much more than a visionary dream. In a great human crisis it was natural that a system like Buddhism would put forth a salvational call which, once gaining momentum, would alarm the temporal rulers. Taoism belonged to the same category, but its crude imitation of Buddhism and incomplete content was well recognized by students of Chinese religion.

Salvational propositions by sectarian societies were far simpler and less consistent than either Buddhism or Taoism. Sectarian reli-gions in China were typically syncretic faiths largely drawing their theology from Buddhism, their magical rituals from Taoism and the classical religion, and their ethical systems from Confucianism. Most of the leading religious societies, from the old Maitreya and White Lotus sects (which were known under a variety of names in different periods to escape persecution) to recent organizations such as Huang-t'ien (Yellow Heaven) and I-kuan (Unity) sects, wor-shiped Buddhistic gods such as Buddha Maitreya and the Unbe-gotten Mother, and had universal messianic prophecies of an un-mistakable Buddhist tone. Their membership was not always open to all, as in Buddhism, but the Buddhistic goal of universal de-liverance was consistently present. From Taoism and the classical religion they drew many of their secondary gods, as well as their magical rituals, such as the use of spiritual media and the planchette, the drawing of magical signs, and the reciting of incantations over water to be drunk by the sick and by those who wanted to be saved. Their ethical systems consisted mainly of Confucian values already familiar to the people. Popular acquaintance with the ethical aspect of the sectarian societies was a factor in their ability to gain ready acceptance by the people. A lone and important exception to this syncretic pattern was the Taiping movement, which took Christianity instead of Buddhism as its main source of theological inspiration, but many of its magical practices, such as the use of charms, were of Taoist or classical origin, and its ethical system—while drastically untraditional in many respects—still failed to break away completely from the Confucian framework.

Whatever its content, the salvational proposition was the core of popular religious movements that rose in answer to a crisis and developed into a political opposition under certain circumstances. The basic claim of the sects was their ability to bring universal deliverance to tortured humanity. But how did they make people believe in their salvational message, how did they gain the faith and confidence of the masses, and how did they attract a following, particularly in view of the risk involved in joining a heterodox movement?

Many factors entered into the picture. One of them was the immediate social and economic benefits offered by the religious organizations, which had the nature of a mutual-aid brotherhood, an important asset in times of crisis, when large numbers of people were dislocated. Another factor, as has already been suggested, was the psychological effect of presenting a "deviating orientation" to stimulate hope at a time when the old ways no longer worked. Still another factor was that, at the heart of the heresy, was the extraordinary claim of the emerging deities' supernatural powers, which could sweep aside all difficulties when the utmost of man's effort had ended in failure and despair. Strange stories of unfamiliar happenings would circulate. Important in this connection were the sectarian leaders, who claimed the role of intermediary between humanity and the new gods (just as the emperor monopolized the role of intermediary between man and Heaven). Many of the leaders appeared to work miracles and perform effective divination to prove their ability to contact the supernatural.

Thus, curing sickness by charms and incantations was a universal claim of the founders of religions and sects, and one made by leaders of most of the sectarian movements persecuted by the Ch'ing dynasty. It was so typical of religious movements, in fact, that the Ch'ing law stipulated against such acts (see p. 186). Yang

Hsiu-ch'ing, a great leader of the Taiping rebellion, was known to the people as a man who could cure sickness with magic, work miracles, and predict the future with uncanny accuracy. Fortune-telling and divination were likewise a familiar occupation for the founders of religious sects. Wang Chüeh-i, the founder of the modern I-kuan (Unity) sect, collected his early following with his art of divination and fortunetelling.[16] Magical curative water from a mysterious well was instrumental in the development of the Yellow Heaven sect as a mass movement.[17] The visionary, as William James said, has a unique political role to play in times of crisis.

Miracle workers had a dual significance. One was their ability to win the public's faith and confidence. The other was their appeal to the individual need for personal salvation. Those who were cured were grateful and became converted, but those who were distant from the scene of the miracles also hoped for personal salvation by joining the organization founded by the miracle workers. Thus, the magic of an independent miracle worker was confined only to the few, but magic worked by sectarian leaders integrated many individuals into a religious movement. Personal salvation thus became a medium for universal salvation from suffering and sin. Performing the same dual functions in the building up of a religious movement was the practice of religious redemption. Many writers, overimpressed with the magical aspect of Chinese religious life, drew the misleading conclusion that there had been no development of the idea of redemption, particularly total redemption, in China. Actually, not only Buddhism and Taoism, but also all the major modern sects, have developed the idea of personal redemption through conversion and total redemption through universal salvation.

THE FUNCTIONAL ROLE OF PROPHECY

While salvational propositions contributed the fundamental motivating force to religious movements, it was through prophecy that a mass call for salvation became the focus of public attention and thereby collected a following. If the salvational proposition was the core of a religious movement, prophecy was an important part of the salvational proposition. By attaching the salvational cause to momentous events of the world in the past, present, and future, prophecy added realism and vividness to the whole movement. Prophecy thrived during crises, and, according to available records, no major critical period in Chinese history was not attended by the rise of some form of prophecy. Typical of a crisis were the mass psychological setting of intense feelings of insecurity, the expectancy of impending disaster, and the uncertainty of what was ahead. As masses of troubled men scanned the horizon for an explanation of their plight and for deliverance from their suffering, prophecy answered them with momentous words of wisdom uttered not by men but by gods. When a traditional Chinese individual was in distress, he would go to the soothsayer, a diviner, or a fortuneteller to obtain an interpretation of his seemingly insoluble problem and to receive some prediction of the outcome to guide his outlook and actions. When society was in distress, prophecy performed a similar function on a collective basis.

The very emergence of Confucius himself was connected with the messianic prophecy of a downtrodden ancient people.[18] The ancient tradition of the Yin-yang school in interpreting extraordinary phenomena of nature as portents of political developments carried the characteristics of prophecy, and many people were executed in every age because they advanced such prophetic interpretations.[19] Records of recent history furnish more detailed accounts of the development of prophecies in critical situations. Thus the rise of the Ming dynasty was heralded by the prophecy that the "Ming Wang" (Brilliant King) was about to be born into the world. In the early part of the fourteenth century, when the Ming dynasty was still struggling to stabilize its newly founded power, the White Lotus sect prophesied that the empire was about to be plunged into chaos and that the Buddha Maitreya was about to descend to the world to save mankind, thus attracting a huge following among the "ignorant people." [20] And the decline of that same dynasty, which was founded by a man who was once a sectarian, was attended by the rise of a prophecy which emerged again and again down to the present time in a variety of revisions but always with the same basic theme. Most modern religious societies took prophesy as part of their salvational theology, as we will see in the following paragraphs.

In the White Lotus uprising during the early years of the nineteenth century, the authorities discovered in the home of a sectarian leader a scripture called *San-chiao Ying-chieh Tsung-kuan T'ung-shu* (Comprehensive Almanac for Facing Calamities by the Three Religions). This mystic book stated that there were three *kalpas*, each marked by the sway of a Buddha over the universe, and great calamities accompanied the transition from one *kalpa* to the next. The first to hold sway over the universe was the Lamplighting Buddha (Jan Teng Fo), who first brought light to the universe; the second was Sakya Buddha, who was holding sway at the present; and the third was the Future Buddha, who would rule the world to come. The Future Buddha was to be born in the village of Shih-fo (Stone Buddha), which was the home community of many White Lotus leaders. Religious tracts distributed by the sectarians at that time called upon the people to send money on every New Year's Day to the house of the sectarian leader so they would receive their blessing and reward when the Future Buddha arrived.[21] On this basis, the sect declared that the Ch'ing dynasty had come to the end of its preordained existence, and that the Ming dynasty was about to be restored. The Christian-inspired Taiping rebellion also made use of the general tone of the prophecy, for its *Kao T'ien-hsia I* (Proclamation to the Empire) declared the end of a cycle of spiritual forces and the arrival of the divine savior.[22]

The same theme of prophecy was handed down to modern sectarian societies that used Buddhistic theology as the core of their doctrines. The I-kuan Tao (Unity sect), which was one of the ramifications of the White Lotus system, for example, disseminated a familiar prophecy. It preached that the Limitless Ultimate (Wu Chih) created Heaven and Earth and all things in the universe and made them operate on *kalpas* or cosmic aeons of 129,600 years each. In each *kalpa* there would be several calamities caused by changes in the heavenly forces. Now, the next to the last *kalpa* had ended and the last *kalpa* was about to begin. Since the creation of Heaven, there had been three *kalpas*. The first was known as the Blue Yang (Blue Sun) *kalpa*, and it began at the time of Fu Hsi (creator of the universe in Chinese classical mythology). The second was the Red Yang *kalpa,* and it began at the time of Emperor Ch'ao in the Chou dynasty (the eleventh century B.C.). The third was the White Yang *kalpa,* and it would begin at the hour between noon and early afternoon. In the period of the Blue Yang, the Lamplighting Buddha controlled the universe. In the period of the Red Yang, the Sakya Buddha controlled the universe. In the period of the White Yang, the Maitreya Buddha would be in control. In each *kalpa,* both the Tao (Way) and calamity were sent down to the world. The Tao was for saving the good and the believers; calamity was for exterminating the evil. When the Tao predominated, calamity would disappear. Calamity came by men's evil conduct, and the Tao was sent down because of it.[23]

This belief represented what was known as the "three changes of the Heavenly *kalpas*" commonly found in recent sectarian theology. Thus, in the founding of the modern Huang-t'ien (Yellow Heaven) sect in the latter part of the nineteenth century, when there was a severe drought in Wanchuan county, the Buddhist monk Chih Ming created public excitement by declaring that the third and final heavenly *kalpa* was about to arrive, a great calamity was about to descend, a wind of destruction was about to sweep down to the world from the sky, and the Unbegotten Mother, foreseeing this, had sent down the Maitreya Buddha to establish the Yellow Heaven sect some three centuries earlier in order to spare mankind from total extinction.[24] From this prophetic pronouncement, and from the alleged miraculous discovery of the stone epitaph from the grave of the incarnated Buddha Maitreya, who had departed from the world after founding the sect, the monk Chih Ming succeeded in arousing widespread public interest and collected enough money to build a gigantic temple. In the 1940's, members of the sect still regarded the prophecy as an important part of their sectarian doctrine.

In addition to the theory of the three heavenly *kalpas* and the pronouncement of the impending arrival of the third *kalpa,* to be accompanied by a great calamity, there were two well-known clairvoyant prophecies current in the modern period. One was the *T'ui Pei T'u* (the Back-pushing Illustration), alleged to have originated in the T'ang dynasty, and the *Shao Ping Ke* (the Baked Cake Ballad), reputedly coming down from the beginning of the Ming dynasty. Each of these prophecies rendered an account of peace and war, and the rise and fall of dynastic powers in the past, present, and future, all veiled in extremely vague language. So far as available records show, the creators of the prophecies were not connected with any religious sects that survived to modern times, and contemporary religious societies expropriated them freely to augment their own prophecies. Thus, the I-kuan (Unity) sect often displayed written versions of both these prophecies in their headquarters.

While the limitation of space precludes examination of the interesting details of these and other prophecies, we may summarize the characteristics commonly found among most of them. First, they presented a basic theory explaining the dynamic changes in the world, such as the three fateful heavenly *kalpas* of the White Lotus system. Such a theory was made to appear as an absolutely immutable law laid down by the highest supernatural power (such as the Limitless Ultimate), thus dismissing any dispute or doubt from the audience. In times of crisis, man was demoralized by events totally beyond his rational control or prediction, and he felt like a being enclosed in an abyss of chaos. To such a state of mind, the offering of an immutable law of events would bring enlightenment and hope, for the world would once more appear as an orderly reality where events had their prearranged sequence; formerly incomprehensible tragedies now became explainable, and, under certain moral conditions, could even be circumvented. Thus, it was partly through their "cosmic laws" that prophecies had strong appeal to the popular mind in troubled times.

Second, they gave an account of mythological and historical events to prove the accuracy of their assertion. Should there still be some doubt regarding the course of events as prearranged by the divine powers, the recounting of great occurrences in the past would reaffirm the people's faith in the prophetic words.

Third, the prophecies explained that the transition from one phase of the world to another, such as from one heavenly cycle to the next, was inevitably accompanied by calamities. Before the arrival of another period of blessing and peace, there would be greater, much greater, calamities than those which had already befallen. If a social crisis had already created widespread suffering and fear, the prediction of even greater calamities, such as a blanketing, destructive wind, would add further anxiety. This was characterized by one of the Ch'ing imperial edicts as "frightening the people and alarming mankind with unfounded heretic talk."

Fourth, there was the inevitable promise of deliverance for the believers and extermination of the wicked who refuse to embrace the truth. By this the sectarian movements attracted a following from those who came under the influence of the prophetic message and wished to be saved. This characteristic was less obvious in the *T'ui Pei T'u* and the *Shao Ping Ke,* which were not firmly associated with any single sectarian organization.

Fifth, the language employed in the prophecies was characteristically obscure and general, thus allowing varied interpretations of a wide range of human events, particularly events involving the immediate interest of the sectarian movement. The *T'ui Pei T'u,* for example, contained a line "when the rooster crows, the sun will set." In 1945, when the Japanese surrendered, there was nationwide talk that the surrender had been predicted by this line, for the year was the Year of the Chicken in the traditional Chinese calendric cycle, and the setting of the sun alluded to the Japanese flag bearing the rising sun. But the same interpretation could fit other events. In the prophecy of the I-kuan Tao, the third heavenly *kalpa* was to arrive between noon and early afternoon, but the year, month, and day were not specified. The classical reason given for the vagueness of the language in the prophecies was to avoid persecution by veiling the identity of the real events. While this is plausible, it can only be one of the reasons for couching prophecies in such obscure style.

Lastly, many of the prophecies laid down periods of change in terms of immense stretches of time, across which only supernatural titans could move. Such vastness of setting suggests an origin in the famed Buddhist scripture *Fa Hua Ching.* By staggering the imagination with time and events of immense proportions, the prophecies impressed upon man the immeasurable superiority of the mighty deities over ephemeral worldly events and the frail human mortals who called themselves rulers. A dynasty of three hundred years and its score of rulers dwindled into insignificance when placed beside a heavenly *kalpa* of 129,600 years and its single titanic ruler, who governed not only the world but also the limitless universe. By thus dwarfing the human historical drama and its human actors, together with man's traditional submission to the supernatural, prophecies gained acceptance among the emotionally overawed audience and helped to create a faith that could not be easily shaken by secular, rational arguments.

This technique of obtaining conversion was especially effective in times of extensive crises when men were throughly confused by controversies, when proffered rational solutions were discredited and weakened by conflicting opinions, when the intellect of great men and the worldly efforts of humble creatures all seemed futile in the face of a worsening situation. But, in the face of the immensity of the prophecy, current disputes and controversies appeared insignificant and would be settled not by methodical weighing of utilitarian advantages against disadvantages, but by being swept aside in the current of the immeasurably greater events transpiring among the gods. The mind of the believer was conquered by the sheer size of the suggested forces.

Because of these characteristics, prophecy was vital to a sectarian organization in seizing command of the popular mind at the psychological moment, in preparing the people for the tragedy of a great struggle, in giving guidance and direction to a confused public, in creating strength among the distressed masses by focusing their attention upon the expected arrival of a savior, a new ruler with the "true commission from Heaven." At the proper time, lines in a prophecy could be used as a signal to set off mass political action. There is little wonder that the traditional Confucian rulers dreaded the "heretic talk that could excite and mislead the people" and periodically persecuted the unorthodox sects. In a political struggle against the rulers, prophecy was indeed a powerful weapon in the hands of the religious societies in crisis-ridden times.

Under the Republic, with the relaxation of government control over organized religious activities, political struggle led by religious

societies was at a minimum as compared with the previous two centuries. Yet, during the ceaseless raging of the civil wars, the age-old
religious prophecies returned to answer the psychological needs of
the time. The southern city of Canton in the 1920's, for instance,
saw the revival of the prophecy, *Shao Ping Ke*. A number of small
sectarian groups warned the people of an impending great calamity
that was to follow the petty civil wars, and promised salvation for
believers who would show faith and contribute money. The sectarians pointed to the line in the prophecy which declared that
there was a cave under the Nine-Oxen Mountain which would
furnish a safe haven for refugees when the calamity struck, that
those who arrived at the cave first would be saved and those arriving late would perish. To this day, pious believers maintain that the
prophecy was fulfilled; they argue that the great calamity of the
eight years of Japanese invasion followed the civil wars, and that
many were saved who took refuge in the mountains. Talk of this
nature was current in many southern localities during the years
following World War II. In the hands of a politically ambitious
religious organization, this would be an excellent instrument for
creating a collective movement in a struggle for power. It is contrary to facts to assert, as Max Weber did, that Chinese religious
life was characterized by the absence of prophecy.[25] Such assertion
is true only if it is applied to Confucianism when it is mistaken
for a full-fledged theistic religion.

POLITICAL STRUGGLE IN THE NAME OF THE GODS

There was another way in which religion contributed strength to
popular movements engaged in political struggle against the ruling
power. This was by generating faith, confidence, and cohesion for
the movement.

To launch a struggle against an established authoritarian government was a risky as well as an extremely difficult undertaking.
The traditional monarchical government not only possessed absolute power that tolerated no opposition but was a deeply entrenched
institution sanctified by the pervasive system of the classical gods.
Thus a ruler governed not merely by the absolute power to condemn

and to kill but also by the people's traditional submission to authority as internalized by their Confucian upbringing, and by their awe for the supernatural power of the classical gods. Under the threat of torture or death, conditioned by traditional values, and awed by supernatural forces, the common people would not lightly take the road of rebellion to redress injustice and to seek relief from suffering. While the disorganizing effect of an economic and political crisis helped to loosen the traditional hold of the government on the people, the inhibitive effect of institutionalized attitudes against rebellions was still a strong discouraging factor in the popular mind.

It was here that religion performed a critical function, for it gave the cause of political opposition the sanction and encouragement of the gods. It was in the name of an extraordinary god that a struggle was launched against a ruling power, which by abusing its office had forfeited its divine commission. Men needed assurance from a supernatural power, as proclaimed by the sectarian leaders, to overcome the awe they had for the established government. For an extraordinary action, men must have extraordinary justification beyond the finite world of secular and utilitarian reasoning. Religion, with all its extraordinary supernatural claims, as illustrated in the contents of prophecy, helped to provide the necessary emotional support. With the gods' sanction, men not only felt justified in their unusual action but also felt sure they would win.

Hence, all religious movements that were engaged in political opposition to the government, such as the series of White Lotus uprisings, closely identified their political cause with the divine mission of universal salvation. The Taiping rebels, in addition to identifying their entire movement with the will of God, called the Ch'ing rulers the incarnation of evil spirits that had to be exterminated in order to clear the path for bringing the kingdom of Heaven to earth.[26] Religion thus added moral and emotional strength to the grievances against the non-Chinese Manchu rulers. The modern I-kuan Tao, which had all the potentialities of a resistance movement, refused to submit to government control, not on social and political but on religious grounds, as pointed out above.

For a dangerous enterprise such as political rebellion, fanaticism was needed to drive men to defy torture and death. While there are many psychological sources of fanaticism, religious conviction is a familiar one in all cultures. The evidence of fanaticism among Chinese sectarians was shown in the records of almost all major rebellions: the large number of White Lotus members who fought to the last ditch in the whole series of uprisings in the nineteenth century,[27] and the Taiping leaders who burned themselves to death en masse rather than surrender to the government when their last stronghold of Nanking fell to the imperial troops.

Available records do not yield much information on the religious techniques used in generating fanaticism among the followers. Extreme emotional devotion and dedication will often drive oppressed sectarian leaders to martyrdom, something that purely rational and utilitarian motives seldom achieve. Stories of religious defiance of persecution by fire and sword were numerous throughout the Ch'ing period. The very failure of bloody persecutions to stop the recurrence of sectarian opposition was an indication of the high degree of devotion inspired by religion. In addition to the inspiration of devotion, there were many minor techniques used by sectarian movements to induce courage among the members. The Boxers and many other ramifications of the White Lotus system taught magical formulas for making the human body supposedly invulnerable to weapons, fire, and drowning. Even in the 1920's the Red Spears made such a claim of magical power. When a member was killed in combat, the myth was protected by the explanation that the victim had committed sin which rendered the magic impotent. The Taipings taught that death was desirable, as it enabled the martyr's soul to ascend to Heaven; Ch'ing official documents repeatedly pointed to this as one of the reasons why the rebels fought fanatically in battle.

In addition to fanatical courage, men engaged in a dangerous struggle needed fortitude and resignation, which only religious dedication could offer. An example was the worship of Kuan-yin, the goddess of mercy, one of the leading patron deities of many religious sects because she "has proved herself a faithful deliverer of all victims of misfortune and oppression who invoke her," as De Groot pointed out.

We possess a number of stories . . . describing apparitions of this goddess especially to persons languishing in prison, with death before their eyes, and to others in imminent danger or distress; such apparitions are always the forerunners of deliverance. No wonder that the sectaries, over whose heads the sword of persecution ever pends, and whom the prospect of martyrdom always harasses, confidently entrust themselves to her. The [Sutra of the High King Kuan-shih-yin] is boldly asserted to bring deliverance to victims of persecution if only it be read often enough; and to this day it is unquestionably recited ardently by sectaries in prison, while their brethren outside do the same on their behalf, thus enabling them to bear their hardship with fortitude and resignation.[28]

It is useful to reiterate an important point here, namely the function of religion in integrating large numbers of individuals into an organized group capable of collective action. Religion performs this function partly by supplying one of the strongest bonds that man has ever forged to cement human relations. The belief in a supernatural power can often furnish the basis of a sacred social relationship that men dare not defy or break lightly. The use of an oath and the burning of a written pledge with the names of members on it were common parts of the initiation rituals of many Chinese secret religious sects in order to impress the members with the fact that their membership was not only a contract between men but also a sacred tie confirmed by the gods and spirits. The Eight Diagrams sect set up eight branches of their organization, each named after one of the eight mystic diagrams. The Nine Mansions sect had nine branches in its organization system, each representing one mansion. The Taiping local political organization was based on the parish system, and the inculcation of the religious doctrine was among the most important means of assimilating new members.[29]

One of the reasons why religion could serve so well as a group integrating factor was its ability to furnish a spiritual orientation as the symbol of a social or political cause, thereby lifting the attention of the group above the conflict of varying utilitarian interests and focusing their views on a higher plane. This was particularly important for a religiopolitical movement of broad dimension, drawing members from many social and economic groups, among whom differences in utilitarian interests were liable to be sharp and difficult to compromise by rational means, thus endangering the cohesion of the movement.

The use of a spiritual or supernatural orientation also has the advantage of imparting lasting vitality to an organization. Independent of ever-changing utilitarian interests, religion focuses the members' attention on a lasting spiritual symbol, the truth of which does not hinge on an individual circumstance. The sect of Buddha Maitreya lasted for 1,200 years, and the White Lotus sect for 600 years. And there was steady re-emergence of many sects under a variety of names over two centuries in the modern period in spite of bloody persecutions. The T'ien Li Hui (Celestial Principle society), a ramification of the White Lotus system, for example, was known under the names of San-yang Chiao (Three Light sect), Lung Hua Hui (Dragon Flower society), and the Pa-kua Chiao (Eight Diagrams sect), attesting to its surprising vitality of survival. Over the range of time, utilitarian interests and realistic causes had shifted ground but the gods and the theology that symbolized broad human interests remained unchanged.

X

RELIGIOUS ASPECTS
OF CONFUCIANISM IN ITS
DOCTRINE AND PRACTICE

CONFUCIANISM HAS BEEN a determining factor in Chinese culture. It laid down the structural principles and supplied the key operational values for the basic Chinese institutions from the family to the state. The Confucianists—the scholars trained in the Confucian doctrine—staffed the officialdom of the government, were the members of the gentry in the local communities, and constituted the elite of traditional society in general. The influence of Confucianism permeated every fiber of Chinese society through some two thousand years of steady development, with only partial interruption for brief periods. Traditional society cannot be properly understood without giving due consideration to the Confucian doctrine and the institutionalized attitudes of the Confucianists.

The religious nature of Confucianism, or whether it is a religion, was an outstanding issue in the Chinese Renaissance which came at the close of World War I. One point seems apparent from the mountains of polemic material on the question. Confucianism may be regarded as a faith in the sense that, through centuries of enforcement and practice as a social doctrine, it won uncritical acceptance by the people and became an emotional attitude as well as a body of rational teaching. But it is not a full-fledged theistic religion, since it poses no god or supernatural dogma as the symbol of its teachings (see chap. i). This, however, does not mean the absence of theistic influence in Confucianism either as a theoretical system or an institutionalized functioning framework. Born of a superstition-ridden period and institutionalized in a society where religion was a pervasive influence, Confucianism adopted many religious elements that helped it to function effectively in the traditional social milieu.

In his work *The Origin and Development of the State Cult of Confucianism,* John Shryock presented the cultic aspect of the doctrine as a practiced institution. Scholars like De Groot pointed to the supernatural elements in the Confucian literary tradition. Of foreign religious influence, none left a more indelible mark on Confucianism than Buddhism. As is well known, neo-Confucianism since the Sung times had broadened its theoretical scope by entertaining the Buddhist problem of mind and matter.[1] As a system of values, Confucianism had incorporated much of the Buddhist world salvational spirit, which urged people to undergo ordeals for the deliverance of mankind.[2] But such Buddhist influence was of a metaphysical and philosophical nature. In this chapter we shall attempt to analyze the supernatural and cultic aspects of Confucianism as a part of its theoretical system and as a practiced tradition.

THEISTIC ASPECTS OF THE TRADITIONAL CONFUCIAN DOCTRINE

The Nature of Confucius' Agnosticism

Much has been said about the rationalistic and agnostic quality of Confucianism. It was assumed that many Confucian scholars of the Ming and Ch'ing periods held the view that the belief in spirits and miracles was incompatible with the teachings of Confucius. In the twentieth century, when the dominance of Western influence brought contempt for superstition and magic as the very sign of national backwardness, a new generation of Chinese scholars, such as Chang T'ai-yen, Liang Ch'i-ch'ao, Ch'en Tu-hsiu, and Hu Shih, came forth to defend the dignity of the Chinese civilization not only by stressing the rationalistic view of the Confucian doctrine but also by claiming that the dominance of the Confucian orthodoxy had helped develop China into a "rationalistic society" where there was neither a powerful priesthood nor protracted struggle between religion and the state.[3]

There is no dispute over the predominance of the this-worldly and even rationalistic quality of the Confucian doctrine. But Confucianism was not so thoroughly rationalistic as to be a body of empirical knowledge with complete "disenchantment of the world," transforming it into a predictable causal mechanism. Instead, in a number of significant respects, Confucianism still regarded the world as a Heaven-ordained entity and a "meaningful and ethically oriented cosmos." [4]

Many statements in Confucius' Analects have been quoted to prove the agnostic nature of Confucianism and to divest it of kinship with the supernatural. Among the most familiar of such statements are: "The Master did not talk about extraordinary forces and disturbing spirits." [5] "While you are not able to serve men, how can you serve their spirits?" [6] "To give one's self earnestly to the duties to men, and, while respecting spiritual beings, to keep aloof [at a distance] from them, may be called wisdom." [7]

Herlee Creel reveals that not one of the pre-Sung Chinese commentaries on these and other similar passages of the *Lun yü* considered Confucius agnostic, and that among the Sung and later commentaries only four passages indicated skepticism. [8] The agnostic impression of Confucius, according to Creel, was mainly the result of a trend toward rationalism within the Confucian school after the Sung times. This "rationalization" of Confucius is particularly apparent in many modern Chinese scholars who have worked under the influence of Western rationalism and of a general secularizing trend in a period of revolution.

Whatever interpretation the commentaries made, it should be noted that these and similar statements by Confucius only advised people to give priority to "knowing life" and "serving men," but they did not attempt to disprove the existence of supernatural forces. Instead, Confucius seemed carefully to have kept the supernatural elements alive in the background in his admonition to "respect the spiritual beings," in his emphasis on sacrifice, and in his attitude toward Heaven and fate. Supernatural conceptions loomed large in people's minds in Confucius' time, [9] and the occasional thoughts of rationalism among leading intellects of that age were far from being a prevailing attitude. Confucius himself could hardly have escaped entirely from such supernatural influence, especially when he encountered problems for which even his genius failed to produce a rational explanation. Nor could he have ignored the supernatural concepts so important to the human affairs of his time. By keeping the supernatural factor alive in the background, the this-worldly orientation of Confucian thought left ample room for the development of theistic religious ideas.

In the centuries after Confucius and Mencius, leading thinkers occasionally rose with a thoroughly agnostic view. Hu Shih, an outstanding proponent of the rationalistic view of Confucianism, quotes from two such thinkers, Fan Chen of the fifth century and Ssuma Kuang of the eleventh century, to prove the point of agnosticism.[10] Thus, said Fan Chen, "The body is the material basis of the spirit, and the spirit is only the functioning of the body. The spirit is to the body what sharpness is to a sharp knife. We have never known the existence of sharpness after the destruction of the knife. How can we admit the survival of the spirit when the body is gone?" And Ssuma Kuang stated in attacking the belief in Heaven and Hell, "When the body has decayed, the spirit fades away. Even if there be such cruel tortures in Hell as chiseling, burning, pounding, and grinding, whereon are these to be inflicted?" Similar agnostic views were often attributed to others like Chu Hsi, the great Confucian scholar of the twelfth century. While such occasional agnostic views exerted a certain amount of influence on the attitude of the Confucians, they were not able to dislodge the influence of religion from the system of Confucian thought and from the traditional social institutions.

The Belief in Heaven and Fate

A close examination of the Confucian doctrine as conceived by Confucius and Mencius and developed by most of the leading Confucians through the succeeding centuries will disclose that it contained a subsystem of religious ideas based on belief in Heaven, predeterminism, divination, and the theory of Yin-yang and the Five Elements. The subsystem began with the belief in Heaven as the anthropomorphic governing force of the universe, including the human world. Hence the belief in fate or predeterminism as a course of events preordained by Heaven as the supreme ruling power. Divination and the theory of Yin-yang and the Five Elements were both devices for knowing Heaven's wish and for peering into the secrets of this preordained course so as to help men attain well-being and avoid calamity. Associated with the attempt to glean information about Heaven and fate were the theory of interaction between Heaven and man, the concepts of *feng shui* (wind and water), and other forms of magic and animism.

There has been controversy over Confucius' conception of the nature of Heaven. In the welter of polemics on this point during the 1920's and 1930's, there seemed to be one common agreement: in the pre-Confucian period, Heaven was considered a supreme personalized force, dictating the events of nature and men, wielding the power of reward and punishment.[11] This is in agreement with the conclusion of the great Ch'ing Confucian scholar, Ch'ien Ta-hsin, who said, "When ancient men spoke of the Way of Heaven, they all meant good luck and misfortune."[12] Did Confucius come under the full influence of this ancient anthropomorphic notion of Heaven? The word *t'ien* or Heaven appears eighteen times in the Analects, and unanimously it is used as the subject of volition, action, or emotion. Even when the Master said, "Heaven does not speak," it is probable that he meant Heaven could speak but need not speak, for Heaven's intentions are demonstrated by the rotation of the seasons and the growth of living things.

Lao Tzu, Confucius' contemporary, did conceive of Heaven as an unfathomable mechanism devoid of any personality or moral meaning. And some two centuries after Confucius' time, Confucianists such as Hsün Tzu even proposed to strip Heaven of its mysticism so as to facilitate understanding it and controlling it for the benefit of man. But such rationalistic views of the universe were rudimentary and far from constituting a system of thought thoroughly worked through to transform the world into a causal mechanism. By the Han period, Wang Ch'ung's *Lun Heng,* a rational exposé of current superstitions, was a lone voice in an atmosphere filled with magic and mysticism, much of which was promoted by the Confucians. What rationalistic trend there was in the Late Chou period scarcely affected the anthropomorphic notion of Heaven in the cosmic view of the Confucian doctrine.

A concomitant to the supernatural concept of Heaven was the belief in predetermination or fate (*ming*), which occupied a prominent place in the Confucian interpretation of life and life crises. The concept of fate was a part of early Chinese culture, and by Confucius' time a variety of theories of fate had emerged.[13] Confucian acceptance of this cultural legacy was reflected in the many statements about fate made by Confucius, Mencius, and subsequent Confucians. One of the popular contemporary adages, "Death and life have their determined appointment; riches and honor depend upon Heaven," originated in the text of Confucian Analects.[14] Confucius spoke of fate thirteen times, and this saying is representative: "If my principles are to advance, it is so ordered. If they are to fall to the ground, it is so ordered."[15] The terms "determined appointment" and "so ordered" are Legge's translations of the same Chinese character *ming* in the original text of both statements.

Mencius was even more explicit in regarding Heaven as a personified predeterminer. For example, ". . . to advance a man or to stop his advance is really beyond the power of other men. My not finding in the prince of Lu a ruler who would confide in me, and put my counsels into practice, is from Heaven."[16] Again from Mencius, "But Heaven does not yet wish that the empire should enjoy tranquillity and good order. If it wished this, who is there besides me to bring it about? How should I be otherwise than dissatisfied?"[17]

These and kindred statements by Confucius and Mencius shared a common ground which indicated that in spite of their this-worldly and rationalistic orientation to many human problems, they never fully abandoned the supernatural, anthropomorphic notion of Heaven as the governor of man's fate. Both men had started with tremendous confidence in the superiority of their own abilities and with a burning ambition to rescue the world from chaos and suffering, but both ended their days without success in putting their doctrines into practice. Why, then, should they still fail, when they as the best of men had done their utmost? The rational and this-worldly part of their doctrine could produce no answer. It must be that beyond man, there is a supreme determinant: fate as ordained by Heaven. As a Chinese proverb goes, *jen ch'iung tse hu t'ien,* "When man is at the end of his means, he cries to Heaven [for help]." Even the two Masters were no exception to this adage, as the end of their life approached with no promise of success in sight. It was perhaps no accident that Confucius, after a long and disappointing career, turned to the mystic book, *I Ching,* in the twilight of his life.

A major premise of the Confucian doctrine was that to achieve harmony and happiness man must adjust the social order to the cosmic order of which he was a part. In early times, when the cosmic order was so imperfectly understood, it seemed inevitable that the ancient mystic interpretation of it, such as the supernatural notion of Heaven, would remain to some degree in people's minds as an explanation for events to which rational thoughts had failed to offer an answer. Even the two Masters attributed their disappointment to Heaven's preordained course.

"Knowing Fate," the *I Ching,* and Yin-yang and the Five Elements

With belief in the supernatural Heaven and fate came the logical attempt to decipher the secrets of the predetermined course of events in order to help man attain well-being and avoid calamity. This attempt to "know fate" was apparently in the thoughts of Confucius, as evidenced by many of his statements. Thus he said, "Without recognizing the ordinances of Heaven [fate], it is impossible to be a superior man." Again he stated, "The mean man does not know the ordinances of Heaven, and consequently does not stand in awe of them." [18] And Confucius claimed he knew the decrees of Heaven by the time he had attained the age of fifty. [19] That the predetermined course of events was knowable was clearly stated in the Doctrine of the Mean:

It is characteristic of the most entire sincerity to be able to foreknow. When a nation or family is about to flourish, there are sure to be happy omens; and when it is about to perish, there are sure to be unlucky omens. Such events are seen in the milfoil and tortoise . . . When calamity or happiness is about to come, the good shall certainly be foreknown by him, and the evil also. Therefore the individual possessed of the most complete sincerity is like a spirit.[20]

While the authorship of this statement is in dispute, there is no question that the Doctrine of the Mean has been a firm part of the Confucian doctrine since Sung times.

But how can fate be known? If they possessed secrets, neither Confucius nor Mencius divulged them. But there is the tradition that Confucius thumbed the *I Ching* so persistently that the binding broke three times. If we trust this traditional account, the question is what Confucius was trying so hard to learn from this mystical volume. The answer depends on the interpretation of the nature of the book. There is the naturalistic interpretation of it as a primitive book of protoscience, attempting to reveal the metaphysical principles that govern the dynamics of the universe, including the human world, and hence the interpretation of the name of the book, *I Ching,* as the Book of Change. From Han times down to the modern period, a whole line of Confucian scholars wrote studies and commentaries on the *I Ching* from this point of view, and it is possible that Confucius shared the same view.

But there is also the supernatural interpretation of the *I Ching* as a book of divination. Yü Yung-liang, for example, offered the very interesting interpretation that deciphering the meaning of the heat cracks on the oracle bones as an early means of divination was too difficult because of the irregularity of the cracks and the lack of standardized interpretation of the various forms of cracks. Consequently, the *I Ching* was written to offer a simplified and standardized method of interpreting the cracks, and hence the version of the name *I Ching* as the "easy book" (of divination).[21] When milfoil stalks came in the Chou period to replace oracle bones as the basic equipment of divination, the standardized method in the *I Ching* proved to be most applicable. There is little doubt that the *I Ching* was the major source of the principles and techniques of Chinese divination that developed in the centuries subsequent to Confucius' time.[22] The *I Ching* exerted a more far-reaching influence in the Confucian as well as the popular mind as a book of divination than as a work of protoscience or metaphysics. Since the Han period the *I Ching* has been classified as one of the six classics of the Confucian doctrine, and has supplied Confucian cosmology with a foundation of magic and mysticism. Aside from the *I Ching,* the other classics frequently discussed divination, attesting to the adoption of this ancient Chinese magical technique into the theoretical system of the Confucian doctrine.

But as a means of "knowing fate" divination was not always dependable. The *I Ching* was obscure; even Confucius wished to have more years to his life in order to study it,[23] and some two thousand years of critical analysis of this work by Chinese scholars have failed to produce a common agreement on a system of meaning of its contents. As a consequence, by the third and second centuries B.C., the theory of Yin-yang (negative and positive) and the Five Elements (metal, wood, water, fire, and earth) rose rapidly to prominence as a means of deciphering the intentions of Heaven and Heaven's predetermined course. Like the *I Ching,* there was a protoscientific aspect to this theory, but the influence of this aspect on Confucian thought was negligible. What was most influential from this theory was its corollary of the interaction between Heaven and man which, as has already been indicated, standardized the interpretation of omens as concrete expressions of Heaven's pleasure or displeasure with man's moral conduct. Equally influential was the designation of human significance to each of the factors of Yin-yang and the Five Elements, thereby formulating a frame of reference for interpreting the operation of the supernatural forces in the sky, the rise and fall of a dynasty, life and death, health and sickness, poverty and prosperity, divination, palmistry and physiognomy, astrology, chronomancy, and geomancy. By omens and by this frame of reference, it was possible to give supernatural explanations for natural phenomena in the universe as well as intimate events in an individual's life. With the development of the Yin-yang and the Five Elements theory, Heaven and fate became concrete expressions that could be grasped by men.

Did the Confucians believe in this theory? It is a fact that the theory was considered a separate school, developed outside the main context of the Confucian doctrine. But, even before the appearance of the theory, Confucius had spoken of omens as he lamented the failure of the phoenix to arrive and of the rivers to yield the mystic charts, as metaphors denoting the hopelessness of realizing his ambitions. That this statement, attributed to Confucius, was an actual part of early Confucian literature is seen in the attack against its superstitious nature by Wang Ch'ung, who lived five centuries after Confucius. Regardless of modern polemics on the point, Mencius was mentioned by men like Hsün Tzu, almost his own contemporary, as one of the originators of the theory of Yin-yang. By the Han period, the wholehearted embracing of this theory by Confucianists was an apparent fact. Books wholly or partly devoted to the discussion of Yin-yang and the Five Elements accounted for one-fourth to one-third of all books in the bibliography section (*I-wen chih*) of the *Ch'ien-han Shu* (History of the Former Han Dynasty).[24] Above all, Tung Chung-shu, the arch-Confucianist who succeeded in enshrining Confucianism as the state orthodoxy, had the distinction of authoring the theory of interaction between Heaven and man, and his celebrated volume, *Ch'un Ch'iu Fan Lu* (Heavy Dews of Spring and Autumn), contained 23 essays on the supernatural nature of Heaven, Yin-yang, and the Five Elements, accounting for one-half the total number of essays in the work.

After the Han period there was widespread application of the theory of Yin-yang and the Five Elements to the interpretation of the Confucian classics by Confucianists, whose thoughts seldom escaped being colored by this theory.[25] This is seen in the historiographical tradition of the Five Emperors,[26] and in the numerous Confucian terms of social relations and social values, such as the Five Cardinal Relations, Five Rituals, Five Virtues, Five Punishments, all bearing the semisacred number extracted from the term Five Elements.[27]

Sacrifice and Ancestor Worship

Sacrifice and ancestor worship were elements of early Chinese culture that had been firmly integrated into Confucianism by Confucius, Mencius, and subsequent Confucians. Sacrifice is a form of ritualistic behavior toward spiritual beings for the purpose of inducing supernatural protection and blessing. Such is plainly the meaning of sacrifice as found in pre-Confucian literature such as the *Shu Ching* and the *Shih Ching*. By the time of Confucius and for two centuries afterwards, a rationalistic trend of thought resulted in growing emphasis on the moral and social functions of sacrifice as a vital part of the Confucian system of *li* (ritualism) for the regulation of social conduct. Early literature such as the *Li Chi* (Book of Rites) and the *Kuo Yü* referred frequently to the secular function of sacrifice as a means of cultivating moral values such as filial piety, honesty, and loyalty. *Ch'ung-te pao-kung* (exalting the virtuous and repaying the great service [of outstanding men]) became a Confucian justification for practicing sacrifice as a basic requirement for the development of civilized life.

Even if we give full recognition to the secular functions of sacrifice, the question arises as to why the religious rites of sacrifice rather than secular means were used to cultivate moral values and to regulate social conduct. On this point, even early classics contained fairly explicit explanations. Thus, the *Li Chi* said, "When the scholars show respect, the people will believe." What was the object of this respect and belief? Plainly, the spirits and gods were the objects of sacrifice. It was essentially the same notion that underlay the commentary to the *I Ching,* attributed to Confucius, "The sage devised guidance by the way of the gods, and [the people of] the land became obedient." It was Hsün Tzu (chap. ii) who put it most clearly:

The Sage plainly understands it [sacrifice]; the scholar and Superior Man accordingly perform it; the official observes it; and among the people it becomes an established custom. Among Superior Men it is considered to be a human practice; among the common people it is considered to be a serving of the spirits. . . .[28]

For two thousand years after Hsün Tzu offered his explanation, sacrifice remained for the common people an affair of serving the spirits, while a few rationalistically inclined Confucians might have regarded it as an affair of men. This dualistic character of sacrifice—skepticism on the part of certain intellectuals, and belief in spirits on the part of the common people—was obviously a device by which the Confucian doctrine used supernatural conceptions as an instrument to enforce social values and to control the masses.

The subject of ancestor worship has been dealt with earlier (chap. ii), and its social significance is clear. There were important secular functions in ancestor worship aimed at encouraging kinship values such as filial piety, family loyalty, and the continuity of the family lineage, and a few rationalistically inclined Confucians might be satisfied with that. But for many of the Confucians and most of the common people, the matter of the soul of the departed loomed large enough to compel them to undertake sacrifice even when they could ill afford the expense. In a world of harshness and uncertainty, the hope of supernatural assistance and the fear of supernatural punishment were powerful influences in stabilizing the kinship system, which occupied a central position in the Confucian scheme of social organization.

The Function of Religious Elements in the Confucian Doctrine

The belief in Heaven and fate, the condoning of divination, the close alliance with the theory of Yin-yang and the Five Elements, the emphasis on sacrifice and ancestor worship as a basic means of social control, and the lack of a thoroughly agnostic and rationalistic attitude toward spiritual matters—all these represented major aspects of the Confucian doctrine. These religious factors were important for the functioning of Confucianism as the guiding doctrine in a society in which gods and spirits were thought to lurk in every corner. In a prescientific age no institutionalized doctrine could stand on secular grounds alone. We have seen that many of the Confucian values became traditions not only on the ground of rationalistic appeal but also on the strength of supernatural sanction.

Confucian belief in a supernatural Heaven and in fate had special significance for the Confucian doctrine as a moral cause. It uplifted the staunch believer to a level on which utilitarian considerations were left behind and on which the believer identified his moral ambitions with Heaven and fate.[29] From this high moral plane he could struggle for doctrinal vindication regardless of earthly adversities. And, in the event of failure, he retained his faith in the doctrine in the name of Heaven and fate, as had Confucius and Mencius, for the doctrine was considered in harmony with the world's preordained course, which, as the eternal truth, would eventually triumph in spite of temporary setbacks, if only man continued the struggle. Thus, on the positive side, the belief in Heaven and fate inspired moral strength, and, on the negative side, it upheld people's faith in the soundness of the doctrine for all generations to come regardless of the temporary dimming of its light or isolated failures of individual believers. It lent a sacred and fateful character to the whole doctrine, which over the centuries struggled to hold its position as the nation's orthodoxy and to enforce its social and moral values in the traditional society.

Modern students of China who maintain a purely rationalistic view of Confucianism are not able to explain away the religious aspects of the doctrine without distorting the meaning of the original texts. It would have been unlikely that a thoroughly rationalistic doctrine could have developed out of the social setting in the Late Chou and Han periods, when supernatural concepts loomed large in men's minds and when there was no modern science but only ancient mysticism to offer answers to momentous questions on the cosmic order and the human world, questions that no major social doctrine could ignore. In fact, if we accept Hu Shih's assumptions in his famous article, *Shuo Ju* (The Confucians), Confucius and his disciples as members of the *ju* groups were professional practitioners of rituals and sacrifice. Such an occupation was a development from the ancient priesthood, and it would have been surprising if Confucius and his disciples had been able to shed completely the supernatural ideas that were a part of such ritualistic performance.

But the religious aspects need not negate the assumption of a predominantly rationalistic character for the doctrine. If formal logic could find contradictions between rationalism and supernatural assumptions, such contradictions did not create serious obstacles in the actual functioning of the doctrine as an institutionalized orthodoxy. The religious aspects in the theoretical system of the doctrine enabled it to work with religious influence as a sanctifying agent for its basic premises. Stripped of its religious aspects and relying alone upon its rationalistic features, the doctrine would probably not have had the success that it had in the past two thousand years as an institutionalized orthodoxy for the operation of the traditional Chinese political and social structure.

FATE AND "KNOWING FATE" IN THE MODERN CONFUCIAN MIND

Much of the preceding discussion reflects Confucian dogma as developed from Confucius' time to the Han period. From then on to the contemporary period, in the intervening two millennia, the doctrine underwent further development, especially in the form of *li hsüeh,* the "study of reason" as embodied in neo-Confucianism in the Sung times. The question arises as to whether the religious aspects reflected in the old classical quotations still constituted effective parts of the Confucian doctrine in the modern period, when the rationalistic nature of the doctrine had become a main issue. The question can be studied by examining the leading religious concepts as they functioned in the mind of modern Confucians.

Heaven and Fate

There is little dispute over the fact that modern Confucians retained complete belief in Heaven and fate as the governing forces expounded in the classics in and before the Han times. The naturalistic notion of Heaven and the rationalistic concept of human events were seldom systematically applied to modern Confucian interpretations of major social institutions and of personal events. Final justification for political power and its rise and fall, for example, was still the Mandate of Heaven, an unmistakable anthropomorphic notion of the universe that permeated Confucian literature in modern as in ancient times. A rationalistic mind like that of Wang Ch'ung, who viewed the cosmos and the ordering of human events as thoroughly materialistic mechanisms, had little influence on this point in the modern period. Even among the Confucians who disbelieved in ghosts and spirits, Heaven and fate were still the ultimate explanation for momentous events in history as well as occurrences in the individual's life.

Among the volumes of popular lore reflecting the mind of the

Confucian scholars, the one considered most faithful to realism was Wu Ching-tzu's *Ju-lin wai-shih* (Unofficial History of the Confucian Scholars), written about the eighteenth-century Confucian world. In the first chapter of this celebrated work of fiction appears a certain Wang Mien, who was pictured as an ideal Confucian scholar. He was forced by tyrannical local officials to flee from his southern home, and temporarily took refuge in a northern town near the bank of the Yellow River, where he made a living by divination and painting pictures. One day he saw refugees streaming into town and learned from them that the river had broken its dikes and had flooded the countryside. He uttered a sigh, "When the river flows north, the empire is about to fall into chaos. Why do I continue to stay here?"[30] He then packed up his belongings and went home. Four years later, as the novel had it, the ruling dynasty collapsed, and local warlords rose in arms to fight for supremacy. Wang Mien was an idealized Confucian scholar; the qualities expected of him included the mystical ability of "knowing fate" as preordained by Heaven, and hence his temporary role as diviner and his uncanny intuition in deciphering the portent of the river flood.

In the interpretation of the individual's life, the official local gazetteers, a product of Confucian scholarship, contained numerous records reflecting the notion of fate as the dictating force. In the gazetteer for the town of Lo-tien in Pao-shan county of Kiangsu province, for instance, there was this recorded event:

In front of the main hall in the city god (Ch'eng-huang) temple stood an old storied building which the people mounted to view shows during the celebration of the god's birthday. On the evening of the tenth day of the tenth month in [1815], the eastern half of the building suddenly collapsed, killing over thirty persons. A native of the district, by the surname of Chang, had returned home from Shanghai for the celebration. On that fateful evening, someone unknown to him came and asked that they go together to see the show. In a dreamy state of mind, he followed the man into the ground floor of the building, and was killed under the falling timbers. Could his death be a matter of fate? [31]

In the gazetteer of the southern town of Fo-shan in Kwangtung province, there was a similar story of the death of over 500 people in a fire in a dyestuff guild hall while they were viewing a show during the celebration of the birthday of the guild's patron god. The inscription on the stele, although admitting the accidental nature of fires and death, asked why these particular persons instead of others had perished in the conflagration, and the answer given was, again, fate.[32]

These and many other similar official records were written by Confucian scholars who clearly retained the idea of fate as preordained by the supernatural power of Heaven. These writers, one may argue, were only the common run of Confucians, and outstanding Confucian scholars would perhaps have taken another view of life and death. Nonetheless, these common scholars were the elite of the local community, giving direction and leadership to local social institutions, and their supernatural notions colored the religious views of the people. But even outstanding modern Confucians seldom escaped the supernatural notion of Heaven and fate. It is related that K'ang Yu-wei, the great modern Confucian reformer, was walking under a scaffold when a falling brick missed his head by just a few inches. But he came through the incident with perfect serenity, saying that his safety had been predetermined.

Belief in Divination

Perhaps the clearest expression of belief in the notion of fate among modern Confucians was their widespread practice of divination of all varieties. Especially common was coscinomancy. In this type of divination, a spiritual medium sat in front of a tray of sifted sand, and his fingers guided the movement of a suspended wooden stick, one end of which touched the sand and served as a planchette. As he went into a trance, it was believed that an invited spirit descended into him; his fingers began to push the stick, writing out messages on the sand. Sometimes the invited spirit was that of a poet, and the writings on the sand produced lines of poetry. The collection of poems, *Pei-shan Shih Ts'un* (Collected Poems of the Northern Hills), edited by the Confucian scholar Lin Kuang-yün, contained poems most of which had been written by spiritual mediums at the planchette tray. Sometimes the invited spirit was asked to guess a riddle, to match a literary couplet, to discuss a literary issue. But more often, the spirit was requested to predict success or failure at examinations, in officialdom, and in other career situations. A medium sitting in front of a planchette tray was a familiar scene at gatherings of Confucian scholars during the nineteenth and early twentieth century. This craze affected not only the common Confucians but also outstanding figures such as Tseng Kuo-fan, who helped to suppress the Taiping rebellion in the name of Confucian civilization.[33] The practice continued to be common among traditional scholars in the Republican period.

"Word analysis," interpreting the structure of a Chinese character picked at random to predict future events, was a widely practiced method of divination among Confucians in modern times. Even the standard forms of divination, like shaking three coins in a tortoise shell and reading the combination of heads and tails, were familiar practices with many Confucian scholars who were well versed in the *I Ching*. The writer's own early teacher, who was a successful Confucian scholar in the sense that he had passed the provincial examination and entered officialdom, was an earnest believer in divination by coins. He believed in and talked much of the *I Ching* as a book of divination. Jingling sounds of the divination coins emitted from his studio every morning; after his death his wife said that he accurately predicted his own end, as shown in his memoirs containing records of his daily divinations. Quite often, when a Confucian scholar failed at the examinations and could not find a school to teach, he would become a diviner at the market place.

Astrology, physiognomy, and palmistry influenced a large number of Confucians, including outstanding ones like Chao Chan-ju, a Minister of Justice at the end of the nineteenth century,[34] and Tseng Kuo-fan, the opponent of the Taiping rebels. Both men were known to have frequently employed physiognomy as a means of judging the character and predicting the future behavior of a subordinate.[35] Similiar stories were current about many high dignitaries of the Nationalist government who had a Confucian educational background and made decisions regarding the hiring or dismissal of a subordinate on the basis of physiognomy. When the Communists drove a large number of the Confucian-minded Nationalist officials to Hong Kong, several well-known diviners in physiognomy and palmistry also drifted into that British colony, following the political refugees as their main clientele. In the momentous change of political fortunes, the old officials felt an even greater need for such supernatural guidance and consolation. Thus, contemporary Confucian scholars believe in fate not only as a strengthening agent of the moral cause but also as a supernatural notion of predeterminism in the course of human events.

PSYCHOSOCIAL FUNCTIONS OF DIVINATION Divination, as Hsü Ti-shan characterized it, is a form of sympathetic magic used to induce supernatural forces to yield their secrets concerning the course of events in nature and men. It has long been an important means by which men in a crisis tried to gain confidence, guidance, and consolation when all rational means had failed to provide a solution. At such critical times, the voice uttered in the name of the gods tended to resolve an emotional conflict and produce confidence. At times, the guidance was based on common sense which happened to be ignored in a situation. There is this illustration:

There was a temple of General Liu-meng (god of insects) in Hsin Ching town of Ch'ing-p'u county in Kiangsu province. During the celebration of the god's birthday, thousands of peasants collected on the temple grounds to see the procession. One year, the bridge at the side of the temple was about to collapse, and repair work was not completed by the celebration date. The county magistrate ordered that there be no procession in order to prevent crowds from gathering on the bridge. The peasants angrily refused to obey. The magistrate was about to go out personally to pacify the crowd when he received a report that the whole issue had been settled. One of the community leaders had performed divination with the planchette, and had told the peasants that the god advised stopping the procession for that year on account of the danger of the dilapidated bridge. The peasants accepted the decision without further question.[36] Thus the voice of the gods stopped a threatened riot when the voice of law and authority had failed.

On the personal basis, the function of divination in imparting confidence, offering consolation, and giving guidance during a crisis is quite apparent. When an individual is beset with difficulties and his empirical means of resolving the situation are exhausted, the influence from religious tradition may guide him to consult supernatural forces for an answer to his anxieties. One of the most common means of divination is sortilege. Most temples have among their furnishings bamboo tubes holding a set of lot sticks, varying from 20 to 103 sticks in a set. Each stick is marked with a number, and each number is identified with a slip of printed verse in a file of slips. The person requesting divine guidance kneels in front of the image of the god; he shakes the bamboo tube holding the lot sticks until one stick drops out. He gives the stick to the temple priest, who pulls a slip out of the file according to the number, and reads and explains the verse.

It is important to note that the contents of these verses are largely words of guidance based on the Confucian system of values. One slip in the Kuan-ti (god of war) lot, for example, contains these lines: "Food and clothing are present wherever there is life, and I advise you not to worry excessively; if you will only practice filial piety, brotherliness, loyalty, and fidelity, then, when wealth and happiness come to you, no more evil will harm you." A commentary follows:

If you ask about fame and wealth, that will come at the proper time; in case of litigation, harmonious settlement will bring good luck; . . . your financial luck is just average at the present, and it is better to delay any plan for marriage; conserve what you have, and avoid skepticism and worry; wealth and nobility are all predetermined, and it is not necessary to worry about it; . . . serve your parents and treat other people on reasonable grounds, and Heaven will bless you against all misfortune; follow the natural course, be content with your status, and act according to conscience, and you will gain peace of mind.[37]

For a man caught in a crisis, hard pressed by poverty, and troubled by adverse social relations, such advice, based on common sense and Confucian ethics, would have a consoling effect that would help to dismiss some of his anxieties. Here, Confucian moral principles were spoken through the voice of the gods, giving them a convincing quality that the human voice alone might not be able

to achieve. Through divination, the Confucian doctrine gave thera-
peutic assistance to minds in distress. Even in coscinomancy, this
help can be observed. The medium was generally well versed in
traditional literature and Confucianism, and, as he guided the
planchette stick in a trance, he wrote on the basis of Confucian
teachings. The I-kuan Tao (Unity sect) employed the planchette
as a major means of obtaining divine guidance, and young boys
were generally used as mediums. Many members sincerely believed
in the magic, for the writing thus produced showed a mature quality far beyond the age of the young boy.[38] But the boy mediums
were rigidly tutored in the sacred scripture and in Confucian
classics, which were reproduced on the tray through sympathetic
suggestibility as the boy started into the trance. Thus Confucian
teachings gained the added strength of supernatural approval.

GEOMANCY Out of the theory of Yin-yang and the Five Elements
came a whole system of metaphysical interpretation of nature that
affected the traditional Chinese view of the universe and even
permeated the theory of medicine. Out of it also grew a whole
range of supernatural interpretations of nature and its relation to
human affairs because of the anthropomorphic notions of the Yin
(negative) and Yang (positive) factors and the Five Elements.
Astrology and the theory of interaction between Heaven and man
are examples of this outgrowth. But one of the most widespread results was the popular belief in geomancy (*feng-shui,* or wind and
water).

Geomancy dealt with the supernatural relation of geographical
locations to human events. The merits or demerits of a location
were interpreted in accordance with the Yin and Yang factors and
the Five Elements, which were considered to be invisibly linked
with the fortune and misfortune of men. Confucians would consult the geomancer before deciding the site and fixing the direction
of a building or, more particularly, a grave, whenever they could
afford such service. Some Confucians did not believe in geomancy,
but they appear to have been in the minority.

Under the administration of Confucian officialdom, few major
public buildings were constructed without advice from geomancers

with regard to the location, the direction they should face, and even the architectural design of windows and doors, as these factors were assumed to affect the fortune or misfortune of the entire community. Ch'ing law provided for the services of geomancers in the construction of public buildings. The gazetteer of Lo-ting county in Kwangtung province contained this official record: In the county city, the Wen-ch'ang (god of literature) temple directly faced the official examination hall, but geomancers had long raised objection to the location of this temple, for it "exerted an oppressive influence" on the examination hall and thereby had an adverse effect on those who took examinations in the hall. In the 1830's, Tai Shih-lun came to the county as its magistrate. Tai, who had entered officialdom because of his accomplishments in Confucian studies, was also well versed in geomancy, and he agreed that the temple was unfavorably located, particularly because it faced the west or negative side, with its back toward the east or positive side. Its facing the negative direction would tend to depress the literary quality of the community, since the temple was across the way from the examination hall. Tai consulted the local leaders, and the temple was moved to the nearby town of Nan-p'ing.[39]

The most critical application of geomancy was in the choice of gravesites, for it was maintained that the location of a grave would affect the careers of the descendants of the deceased. The common people, who were convinced of the influence of the ancestors' souls upon the prosperity or misfortune of the descendants, held the theory with deep conviction. But did the Confucian scholars believe in it? Some did not, but there were a very large number who did. Their attitude in this respect is reflected in their writings in the family genealogies. Thus stated one genealogy: "Although we should not completely believe in geomancy, yet if a location is damaged, those involved seldom escape from the harmful effect . . . No holes or ditches are to be dug around the ancestral hall and near the village, in order to avoid damaging the geomantic factors. . . ."[40] Another genealogy stated that the location of a grave might affect the fortunes of the descendants, and it advised the clansmen to look for good gravesites and buy them for later use.[41] Some Confucians raised objections to following the belief, not so much because of the rationalistic refutation of the superstition as because the frequently long delays while searching for a favorable gravesite violated the rules of filial piety, which required the prompt and proper burial of deceased parents.[42]

Geomancy, like other forms of divination, increased man's confidence as he turned to face an uncertain world. By locating a building or a grave on a proper site and facing it in the auspicious direction in accordance with the rules of geomancy, he minimized his doubts and fears and assumed the future to be predictable and good for himself and for his descendants, as the invisible factors of chance were thought to be under control.

SUPERNATURAL FACTORS IN THE EXAMINATION SYSTEM AND THE LITERARY TRADITION

One of the most important contributions of the Confucian doctrine to the Chinese sociopolitical structure was the development of the examination system through which learned men were raised to political power and social prestige. Based on the principle of government by men of merit, the examination system helped to guide ancient Chinese society away from domination by hereditary power and prestige based on the nobility of birth. As a social system, it represented one of the most rationalistic aspects of the Confucian doctrine. But in actual operation, it borrowed considerable strength from religion in order to make it workable and respected in a society permeated with religious ideas. A study of the religious elements integrated into the system will further illustrate the supernatural aspects of the Confucian doctrine as an institutionalized orthodoxy.

The Notion of Fate in the Examinations

Success or failure in the government examinations was theoretically a rationalistic means of measuring a person's qualifications for the status conferred by the system. But supernatural notions crept into the system at this very point. If belief in fate was the most basic religious idea among the Chinese people, including the Confucians, it gained clear expression in the supernatural lore regarding an individual's fortune in the examination system. Although the examinations were intended to measure an individual's intelligence and knowledge, it was widely believed among Confucian scholars that success or failure in the examinations was preordained.

Volumes of popular lore describe the operation of this idea of fate in the minds of Confucian scholars, but let us quote from Wu Ching-tzu's celebrated *Ju-lin wai-shih* again. In the second chapter, a scholar named Wang was asked about his essay, which brought him success in the provincial examination and earned him the degree of *chu jen*. Wang answered calmly that the last two sections of the essay, the best in the whole piece, were written neither by himself nor by any human being. He related,

It was the first session of the examination. Twilight was approaching, and I had not yet finished the first essay . . . I dozed off at my desk in fatigue. Then I saw five blue-faced men leap into the room. The one in the middle held a large brush in his hand and put a dot on my forehead, and then the five of them leaped out of the room. Then a man wearing a gauze hat, a red coat, and a golden belt lifted the curtain, walked in, patted me, and said, "Lord Wang, please rise." I was frightened; cold sweat was on my back. When I woke up, I picked up the brush and wrote the last two passages without being conscious of doing so.

In the same chapter, Wang told of a dream of passing the national examination together with a little boy who at the time of the dream was only seven years old; and later the dream came true.

This is typical of numerous stories familiar to Confucian scholars showing predetermination of success or failure in examinations. But one's fate might be affected by his moral conduct: men of evil deeds might fail the examinations in spite of intellectual brilliance. It was a popular belief that spirits unjustly treated in their human existence would visit the examination hall as a favorable ground for seeking revenge upon the culprit. On the other hand, men of exemplary moral conduct would eventually be rewarded with success at the examinations. *K'o-ch'ang i-wen lu* (Strange Stories from the Examination Halls), a volume familiar to Confucian scholars in the last part of the Ch'ing period, contained this typical account:

A poor neighbor, Lin Wei-shih . . . was orphaned when very young. He was still single after he had reached marriageable age, but he saved hard for his own marriage. When he had accumulated almost enough for the purpose, his elder brother died, and the money had to be spent for the burial. His marriage was much delayed, but he finally took a wife and had several sons. When his eldest son was grown, he took his savings of fourteen ounces of silver and was on his way to pay it to a family as the ceremonial price for a bride for the son. He passed a pond where a man was attempting suicide by drowning because of poverty. He consoled the man and gave him the fourteen ounces of silver. A woman tried to hang herself in a temple because her son indulged in gambling. He saved the woman and inspired the moral conscience of the son with the result that the latter joined the army and became a morally disciplined man . . . In his late years, a god told him in a dream that he would attain success in the examination, and he did. When his son entered the examination hall, he also had a strange dream; when the results were posted, he ranked sixth among the successful scholars in the whole province.[43]

In these and similar stories is the incorporation of the Buddhist idea of causal retribution.

The supernatural belief in fate and retribution in the examination system had many functions. An ambitious scholar would believe he was destined to succeed, and would confidently spur himself on in his scholastic efforts, and at the same time improve his moral conduct. But for older scholars who had met repeated failure in the examinations, either the belief inspired persistence in them if they had enough ambition to think that fate would eventually bring them success, or it gave them consolation that fate was against their success and that it would be better for them to be contented with life as it was. Thus, the belief gave the ambitious confidence and strength and gave the unsuccessful an attitude of peaceful resignation that helped mitigate the shock of failure. Thus, the talented eighteenth-century Cheng Pan-chiao found satisfaction in the theory of Heaven's predetermined course of one's worldly success as the explanation for the lifetime of poverty and misery he suffered for defying the corrupt influence of the careerist scholars who sought status instead of knowledge (see the letter he wrote his younger brother in 1733 in his *Cheng Pan-ch'iao ch'uan-chih*).

In the traditional society, a scholar had a very narrow range of occupational opportunities that befitted his dignity and ambition. The business class was despised; teaching was a poorly paid occupation with little prospect of social or economic advancement. The scholar was left with the government examinations as the outstanding objective of decades of hard study, in which he was urged on by dreams of the prestige, power, and often wealth that awaited successful candidates. Not only was his whole life dream at stake, but the eyes of his kinsmen and the entire community were trained on him as he entered the examination hall. Under this many-sided pressure an individual's failure in an examination had a powerful impact, but, by putting the final control in the hands of the gods, the subject was thus exonerated from the sole responsibility for failure. Derision from his fellow man was mitigated, a stop might be put to further yearning for an unattainable goal, and the torturing suspension between dream and reality might be eased. With belief in fate, the subject could humbly submit to a power higher than man and thereby accept failure without excessive self-criticism or bitterness.

The belief in fate also performed a protective function for the examination system itself. Unfairness, favoritism, corruption, and mediocrity of the examination officials were familiar charges against the system, particularly during periods when the efficiency of the government was declining. Many scholars of recognized excellence failed to pass, while inferior ones, with money or influence, emerged with resounding titles. Although there might be few cases of intellectually unaccountable success or failure, they tended to endanger the prestige of the system and its ability to command the devotion of the talents of the land to the Confucian orthodoxy and classical studies. But the belief in fate, by assigning the final decision to the gods, helped to dilute public disillusionment at the many human frailties involved in the operation of the examination system.

Sanctioning the Status of the Literati

For the examination system to function as the most important means of upholding the Confucian orthodoxy, there was a need to enhance the literary tradition and the status of those who passed the examination. Honorific titles, social status, and political power awarded to successful candidates were secular means to this end. But, in addition, elements of religious sanction were also a factor.

The supernatural notion that the successful candidates in the examinations were favored by fate bestowed a sacred character on those fortunate individuals and enabled them to serve as community leaders not only with approbation from man but also by sanction of the gods. In the traditional days, the common people also believed that those who passed the higher examinations were incarnations of the star gods. Confucian scholars were perhaps not a party to this superstition, but its currency among the common people had the effect of sanctioning the high social and political status of the literati.

In Chapter 3 of the *Ju-lin wai-shih,* for instance, we read of a certain Fan Chin, who was shocked into a trance by his unexpected success in the provincial examination at the late age of fifty-four. It was suggested that Fan Chin could be brought out of his trance by being slapped on the face by someone whom he usually feared. His father-in-law, a butcher, was selected for the job. But the butcher refused: "Though he is my son-in-law, he is the incarnation of the star god, as shown by his passing the provincial examination, and you cannot slap the star god. The Buddhists say that slapping the star god would condemn a person to one hundred strokes by an iron rod in Hades and banishment to the eighteenth layer of hell, never to be let out again. I don't dare do such a thing." Finally persuaded, he slapped Fan Chin once on the face, but did not dare to slap him a second time. The slap, however, brought the scholar out of the trance. Standing in the midst of an excited crowd, the butcher felt a pain in his hand, which soon became temporarily paralyzed. He thought to himself: "You really cannot slap a literary star from the sky. Now the spirits are taking their revenge." [44]

This popular superstition of the incarnation of the gods in the person of scholars who passed the higher examinations was based on the notion that an influential man or an extraordinary person possessed mana or charisma—a notion widely present in many cultures. It was related to the idea that the Chinese emperor was the incarnation of the dragon. The supernatural quality of the person sometimes was thought to remain with major objects associated with him, long after his death. For example, in every town there were memorial arches set up over the streets to commemorate illustrious sons of the community who had achieved high status in the examinations. In the southern city of Canton, one such stone arch was dismantled in order to modernize the street. Local belief that the structure had magical power led people to refuse to have it set up elsewhere. Because of its artistic value, it was finally removed to Lingnan University on the outskirts of the city. There the arch was set up again on a hill, but campus talk as late as 1948 was that the ancient arch cast a spell on the houses facing it, resulting in the birth of only girl babies among the residents of the houses, and the untutored working people still regarded the arch with awe.

Attaching a supernatural quality to the outstanding literati and commemorative objects associated with them had the effect of producing a lasting respect for the status system created by the examinations. The use of magic and supernatural beliefs as justification for unusual influence and privileges is commonly found in other cultures also. The supernatural lore that grew around the imperial examination system inevitably gave birth to an array of gods and spirits that were patrons of both the literati and the system itself. The patron deities of literature are familiar to students of Chinese religion. There was Wen-ch'ang, foremost among the gods of literature and the third star in the Ursa Major group; there was K'uei-sheng, god of a star in the constellation Andromeda but later transferred to one in Ursa Major. Both deities presided over the examinations and were dispensers of examination degrees; they generally shared the same temple. There were the lesser patron spirits, such as Chu-i (Red Coat) who served with K'uei-sheng as Wen-ch'ang's attendant; he helped backward and dull scholars to pass the examinations. The literary spirit of Lü Tung-pin performed the same function.

Since these were deities who helped scholars in the examinations, they were widely worshiped by Confucians. The present writer was taken by his family to a Wen-ch'ang temple when he started school at the age of six. Besides blessing the individual, these gods were patrons for the literary tradition, helping to promote literary studies in the community. There was hardly a sizable traditional community that did not have a Wen-ch'ang temple, where the other lesser literary gods were also enshrined. This temple generally served as the meeting place for scholarly groups in their writing contests and other literary activities. Wen-ch'ang's birthday was an especially important date for literary exercises. The inscription on the stele in the Wen-ch'ang temple in Sui-ning county of Szechwan province carried this account:

. . . Wen-ch'ang is the leader in the six-star constellation. In order to promote literature and Confucian teachings, to foster scholars, and to induce literary success, officials established a temple for the god within the administrative district. . . . the temple was used for lectures, literary gatherings, and poetry groups on the first and the fifteenth of the month . . . On the birthday of the god, there was a large gathering of scholars and the gentry for the celebration and for testing the scholars . . . The collection of all the talents in one place and instruction by famous teachers greatly raised the morale of the scholars. In recent years, there has been a steady stream of successful candidates at the spring and autumn examinations . . . It is no falsehood that the temple is a symbol of good luck, that the local literary success is a response of the star, and that there is a relation between Heaven and man.[45]

This was typical of stele inscriptions about the Wen-ch'ang god and the use of his temple, as quoted in the numerous local gazetteers in all parts of the country. The use of the Wen-ch'ang temple as the center for literary group activities had the effect of rendering a sacred character to the entire literary tradition. This same influence accounted for the belief that the written or printed word had magical power against evil spirits, and the tradition of regarding as desecration any disrespectful treatment of paper having written or printed words on it. The fact that the Chinese people revered Confucianism and its tradition of glorifying literary learning was due not only to the secular rewards attached to it but also to the effect of sanctioning the literary cults.

Man's Role in Determining His Fate

In the previous paragraphs we have shown the presence of religious concepts in the theoretical system of Confucianism, and the operation of these concepts in the contemporary Confucian mind as well as in the examination system and the literary tradition which conditioned the whole life pattern of Confucian scholars. As a social group, the Confucians embraced the idea of fate, engaged in a variety of magical practices as a means of "knowing fate," oriented many of their literary activities around patron deities, and owed much of the prestige of their social status to the supernatural sanctification of Confucianism as an institutionalized orthodoxy. As the ruling elite of society, the Confucians relied heavily on religion to maintain the ethicopolitical order. It is far from the truth that Confucians, as late as the early twentieth century, were thoroughly rationalistic thinkers or agnostics. Many of the anti-superstition statements that have been quoted to prove their rationalistic intellectualism were motivated more by their struggle against organized religious movements which threatened their status than by well-reasoned, genuine skepticism about supernatural matters.

But the Confucians were not dominated by mysticism, and their attitude toward life was not totally subordinated to the notion of fate as controlled by supernatural agents. While relying on the concept of fate to steel themselves in the face of momentous crises or to help them resolve conflict in life situations, the Confucians reserved for man an important role in the shaping of fate. In this reservation lay the realism and positive spirit of the Confucian mentality toward life, making the Confucians, and the Chinese people in general, different from members of cultures in which there is a distinctly negative quality and in which the whole course of life is resigned to the control of supernatural agents, as in the theocracy of Tibet or among certain castes of India.

The most basic expression of man's share in determining fate was the Confucian concept of "establishing fate." [46] This concept is best elucidated by the sayings, *chin jen-shih i t'ing t'ien-ming* ("Exert the utmost of human abilities, and then resign the rest to the decree of Heaven"); and *mou-shih tsai jen, ch'eng-shih tsai t'ien* ("It is up to man to plan things, but it is up to Heaven to decide their success"). In other words, man must plan and do his utmost, but must accept success or failure as the decree of fate. After all, if man has done his best and still meets failure, what can he do aside from becoming the prey of continued illusion or the victim of conflict between illusive dream and disheartening reality. It was here that the supernatural notion of fate played its vital role. On the other hand, *t'ing t'ien yu ming* or "rely on Heaven and follow fate" was a popular expression of disapproval of persons who refused to work hard to establish themselves in the world but simply drifted along. Many Buddhist priests were regarded as *lan ho-shang* or "lazy monks" because they did not exert themselves to cope with realistic problems but devoted themselves instead to pleasing the gods and spirits. This popular attitude contributed partly toward the social degradation of the monks in the eyes of the Confucians and the secular public. Hence the idea that man must first lay out the path toward his goal, and only then should he stand ready to receive the ordination of fate.

The concept that man can share in determining fate stemmed from the Confucian dogma that gave man a high place in the cosmic order. Man, together with Heaven and earth, was a member of the *san kang,* or trinity of the universe. In the Confucian view, the same ethereal substance, *ch'i,* that went into the making of Heaven and earth also went into the making of man. This common substance was what permitted the interpenetration between *t'ien tao,* the Way of Heaven, and *jen tao,* the Way of Man. This same substance was also the innate goodness in man that made him morally and intellectually perfectible to the point at which he could understand the great transforming and nourishing processes of Heaven and earth for the establishment of the foundations of civilized society.[47] Perfected men are sages, but nonetheless men, and the perfectibility of men led Mencius to assert that any man could become a sage through cultivation and discipline, thus placing the moral responsibility for self-perfection not on a few exceptional men but on all humanity.

It was this belief in the high position of man in the cosmic order that imparted a positive meaning to the Confucian idea of fate and inspired man to identify his moral cause with a sense of super-humanity, with Heaven itself. The positive meaning of fate inspired Wen T'ien-hsiang to write his immortal piece *Cheng ch'i ko* (Ballad of the Great Spirit) while on the brink of death in captivity under Kublai Khan. In this piece he reiterated the Confucian tenet that man was made from the same substance that went into the making of the sun, the stars, the rivers and mountains, and declared that his moral effort was what upheld Heaven and earth, transcending life and death. The same conviction of the super-humanity of man and his moral responsibility sent untold numbers of heroic Confucians into calm martyrdom for causes that were obviously doomed to failure for the time being.

The exaltation of the position of man gave rise to the idea that the morally qualified man, though subordinate to Heaven, was capable of warding off evil spirits, for man is a part of the Yang (positive) forces, which are superior to the Yin (negative) forces. It was the same sense of self-importance that made men of wisdom bold enough to "devise guidance through the Way of the Gods," to employ supernatural sanction to uphold the moral order of society, unafraid of Heaven's wrath at their usurpation of divine power. The same concept perhaps led to the claim of magical power for the written word and for the classics, which were supposed to stem from the sages who had come to understand both the Way of Man and the Way of Heaven.

In his exalted position, man could certainly share in determining his own fate through effort and cultivation. It was also understandable that the numerous superstitions about the performance of moral deeds as a means of improving one's fate were in harmony with the concept of "establishing fate."

CLASS DIFFERENCES IN RELIGION

It is possible to maintain, as do a number of writers, that the Confucians as a social class held a religious attitude different from that of the common uneducated people, whose life and views were chained by superstition. It is a sound observation that the highly educated Confucians were subjected to fewer supernatural notions than were the untutored common people. Here, we will examine some of the causes of this difference.

Class difference in religious life was a basic fact that extended beyond the educational and philosophic distinctions between the Confucians and the rest of Chinese society. Religious differences were quite apparent among occupational groups. The business class were accustomed to calculated risk in their occupation, and so they were relatively less superstitious about life, worshiping mainly the gods of wealth and a few associated deities. The peasants, on the other hand, faced much greater odds in their primitive struggle with the unpredictable and unsurmountable forces of nature. In their life, human control over the environment was less calculable and dependable. Consequently, they were generally more concerned with supernatural notions, worshiping a mass of functional gods concerned mainly with the elemental forces of nature. In the even more hazardous occupations such as sailing and mining, where the factor of chance played a prominent role, people were known for their superstitiousness. With the Confucians, whose social and economic status was more secure and whose literate education gave them more rational understanding of the world, it is to be fully expected that they should entertain fewer supernatural notions. But even with them, the basic Chinese beliefs such as Heaven, fate, and the magic of divination remained firm. And in the matter of success or failure in the examinations, supernatural notions were widespread among them.

The various occupational groups, as pointed out in a previous chapter, had their own patron gods, which helped the members identify themselves as a common group. Modern religious societies had fairly clear class delineations. The T'ung-shan She (Fellowship of Goodness), for example, drew most of its members from the political and military elite. The Li Men (Reason sect) and the Kuei-i Tao (Refuge sect) were organizations of the poor.[48] The I-kuan Tao, which was made up mainly of merchants but with some politicians and a variety of other people, specifically excluded certain social groups, such as barbers, actors, and prostitutes. These religious organizations served as identification of social status, and even functioned as channels of contact for social and economic opportunities. Many Confucians, taking politics as their major occupation, belonged to those religious organizations that were identified with their class status. In the traditional days, the literary gatherings in the Wen-ch'ang temples and the sacrificial activities in the Confucian temples were prerogatives of their class, and others of nonliterary status who wanted to participate had to buy an examination degree before they were admitted,[49] as purchase of a degree was permissible in the Late Ch'ing period.

Even taking into consideration the relative difference in the belief in magic and miracles, the Confucians did not constitute a group separate from the general current of religious life of traditional Chinese society. They shared with the rest of the population a basic system of religious belief in Heaven, fate, and other supernatural concepts. More important was the steady interflow of religious ideas between the Confucians and the general population. Works of fiction and memoirs containing religious ideas were written by the Confucians and were read by the public as major vehicles of religious information. But many of these religious stories did not originate with the Confucians, but rather were collected from the lore of the common folk and edited and embellished by literary Confucians. The foremost supernatural fantasy in Chinese literature, *The Monkey,* grew as folklore for several hundred years before the Confucian scholar Wu Ch'eng-en finally put it into superb written form. The *Liao-chai chih-i* (Strange Stories from a Chinese Studio), another famous work of supernatural fiction, was based mainly on folk tales of Shangtung province. In this way supernatural ideas also flowed from the common people to the Confucians, who read such tales as avidly as the illiterate peasants listened to them from storytellers.

It is difficult to judge how many of these miracle stories were distrusted by the Confucian readers. The great eighteenth-century Confucian scholar Chi Hsiao-lan, for example, obviously invented many of the ghost stories in his celebrated collection, *Yüeh-wei ts'ao-t'ang pi-chih,* but for those who have read the whole work carefully, it is truly difficult to decide just how much the author intended to frighten the "ignorant people" and how much he believed in the basic supernatural ideas underlying his own inventions. He wrote many articles arguing that, while it was impossible to prove the reality of ghosts, it was equally impossible to prove their nonexistence. In one article, he seemed quite sincere in his question: While admittedly there was only one kitchen god, how could he supervise man's conduct everywhere at once when every household in the empire had an altar for him in the kitchen? The Confucians, therefore, cannot be regarded as a distinctively different group on religious grounds, but must be regarded as part of the general pattern of Chinese religious life with only relative differences due to their social and economic position.

XI

RELIGION AND THE
TRADITIONAL MORAL ORDER

IN HIS WELL-KNOWN STUDY of Chinese religious persecutions, De Groot noted the "two-faced" policy of the Chinese government toward religion: repeated persecution on the one hand, and lack of thorough suppression on the other. This indeed characterized the long struggle between religious forces and the Confucian ruling group. In the interests of the secular ruling group and the state, religious forces were prevented from attaining an independent influential position. But religion could not be eliminated altogether, partly because of the function of religion in the moral order of society, as the Confucians clearly saw. Religious groups generally tried to justify their social existence by proclaiming their objective as the "promotion of moral virtues." [1] Our previous discussion of the ethicopolitical cults (chap. vii) has brought out the importance of the religious element in the functioning of the traditional moral order.

However, in its relation to the moral order, religion played the role of supernatural sanctioning agent. Religion in itself was neither the dominant source of ethical values, nor the seat of disciplining authority against the violation of moral rules. Hence, religion functioned as a part of the traditional moral order, but it did not occupy the status of a dominant, independent moral institution. This is seen in the limited position of religion in the system of traditional ethical values, in the way religion tried to enforce moral standards and to promote moral ideals, and in the general lack of a prominent moral position among the priesthood.

DOMINANCE OF CONFUCIAN ETHICAL VALUES

From an early date in Chinese culture, the major role of religion was not as the fountainhead of moral ideals but the magical one of inducing the gods and spirits to help bring happiness to man, to ward off evil, to cure sickness, to obtain rain in a drought, to achieve victory in war and peace in a crisis. Heaven was always a sanctioning force for man's moral conduct, but not the embodiment of any specific moral concepts. The rationalistic tendencies in Late Chou times accentuated the confinement of religious matters to magic and moral sanction, and even the moral meaning of Heaven came into question. Confucians like Hsün Tzu made the well-known pronouncement: "The *tao* [Way] is neither the *tao* of Heaven, nor the *tao* of earth, but the *tao* of man." And Lao Tzu, the founder of Taoistic thought, stripped the supernatural, anthropomorphic character from the universe by regarding it as a *hsüan chi* or unfathomable mechanism. It was not until Han times that the moral meaning of Heaven was once more enforced by the Yin-yang school in its theory of interaction between Heaven and man. But by then the Confucian system of ethical values was well on its way to becoming the moral orthodoxy of Chinese society for all generations until the twentieth century.

The dominance of Confucian ethical values in the traditional moral order needs no elaboration. For two thousand years, they provided the standard motivation for social behavior and the criteria for judging right from wrong. New moral values that harmonized with Confucian values were easily absorbed into the traditional social code, but those in conflict with them had great difficulty in being assimilated. One reason for the success of the Confucian system of ethical values was its adaptation to the practical needs of the secular society, particularly the needs of kinship relation, which was the structural core of Chinese agrarian society. The ethical values of many religious groups, such as the monastic orders and the religious societies, appealed to the need of a wider brotherhood beyond the kinship system. This appeal, as was pointed out earlier, met the needs of certain historical situations, such as the period of disunion, when, because of general political chaos and economic misery, the kinship relations failed to provide physical and emotional security and thus forced individuals to seek salvation from non-kinship brotherhoods. But such situations were episodic rather than enduring in Chinese history. In the long normal periods of peace and order, individuals for whom the kinship relations failed to function properly would join non-kinship brotherhoods for relief. Such individuals were usually orphans, widows, or members of extremely poor families. But in normal times, the kinship organization provided adequately for the basic needs of the vast majority of individuals. The lack of systematic development of Confucian values with regard to the wider brotherhood of man did not seriously impair the dominant position of Confucianism as the source of moral values in a kinship-oriented society. Under the dominance of the Confucian ethical system, religion was confined mainly to the role of supplying sanction for Confucian values, the fulfillment of which was the chief condition for attaining social security and mental serenity.

PRACTICAL LIMITATIONS OF ETHICAL VALUES IN INSTITUTIONAL RELIGION

However inspiring were some of the moral values offered by religions in China, two facts stand out quite clearly. First, no major religion in Chinese history developed an ethical system comparable to Confucianism in comprehensiveness and in systematic adaptation to the characteristics of the indigenous social structure. Second, major religions in China adopted some of the most strategic Confucian ethical values or made compromises with them.

Buddhism of course has a comprehensive system of ethical values which in many respects is more elaborate in detail than Confucianism, and it seems to have functioned well within monastic societies. But it was never the source of ethical values for secular social relations that Christianity was in European society. Its firm conviction of the tenacious character of human lust in secular life led it to renounce the world and to regard the improvement of a realistic social order through moral regulation as an impossible task. Its message on the ephemeral nature of all human struggles served to trim the burning desires of men and prevent them from committing excessive measures in disregard of the interests of others. In this respect, "fleeing into the door of emptiness" (conversion to Buddhism) and "coolness toward prestige and material gain" had a moral meaning. But this was negative escape, and not the positive spirit for remaking the existing world that characterized the Confucian ethical system. Inspiring indeed were the Buddhist teaching of universal pity and the Mahayanist admonition of "entering the world with the spirit of renunciation of it" (working to save the world with complete selflessness). But the love of humanity, the spirit of universal salvation, the disregard for personal consequence in the cause of moral uplifting of the world, and the Mahayanist obliteration of the technical distinction between entering the world and renouncing it were in close consonance with the key Confucian value of *jen* or universal benevolence. Buddhist teachings consequently became intimately fused with the moral outlook of the Confucian mind. It was largely through its fusion with Confucianism after the Sung times that the positive aspect of Buddhism became instrumental in the secular life of Chinese society.

Because of the distance between many Buddhist ethical values and the practical situations of secular life, Buddhists often had to face the world by tacitly accepting some of the dominant secular values, even when such values were in contradiction to the Buddhist creeds. Thus, while Buddhism proclaimed the renunciation of the family and the state, there were Buddhist convents in many parts of China bearing such names as Kuang-hsiao Ssu (the Monastery for the Glorification of Filial Piety), Pao-chung Ssu (the Monastery for Honoring the Loyal [to the state]), and Hu-kuo Ssu (the Monastery for Protection of the State). Such monastic names carried the apparent intention of trying to improve the status of world-renouncing Buddhism in the secular world by condoning Confucian values.

The Taoist religion as an ethical system for the secular world was even weaker than Buddhism. The chief Taoist moral creed consisted of the Five Commandments and the Ten Virtues. The Five Commandments were against killing any living thing, alcoholism, hypocrisy, thievery, and licentiousness. The Ten Virtues were filial piety; loyalty to the emperor and one's own teacher; mercy toward all things; tolerance for unjust treatment; helping to settle disputes and remove hatred; sacrifice for the relief of the needy; releasing captured animals and nourishing living things; planting trees along roads and around houses and wells, and building bridges; helping with beneficial enterprises for and removing harmful things from the community, and enlightening the ignorant; and lastly, reading the *San Pao Ching Lü* (Three Precious Scriptural Rules) and constantly placing fragrant flowers before it.[2]

Except for their rather unique listing of tree planting and bridge building as ethical merits, the Five Commandments and Ten Virtues (as well as other more elaborate ramifications of the same basic ideas) do not compare favorably with the Confucian ethical system in consistency, in comprehensiveness, or in realistic adaptation to the particular needs of Chinese secular society. They largely represent adaptations from Confucian and Buddhist values.

If Buddhism and Taoism, the two greatest institutional religions in China, did not develop ethical systems of their own which became effective in the secular life, the syncretic religious societies accomplished even less in this respect. It has been indicated before that the ethical part of their doctrine was adopted mainly from Confucianism. All major Confucian values found their way into sectarian doctrines and received sanction from the sectarian gods and spirits. "Those who want to become Buddhas or [Taoist] fairies must start by practicing loyalty and filial piety," [3] the two most basic values in the Confucian ethical system. One of the largest modern religious societies, the I-kuan Tao, proclaimed itself to be the *k'ung-chiao ch'uan-kung,* the complete attainment of the Confucian doctrine, and its moral teachings consisted predominantly of Confucian values.

Ethical systems for institutional religion might have been adequate for the regulation of monastic societies or the lives of priests and devotees, but they were not systematically practiced by the common people in secular life in the way that Confucian ethical values were observed. For the common people, the dominant purpose of religion was its magical value in obtaining happiness and warding off evil. Magic was a technique for achieving tangible results in a particular situation. It contained no moral dogma of universal validity for social life.[4] As such, magic placed no opposition to the practicing of secular moral values. Hence, a common man could worship a Buddhist god for the general happiness of himself and his family, pray to a Taoist deity for the return of his health, and at the same time practice Confucian morality. The relation of magic to morality was not as a source of moral ideas, but mainly as a sanctioning agent for ethical standards. A man believing in magic usually feared the spirits, and thus respected the morality that the spirits were supposed to sanction in the popular cults.

CONFUCIAN ETHICAL VALUES IN MYTHOLOGICAL LORE

Because there was little public preaching to organized congregations, mythological lore was an important verbal and literary vehicle for the dissemination of religious ideas. The common people received a considerable part of their religious information by listening to stories and reading literature of a mythological nature, while very few had read the sacred scriptures of Buddhism, Taoism, or any other religion. The religious nature of such lore was mainly syncretic, and the main theme was the relationship between supernatural forces and man's moral conduct.

Here again, the criteria for man's moral conduct were taken from the Confucian rather than the religious system of ethical values. This can be seen in many local gazetteers and in the rich store of mythological literature. In *Lo-tien chen chih* (Gazetteer of Lo-tien Town, Pao-shan County, Kiangsu Province), one of the many mythological stories dwelt on supernatural enforcement of the Confucian value of fidelity in the observation of a business contract.

In the Ch'ien Lung period [the latter half of the seventeenth century], two men bearing the surnames of Chao and Hsü lived in this neighborhood, and the two families enjoyed close and friendly relations. Hsü was skillful in business and gradually became rich. He took Chao into partnership in a rice business. Some years later, Hsü passed away. Chao took advantage of the infancy of Hsü's son, and embezzled six hundred ounces of silver of Hsü's share of the business. When Hsü's widow demanded the money, Chao refused to give it to her, and in addition insulted her by charging her with immoral conduct. Hsü's clansmen also mistreated her. When the inheritance was nearly gone, she tried to commit suicide. Chao then was suddenly afflicted with lung cancer, and, spitting blood, said that the spirit of Hsü had come to punish him for the embezzlement of joint property and for soiling the reputation of the widow. Such crime, the spirit charged, was committed in complete disregard of conscience, and could not possibly be pardoned. Chao soon died with the cancer festering through the chest.[5]

The Pao-shan county gazetteer gave a terse account of supernatural enforcement of the Confucian value of harmony among brothers.

On the tenth day of the tenth month in 1524, the district was lashed by a violent thunderstorm and torrential rains. There were three brothers whose houses were next to each other. There had been continuous conflict among them. On that day, all three houses were swept away by the storm, with the people in them. But the neighboring houses remained untouched.[6]

Moralistic lore frequently concentrated on the key Confucian value of filial piety, as can be seen in collected volumes of mythology such as the *Liao-chai chih-i,* of which Herbert Giles did an abridged translation under the title of *Strange Stories from a Chinese Studio.* But there is as yet no English translation of the well-known collected work of *Yüeh-wei ts'ao-t'ang pi-chih* (Notes from the Yüehwei Thatched Hall) by the famed eighteenth-century writer Chi Hsiao-lan, whose work contains chiefly supernatural tales created with explicit moral lessons in view. Here is a sample, telling of a werefox, the most popular spirit of mischief in the Chinese mythological tradition:

In the Ts'ang-chou district, a member of the gentry, Liu Shih-yü, had a studio. It was occupied by a werefox which argued with people in broad daylight and threw stones at them, while remaining invisible to human eyes. The district magistrate, Tung Ssu-jen, was a good official. Hearing of the difficulty, he went to the studio himself to chase away the werefox. He was propounding the principle that men and spirits tread different paths when a clear voice uttered from the eaves: "As an official, your Honor has considerable love for the people; you have taken no bribery, so I do not dare to strike you. But, your Honor's love for the people is to win a reputation, and your refusal to take bribery is motivated by fear of the consequences, so I do not need to keep out of your way. You had better remain quiet, and do not utter too many words which could get you into trouble." The magistrate went away in embarrassment. But Liu, the studio owner, had a rough and ignorant female servant who alone was not afraid of the fox, and neither did the fox attack her. When the fox was talking to the people, someone asked about the maid. The fox said, "Though a lowly servant, she is a genuinely filial woman. Her great virtue causes even the gods and spirits to avoid blocking her path, and who are we to bother her?" Liu then asked the maid to live in the studio, and the werefox left on the same day.[7]

Then there was the tale of a young man who had committed suicide. His spirit returned to tell his wife in her dreams that his crimes had caused him to be condemned to live forever in the soil. But, during his lifetime, he had been a filial son to his mother, and this mitigated his punishment a bit, so that he was now on his way to be reborn as a snake. He further told her that the severest punishment in Hell was given for violation of filial piety, and that, in her remarriage, she should be filial toward her new parents-in-law.[8]

Lack of Independent Ethical Values in Diffused Religion

Diffused religion that has become a part of secular social institutions lacks any independent ethical position of its own, for its chief function lies in furnishing supernatural support for the ethical values in the basic concepts of the secular institutions. Diffused religion itself is not the source of ethical values for the operation of the secular institutions, as can be seen in the role of religion in the family, in social and economic groups, and in the state.

Ancestor worship in itself, for example, was not an independent factor that gave rise to a system of kinship ethics, but rather it used its supernatural premises to justify and enforce the Confucian values designed for the operation of the kinship group. Thus, the supernatural notion of the existence of the ancestors' souls justified the ethical requirement of ancestor worship as an expression of the sentiment of filial piety. Filial piety was a product of the practical needs of the kinship group as interpreted by the Confucian doctrine, and not a product of supernatural assumptions about the existence of the soul of the dead. The worship of the patron god in a trade guild served to strengthen the secular moral values of fidelity in business transactions and faithfulness in observation of guild rules, but the supernatural idea of the patron deity in itself was not the basic reason for the formulation of these values, which represented, rather, the functional product of the needs of the group. The frequent worship of Kuan Yü in secret societies was due to the fact that the life story of this great soldier symbolized the secular values of fidelity and justice, which were so essential to the functioning of underground groups. The Mandate of Heaven was a supernatural concept to command public acceptance of political power and to foster the values of loyalty and subservience. In the historical development of the Chinese political institution, the Mandate of Heaven was a blank paper on which the Confucians wrote ethicopolitical details. The obligations and privileges of the rulers were defined in terms of Confucian values, to which Heaven and its associated deities lent their sanction and support. Diffused religion, therefore, had no independent system of ethical values apart from those developed by the secular institutions.

Religious Enforcement of Ethical Values

From elsewhere in this work as well as from the foregoing discussion in this chapter, it has been shown that the chief moral role of religion lay not in its being a premise of ethical values, but in its assistance in the enforcement of the secular moral standards. In the performance of this function, religion in China relied mainly on supernatural sanction as a means of both encouragement and deterrence. But specifically, religious groups such as the priesthood exercised no authority in the maintenance of the moral order in secular society.

Postive Encouragement and Negative Deterrence

One form of encouragement of moral conduct, as already suggested, was the classical conception of fate, which inspired the Confucian identification of man's moral efforts with the Heaven-ordained course. In the name of this preordained course, man was to proceed with his moral duties regardless of success or failure in his own lifetime, for the predestined course would eventually triumph, and his own possible failure was a necessary sacrifice for the final victory.

Another means of encouragement of moral standards was the deification of men who had shown exemplary moral conduct and thereby became models of moral ideals (chap. vii). In the town of Yang-hang Chen in Pao-shan county, there was a temple dedicated to two brothers, Wang Hao-yao and Wang Yüan-yao who died defending their home territory against invasion by Japanese pirates in the Ming dynasty. In the latter part of the nineteenth century the temple was renovated, and the stone stele erected in commemoration of the event carried typical remarks, praising the two brothers for having exemplified the virtues of loyalty, filial piety, righteousness, and moral chastity. The two historical figures were compared to the lofty peak of a mountain, standing to be adored by subsequent generations for its towering height. The county erected the temple and offered sacrifice to the two men "not only for their sake" but also for the moral inspiration of posterity.[9]

The command of fate and the inspiration of exemplary men probably reached for the most part only the educated minority. For most of the common people, self-sacrificing moral dedication was not a social status requirement, and positive encouragement of moral conduct took the materialistic form of the enticement of happiness in this life and paradise after death for those who observed the ethical admonitions. Good deeds were the "accumulation of merits for the other world" (*chi yin-te*). The Taoists even set up quotas of merits for the attainment of fairyhood, as stated in the Taoist scripture, *Pao P'u Tzu:*

Those wishing to attain fairyhood on earth must establish 300 merits of virtue; those wishing to attain fairyhood in Heaven must establish 1,200 merits of virtue. Even if one has established 1,199 merits, but suddenly commits one evil deed, all the previous merits are wiped out, and one must start all over again.

But just as important, if not more so, was deterrence as a means of enforcement of the moral order in secular society. Enter any Buddhist or Taoist temple, and one encounters many images of gods and spirits with terrifying faces, holding menacing weapons. No child frequenting Buddhist temples could easily forget the images of the four door guards, each over ten feet tall, carrying huge swords, flashing rows of saberlike teeth, and staring down with ferocious eyes. Their gigantic seize and horrifying features symbolized to the worshipers the terrible power of supernatural beings, ever ready to punish wrongdoers. And in addition there were the frescoes of the Ten Courts of Hell, where men were punished by being boiled in oil, by being driven over hills studded with sharp knives, and by many other unimaginable tortures. Above all, there was widespread belief in the Buddhist warning of afterlife retribution for all evil deeds. Even the image of K'uei-sheng, the star god of literary success, was sculptured with a ferocious face and angry bulging eyes, probably to warn those who might want to attain literary success through devious immoral means. These demonic forms may well have represented man's reflections of the wickedness in the will of his own nature, as concretely symbolized in the distorted proportions of such structures as the body, the eyes, the teeth, and the limbs, which posed distinct threats to the solidarity of social relations.

If the Taoist scripture set up quotas of good deeds for the encouragement of moral conduct, it similarly warned men against evil doing:

On earth and in Heaven there are gods who oversee the wrongdoings of men and take away the counts (*suan*) from a person in accordance with the seriousness of the evil deed. When a person's counts are reduced, poverty, sickness, and misfortune will descend on him. When all the counts are gone, the person dies. There are hundreds of wrongdoings, too many to enumerate, for which counts may be taken away.

Should a person commit an evil deed, stated another Taoist passage, records (*chih*) or counts are taken away from him, depending on the seriousness of the evil, one record being equal to 300 days of his life, and one count, three days.[10] This was adding teeth to morality. It is interesting to note that, while punishments for wrongdoings were carefully listed, the punishable wrongdoings themselves were not pointed out, thus leaving room for folkways and mores to operate. This made the Taoist religion a very suitable sanctioning agent for the ethical values of secular institutions.

This negative aspect of the moral function of Chinese religion was stressed by modern Chinese leaders. Thus stated T'an Ssu-t'ung, who died in the Hundred-Day Reform in 1898:

Should the power of Heaven and Hell stand out in the people's minds, they will not dare to cheat and to act without inhibition. Instead, they will move toward the moral grounds through self-warning . . . Should there be no supernatural power to control the ignorant public, there will be the danger of absence of restraint against killing, arson, thievery, licentiousness, and all other kinds of evils. Now, if we accost any ignorant peasant and ask him . . . why he did not default on debt, and he will likely answer, "Defaulting on debt in this life must be repaid in the next life by being reborn into horses and mules to work it out." [11]

Wang Ts'ung-hui, one-time Minister of Justice in the Nationalist government, stated: "Man's mind needs control, without which it will run rampant. The most blessed means of controlling the human mind is religion." [12]

Lack of Religious Authority for Enforcement

The role of religion in the enforcement of moral values was limited to psychological encouragement and deterrence. The weak structural position of the priesthood and religious organizations in Chinese society precluded the development of organized religious authority to enforce moral discipline among the secular population. Since religion was not the chief source of secular ethical values, religious bodies could not be the authoritative groups to pass judgment on what was right or wrong when disputes arose about the moral nature of certain aspects of social conduct. The authority for such judgment was the jealously guarded prerogative of the government and the Confucian scholar-officials whose power from the beginning had an ethocratic orientation.

The priesthood, on the other hand, faced many limitations in the development of any authority for moral judgments. In the first place, most modern priests were ignorant and illiterate. Their position in rendering moral judgment was obviously inferior to that of the highly educated and sophisticated Confucian group, who devoted years to the study of the classics and the moral lessons in history. It was no accident that it was the Confucian rulers who recognized the religious element only as a tool to strengthen the ethicopolitical order of traditional society.

Secondly, the priests, at least in the modern period, did not distinguish themselves by high moral reputation. While the average Buddhist or Taoist priest was the equal of the common people in moral conduct, many of them were notorieties. Poverty drove some of them to steal. More often, not a few Buddhists became licentious. Some Taoists looked upon promiscuity as a magical practice to attain longevity. The temple grounds were long regarded as a romantic place for women, resulting in the repeated legal prohibition of women from the temples.[13] The distinctive function of the priests, in the eyes of the people, was not the exercise of moral discipline, and not even the teaching of moral values, but the performance of religious services with a predominantly magical note.

SEPARATION OF ETHICS FROM RELIGION

In spite of the weakness of religion as a source of ethical values and the lack of moral authority of the priesthood, it would be unsound to underestimate the role of religion in the traditional moral order. Even with its limitations, religion helped uphold moral values which the social institutions, using secular means alone, would not have been able to maintain. The stele inscription in the Yüan-chün Sheng-mu miao (temple of the Sacred Mother, the Original Ruler) made this observation:

The deity is the great mother of all things . . . hence the universal sacrifice to her . . . this is why we enshrine her in a building of halls and courtyards, furnish the temple with desks and the altar with stationery, staff it with images of men and spirits, dignify the walls with pictures of fire, grinding stones, knife-studded hills, and sword-branched trees [scenes of Hell] . . . This is the essential idea of guidance by the Way of the Gods as designed by the Sage. Now, the government has a complete system of reward, but the people do not necessarily become enthusiastic; but if we tell them about the ability of the gods to bring them happiness and benefit, then they all become attracted. The government has all kinds of punishment and threats, but the people are not necessarily deterred; yet, if we tell them about the power of the gods to punish crimes, then they all have fear . . . This is the way to encourage the good and to punish the evil, and to transform the people by good customs. . . .[14]

This inscription makes it clear that the moral order could not stand on secular grounds alone without assistance from religious influence; it also indicates that religion was not the embodiment of ethics, but a sanctioning force for it. Religion and ethics, then, belong to two separate aspects of the institutional structure of traditional Chinese society, although the two functioned together, with the ethics of the Confucian doctrine and the secular institutions deriving its sacred and awe-inspiring quality from religion.

As indicated previously, through the prospect of reward or punishment in the afterlife, especially through popularization of the idea of karma, religion not merely made moral rules sacred and awe-inspiring, but it also helped to remedy the fallibility of ethical values in their actual operation. Here again, the moral order that received religious support was secular in nature, and it stood apart from religion as a structural entity, despite the delicate interweaving of morality and religion. This important feature distinguishes Chinese religion from Western religion, which combines an ethical system and worship of the supernatural into a single structure.

It is interesting to read another of Chi Hsiao-lan's mythological tales on the moral function of religion as conceived by this great eighteenth-century editor of the imperial Four-Chamber Library. In the following liberal rendering from the Chinese version, one must keep in mind that the traditional Chinese world was one where men mingled freely with spirits, and where the question of whether there were ghosts was a familiar but unanswered query, perhaps intentionally left unsettled by many great Confucians who saw definite moral usefulness in keeping the popular mind in doubt on the point. Thus runs the story:

In the southern province of Fukien, where rainfalls are heavy, there were covered bridges to provide shelter for passers-by. According to the story, there was a person who was out at night and ran into a shower. He hastened to a bridge for shelter. Behind him came an official-looking man, carrying a sheath of documents, and with him were several armed guards accompanying some prisoners, whose chains clanged as they walked onto the bridge, also seeking shelter. The first man, seeing that it was an official convoying a group of criminals, cowered wtih fear into a corner.

One of the prisoners was crying. The official shouted, "If you are afraid now, why did you do it in the first place?" The prisoner replied, sobbing, "My teacher misled me. In his daily lectures, he dismissed all talk of gods and spirits and retribution as lies from Buddha. I trusted him, and I thought that, if I worked my machinations and tricks carefully and cleverly, I could do anything I wished without being detected in my lifetime. After my death, my soul would evaporate into the ethereal sphere, and I would know nothing further about people's praise or blame of me. There was nothing to deter me from trying to gratify all my wishes. Little did I expect to discover that Hell is no lie, and and that there is really a king of Hades. Now I know I was betrayed by my teacher; I am sorry and repentant."

Another prisoner chimed in: "Your belief in Confucianism caused your downfall, but I was misled by Buddhism. According to Buddhist teaching, an evil deed could be redeemed by religious service, and a soul fallen into Hell could be ransomed by one's living relatives chanting the sutra. I thought it was well within my means to burn incense and give alms during my life, and to hire monks to conduct services at my death. With this protection from Buddhist law, the subterranean authorities would not be able to control me in spite of all of my wrongdoings. Little did I know that reward and punishment are based on good or evil deeds, and not on the amount of wealth one dispenses. All the money I gave away has not saved me from the hammer and the boiling caldron. Without relying on Buddha, I would not have become as uninhibited as I did." The prisoner finished his statement with a bawl, and the other prisoners joined in the crying. The first man then knew that these were not human beings.[15]

The moral of the story is pointed out by the author:

Throughout the Six Classics, there is no statement in which the existence of gods and spirits is refuted, and in the Tripitaka, there is no talk of taking money and bribes. When the Confucians were seeking personal recognition and the Buddhists were seeking pecuniary gains, they produced extremely bad results. Buddhism was originally a foreign doctrine, and we may not blame the priests who rely on it as a livelihood. But it is not necessary that Confucians talk in an agnostic tone.

Thus a great Confucian scholar believed that the gods and spirits, and Heaven and Hell, were all essential agents of moral control; he blamed the Confucians for doubting them, and lamented the degeneration of the Buddhist priesthood into a profit-seeking group.

XII

DIFFUSED AND INSTITUTIONAL
RELIGION IN CHINESE SOCIETY

THE DATA AND DISCUSSIONS in the previous chapters have shown the importance of the religious element in all major aspects of Chinese social life. In Chinese society, however, religion has been less prominent or less readily observable as an independent factor than in many other cultures, such as the European or the Arabian culture. This less apparent role of religion as an independent system may be explained by the dominance of diffused religion and the relative weakness of institutional religion in Chinese society.

In his celebrated work, *Sociology of Religion,* Joachim Wach distinguished two types of religious groups: those that are identical with "natural groups" and those that are "specifically religious" organizations.[1] The distinction is an extremely useful tool for understanding religious life in Chinese society, and in Asiatic societies in general. Because of its significance and general applicability, Wach's concept is hereby broadened into the distinction between two types of religion: institutional religion and diffused religion.

For the purpose of this study, institutional religion in the theistic sense is considered as a system of religious life having (1) an independent theology or cosmic interpretation of the universe and human events, (2) an independent form of worship consisting of symbols (gods, spirits, and their images) and rituals, and (3) an independent organization of personnel to facilitate the interpretation of theological views and to pursue cultic worship. With separate concept, ritual, and structure, a religion assumes the nature of a separate social institution, and hence its designation as an institutional religion. On the other hand, diffused religion is conceived of as a religion having its theology, cultus, and personnel so intimately diffused into one or more secular social institutions that they become a part of the concept, rituals, and structure of the latter, thus having no significant independent existence. This diffused form of religion has been well presented by Emile Durkheim.[2] Institutional religion functions independently as a separate system, while diffused religion functions as a part of the secular social institutions. In its origin, religion in any form stems from psychological sources which are independent of the structure of secular life. But in its subsequent development, religion may take either one of the two forms. An institutional religion may be readily observable in its independent existence, and yet its role in the social organization may not be very important. Diffused religion, on the other hand, may be less apparent as a separate factor, but it may be very important as an undergirding force for secular institutions and the general social order as a whole. The purpose of this chapter is to employ this viewpoint to interpret the functional role of religion in Chinese social life and organization.

In China, institutional religion was represented by major universal religions such as Buddhism and Taoism and by religious or sectarian societies. The cults of professional magicians and sorcerers also belonged to this category, for such cults did not function as part of the secular social institutions. In many situations institutional and diffused religions were interdependent. Diffused religion relied upon institutional religion for the development of mythical or theological concepts, for the supply of gods, spirits, and other symbols of worship, for the devising of rituals and sacrifice, and for the services of technically trained personnel, the priests. Thus Buddhist and Taoist theology, gods, rituals, and priests were used in different forms of diffused religion such as ancestor worship, the worship of community deities, and the ethicopolitical cults. On the other hand, institutional religion relied on rendering such services to secular institutions in order to sustain its existence and development. The two forms of religious structure were thus mutually related in their functional role in the religious life of Chinese society.

DIFFUSED RELIGION IN CHINESE SOCIETY

Examining the religious characteristics of traditional Chinese society in this light, we shall see that diffused religion was a pervasive factor in all major aspects of social life, contributing to the stability of social institutions, and that institutional religion, although important in its own way, lacked organizational strength to make it a powerful structural factor in the over-all Chinese social organization.

Pervasiveness of Diffused Religion

The data and discussions in the foregoing chapters have made it clear that the religious element was diffused into all major social institutions and into the organized life of every community in China. It was in its diffused form that people made their most intimate contact with religion. Many students of Chinese society have either ignored the religious aspect of Chinese social institutions altogether, have dismissed diffused religion as superstition, or have given it some other label to avoid the term religion. In our analysis, the religious aspect of institutional and community life represents religion in its diffused structural form.

Thus, in the family, the basic unit of organized life in Chinese society, ancestor worship had all the primary qualities of religion diffused into the institutional structure. The belief in the souls of the dead, their power to influence the living morally and physically, and the need for perpetual sacrifice by the descendants was a part of the classical theology that had been inseparably woven into the matrix of kinship values and the very concept of the traditional family. The mortuary and sacrificial rites and other social and economic arrangements of the family that were associated with the dead ancestors formed an integral part of the system of rituals of the family. The head of the family or clan administered the affairs of ancestor worship and officiated at the sacrifices in the capacity of a priest. The kinship group constituted the congregation, and members performed their rituals in an order based on their age and sex status in the family. Hence, ancestor worship, the chief aspect of family religious life, was thoroughly diffused into the family in its theology, its cultic symbols and practices, and its organization. Family religion was thus organizationally as strong as the family itself. As will be noted later, ancestral temples were among the best-endowed religious establishments in the country. At times, professional priests were hired to participate in some of the rituals, but they did not officiate at the worship.

Reviewing the religious aspect of social and economic groups (chap. iii), we find basically the same situation when religion was theologically, cultically, and organizationally diffused into the secular group. In the trade guilds the theological interpretation of the patron god was part of the fundamental concept of the existence and development of the trade and its guild organization. The image of the god and the worship ritual were inseparable from the operational equipment and procedure of the guild meetings and the functioning of the organization. The leading officers of the guild, and not professional priests, administered and officiated at the worship. And the general membership of the guild constituted the congregation.

The earlier chapter on the religious aspect of community organization (chap. iv) reveals substantially the same pattern. The theology of the community patron gods was an integral part of the general concept of the traditional community, for the collective existence of the community was symbolized by them. The mass celebrations and processions in honor of the patron gods, together with all the images and paraphernalia, formed an intimate part of the equipment and collective rituals in the routine operation of traditional community life. The community leaders acted as officiating priests, and the entire population of the community was the congregation.

Our chapters on the religious aspects of the state (chaps. vii, viii, and ix) present a similar pattern of the diffusion of religion into the central and local political order. The theology of Heaven and Earth, the Yin-yang school, and the interpretation of the interaction between Heaven and man had long been a firm part of the traditional political orthodoxy. The theory behind the ethicopolitical cults was similarly woven into the matrix of traditional ethicopolitical values. The performance of cultic rituals was a part of the administrative routine of the governing officials and the local gentry.

The emperor and his officialdom constituted the priesthood for ethicopolitical worship, and the entire population of the empire was theoretically the grand congregation. The whole story of the control and persecution of Buddhism and the sectarian societies was in a sense a constant effort to preserve the diffusion of religion in the secular institution of government and to prevent the development of independent religious organizations that might concern themselves with affairs of state.

Diffused Religion and the Stability of Social Institutions

The diffusion of religion into secular social institutions and community life had many consequences. One was the functioning of religion in society without presenting a separate dominant religious institution, as already suggested. Another was the imparting of a sacred character to social institutions. The presence of symbols of gods and spirits and the performance of religious rituals in all major aspects of organized social life created a general feeling of awe and respect for institutionalized practices. Enter a house, participate in the ceremonial activities of any group, walk through a neighborhood or a public square, look at a memorial arch, go through a city gate, climb a large bridge, view a sizable public building of any nature, and one would nearly always see an altar, an idol, the picture of a god or spirit, a magical charm, or some mythological lore of the gods and spirits connected with the nature and history of the object. Every traditional institutional value and structure was similarly imbued with a rich folklore of a supernatural character. The social environment as a whole had a sacred atmosphere which inspired the feeling that the gods and spirits, as well as man, participated in molding the established ways of life in the traditional world.

The feeling of awe toward the established ways had the effect of stabilizing and strengthening social institutions. Religion in its diffused form became a strong supporting influence for the values and tradition of an established institution. Rendering support for the past was a characteristic of diffused religion and its vast pantheon of functional gods, who were considered creators or guardians of their respective institutions. This was in sharp contrast to institutional religion, which frequently required a break with the past and participation in a radically new way of life. The Buddhist tonsure and the Taoist knotted hairdo, the priestly robe, the vegetarian diet, the assumption of life in a monastery or temple, the foreswearing of family and other social ties—these and many other ritual acts served the purpose of marking a person off from the secular population and severing his ties with the past, with the established ways of life accepted by society. From this interpretation, the well-known quality of conservatism and stability of Chinese society may be partly attributed to the broad development of diffused religion in all major Chinese social institutions. The deep devotion to the past and the presentation of occasional innovation only in the name of ancient wisdom were inspired by the feeling that the will of the gods and the wisdom of the sages had devised the instituted ways of life, and that any change would invite the wrath of the spirits and violate the rules of the predecessors. Many rationalistic Confucian thinkers in the past challenged the supernatural aspect of social institutions, but few of them dared to launch a systematic attack, mainly because they recognized the stabilizing and conserving quality of the functional cults. The Confucian attitude toward sacrificial rites was an illustration of this.

Diffused religion was dependent on the effective functioning of the secular institutions for its strength, and even its existence. When a secular institution functioned effectively in meeting the basic needs of man, the functional cults diffused in it enjoyed the devotion of the people. But when the secular institution failed to meet prolonged crises and left basic institutional needs unfulfilled, people lost faith and confidence in both the institution and its functional cults. Thus, in times of peace and order, the classical cult of Heaven and Earth effectively inspired hope and confidence in the government. But during protracted chaos and disorder, such as during the Late Chou period and the period of disunion, in which there were in each case some four centuries of continuous confusion and widespread suffering, pessimism predominated, life seemed hopeless, and people tended to lose faith both in the classical institution of government and in the cult of Heaven and Earth. As a consequence, in the Late Chou period, people lamented that Heaven was blind and indiscriminate in sowing misfortune that struck both the good and the evil, and rationalistic thought arose to challenge the soundness of religion and to formulate new doctrines for the institution of government. In the period of disunion, the loss of faith in the ability of the classical political cults to bring peace and happiness partly accounted for the rise of the faiths of Taoism and Buddhism as new roads to salvation. When secular institutions showed prolonged failure in meeting new situations, the religion diffused in such institutions consequently lost popular support.

In the modern period, the same process could be witnessed. From the turn of the present century, it became increasingly obvious that the traditional social institutions were inadequate to meet the changing needs of the modern world. Chaos grew as social, economic, and political crises deepened through the years. The people had less respect for the old institutions, and one of the most notable facts was the loss of the sacred character which once marked such institutions. As the government floundered from crisis to crisis, and the Republic came to succeed the age-old monarchy, the impressive altars of Heaven and Earth and the great temples of the many ethicopolitical cults ceased to function as religious establishments; they lay empty and deserted, their sacrificial equipment collected dust, and their grounds became overgrown with weeds. As the urban families began to lose their cohesion under Western influences, ancestor worship waned rapidly. Modern homes no longer had the once-inevitable ancestral altar in the main hall, and what had been man's most sacred duty, ancestral sacrifice, was often ignored by the younger generations.

Thus diffused religion depended largely on the fate of the secular institutions, and did not have the enduring quality of the great universal religions which formed separate institutions of religious life. As the strength and efficiency of the secular institutions waxed and waned, new functional cults arose to succeed the old. But in the contemporary period, with its emphasis on science and its strong trend toward secularization, the religious aspect of social institutions has been fast retreating into the pages of history with little likelihood of return. Diffused religion, once a dominant factor in Chinese society, seems to have lost irrecoverable grounds.

INSTITUTIONAL RELIGION AND ITS WEAK POSITION IN MODERN CHINESE SOCIETY

In contrast to the traditional dominance of diffused religion, institutional religion has played a comparatively weak role in Chinese society since the Sung period of the eleventh century. This comparative weakness has become particularly apparent in the nineteenth and twentieth centuries, for which more data are available for the construction of a coherent picture.

Varieties and Leading Functions of Institutional Religion

Institutional religion, as characterized earlier, existed in three major forms in traditional China. The first was that part of the ancient classical religion which was carried on by specialized personnel, such as geomancers, diviners, sorcerers (*wu*), and other types of magicians long known to the classical religious tradition. This group acted as the living depository of the theoretical knowledge and magical skills of classical religion, and its members generally took their religious practice as a trade or profession, thus playing a role independent of their capacity as members of the secular social institutions. The second form of institutional religion was that of the great religions of universal salvation (or universal religions) that had gained legal recognition and the right to carry on an open existence; the leading religions here were Buddhism and Taoism. The third form of institutional religion was that of the syncretic religious societies, which were forced by long political suppression to lead an underground or half-hidden existence. Both the universal religions and the religious sects developed their theology, cults, and organizational systems independent of the function and structure of the secular social institutions.

All three forms of institutional religion performed important religious functions in traditional social life. First, they served the spiritual needs of the individual, in contrast to diffused religion, which focused its function upon the interests of the group, disregarding to a large extent the particular problems of the members as individuals. A member of a family might on occasions pray to the ancestors for his personal welfare, but the theory, structure, and collective rituals of ancestor worship were designed mainly for promoting the interest of the family group as a whole, without favoritism toward any particular individual. The same was true of diffused religion in social and economic groups, in the community, and in the state. This left ample room for institutional religion to serve the spiritual needs of the private individual. Thus, when an individual was in distress, he went to a diviner or sorcerer for advice and help; he went to a temple to pray; in prolonged and seemingly unrelievable misfortune he sought spiritual salvation and material relief through conversion to a faith (generally Buddhism or Taoism) outside the traditional orthodoxy and the secular institutional framework of life which had brought no deliverance to him as an individual. When the standardizing process of social institutions left unattended many problems of the individual resulting from the fortuity of circumstances, he was able to turn to institutional religion for assistance.

An equally important feature of institutional religion was the systematic development of theology, cultic practices, and organization under the efforts of a devoted, specialized personnel unencumbered by considerations of the secular institutional framework of life. Diffused religion always faced one major restriction in its development of the spiritual life: it was too intimately integrated with the utilitarian interests of the secular institutions. Religion under this restriction was confined to a finite view of the world. Without stimulation and help from institutional religion, with its devotion to the world beyond, religious life in traditional China might never have developed beyond the naïve, magical level of early classical religion. Because of its higher theological, cultic, and organizational plane, institutional religion was able to break through the finitude of the mundane world and make important contributions to the theology and functional cults of diffused religion in various secular institutions. Many of the modern Confucian interpretations of the ritualistic practices of the functional cults previously quoted clearly bore influences from Buddhism and Taoism. The development of diffused religion in China in its present form would not have been possible without contributions from institutional religion.

In these functions lay the vast importance of religion in the form of a separate institution. But in the general scheme of traditional social organization, the structural position of institutional religion was not commensurate with its functional importance. Under the dominance of diffused religion and the Confucian orthodoxy, institutional religion was forced into a weak structural position which severely restricted its direct influence on the operation of secular social institutions. The religious societies were a partial exception, in the sense that they possessed a strong internal organizational system, but their position in traditional society was seriously weakened by constant political persecution. The following pages will be devoted to the weakness of the social position of institutional religion in traditional Chinese society.

Priests of Classical Religion and Their Social Status

As an institutional religion, classical religion found its structural expression mainly in the group of practitioners who were actually the priests of the classical religion and whose social status revealed the structural position of classical religion in Chinese society.

While there were several categories of classical priests, the most important type throughout Chinese history was the *wu* or sorcerer, who worked magic and acted as a medium between the spirits and man. As in other early civilizations, sorcerers occupied a prominent social position at the inception of Chinese society. Oracle bones show the early priests to have been the literate members of society and the recorders of important events of state. Ancient literature such as *Kuo Yü* and *Tso Chuan* pictured them as having formal official positions in the state. In the Shang period the leading *wu* was "second to the chief of state," and early records show that at least two *wu* held the position of prime minister during this period. Even in the Late Chou period (sixth to third centuries B.C.), the *wu* still held official positions in the state and were frequently found participating in important public affairs. For example, one of the feudal princes had his sorcerer ferret out critics of his rule when his misgovernment had aroused widespread criticism. These early priests were in charge of vital religious functions such as divining for important actions of the state, helping to conduct great sacrifices, praying for rain, and exorcising evils from the community.

The rising influence of rationalism in the Late Chou period

marked the decline of the *wu* and of classical religion as an independent institution. The early classical religion was overwhelmingly magical in nature. The rise of rationalism repeatedly put its magical power to test, and the downfall of the *wu* came when they failed to prove the efficacy of their magic in the centuries of mounting sociopolitical disorganization. In this period, records show at least three interesting events. In the feudal state of Lu, the prince threatened to expose the sorceress under the hot sun for dereliction of duty when prayers for rain failed to achieve results, but her punishment was forestalled by an official who commented, "The sorceress is only an ignorant woman. What good will it do to expose her to the sun?" The prince of the state of Tsin killed a sorcerer when his prophecy proved wrong. In still another feudal state, a sorcerer was ordered drowned in the river for the failure of his magic. In this period a new word was added to the Chinese vocabulary, the word *wu,* meaning falsification, which is composed of two radicals, one meaning sorcerer and the other meaning speech.[3]

From the Late Chou period on, the theology and cultic practices of the classical religion were largely incorporated into the secular social institutions as a form of diffused religion. This was particularly evident with ancestor worship and the ethicopolitical cults. The cultic aspect of the classical religion became a part of Confucian sacrificial rituals. But the *wu,* who had played an important role in such religious acts, were largely displaced by leaders of the secular social institutions, who became the sole officiating agents in the sacrifices. Even as the custodians of technical skill in religious rituals, the *wu* failed to hold their own position against the competition from the new institutional religions, Buddhism and Taoism, from the third century on. In public religious rituals, it was increasingly the Buddhist and Taoist priests rather than the ancient sorcerers who were hired to help conduct the rituals and render magical service.

In the modern period priests of the classical religion continued to exist in the form of sorcerers, geomancers, diviners, and miscellaneous magicians. No longer did they wield direct influence upon group life by occupying a formal position in the social institutions. Their function was restricted to rendering various religious services to private individuals and groups whenever hired to do so. In the market place of every town, there were the inevitable diviners who sat behind a small portable desk, waiting to tell the fortunes of those cornered by the adverse circumstances of life or those who wanted to choose the best time or course of action for a new adventure. In urban neighborhoods and rural villages an occasional sorcerer or sorceress plied the trade of praying for others' well-being, curing sickness, exorcising evil spirits, and warding off misfortune. Some of them played the role of spiritual medium so that people could converse with the dead. The influence of the geomancers still pervaded in locating the most auspicious spot for graves and public as well as private buildings. In northern rural areas the widespread existence of sorcerers as magical healers of sickness in the 1940's was indicated by the Communists' anti-sorcery campaign, which charged the sorcerers with swindling. When the sorcerers themselves got sick, said the campaign literature, they did not rely upon their own magic, but went to medical doctors for treatment.[4]

The classical priests thus had intimate contact with the life of the people and enjoyed a considerable degree of functional importance. Their religious practices represented the part of ancient classical religion that continued to exist as a religious institution separate from the functions and structure of the secular institutions. But these practitioners carried on their trade mainly as individuals, not as members of an organized group. Even the geomancers, who, more frequently than other types of classical priests, had their own organization, worked as individual employees for clients, so that people seldom knew of their special organizations.

There is no statistical information on their possible number, but general observation seems to suggest that the classical priests numbered far fewer than the Buddhist and Taoist priests. Since their religious practices in the modern period were a paying trade, they showed little eagerness in propagating their skills, which were always carefully kept secrets. Consequently, there were not many neophytes coming into their circle. Their practice was often hereditary. If one of them wished to hand down his secrets to an outsider, he usually did not teach more than one or two pupils. Their total number could not have been very large, and the numerical base of their social influence was thus limited. In class status, with the exception of the geomancers, they were looked down upon by the people, and generally only those pressed by poverty entered this type of magical work.

Lacking an organizational system, small in number and generally despised by society, and regarded suspiciously by people as possible professional liars and swindlers, the classical priesthood occupied a very low structural position in the institutional framework of modern Chinese society. Their position sank lower as the impact of Western science nullified the magical power of their trade. Added to their structural weakness was the lack of an organized laity or following. An individual who patronized a classical priest for whatever personal purpose did so mainly on a single-encounter business relationship. When the requested aid had been given, the client left with no further obligatory tie to the priest. He might return for further service upon satisfactory results, and an effective diviner or magician might command a clientele, but the clients did not compose a formal organization resembling a congregation, nor did the laity of Buddhism and Taoism.

One may question how the classical priests managed to command a wide patronage when their magic was regarded with suspicion. An obvious factor was the lack of widespread scientific knowledge to enlighten the populace regarding the cause and effect of physical and social phenomena. As has been shown earlier, people used magical practices not so much because of their proven effectiveness as because of their psychological stimulation of hope and confidence at times when the best of human efforts was uncertain of success in surmounting a situation. The greater the difficulties in life, the more were people driven to magic and religion. The poorer the class, the more superstitious its members. Hence, in traditional Chinese society, where life was hard and the average man was beset with seemingly unsurmountable difficulties, there was no shortage of patronage of the classical priests in spite of doubts raised about their magic.

Weakness of the Structural Position of Buddhist and Taoist Priesthood

If the classical religion largely merged with the secular institutions, leaving only a certain part of its magical cults in an independent institutional status, Buddhism and to a lesser extent Taoism maintained their position as institutional religions. Their theology, cultic practices, and organization pursued a course of development separate from the secular institutions. Their independent status was especially clear with respect to their theology and organization. Confining our attention to the structural position of institutional religion in modern Chinese society, we will examine the situation of the Buddhist and Taoist priesthood.

In many historical periods, when prolonged disturbances or foreign rule caused a weakening of Chinese secular institutions and their diffused religion, people flocked in large numbers to the institutional religions for deliverance. Institutional religion developed a strong structural position which exerted direct influence upon various aspects of organized social life. This was especially true of Buddhism, which was less integrated into the function and structure of the secular institutions than was Taoism. During the Liao period in north China in the eleventh century, for example, Chinese social institutions were seriously weakened by foreign rule, and Buddhist influence became widespread in political, economic, and social life. A large priesthood, concentrated in numerous great Buddhist convents and temples, owned vast properties, including agricultural land and commercial firms like pawnshops, which became important credit agencies in the local communities. The Buddhists operated free schools and charitable organizations, which met the needs of the poor and the destitute.[5] But such periods were exceptions rather than the rule in the course of Chinese history over the past two thousand years. Since the Sung times, and especially in the nineteenth and twentieth centuries, both the functions and structure of Buddhism and Taoism have been markedly reduced.

SMALL NUMERICAL SIZE OF PRIESTHOOD   The weak structural position of institutional religion in the modern period is indicated first of all by the small size of the priesthood. To the traditional Chinese society in recent times, the term priest had the connotation of a legally recognized status, and it generally meant either a Buddhist monk or professional Taoist. A Buddhist monk had to be properly ordained, with an ordination certificate from the secular authorities. Professional Taoists fell into two types. One type had formal ordination, and the government granted them ordination certificates, as it did for the Buddhist monks. These Taoists lived in convents and came into contact with secular society only in the performance of religious services for individuals or social groups, aside from their necessary purchases of food in the market. The second type of Taoists gained their status by serving an apprenticeship of three years or longer under a Taoist master, which entitled them to membership in a local Taoist organization. They received no official ordination certificate but lived at home, practicing their magical trade as their sole or partial means of livelihood. Some of them had a secular trade as farmers, artisans, or small merchants, and would don their Taoist garb only for religious services.[6]

Because of the organized existence of the Buddhist and Taoist priests, there have been some rough estimates of their numerical size. For China as a whole in the twentieth century, Buddhist and Taoist priests were estimated to number from 500,000 to 1,000,000 persons, depending on the particular estimate.[7] Taking the Communist figure of 582,000,000 as the total population for the country in 1953, this means that between 0.06 and 0.17 per cent of the population were in the priesthood. There are also some local statistics on this subject. In Hunan province in 1933, for example, there were about 10,000 Buddhist and Taoist priests to the total provincial population of about 30,000,000, or about 0.0033 per cent of the population.[8] On the county level, Ting Hsien in Hopei province in 1927 had only 39 Buddhist priests among the county's population of 408,000, yielding the low ratio of less than one priest for every 10,000 population. Among the reasons for this particularly low ratio as compared with many of the richer southern localities is the poverty of the northern provinces and their limited ability to support a large priesthood.

There is no nationwide data for the nineteenth century to afford a comparison. In the chapter on government control (chap. viii) we noted the restrictions placed upon the growth of the priesthood through the requirement of ordination certificates, the limitation of training only one neophyte by one priest, the prohibition of proselytism, and similar obstacles. Under such circumstances, the priesthood was unlikely to have experienced any significant growth in the nineteenth century. Religious controls were greatly relaxed during the Republican period, but the strong trend toward seculari-zation brought about by contact with the West was a devastating counterinfluence, as witnessed by the wholesale confiscation of temple and conventual properties for secular use.[9] There is little indication that the priesthood gained any important growth during the Republic.

From the above figures, it seems clear that the priesthood could not develop strength in their social position through numerical size. A small priesthood at times can occupy an important functional position if they lead a large organized laity or perform strategic social functions. But the Buddhist and Taoist priesthood in con-temporary China did neither.

STRUCTURAL POSITION OF TEMPLES AND CONVENTS Temples and, with some exceptions, monasteries and cloisters were public places of worship, and they therefore represented the foci of collective re-ligious activities. One might expect that, as centers of religious life, temples and convents would be the primary units of a system of religious organization, with priests as the administrative staff and an organized laity as its membership. But the actual modern picture of temples and convents bore little resemblance to this expectation. The absence of an organized laity will be a subject for consideration later in this chapter. Here, we will examine the relation of the priesthood to temples and convents.

Absence of Priests in Most Rural Temples and Convents The first notable fact was that there were no priests in most of the religious establishments. Many religious establishments bearing the labels of *ssu* (Buddhist monasteries), *an* (Buddhist nunneries), *kuan* (Taoist monasteries), and *nü Tao yuan* or *nü Tao kuan* (Taoist cloisters for female ordained Taoists) had become common temples for public worship, with or without priests in them.

Many educated Chinese were not aware of the absence of priests in most of the temples and convents, particularly in north China. This was the condition in the northern county of Wang-tu in Hopei province during the early years of the twentieth century:

Frequently a village reported having more than ten temples, leading us to wonder about the large number of heretic cults among the people. But careful investigation showed that most of the so-called temples were merely small shrines just large enough to hang a picture of the god . . . Even the well-known temples as recorded in the local gazetteer are mostly without any priest to take charge of the affairs. The local gentry simply hire a common laborer to maintain the temple property. . . .[10]

Ting county in the same province had 104 temples (excluding small shrines) but only 39 Buddhist and Taoist priests in 1928. Most of the temples had no priest in attendance. On special religious occasions, such as the birthday celebration for the chief god of a temple, a priest would be hired for the event. During ordinary times, the village temples were usually empty, with an occasional worshiper coming in to burn incense and pray, and with the villagers maintaining the temple property.[11] Among the 570 temples in Wanchuan county in Chahar province in 1948, only four or five, or less than 1 per cent, had priests in attendance.[12] Even in the southern county of Ch'uan-sha in the vicinity of Shanghai, only 17 of the 94 temples had priests in them.[13]

The absence of priests in most of the temples is a significant fact, for it indicates that religious activities, even those centered around the temples, were conducted by the people themselves without priests in the guiding role, attesting to the weakness of the structural position of the priesthood in organized institutional religion.

Small Number of Priests in Staffed Temples and Convents A second significant fact is the small number of priests in those temples that were staffed. In Wang-tu county each staffed temple had an average of only one or two priests. The 17 staffed temples in Ch'uan-sha county had a total of 42 Buddhist and Taoist priests, averaging 2.5 priests each. Table 5 shows the average number of priests per staffed religious establishment in Pao-shan county in the vicinity of Shanghai in 1921; except for one cloister, the tem-

TABLE 5

Average Number of Priests in Each Temple or Convent
in Pao-shan County, Kiangsu Province, in 1913

RELIGIOUS ESTABLISHMENTS	NUMBER OF ESTABLISHMENTS	TOTAL NUMBER OF PRIESTS IN ALL ESTABLISHMENTS	AVERAGE NUMBER OF PRIESTS IN EACH ESTABLISHMENT
Temples	44	75	1.7
Buddhist monasteries	55	140	2.5
Buddhist convents	32	78	2.4
Taoist convents	27	106	4.0
Female Taoist convents	1	11	11.0

Source: *Pao-shan hsien hsü-chih* (Supplementary Gazetteer of Pao-shan County) (1921 edition).

ples and convents averaged under five priests. Table 6 shows the frequency distribution of staffed temples and convents according to the number of priests in Hunan province in 1933. Here, one-third of all temples and convents had only one priest, one-half of them had three or less priests, and 79 per cent had five or less. Larger establishments were few in number and only two Buddhist monasteries in the whole province of 33,000,000 population had more than 100 monks.

These statistics confirm the general observation that most staffed temples and convents had no more than two or three priests, and that those having a large colony of priests were rare. Temples and convents were the primary units of organization of the priesthood. Since most of these basic units, which had the broadest contact with the religious life of the people, were so small as to have less than three priests each and were without the support of an organized laity, it would have been very difficult for them to develop a strong structural position in the general scheme of social organization and

TABLE 6

Number of Priests in Each Temple or Convent
in Hunan Province in 1933

NUMBER OF PRIESTS	BUDDHIST MONASTERIES	BUDDHIST NUNNERIES	TAOIST CONVENTS	TEMPLES	TOTAL
1	69	3	9	4	85
2	34	3	4	5	46
3	21		1	3	25
4	20	1	2	3	26
5	15	3		3	21
6	11	1			12
7	8				8
8	7		2	1	10
9	3	1		2	6
10	2				2
11–20	14	1		1	16
21–30	5	2	4		11
31–40	2			1	3
41–50	4				4
51–60	2				2
81–90	1				1
101–110	1				1
111–120	1				1
Total	220	15	22	23	280

Source: *Hunan Yearbook* (1933), pp. 837–856.

exert a prominent influence on the major organized aspects of social life.

Lack of Centralized Organization Among the Priesthood   While a well-organized network of small but interconnected basic units can develop an influential structural position among social institutions, this was not the case with the modern organization of institutional religion in China. The primary units, the temples and convents, were not only small but were also lacking in centralized organization of any significant size and any effective hierarchical structure.

In actual operation, each temple or convent functioned largely as an autonomous unit.

Buddhism in the Ch'ing period did not have even a nominal national headquarters. There were nationally prominent monasteries located in various celebrated mountains such as the scenic hills of Hangchow, the Omei Mountain in Szechwan, and the T'ient'ai Mountain in Shansi, some of the establishments claiming to be the custodian of the theological tradition of certain Buddhist sectarian schools. But these great Buddhist establishments were only pilgrimage centers for the laity and wielded their influence over monks of the same sect in other temples and monasteries chiefly through their theological prestige, possessing no hierarchical authority over them. Theological prestige influenced only a small number of learned monks, as the religious knowledge of most of the monks did not go beyond the rote memory of the popular sutra and the commandments. In Wanchuan county of Chahar province, for example, the priests of some temples were unable to identify by name some of the gods of the temple or to tell whether they belonged to the Buddhist or the Taoist faith. The theological influence of prominent religious centers on such priests would be practically nil.[14]

The existence of these prominent centers did not alter the autonomous status of the individual temples and monasteries. The abbot of a monastery was selected by consensus of the monks of that monastery, with participation from abbots of outstanding convents in the same locality, and at times from local community leaders. The latter were especially influential if the convent had few or no priests.[15] Should a new temple be built by the secular community, a head priest would come by invitation from the community leaders and recommendation of senior priests in the locality. This procedure for setting up the chief authority of a temple or convent remained largely unchanged in the Republican period. Once installed, the head priest, with or without subordinate priests under him, administered the religious and economic affairs of the temple or convent without any compulsory superior religious authority from the outside.

Occasionally Buddhist priests formed associations in local communities. An example was the Ho-nan Hui (Harmonious South Association) in Hsin-ning county of Hunan province, which had about 100 members in 1933.[16] Such associations were in the nature of trade guilds designed for the regulation of the performance of religious services, chiefly sacrificial rites for the dead. In spite of their rather strict regulations for the membership and the rendering of religious services, the organization was based on the free affiliation of individual members, and in no way interfered with the operation of temples or convents as autonomous units.

The Republican period saw the rise of a number of local and national organizations of Buddhists, including both ordained priests and laity, for the general promotion of Buddhism. Aside from the All-China Buddhist Association, some 25 local Buddhist associations sprang up in Hunan province alone during the 1920's, generally with a membership of under 100 each, but some attracting over 1,000 members.[17] Similar associations were common in other provinces in the 1920's and 1930's, but these were likewise free associations of individual members, having no hierarchical authority over temples and convents, either administratively or financially. From their rise in the 1920's until the outbreak of the total Japanese invasion in 1937, these Buddhist organizations had less than two decades in which to develop their functions, so that the long accumulation of structural weaknesses of Buddhism as an organized institution, coupled with the secularizing influence in modern Chinese society, prevented any success in building an effective national religious structure.

The same applies largely to the Taoist priesthood. Taoism had a nominal national leader in the office of Chang T'ien-shih (Chang the Heavenly Teacher), the so-called Taoist pope. The imperial government gave him a staff of assistants and invested in him the task of helping to suppress rebellious heresy (chap. viii). The famed Pai-yün Kuan (White Cloud Convent) in the vicinity of Peking claimed supremacy over the Taoist priesthood in the northern provinces,[18] and there was a long-standing contention for national leadership between these two Taoist centers. But what each center actually wielded was theological and magical prestige, not hierarchical authority. Administratively and financially, the individual Taoist temples and convents in the country were autonomous.

Like the Buddhists, Taoist priests at times had local associations in the nature of trade guilds. One of these associations in the vicinity of Canton was still operating in 1949 to regulate apprenticeship requirements for the local Taoist priesthood and the distribution of their services. The association had no name, obviously to avoid the attention of the authorities because of the tradition of political persecution of organizations of this nature. But its headquarters were in the village of Sha-chiao in the southern suburb of Canton, and priests of many temples as well as Taoist magicians were members. Such associations were common in other southern provinces like Hunan. Functioning chiefly to regulate remunerative religious services, these local organizations of Taoist priests were not a strong religious structure influencing various organized aspects of social life, nor did they alter the basically independent status of the individual temples and convents.

With unstaffed temples and convents, whether Buddhist or Taoist, the administration of religious affairs and the management of endowed properties were in the hands of secular community leaders, as will be elaborated on. In view of the fact that most temples and convents in the countryside belonged to this category, organized institutional religion, with a priesthood as its backbone, played only a limited role in the total religious life of Chinese society.

Financial Position of Temples and Priests It is apparent that in order to develop extensive functions and a strong structural position, religious organizations, like any social organization, would need an adequate financial foundation. In periods when Buddhism was an important factor in public life, a substantial financial position was a concomitant condition. But a striking characteristic of institutional religion in modern China was its inadequate financial support and the inability of the clergy to control financial resources. Temples and convents with large endowments under clerical control existed, but they were few in number and far from representing the general picture.

The economic foundation of a temple or convent lay in its endowment, usually in the form of agricultural land but occasionally in buildings in the case of urban temples. Both land and buildings yielded rent as income for the maintenance of the temple and the support of the priests, if any. Donations of money for the yielding of interest were sometimes given, but very often such money would eventually be used to purchase real property, mainly because of the merits of stability and comparative ease of management.

Some sample data on the landed property of temples and convents are available. In the northern county of Wang-tu, for instance, there are figures on the property owned by 39 of the major temples, as tabulated in Table 7. The county gazetteer gives the useful informa-

TABLE 7

Amount of Agricultural Land Owned by 39 Staffed Convents and Temples in Wang-tu County, Hopei Province, in 1905

NUMBER OF MOW *

OWNED	CONVENTS	TEMPLES	TOTAL
1–5	3		3
6–10	4	4	8
11–20	6	3	9
21–30	2	1	3
31–40	4	4	8
41–50	1	1	2
51–100	3	2	5
260	1		1
Total	24	15	39

Source: *Wang-tu hsien hsiang-t'u t'u-shuo* (Illustrated Gazetteer of Wang-tu County) (1905 edition).
* 1 mow = 0.1647 acre.

tion that the land in this locality was relatively unproductive, and that those families possessing less than 20 mow (about 3½ acres) belonged to the poor class, those having 20 to 50 mow belonged to the middle class, those owning 50 to 100 mow were well-to-do, and those with over 100 mow were considered wealthy.[19] Regrouping the detailed data according to these criteria, we find 20 temples and convents, or 51 per cent of the total, had less than 20 mow; 13, or about 33 per cent, had 21 to 50 mow; 5, or 13 per cent, had 51 to 100 mow; and only one, or 4 per cent, had 260 mow. This means that half the temples and convents had an endowed property capable of supporting only one family on the level of the poor class; one-third had enough land to support a family of the middle class; and only 13 per cent had property in the category of a well-to-do family. The lone case of a Buddhist monastery, Ku-kuo Ssu (State-Strengthening Monastery), having 260 mow of land, was due to its being a government-endowed institution; its god had given efficacious blessing for the suppression of a rebellion.

The gazetteer of Ch'uan-sha county (1936 edition) gives the property data for five temples and twelve ancestral halls, as shown in Table 8. The land in this southern community was rich and

TABLE 8

*Amount of Agricultural Land Owned by Staffed Temples
and Ancestral Halls in Ch'uan-sha County,
Kiangsu Province, in 1936*

NUMBER OF MOW OWNED	TEMPLES	ANCESTRAL HALLS	TOTAL
1–5	2	4	6
6–10	1	2	3
11–20	2	2	4
21–30		1	1
101–150		2	2
450		1	1
TOTAL	5	12	17

Source: *Ch'uan-sha hsien chih* (Gazetteer of Ch'uan-sha County) (1936 edition), chüan 12, pp. 1–26.

productive. Of the five temples, two having under 5 mow of agricultural land belonged to the category of poor families, and three with 6 to 20 mow belonged to the status of middle-class families.

The two samples show that about one half of all temples and convents had the property status of a poor family, and that the larger part of the rest belonged to the economic category of middle-class families. Wealthier establishments were exceptions. When the average temple or convent in these recorded accounts had enough property to support only a family of the lower or middle class, the financial resources could defray only the cost of subsistence of one to three attending priests, as these were average figures for staffed temples or convents. This left no financial means for elaborate religious services or the performance of extensive functions in organized community religious life.

Furthermore, in both samples, temples and convents having a record of property in the gazetteers constituted only a part of all the recorded temples. In Wang-tu, the gazetteer listed a total of 116 temples and convents, out of which 39 or 33.6 per cent had an account of their property. In Ch'uan-sha, out of 132 temples and convents (exclusive of ancestral halls) listed, only five or 3.8 per cent had records of their property. What happened to the other records is an unanswered question. There is a distinct possibility that the temple property which the gazetteers did not record was not too large, for the property of a wealthy temple was a notable object in the eyes of the local authority and there was little chance of its not being recorded. But general observation tells us that a large number of temples and convents in the countryside had no property, and this might have been the case with a large proportion of the temples and convents having no property records. In fact, this would help explain the number of temples which had no priests, for there was no income-yielding property to support them and other sources of religious income proved insufficient for their sustenance.

Under these circumstances, only the priests of a few well-endowed temples and convents could lead an exclusively religious life by drawing on income from institutional property for sustenance. The livelihood of most priests had to depend on or be supplemented by one or all of three sources of income: small donations from worshipers in the form of "incense and oil money"; remuneration for performing religious services for individuals and groups; and secular occupations or trades. In Hunan province a large proportion of the Taoist priests had secular occupations, their magical services bringing only a supplementary income.[20] Even though the temple agricultural land was the equivalent to that owned by a poor or middle-class family, the rent from it alone might not be sufficient to support the priests, for rent represented only a part of the total yield of the land. That meant the priests would have to devote most of their time to farming the land, working like any other farmer, so as to get the full yield, thus having only limited time for religious life. In Ting county in Hopei province, for instance,

The twenty-four Buddhist monks in the county farmed on the temple land in normal times, while occasionally they went on calls to mourning families to conduct services for the dead . . . There were fifteen Taoist priests in the county . . . who also tilled the land in ordinary days, and at times went to mourning families to render religious service.[21]

Thus, the priests and the institutional religion they represented faced severe financial limitations in the development of any prominent structural position in the general scheme of social organization. It is interesting to note that, in comparison, many forms of well-developed diffused religion such as ancestor worship enjoyed adequate financial support. There was seldom an ancestral hall without endowed property for its maintenance and the sacrificial rites. Table 8 shows that most of the twelve ancestral temples in Ch'uan-sha county had property equivalent to that of poor or middle-class families, but three of them had more extensive possessions than those of any temples of institutional religion in that locality. The ancestral temples had no professional priesthood to support, and the maintenance of ancestral halls and the expenses of sacrificial rites had priority in using the income from the endowed property. If the income proved insufficient for such purposes, the members of a clan always were ready to make a contribution or to take up a levy to supplement it. A successful son of a clan was generally expected to come home and renovate or build an ancestral hall or give a substantial endowment for carrying on its functions. To be able to perform such an act was the consuming ambition of many worthy sons of the traditional clans.

Temples of social and economic groups, such as the Lu-pan temple of the carpenters' guild in Ch'uan-sha county, and many temples of ethicopolitical cults, such as the Hsüan-wu and Confucius temples, had extensive property endowments, to which social groups or the state were ready to contribute whenever there was a special need. Moreover, cults of diffused religion were often carried on in homes or in the meeting quarters of social groups who did not set up temples, thus avoiding a heavy item of expenditure. In any case, by being a part of organized secular institutions, diffused religion was better financed and more adequately staffed than was institutional religion.

More light can be shed on the position of institutional religion in the general scheme of social organization by examining the sources

TABLE 9

Sources of Donations for the Building, Reconstruction, and Renovation of Temples and Convents in Ch'uan-sha County, Kiangsu Province

SOURCES OF DONATION	FOR BUILDING AND RECONSTRUCTION			FOR RENOVATION			
	Temples	Buddhist convents	Taoist convents	Temples	Buddhist convents	Taoist convents	Total
Local officials	2						2
Local officials in coöperation with gentry and merchants	1			2			3
Single individuals	1	2	1	17			21
Public subscription in local community	8	1	5	13	8	5	40
Public solicitation by priest		1		3	3		7
Religious organization				1			1
Guilds	1						1
Total	13	4	6	36	11	5	75

Source: *Ch'uan-sha hsien chih* (Gazetteer of Ch'uan-sha County) (1936 edition), chüan 12, pp. 1–26; chüan 13, pp. 1–10. Temples and convents in this table existed in 1936, but most of them were built, reconstructed, or renovated during the latter part of the nineteenth and the early part of the twentieth century.

of donations for the founding or renovation of temples and convents. Examples in three southern counties (Tables 9, 10, and 11)

TABLE 10

Sources of Donations for the Building, Reconstruction, and Renovation of Temples and Convents in Pao-shan County, Kiangsu Province

SOURCES OF DONATION	FOR BUILDING AND RECONSTRUCTION			FOR RENOVATION			
	Temples	Buddhist convents	Taoist convents	Temples	Buddhist convents	Taoist convents	Total
Single individuals	2				1		3
Public subscription in local community	5			1	4		10
Public levy					1		1
Public solicitation by priest		1		1	1		3
Guilds	1						1
Total	8	1		2	7		18

Source: *Pao-shan hsien chih* (Gazetteer of Pao-shan County) (1921 edition), chüan 5, pp. 23–31. Temples and convents in this table existed in 1921, but most of them were built, reconstructed, and renovated during the latter part of the nineteenth and the early part of the twentieth century.

have a common characteristic, namely the dominance of secular sources of donations. Most of the temples and convents drew donations from general community money-raising projects organized by secular local leaders. A sole donation from a single individual accounted for the founding or renovation of a sizable number of religious establishments. Donations in this category were from wealthy men or women who gave generously either because of religious piety or because of the belief that divine assistance had helped them to avert disaster, gain a fortune, or beget a male heir. Typical were persons who made large donations because of a warning received in a dream which saved them from going on a boat that sank or to a building that burned. As in many other cul-

TABLE 11

Sources of Donations for the Building, Reconstruction, and Renovation of Temples and Convents in Lo-ting County, Kwangtung Province

SOURCES OF DONATION	FOR BUILDING AND RECONSTRUCTION			FOR RENOVATION			Total
	Temples	Buddhist convents	Taoist convents	Temples	Buddhist convents	Taoist convents	
Local officials	9			5			14
Local officials in coöperation with gentry and merchants					1		1
Public subscription in community	13			2			15
Public solicitation by priest	2						2
Total	24			8			32

Source: *Lo-ting hsien chih* (Gazetteer of Lo-ting County) (1935 edition), chüan 2, pp. 1–7. Temples and convents in this table existed in 1935, but most of them were built, reconstructed, or renovated in the latter part of the nineteenth and the early part of the twentieth century.

tures, wealthy individuals were similarly important in the financial support of religious enterprises. Even in cases of collective contributions from the community, a few wealthy individuals and families gave a far larger share than their number. In the rebuilding of the Taoist convent, Ch'un-yang Kuan, in Ch'uan-sha county in 1932, for example, Table 12 shows that 20 per cent of the donors, each contributing $100 Chinese currency (about $33 U.S. at the exchange rate of that time) or more, gave 73 per cent of the total fund.

Donations from local magistrates alone or in coöperation with the gentry and merchants were not many; their gifts were limited to Buddhist or Taoist temples of some ethicopolitical significance. This particular source of funds, however, was important in Lo-ting county in Kwangtung province. Deep in the southern mountains in the territory of the non-Chinese Miao and Yao peoples, magis-

TABLE 12

Sizes of Donations for the Reconstruction of the Taoist Convent,
Ch'un-yang Kuan, in Ch'uan-sha County in 1932

Sizes of donation *	Number of donating families	Total contributed	Cumulative total
$300–800	1	$2,660	$2,660
200–299	2	410	3,070
100–199	13	1,382	4,452
50–99	13	815	5,267
11–49	25	503	5,770
1–10	41	320	6,090
Total	95	$6,090	$6,090

Source: *Ch'uan-shah hsien chih* (Gazetteer of Ch'uan-sha County), chüan 13, p. 6.

* In Chinese currency, roughly three dollars for each U.S. dollar at the rate of exchange in 1932.

trates there had the special duty of popularizing Chinese social institutions, and the building of temples was one way to spread Chinese culture.

Only in a few cases did funds for the construction or renovation of a temple in China come from public solicitation led or sponsored by priests, or from religious organizations. Funds usually came individually or collectively through secular sponsorship. Occasionally a monk or a Taoist priest solicited from door to door for funds to build or renovate a temple, and now and then there was a monk whose prophetic words and magic aroused extremely generous impulses among the people.[22] But such cases were rare. In the above-mentioned three counties, only one temple was renovated from funds of a religious organization. This was a Taoist temple, Tung-yo miao (East Peak temple), in Ch'uan-sha county, which was refurbished in 1907 by a Taoist organization, the Shen-tao Hui (God's Principle society), which used the temple as headquarters for meetings and worship.[23] If we keep in mind the traditional suppression of organized religious groups, we can see that the financing of construction or renovation of temples by religious organizations would be necessarily rare, and often disguised from public view. The chief temple of the Yellow Heaven sect in Wanchuan county of Chahar province was built and maintained by a monk and his sectarian members,[24] but cases of this type were exceptional.

In the southern county of Pao-shan the funds for the renovation or major repair of one temple came from taxing all families in the village where the temple was located. This method of financing the repairs of a temple was rather common in north China, generally for temples having little or no property of their own, in which case the temples were regarded as community property. In the village of Han-chia Chuang in Wang-tu county of Hopei province, for instance, "there were six temples, all having no property, and in case of financial need for repairs the funds came from taxing all families in the village according to the amount of land owned by each family."[25] The same situation was found in Ting county of Hopei province.

Such temples in north China were almost all part of the ethico-political cults belonging to the general category of diffused religion intimately connected with secular social institutions. There was no compulsory support for the temples or priests of distinctively independent faiths such as Buddhism. The tithing system of medieval England, which gave the Christian church there a strong economic foundation, did not develop in China. Even in north China, where compulsory levies were made, the money was devoted to building and maintaining the temples themselves and at times to defraying the cost of public religious services such as temple fairs, but not to the support of the priests and the development of their religious position.

Since the property of most temples and convents came from secular sources, it might be expected that the priests did not have much control over the temple property, and such was usually the case. Thus said Gamble of the temples in Ting county:

The temples seemed to be relatively independent units. Most of them had been erected by the people living in the village. The building was financed sometimes by popular subscription, sometimes from village funds, occasionally by an individual who had acquired wealth and wanted to do something for his native village. When built, the temple was dedicated to the deity who offered the type of protection the people felt they needed or who personified the characteristics they honored and revered. Priests were in attendance only for special services. These priests had had, of course, the official Buddhist or Taoist training.[26]

Investigation of temples in Wanchuan county of Chahar province revealed substantially the same situation.[27] In general, the village leaders constituted an informal board for the control and administration of the temple property and its income. This was necessary, since most of the temples and convents had no priests. Even when there were priests in attendance and when they were permitted to farm the temple land for sustenance, the final control of the property was vested in the village leadership.

Secular control over temple property was shown in the increasing trend toward using it or its income for nonreligious purposes. An example was the account of the disposal of property income of 39 temples in Wang-tu county in 1905 (Table 13). In 1904, when the development of modern education was a new issue and money was needed for this purpose, the imperial government issued a general order to use temple property wherever available for the estab-

TABLE 13

Uses of Income from Temple Lands in Wang-tu County,
Hopei Province, in 1905

TYPES OF USES	NUMBER OF CASES (temples and convents)	PERCENTAGE
Operation of schools	18	48.0
Corvée expenditure	4	10.0
Support of priests, temple caretakers, maintenance of temple, and operation of schools	5	12.0
Support of priests, temple caretakers, temple maintenance and repairs	7	18.0
Unsettled	5	12.0
Total	39	100.0

Source: *Wang-tu hsien hsiang-t'u t'u-shoh* (Illustrated Gazetteer of Wang-tu County) (1905 edition).

lishment of schools. The result was that nearly one-half of the 39 temples had their income from property devoted to school operation. The item of *corvée* expenditure referred to the traditional conscription of unpaid labor from the villages for public works, for which each village was assigned a quota according to the size of its male adult population. When the call from the government came, it was quite common for a village to pay the cash price of such labor to the government so as to free the villagers from the burden of labor. Income from community property, including temple land, was often used for such purposes. As shown in the table, only seven, or 18 per cent, of the 39 temples in Wang-tu county had their income from property devoted entirely to the support of priests and the maintenance of the temples. Five temples, or 12 per cent, had income from property divided between the same purpose and the operation of schools.

The use of temple property and its income for various community purposes was quite common in all parts of China, especially in north China, where the population was poorer than in the southern part of the country. In the early 1920's, when Sun Yat-sen needed money to finance his revolutionary government, he expropriated the property of a large number of temples in Canton for the purpose. The Nationalist government in the 1930's issued regulations permitting the expropriation of temple property for schools and for public charity.[28] By the 1930's numerous temples in all parts of the country had been converted into schools, offices for local government and other public organizations, and temporary barracks for troops. To be sure, the priests in many large convents had administrative control of their temple property, but their control lacked final authority. All temple properties under the Ch'ing as well as the Republican governments were required to be registered as public property and were regarded by the officials as such. There was no legal protection against expropriation by the government.

Thus, what limited endowed property the temples and convents had came largely from secular sources, and in the twentieth century was largely under the control and administration of secular agents who diverted it to a variety of purposes, of which religion was only one, frequently a minor one. It was the exception rather than the rule to find a temple or convent having heavy endowments and supporting a sizable number of priests who had full control of the property for the development of religious functions for themselves and for the secular community. Except for secret religious societies, there was no central religious organization which received financial contributions from local units and which could subsidize the founding of new units or the maintenance of old ones.

Lack of Organized Laity

It has been indicated that the structural position of institutional religion was weakened by, among many factors, the absence of a broad organized laity. Exceptions were the religious societies and the so-called *chü-shih* or devotees. The membership of religious societies was well integrated into an organized system under a hierarchy of officers ordained in accordance with the society's rules. Devotees had definite association with a single faith, generally Buddhism or Taoism, and they usually maintained affiliations with priests in certain temples or convents. While there is not even an estimate on the size of membership in the religious societies throughout China, there were some 4,000,000 devotees (mainly Buddhists) in the country in the 1930's.[29] One thing is certain: the membership in both groups accounted for only a tiny minority of the total population.

The secular population at large lacked any formally organized relationship with the priests and temples or convents. If the well-known facts of religious life in China are analyzed, the first striking characteristic is the general absence of any membership requirement for worshiping in a temple or convent. With the exception of a few convents which were closed to the public, anyone could enter a temple or convent to pray, to make a vow, to seek divine guidance, or to conduct any other type of worship without restriction. There was no special identification marking him off as a member who worshiped in a certain temple. The priest in the temple might or might not know him. After performing the religious rituals, the worshiper generally paid the attending priest for the incense and for oil for the sacred lamp; the making of this payment discharged any further obligation between the worshiper and the priest. The worshipers enjoyed no stable, binding tie with the temple or the priest. An important factor in this connection was the absence of priests in most temples and convents, and thus the absence of any active agent uniting the worshipers into an organized body.

The polytheistic factor in the Chinese religious tradition led laymen to worship in different temples of different faiths on different occasions. To obtain a male heir, a layman might go to a Buddhist temple to pray to the goddess of mercy or the goddess Niang-niang; but to pray for the return of his health, he might go to a temple dedicated to the Taoist patron of medicine, Hua-t'o. Selection of a temple was guided not by faithful attachment to a single religious faith, but by the reputed magical efficacy of a certain god for a certain purpose. Thus, the polytheistic tradition and the dominance of the magical factor in Chinese religious life prevented the development of an organized laity for a particular temple, with its priests as an integrating nucleus.

Aside from the priests and the temple, few factors operated to unite the laymen as a functioning religious group. Worshipers attended the temple individually or occasionally as a family, but not collectively as an organized group. Each went at a time most convenient to him. Friendship or other types of social relations might develop in the temple as a meeting ground, but these did not usually lead to the development of a religious organization. There was no regular meeting of the laymen where group identification and solidarity among worshipers could develop. In mass religious events, such as temple fairs or the celebration of the birthday of a patron god, large numbers of people went to the temple at the same time. But in such cases, a particular cult had become a part of the organized community life or of a secular social institution, and the crowds were part of the secular institutional framework and not an independent religious group.

If polytheism and the functional nature of magic were contributing factors to the general lack of a stable bond between laymen and priests as well as among laymen themselves, it must be remembered that organized religious followings were suppressed throughout the Ch'ing period and, to a lesser extent, even in Republican times. Temple priests commanding a following of organized laity would have been interpreted by the imperial government as a potential rebellion, and religious circles were well aware of such interpretations, as this had been consistently demonstrated by periodic persecutions. Even proselytizing was prohibited under traditional law. In the Republican period, when the oppressive laws were relaxed, Buddhist, Taoist, and sectarian societies mushroomed in various parts of the country, all with some form of organized following. But the three decades following the beginning of the movement after World War I constituted a relatively short period full of interruption by civil wars, so that there was a general paucity of adequately educated leadership in the new religious movements. Consequently, there was no substantial alteration of the traditional pattern of an unorganized laity.

To realize the full significance of the absence of an organized laity, we may contrast this with the tradition of church affiliation in Europe and in the early years of certain of the American colonies, when everyone belonged to a church denomination, when such affiliation was an identifying mark not only of a religious bond but also of a social and economic relationship within a communal group.[30] A well-organized laity was an important source of the once strong functional and structural position of the Christian church in European and American societies. Reduce the laity to unorganized individuals, and it would have been difficult for the Christian church to develop the influence it had on secular social institutions.

Some Limitations on the Functional Position of Institutional Religion

Institutional religion in contemporary China was restricted not only by its structural weaknesses, as evidenced in the small and noncentralized priesthood, the limited financial resources, and the lack of an organized laity, but also by many limitations on its organized position in the structural framework of traditional Chinese society. Among the limitations were the restricted position of the priesthood and the monastic orders, the lack of priestly participation in the formal educational system, and the weakness of institutional religion in the ethical system. By contrast, in the history of Christianity in European society were the factors of the strong functional position of the Christian priesthood and its hierarchical organization, the role of the Church in the development of formal education, and the influence of Christianity on the Western ethical system.

LIMITATIONS ON THE SOCIAL FUNCTIONS OF THE PRIESTHOOD AND MONASTIC ORDERS   Between the third and the tenth centuries, when institutional religions such as Buddhism and Taoism were strong, the priesthood and the monastic orders performed extensive social and economic functions,[31] thus affecting the general developments of the time. But from the T'ang period down to the modern age, the chief direct social functions of the priesthood and the monastic orders were reduced to offering a refuge for disillusioned individuals and providing some degree of security for a small number of the economically destitute.[32]

Entrance into priesthood as an escape from frustrations in secular life were a traditional safety valve for Chinese society, and the monastic orders in this sense represented a structural addition to the Chinese social order. This escape was important even for members of the well-to-do class and sophisticated intellectuals whose most pressing concern was not material subsistence but the fulfillment of social ambitions. The Confucian pattern of social organization provided no specially organized device to place those individuals who could no longer find a satisfactory role in the secular world. Few were those who could find contentment in the Confucian conception of fate and could continue the struggle on behalf of posterity while knowing that all doors to realistic success in one's lifetime were shut. Here, priesthood in a monastic order, particularly that of Buddhism, offered a ready answer for those who wished to forget the past and start life again in a new world.

Thus, many a thwarted statesman, a frustrated scholar, a bankrupt merchant, a jilted lover, a person who had failed to withstand the onslaught from life, even the successful outlaw who had failed to find satisfaction in his accumulated loot and in his vengeance against society, would suddenly waken to the futility of the struggle and "flee into the door of emptiness," the traditional phrase for conversion to Buddhist priesthood. In traditional fictional literature, such as the celebrated *Red Chamber Dream,* one of the standard actions for the hero or heroine confronted by insurmountable difficulties or insoluble conflicts was to take refuge in Buddhism. With impressive ritualistic foreswearing of all secular social ties, one walked into a secluded world of meditative quiet where he could contemplate the futility of the ephemeral mundane life in the light of eternal religious truths, and where he could commiserate with the brotherhood of fellow refugees who had also come to seek escape from the perplexities of the "world of dust and noise." Inside this secluded sphere operated another set of motivations, laws, and a routine of life leading to eternal salvation for the truly pious. Herein lay the ideal order of life capable of banishing all the crises and ills of secular society.

The providing of such a peaceful retreat for those shipwrecked in life performed a stabilizing function for the secular social order. But such a retreat was available to only a small number of people, for several reasons to be mentioned later. The limited size of the modern priesthood was testimony to the fact that in a world in which the struggle for life was hard and the cases of failure were many, relatively few chose the road of priesthood as a solution. Buddhism and to a lesser extent Taoism were of wider influence on the many who remained in the world. The sense of eternity that dwarfed the vicissitudes of the mundane world helped to stabilize fiery emotions or stayed hands overeager in the pursuit of life. In the twilight of life, most sophisticated persons acquired a Buddhistic tinge of futility in their attitude toward the world. "At the end [one's own death], all becomes empty." Above all, Buddhist altruism and universal pity gave significant reinforcement to the Confucian virtue of benevolence. Thus, institutional religion attained importance through the diffusion of its theological doctrines among the populace, and not by the functional position of its priesthood.

Priesthood and the monastic orders claimed a large number of converts from socially and economically helpless individuals, giving them in effect not so much spiritual as material salvation. Thus, most of the priests came from poor families or were orphans and widowers, without intimate family ties. One source said that 60 to 70 per cent of the nuns were women who entered the cloister for lack of any other alternative.[33] There is no statistical information on monks, but general observation by students of Chinese religious life pointed toward a similar situation. Priesthood and conventual life served as a religious brotherhood for those who failed to derive support from the kinship system. At the base of the functionally diffused social organization was the kinship system, and at the top was the state. But between the family and the state there were not many intermediary groups to attend to the needs of those individuals whose kinship ties were inadequate or had broken down and whose interests were not cared for by the political system of the traditional state. The traditional Chinese language has no equivalent for the word society; beyond the family was the term *kuo-chia* (state-family), which stands for the concept of the state as well as the greater society. In the Confucian teaching, one's moral duty lay in achieving perfection for the individual, the family, and the state, with no systematic consideration for intermediate social units between the family and the state.

The monastic order fulfilled an important social function as an extrafamilial group. This was why the monastic orders drew their members mainly from the poor class, in which families were too poor to support many individuals or were broken because of the death of the breadwinner. Judging from the general prevalence of poverty in a preindustrial society such as the Chinese, especially in times of political disorder and economic crisis, one would have expected that a far larger number would have joined the priesthood than actually did.

That the priesthood was so small was due to several reasons. The leading one was political restriction, which purposively restrained the growth of the priesthood and the monastic orders to prevent the rise of competitive centers of power. The poor financial condition of the convents was a severe limitation on the number of priests that could be admitted. It was rather common for nunneries to require a sizable financial contribution as the price of admittance. A widow who joined a nunnery might contribute the inheritance left her by her deceased husband.

The Buddhist vow of foreswearing one's own kinship and all other secular ties proved difficult for many, unless the last ray of hope was gone. The severing of kinship ties was particularly hard for a people to whom the family assumed such basic personal and social importance. Other social ties might be fraught with obstacles and frustrations, but they were also channels of success in the struggle for status and privilege. The Buddhists had long derided man for his willing self-enslavement to the "rein of fame and the lock of material benefits." The few who were able to forsake all secular social ties had surmounted a tremendous psychological crisis. This may provide a partial explanation for the fact that an appreciable number of the priests in monastic orders had been given as children by their parents or relatives to be raised in secluded surroundings where religious values could be inculcated in place of secular values.

The generally low social status of priests in traditional society was an obstacle to the growth of the priesthood, for ordination into monastic life represented no improvement of social status for the poor and it meant class degradation for members of the middle and upper classes. To be sure, a learned Buddhist or Taoist priest ranked with the scholars as members of the elite in traditional China, but these were few in number and exceptions to the rule. Observers of Chinese social life early in the twentieth century noted that a family would be despised by the community if Buddhist and Taoist priests came to call frequently in addition to performing religious services.[34] A nineteenth-century admonition to the members of a clan contained this passage:

As the proverb goes, "A reputable family is one which has no smart servants in its halls, no flowers in its garden, nor Buddhist or Taoist priests coming to call." Recently people have associated with Buddhist and Taoist priests, nominally in order to obtain male heirs and a long life [through religious worship]. Little do they know that such social association might lead to the collapse of the family reputation. Neither should nuns be allowed to enter the homes, for as Chu Hsi has said, females priests are the medium for licentiousness and thievery.[35]

One effect of the low social esteem of priests was that the common people were discouraged from joining the priesthood unless there was no alternative. The lowering of social status also deterred many intellectuals from taking the vow of priesthood, thus depriving institutional religion of a supply of educated leadership in its struggle for an influential position in society.

A number of possible factors contributed to the low class status of the priesthood. A dominant one was the antagonism to heterodoxy held by the government and by the Confucian doctrine which had a controlling influence on social values. Repeated persecutions of priestly religion also led people to shun the company of priests, for fear of inviting trouble from the authorities. Forsaking of family and secular social ties was definitely a factor in conflict with the secular social values, especially since to gain esteem a man was required to have a large family. The traditional disdain for the discredited classical priests, especially the sorcerers, reflected upon the relatively newer Buddhist and Taoist priesthood. Finally, most of the priests were poor and ignorant men from the lower social class.

Because of these political, economic, and social limitations on the priesthood and the monastic orders, a large number of people who felt the need of religious salvation became secular devotees or joined religious societies, in spite of the frequent persecution of the latter. There was no open ceremony of ordination to attract official attention, no ordination certificate to be obtained from an antagonistic government, and no limitation of membership, such as the legal restriction of only one pupil to one instructing priest. The number of people who could join religious societies was not restricted by the size of endowment, as was the case for the priesthood in a temple or convent. Each member of a religious sect had his own livelihood. As the leaders generally lived on membership contributions, the more members there were, the better off would be the leaders and the more could the organization afford to expand. That was why the traditional government was always wary about the collection of dues from members of a religious organization, for this might enable the organization to grow to uncontrollable proportions. Members of religious societies could remain with their families, keep their social ties, and continue the pursuit of their secular ambitions and interests. Membership in religious sects did not usually affect one's own social status, partly because many societies drew their members from the same class. If many respectable people traditionally shied away from participation in such groups, they did so because of the political danger involved rather than any class stigma. Persecution was indeed an ever-pending hazard. But, as was pointed out before, the chance of evading police attention was good, making it possible for many religious societies to grow into extensive organizations. As a part of institutional religion, they represented a stronger factor in traditional society than did the organizational units of legitimate and open religions such as Buddhism and Taoism.

LACK OF PARTICIPATION IN COMMUNITY CHARITY Universal religions are dedicated to the general alleviation of human sufferings; hence, extensive charity work has been one of the channels through which religious organizations in many cultures have established their functional position and influence in the secular community. We see this in the Christian church and its missionary enterprises in non-Christian lands. We also see it in the work of the Buddhist organizations in periods of Chinese history when they enjoyed a relatively unhampered development and wielded appreciable social influence. Extensive community charity work was a well-known feature of Chinese Buddhism between the third and the tenth centuries, with large numbers of people partly dependent upon its assistance in critical times.[36] Taoist organizations in their thriving periods gave relief to the needy and participated in the construction of public facilities like roads and bridges.

But the modern Buddhist and Taoist organizations, like Chinese religious societies in general, showed a singular lack of participation in charitable work. In contemporary times, it was a regular part of the function of the local magistrates, in coöperation with the gentry and merchants, to establish and maintain institutions for the care of orphans, widows, the aged, and the disabled. Though always inadequate to accommodate the large number of cases, such undertakings were a regular part of secular government and community leadership, with little participation from religious organizations. The dispensing of free medical aid, free drugs in times of epidemics, free rice, porridge, and clothing in the winter and in famine, and free coffins and burial plots for the poor was sponsored and organized by secular social leaders. Information on such activities abounded in the local gazetteers. In Ch'uan-sha county, for example, the Chih-yuan T'ang, the headquarters for all county relief work, was renovated and charity endowments were increased in 1898 so as to strengthen its activities in helping orphans, widows, and the aged and in giving free burial plots, medical aid, rice, and clothing to the needy. The 63 contributors who donated agricultural land and houses to the foundation included 3 officials and 60 private individuals and families, but no priests or religious organizations. Among the 107 contributors of money to the work of renovation, 41 were private individuals and families, 36 were shops and stores, 3 were local officials, but again none were priests of religious organizations.[37] This tradition of secular sponsorship of charity and relief work without appreciable participation from religious organizations continued in the Republican period. In the town of Yüeh-p'u in Pao-shan county near Shanghai, relief work for the famine of 1920 and for civil war destruction in 1924 was exclusively organized by the local gentry and merchants.[38] In 1929 a central organization for charity was set up in Changsha, the provincial capital of Hunan, by combining many formerly independent charity organizations such as the home for the aged, the widows' home, the orphans' home, the orphans' school, and the community granary. New financial support came partly from the old foundations for each of the units, and partly from a small additional levy on the sale of salt in the locality.[39] Both the sponsorship and the financial resources of the undertaking were exclusively secular in nature, with no religious organizations participating. Similar instances could be multiplied indefinitely in all parts of China.

Lack of participation in community charity work was an obvious consequence of the weak organizational and financial position of Buddhism and Taoism. With financial endowments hardly sufficient to keep the priests alive, they themselves were the objects of relief instead of being in a position to give aid to others. In fact, alms seeking by mendicants was an important tradition of Buddhism. The emphasis on self-salvation kept most of the monks and

Taoist priests from engaging in charity enterprises as a part of religious duty. Indeed, the universal salvational spirit of Mahayana Buddhism and the belief in *chi-yin-teh* (accumulating virtues for better existence in the other world) contributed strongly to the benevolent motivation and almsgiving by the average Chinese, but this represented theological and cultic influence from Buddhism rather than structural influence from the Buddhist organization. As an organized religious force, Buddhism's lack of participation in community charity work definitely reduced its functional position in secular society.

LACK OF PARTICIPATION IN SECULAR EDUCATION   Scholars of Chinese religion have occasionally noted the lack of participation of priests in the Chinese educational system.[40] This is in striking contrast to European history, where modern educational institutions stemmed from the church's educational function, where medieval monasteries were centers of learning, and where monks were teachers when kings and nobles were illiterates, and education and political power were separate. It took the Renaissance to remove the task of education from the Church. In the early United States, denominational schools were frequently the precursors of the public school system. Even today, the influence of priestly education in the Christian world is considerable.

This educational function of religion did not develop in China. By the early Chou period, priests had been eliminated from education, and the *ju* or Confucians had taken over the educational function in grand style. Long before Ch'ü Yuan, one of the fountainheads of Taoist mysticism, exclaimed in his eternal poetic lines, "The Tao [metaphysical principle] can be caught but cannot be taught," Confucius was preaching to his disciples that one of the three joys of life was "to gather all the talented in the land and educate them."

The Master's words were faithfully followed by all subsequent generations of Confucians, whose primary occupation outside of officialdom was teaching pupils. Education became a veritable Confucian monopoly. Without education as its propagating agent, the establishment of Confucianism as the great orthodoxy of the land would have been difficult if not impossible. Education, furthermore, was made a condition of political power. But in this development, religion and the priests were left out of the educational system.

Even in Confucius' lifetime, the secularization of education was apparent, for there was little religion in the six classical subjects of education: rites, music, archery, chariot-driving, writing, and mathematics. From the Han period on, the state examination system, the gateway to officialdom, did not include religion as one of the subjects in which the candidates for power and status were examined. Learned priests, however well informed on religious subjects, were excluded from the examination halls, which were the portal to fame and political influence. Occasionally a distinguished secular scholar, purified of social and political ambitions, became a priest.

Most of them ignorant and many illiterate, the Buddhist monks and Taoist priests in the contemporary period had no qualifications as teachers. On rare occasions a learned priest might tutor a pupil on secular literary subjects with resounding success, but priests did not operate schools, not even free schools for the poor, as the Buddhists had done during the Liao dynasty in the northern part of China.

Thus, without a place in the educational system, Buddhism and Taoism, the two major forms of institutional religion in China, were deprived of one of the most effective vehicles for propagating religion to the minds of the young, and were kept from developing an influential status in the political and social structure through the state examinations. This, of course, is not to ignore the learned quality of these two great religions, as attested by their voluminous Tripitaka. But the vast Buddhist and Taoist literature concerned only purely religious subjects and stood apart from the secular literature, thus failing to become an important part of the educational material of laymen. Aside from the Moslem religion, which never became fully integrated into the Chinese culture, Christianity was the first major institutional religion that took an active part in education and cultural enterprises. But, as modern history has shown, this did not take place without considerable friction with the Chinese political authorities, particularly in the 1920's and the 1930's, when nationalistic sentiments reasserted the tradition of secular sponsorship of education.

LACK OF ORGANIZED AUTHORITY OVER MORALITY   The functional importance of religion in the moral order of traditional Chinese society has been stressed frequently in this work. But in connection with the structural weakness of institutional religion in China, it is necessary to bring this point up again to illustrate the fact that the functional importance of religion was not always accompanied by a strong structural position in society. The function of religion in the moral order of society lay mainly in providing sanction for ethical values that stemmed mainly from secular sources. Religion itself was not the chief source of the traditional ethical system, and institutional religion had no organized authority to enforce social morality. This situation is in contrast to the Christian church before the seventeenth century, when it was said that "social morality is in the province of the Church, and [all sectarian groups] are prepared both to teach it, and to enforce it, when necessary, by suitable discipline." [41]

SUMMARY: A DECENTRALIZED PATTERN OF RELIGIOUS LIFE

From the above data and discussion, we see that religion as a separate social institution in China emerged in a highly decentralized pattern. As an organized body, modern institutional religion had a very small priesthood, divided into minute units of two or three priests each, largely unconnected with each other. It had barely enough financial resources for subsistence for this scanty personnel. It was deprived of the support of an organized laity. It faced a number of limitations in the development of social functions by the monastic orders. It did not participate in various organized aspects of community life such as charity, education, and the enforcement of moral discipline. There was no powerful centralized priesthood to dominate religious life or to direct operation of the secular social institutions. Each Buddhist or Taoist temple or convent was to a large extent an independent unit of religious organization, frequently with its own complement of gods and its own interpretation of theological themes, even though the temples might bear the same name and worship the same chief deity.[42] Consequently, no centralized priesthood dominated the religious life of either the priests or the people. In this sense, institutional religion was free from hierarchical control.

The lack of a powerful priestly religion did not mean the weakness of religious influence in social life. The Chinese common people, especially the women, hardly passed a day or faced a crisis without resorting to religious assistance. Burning incense to the house gods in the morning and evening, going to the temples to pray on numerous public and private occasions, visiting a classical priest for divine guidance on big or little problems, attending temple fairs and religious festivals, consulting the religious sections of the almanac for an auspicious time for making a major or minor move, and reflecting on the supernatural influence on life and the universe—all these added up to an intimate relationship between religion and life under the traditional social order. Yet all these activities proceeded without the organized direction of any priesthood. People visited a particular temple, worshiped a particular spirit, called on a particular priest, all in accordance with the practical function of religion for the particular occasion. To what religion a temple or a god belonged might be a puzzle to many academicians, but such questions had no functional significance in the religious life of the common people. Hence, weakness in the structural position of institutional religion was not synonymous with the functional weakness of religion in social life.

Religion under such a decentralized pattern derived its organized strength largely by serving the secular social institutions under the form of diffused religion. By diffusing itself into the secular social institutions, religion, its theology, its gods and spirits, and its rituals, received organized support from the institutional framework of traditional society and exerted systematic influence on the life of the people, whose activities in life were grouped around the major institutions. By functioning as a part of the social institutions, religion became a pervading influence without having a strong independent structure itself.

XIII

THE CHANGING ROLE OF
RELIGION IN PRE-COMMUNIST
CHINESE SOCIETY

IN THE PREVIOUS DISCUSSION of each aspect of Chinese religious life, recent developments have only been touched upon. It remains for the present chapter to summarize the broad trends of religious development during the modern period from the latter half of the nineteenth century to the current Communist rule.

A notable event of the modern age has undoubtedly been the trend toward secularization, which has weakened the influence of religion in many strategic aspects of Chinese social life and has particularly affected the views of the modern educated Chinese intellectuals, with whom social and political leadership rested. On the other hand, we witness the persistent influence of religion in the life of the common people. Before the Communist accession to power, the continued belief in Heaven and fate, the most basic element in Chinese religion, was indicated by the ubiquitous presence of all varieties of diviners in the country, and by the wide sales of the old Almanac, containing mostly chronomantic guidance for the conduct of life. The complex pantheon of functional gods that operated as the long arm of Heaven and fate still retained a strong hold on the people's mind. It is, therefore, necessary to examine the factual situation in the religious life of the common people as well as the trend toward secularization, which together made up the religious picture of the modern period, particularly during the Republic, in which so many critical social changes occurred.

CONSTRUCTION AND REPAIR OF TEMPLES IN THE MODERN PERIOD

Temples are centers of public worship, and their construction and repair are an indication of the continued vitality of functional gods in the life of a community. The building of new temples may slacken in modern times, but major repairs and renovation serve to retain the usefulness of the old ones. Statistical information in Tables 14

TABLE 14

Number of Temples Founded in Different Periods in Hunan Province

PERIODS OF FOUNDING	NUMBER OF TEMPLES
Before Ming	24
Ming (1368–1644)	52
Ch'ing: 1644–1849	68
1850–1911	22
Republic (1912–1928)	15
Total	181

Source: *Hunan nien-chien* (Hunan Yearbook), (1933), pp. 837–854.

to 19 is based on records from one provincial yearbook and five local gazetteers. Information on the original founding and major repairs or renovation is given only for the larger temples, which constitute only a small portion of the total number of temples in these localities. The information, nevertheless, gives an indication of significant happenings in the religious life of different periods.

The tables represent three types of areas. Table 14 gives data for a regional unit, a province. Tables 15, 16, and 17 give data for three local communities in the vicinity of a great modern city, Shanghai, with its growth of wealth and modern materialistic influences. Tables 18 and 19 give data for two inland counties, one in the north and one in the south, both relatively poor and distant from centers of modern social and economic influences. Unfortunately, there is no comparable information on the situation within the cities, which are the very centers from which modern influences radiated.

TABLE 15

Types and Number of Temples Founded and Repaired in Different Periods in Ch'uan-sha County, Kiangsu Province

	SOCIAL ORDER								
PERIODS OF FOUNDING	Family (ancestral halls)	Community	State	Moral order	ECONOMIC FUNCTION	HEALTH	GENERAL WELFARE	CONVENTS	TOTAL
Ming (1368–1644)				2				1	3
Ch'ing: 1644–1849	5						1		6
1850–1911	15		3	1	7		5	3	34
Republic: 1912–1925	6				1				7
1926–1936	3								3
Total	29		3	3	8		6	4	53
Periods of major repairs or renovation									
Ming (1368–1644)									
Ch'ing: 1644–1849									
1850–1911		2	2	9	6	1	21	3	44
Republic: 1912–1925	3	2	2	4	1	1	7	5	25
1926–1936	1						4		5
Total	4	4	4	13	7	2	32	8	74

Source: *Ch'uan-sha hsien chih* (1936 edition), chüan 12 and 13.

TABLE 16

Types and Number of Temples Founded and Repaired in Different Periods in Pao-shan County, Kiangsu Province

PERIODS OF FOUNDING	SOCIAL ORDER								
	Family (ancestral halls)	Community	State	Moral order	Economic function	Health	General welfare	Convents	Total
Ming (1368–1644)				1				1	2
Ch'ing: 1644–1849								1	1
1850–1911	2		1		2		1	8	14
Republic: 1912–1925					2		1		3
1926–1936									
Total	2		1	1	4		2	10	20
Periods of major repairs or renovation									
Ming (1368–1644)								1	1
Ch'ing: 1644–1849	2	5	3	9	3	2	7	4	35
1850–1911		1	1	3	2		6	5	18
Republic: 1912–1925									
1926–1936									
Total	2	6	4	12	5	2	13	10	54

Source: *Pao-shan hsien hsü chih* (1921 edition), chüan 3, pp. 17–20; chüan 5, pp. 8–23.

TABLE 17

Types and Number of Temples Founded and Repaired in Different Periods in Yüeh-p'u Township of Pao-shan County, Kiangsu Province

PERIODS OF FOUNDING	SOCIAL ORDER				ECONOMIC FUNCTION	HEALTH	GENERAL WELFARE	CONVENTS	TOTAL
	Family (ancestral halls)	Community	State	Moral order					
Before Ming (1368–1644)			1					2	3
Ch'ing: 1644–1849			1	1			1		3
1850–1911			1	1			1		3
Republic: 1912–1925									
1926–1936									
Total			3	2			2	2	9
Periods of major repairs or renovation									
Before Ming									
Ming (1368–1644)									
Ch'ing: 1644–1849			1						1
1850–1911		1	2				1	2	6
Republic: 1912–1925							5		5
1926–1936			1	3					4
Total		1	4	3			6	2	16

Source: *Yüeh-p'u li chih* (1933 edition), chüan 4, pp. 5–7.

TABLE 18

Types and Number of Temples Founded and Repaired in Different Periods in Lo-ting County, Kwangtung Province

PERIODS OF FOUNDING	SOCIAL ORDER			Moral order	ECONOMIC FUNCTION	HEALTH	GENERAL WELFARE	CONVENTS	TOTAL
	Family (ancestral halls)	Community	State						
Ming (1368–1644)			4	5	2		4	3	18
Ch'ing: 1644–1849			6	4	1		1	2	14
1850–1911		1			1		3	1	6
Republic: 1912–1925									
1926–1936									
Total		1	10	9	4		8	6	38
Periods of major repairs or renovation									
Ming (1368–1644)				1					1
Ch'ing: 1644–1849			3	2		1	4	1	11
1850–1911			1				2		3
Republic: 1912–1925									
1926–1936									
Total			4	3		1	6	1	15

[346]

Source: *Lo-ting hsien chih* (1935 edition), chüan 2, pp. 1–16.

TABLE 19

Types and Number of Temples Founded and Repaired in Different Periods in Wang-tu County, Hopei Province

PERIODS OF FOUNDING	SOCIAL ORDER							CONVENTS	TOTAL
	Family (ancestral halls)	Community	State	Moral order	ECONOMIC FUNCTION	HEALTH	GENERAL WELFARE		
Before Ming									
Ming (1368–1644)			1						1
Ch'ing: 1644–1849			1					2	3
1850–1911									
Republic: 1912–1925									
1926–1936									
Total			2					2	4
Periods of major repairs or renovation									
Before Ming									
Ming (1368–1644)									
Ch'ing: 1644–1849			5	3	1		1	3	13
1850–1911			1						1
Republic: 1912–1925									
1926–1936									
Total			6	3	1		1	3	14

[347]

Source: *Wang-tu hsien chih* (1934 edition), chüan 3, pp. 32–41.

The division of historical periods, particularly the recent ones, is based on major events affecting the number of temples. Relatively few existing temples trace their original founding before the Ming dynasty, which began in 1368. This is due in part to the damp climate of the coastal regions, especially in the warm south, which caused deterioration in the wood and brick structure of most of the temples. The Ming dynasty was a prominent period of temple building as a part of the nationwide cultural restoration from the extensive destruction by the Mongols. The dynastic change from Ming to Ch'ing was not attended by extensive temple destruction, and the construction of temples continued at normal rates throughout the Ch'ing period. The great Taiping rebellion of 1850, motivated by zeal against idol worship, leveled a large number of temples, but after the rebellion was put down the building of new temples and the reconstruction of old ones proceeded steadily until the end of the Ch'ing dynasty in 1911. During the early years of the Republic (1912–1925), the number of temples built compared favorably with the number constructed in a similar length of time in previous periods. It was not until the full strength of the Second Revolution, together with its antireligious movement, made itself felt after 1925 that the pace of temple building and repairs noticeably slowed down, but it by no means discontinued. This was the general picture in Hunan province, in the rich counties of Ch'uan-sha and Poa-shan, and in the town of Yüeh-p'u in the latter county, all in Kiangsu province (Tables 14 to 17).

The situation in Lo-ting county of Kwangtung province in Table 18 was different in that little building and repair of major temples were done after 1850, and none in the Republican period. The northern county of Wang-tu in Hopei province (Table 19) presented even a sharper contrast, for available records show that the few major temples in that district were founded in or before the Ming period and that none were built in the three centuries during the Ch'ing period and the Republic. Most of the major repairs were done in the Ch'ing period before 1850, and none during the Republic. This, however, does not indicate that there had been no recent building or repair of minor temples and small shrines in either of these districts, for the gazetteers included only major temples. Nor was the lack of construction and repair of major temples a sign of the collapse of popular worship in large temples, for the people could worship in these places in spite of their disrepair.

A common feature among all these localities is that the temples and convents of the modern period were the result of over six centuries of gradual accumulation rather than the product of any single period. This is particularly clear in the even pace of major temple building in Hunan province (Table 14). In the modern period the difference in the rate of construction and repair of temples between Ch'uan-sha and Pao-shan counties (Tables 15, 16, and 17) on the one hand and Lo-ting and Wang-tu counties (Tables 18 and 19) on the other was due to historical events and economic circumstance. One thing is certain: the lack of temple building and renovation in the two inland counties is unrelated to the modern secularizing influence, which arose only in the twentieth century.

Both Ch'uan-sha and Pao-shan counties were in the path of advance of the Taiping rebels, and there was fairly extensive destruction of temples. The obviously incomplete records of the gazetteers show that 16 out of 65 major temples and convents, or roughly one-fourth of the total in Ch'uan-sha county, were entirely leveled.[1] In Lo-tien town of Pao-shan county, 16 out of 45 temples were reduced to ruin.[2] The consequence was a pronounced increase in temple building and repairs in the period 1850–1911 in both counties. While certain counties in Hunan province were similarly affected by the rebellion, with the probable result of a period of temple restoration, such effect is averaged off in the broader base of statistical figures of the province as a whole (Table 14). But neither Lo-ting nor Wang-tu county was the scene of fighting and destruction in the Taiping rebellion, and the general absence of major temple construction in the two districts since 1850 was partly due to this fact.

But there is also an economic factor to be considered. Both Lo-ting and Wang-tu are inland agricultural counties where the fertility of the soil is generally poor and the productivity of the economy is relatively low, thus seriously limiting major construction or repairs.

The editor of the 1934 Wang-tu gazetteer, in surveying the dilapidated appearance of the county's temples, remarked on the lack of
financial means for their renovation.[3]

In contrast, both Pao-shan and Ch'uan-sha are part of the metro-
politan area of Shanghai, sharing in the tremendous economic
growth of the city in the last century. Successful men in business
and in other walks of life made sizable donations to projects of
temple building or renovation. Even the common people had sufficient economic surplus to engage in collective projects of temple
construction. The Lu-pan miao (temple of the patron god of
carpentry and masonry) in Ch'uan-sha county was built in 1899;
one was built in Pao-shan county in 1906, and another in the same
locality in 1916, all by the construction trade guilds whose members became prosperous from building the rapidly growing city of
Shanghai.[4] The notorious Shanghai racketeer, Huang Chin-jung,
donated sizable sums to the refurbishing of a large temple in P'u-t'o
Shan in the 1930's. A gambling boss in Canton, Ho Ju-fa, invested
a part of his loot in founding a small Buddhist temple in a village
20 miles south of that metropolis in 1948. Examples are inexhaustible
in which people enriched by the economy of modern cities became
principal donors to the building and repair of temples and convents.
This shows that modern cities as centers of secularization had only a
limited effect on the common people's attitude toward religion. That
the wealth of modern cities was used for places of worship is one of
the notable conclusions to be drawn from these tables.

The data in Tables 15 to 19 show no consistent concentration of
construction or repair of temples in any single functional category.
Instead, they appear to have been dispersed irregularly among all
the categories. In view of this, and considering the small size of the
statistical samples, the tables give the impression that all functional
categories of temples retained a fair amount of vitality in the modern period as shown by the continued building of new temples and
major repairs to old temples. There are some exceptions to this
observation. While the building and repair of temples of the fertility and marriage cults related to the family seemed to be rare, the
founding and upkeep of ancestral halls (or ancestral temples) remained an active undertaking down to very recent years in the

southern communities, and was limited only by available economic means. Of the gazetteers used in these tables, only that of Ch'uan-sha county contained a detailed account of the ancestral halls, and it bears witness to this observation. If modern influences affected the ancestral cult among the intellectuals, it remained among the common people. In the southern villages, if the vast majority of ancestral temples were at least a half-century old, an occasional new one could still be seen in communities where a fortunate son had scored an unusual financial success; and the ancestral temples have been better maintained than most of the other types of temples.

Temples were built and repaired either by permanent organized social groups or by temporarily organized community campaigns or individual efforts. Thus ancestral temples were built or repaired by the family groups; the temples of patron gods by trade guilds; and temples of official ethicopolitical cults by the government. Such temples were a part of diffused religion in these social institutions. The continued building and repairing of ancestral temples not only showed the persistence of religious influence in the family institution but also indicated the vitality of the family in the traditional pattern which regularly included the religious element. The same applied to the building of temples of patron gods by the trade guilds in the twentieth century. Burgess' study of guilds in Peking in the 1920's [5] showed that only a small proportion of the guilds had succumbed to the modern trend toward secularization by discontinuing the worship of patron cults; most of the guilds continued to function in the traditional pattern by retaining their cultic worship. But the increasing transformation of the guilds into modern chambers of commerce and labor unions in the late 1920's and the 1930's was accompanied by the elimination of the traditional cultic element in the structure and functioning of the new organizations. The discontinuation of official ethicopolitical cults and consequently the lack of official building and repair of their temples during the Republican period had the same significance as the decline of the traditional political institution with which it had been associated.

Temples that were not part of formally organized social groups but existed for general public worship were built or repaired by community subscription or occasionally by individual donors. The cults in such temples were kept alive mainly by public belief in the magical efficacy of their gods. The efficacy of a god, we must assume, depended on fortuity of circumstance. If for some time no one had received an effective answer to his prayers, it was considered that the spirit or god had departed from that temple, and the temple ceased to draw worshipers; its incense urns no longer spiraled smoke, and its altars became buried in layers of dust. Such a temple might fall into ruin; but it might be revitalized if perchance someone's prayers in the temple were answered and others later had the same good fortune in matters such as health, wealth, or the bearing of a male heir. Or the temple might be revivified by the spreading of a mythological story. Either situation might lead to the renovation of a dilapidated temple or the building of a new one to house the resurrected god. The power of a myth is illustrated in the renovation and the adding of a new wing to the Yung Shou Kung (Longevity Convent) in Lo-tien town of Pao-shan county.[6] In the convent was an idol of Lord Yang, who was deified in the fourteenth century for extraordinary performance of official duty; however, this god had long been forgotten by the local people. One day a traveler from a distant locality came into town, looking for a Mr. Yang. The neighbors told him that there was no one in the vicinity bearing such a surname. The traveler insisted that a healer had come to his home and cured a member of his family who had been near death. The healer had refused any remuneration, leaving only his surname and his home address, which was this town. The local people decided that this must have been the spirit of Lord Yang showing its efficacy. The traveler worshiped in the temple with incense and candles and departed. As the miracle story spread, the community organized a festival in honor of the god's birthday. Large numbers of worshipers were now constantly in the temple, and finally the public decided to renovate the structure.

Although this took place in the nineteenth century, similar incidents occurred in different parts of the country down to the Republican period, accounting for the repair of many old temples. The magical factor was important in the unorganized popular cults, and the length of life of their temples depended much on the demonstration of magical efficacy. The repairing of many old temples of unorganized cults was a part of this process of the rise and fall of the functional gods. If a temple was favored by chance, in the sense that from time to time someone among the large number of worshipers had his prayers fulfilled, the magical prestige of the god was maintained and the temple continued to exist. On the other hand, if such fortune happened only infrequently and there was no miracle story in circulation, the number of worshipers might drop, thus progressively reducing the numerical base of the chance for good luck and leading finally to the decline of a temple.

In addition, there was the continual emergence of new cults, leading to the establishment of new centers of public worship. The nineteenth century still saw the deification of many men who had performed unusual deeds, leading to the establishment of temples dedicated to them, as in the case of the two garrison generals in Chekiang province (see chap. vii). The deification of public leaders died out as a cultic tradition during the Republic, but miracle stories of other varieties continued to rise in various localities, giving birth to new gods and spirits. In the 1920's in Ting county of Hopei province, there was the tale of a sick man who was told in a dream that he should make a drink from the bark of a certain old tree at the edge of a village. He did this and got well. The story spread; others stricken with sickness did the same, and some got well. Soon the tree became a busy shrine, bedecked with many banners presented by grateful worshipers to exalt the magical power of the tree god.[7] While temples to tree gods were encountered frequently in various parts of the country, most of the local miracles gave rise to new cults housed in small, obscure shrines unrecorded in the official gazetteers. Nevertheless, miracle stories were common in China throughout the Republican period, giving rise to new local cults housed in small shrines which played a more intimate and vital part in the common people's life than did many of the impressive temples of official cults, like the temple of Confucius, in which religious activities were restricted to the small ruling class.

THE RISE OF MODERN RELIGIOUS MOVEMENTS

In addition to the building of new temples and the repair of old ones, the early twentieth century also saw the rise of many major and minor religious movements. In the light of the lesson of history, the general social setting was conducive to the development of religious movements. In one century, China as a nation had suffered a series of humiliating military defeats and was hard pressed by a host of influences from the Western world, which had demonstrated its competitive superiority over the Chinese culture. This resulted in, among many things, a sharp sense of national insecurity and inadequacy, of which the intellectuals were particularly conscious because they had to justify their own status as the nation's ruling class. Internally, the country was plagued by continual destructive civil strife, spreading economic deterioration, and social disintegration. This caused further national insecurity and an increase in personal hardship and misfortune for the masses. In the midst of social calamities and personal crises, the routine utilitarian factors that had held social groups together were shattered or became too weak to orient the individual toward the group. The individual, now loosened from weakened traditional group ties, tended more to fend for himself than to take part in institutionalized group life. The once-dominant Confucian orthodoxy and the traditional pattern of social institutions proved grossly inadequate in the new situation.

These circumstances were conducive to the development of popular movements stemming from notions of superhuman powers, miracles, and a host of other supernatural ideas and phenomena that transcended the limits of man's earthly abilities and efforts to wrestle with overpowering situations. In a society long pervaded with religious influence, such movements easily captured attention at a time when people could find no solution to a pressing situation, when men searched hard for a new orientation to life which would alleviate their anxiety, deliver them from suffering, and redirect their outlook toward a common bond. Similar conditions—the threat of foreign influence from without and spreading chaos from within—had brought about the expansion of the Buddhist and Taoist movements in the period of disunion. And similar times, in shorter interludes between major dynasties, had set a variety of religious movements afoot. Now, once again, a similar situation faced the Chinese people, and it would have been a surprise if some sort of religious movement had not emerged to take its familiar role in the historic scene.

The whole series of minor religious movements in the first half of the nineteenth century, the great Taiping rebellion of 1850, and the Boxer rebellion of 1900 were all religious responses to the socio-political crises in the declining period of a dynasty. In the Republican period, political chaos, ineffective government, and some democratic premises injected into the old concept of power converged to relax traditional control over organized religion, thus giving religious movements a further opportunity to develop among all social classes. Hence there was a movement to convert the Confucian orthodoxy into a religion among the intellectuals, there was the attempt to revitalize Buddhism into an organized national movement, and there were the large number of local and national sectarian movements which were once dreaded by the imperial authorities and a primary target for suppression. The religious movements of the nineteenth century have been analyzed in the previous chapters. W. T. Chan has rendered an excellent account of the religious movements in the Republic in his *Religious Trends in Modern China*. The present discussion is limited to sociological interpretations of what is already well established as history.

The Confucian Religious Movement

The first major national movement in the early years of the Republic was the attempt by some Confucian scholars to convert Confucianism into a systematically organized religion. One significant feature of this movement was that it represented a collective effort to strengthen the Confucian orthodoxy and to justify the position of Chinese civilization in the face of the superior power of the Western world, which had invaded China with the Christian religion as its vanguard. The Confucian movement was clearly a product of the political crisis, and religion was invoked as a means of reasserting the position of a once-unchallenged national tradition in the midst of an increasingly fierce ideological struggle. The Confucian scholars, the intellectual elite of the nation, had more at stake in the struggle than did any other social group because of the responsibility of their traditional political leadership and because of the unmistakable threat to their position. The fact that it was Confucian political reformers like K'ang Yu-wei who led the movement, rather than prophets and mystics, indicated the causal relationship between the effort to establish a Confucian religion and the national political crisis.

But this movement went little beyond the colorful polemics which stirred the intellectual atmosphere for less than a decade, during which time the Chinese leaders tried to find a road to a new social order in an age of revolution. Aside from a short-lived organization that included a national headquarters, a number of local associations, and the sporadic performance of ritualistic sacrifice in front of the Confucian altar, there was little success in mobilizing mass action or in establishing a new system of theistic religious life. No new theological view of Confucianism and no fresh supernatural inspiration developed because there was no mystic prophet among the leadership. Cultically, there was no renewed attempt to make a god out of Confucius, and there was no innovation in the age-old ritualistic sacrifice, the vitality of which was already drained by the changing times. Structurally, there was no well-organized and well-financed leadership that would offer its full time and zeal to the task of systematically building up the movement. At best, the movement must be regarded as an abortive attempt to strengthen the religious factor in Confucianism as an institutionalized orthodoxy, for it was essentially an effort to revitalize a national faith so as to save the traditional ethicopolitical order for the hard-pressed Chinese civilization. The entire episode showed no characteristics of the beginning of a new institutional religion.

It is interesting to recall that the attempt to make a religion out of Confucianism was not new. A notable research by Ch'en Shou-i has shown that there was a similar attempt some three centuries ago, at a time when the nation was troubled by political strife and misgovernment under the rapidly tottering Ming rule, and when

Catholic Christianity was gaining strength as a new and foreign orientation to life. At that time Wang Ch'i-yuan attempted to promote Confucianism as a religion, regarding Confucius as a prophet sent by Heaven and Confucianism as a comprehensive system that covered all problems concerning "Heaven and earth and all things that exist," a system beyond the ability of man to devise. Wang's movement was intended explicitly to meet the challenge of the rising tide of Christianity among the intellectuals.[8] On theological grounds, Wang went farther than the modern K'ang Yu-wei. But, like its contemporary counterpart, the movement rested as a largely forgotten episode in the pages of history, leaving no trace in the institutional framework of Chinese society.

The causes contributing to the failure of the modern movement to make a religion out of Confucianism are fairly obvious. The Confucians who filled the ranks of the movement were traditionally antagonistic toward organized religious systems as an independent force in the ethicopolitical order. Now, when their views were being broadened by an initial acquaintance with European civilization, the lesson of the Western struggle between Church and state was held up as a warning by opponents of this movement, which ostensibly aimed at the establishment of a "national religion." This was clearly the argument in numerous articles such as Ting I-hua's "Will the Evil of Religious Struggle Emerge in China?"[9] which appeared in newspapers and periodicals in the early years of the Republic, when the movement was a heated issue among the intellectuals.

This movement to strengthen the religious aspect of Confucianism as an institutionalized orthodoxy suffered from the disadvantage of diffused religion, which depended on the vitality of the secular institution for its functional development and existence. When a secular institution is seriously weakened and proves incapable of meeting the needs of a new situation, its religious component is likely to lose its structural basis of operation. Confucianism as an institutionalized orthodoxy proved to be inadequate as the foundation of a new ethicopolitical order in a modern world dominated by democratic social and political trends. Its stifling ritualism, its authoritarianism, its intimate association with the

monarchical political system, all lost favor with the younger generation of intellectuals who were emerging to take command of a new
phase of Chinese history.[10] A new religious movement founded
on the basis of a declining social order was doomed to failure.

The movement to recast Confucianism into a religion also met
a challenge from Christianity which, as a religious force, appeared
to be better suited to the needs of a progressive and liberal modern
social setting. For example, its dogma of the dignity of the individual as the creation of God fitted the democratic trends, and its
Calvinist development adapted it to the capitalistic industrial order.
Christian missionary efforts claimed many converts from the ranks
of the intellectuals (though such converts were a small minority
among all intellectuals), and their opposition to a "national religion" based on Confucianism was certainly among the forces that
converged to doom the movement to failure. The most vital attack
against the movement was rather silently launched by the secularizing influence of science and technology, which presented a powerful
challenge to any mass movement based on supernatural ideas. As
modern Chinese intellectuals wholeheartedly embraced Western
science, it was to be expected that religious movements would not
find a fertile field among them.

The Buddhist Movement

The Confucian effort was only a pseudo religious movement involving a relatively small group of scholars without touching the
life of the broad masses, but the movement to revitalize Buddhism
was a truly religious movement in the Republican period, and
much has been written about it. Buddhism had developed a rich
independent theological foundation in China, and modern Buddhist thinkers like Hsiung Shih-li were able to add new interpretations to it in response to contemporary intellectual developments
(see, for example, Hsiung's *Shih-li Yü-yao,* or Critical Statements
from Shih-li). Even the popular abbot T'ai-hsü tried to interpret
Buddhist theology in terms of modern needs. Cultically, no new
symbols, no new gods or new rituals were invented in Republican
times, and this might be regarded as a weakness of the Buddhist
movement. Cultic symbols and practices are psychological devices

to awaken people's spirit, to provide a focus of public attention, and to organize group action. Herein lies the power of a new god and the performance of new rituals when old deities and cultic procedures have become time-worn and lost their vitality. The failure to devise new symbols and rituals in the face of new needs of the age perhaps accounted for the modern Buddhist movement's lack of a greater mass following. But the movement scored new developments in the organization of the Buddhist religion, which previously had been under rigid control by the imperial government.

With the relaxing of religious control under the Republic, mass religious gatherings led by celebrated Buddhists like T'ai-hsü were frequent occurrences in various parts of the country in the 1930's, attracting large crowds. But more important was the organization of Buddhist societies, with a national organization and local bodies in the provinces, which would have been suppressed as heretic societies under the imperial authorities. While there is no national statistical information, sources such as the *Hunan nien-chien* do provide limited data on Buddhist organizations. In Hunan no Buddhist society was recorded in the Ch'ing period. In the first year of the Republic, 1912, two Fo-chiao Hui or Buddhist societies appeared. The number increased slowly until the late 1920's, when there was a rapid increase under the encouragement of the military governor T'ang Sheng-chih, a Buddhist devotee. By 1932, there were 25 societies in different parts of the province, with a thriving headquarters in the provincial capital of Changsha.[11] Table 20 shows the size of membership in these societies. While most of the societies were by no means large, there were five with memberships between 500 and 2000, providing a sharp contrast to the highly decentralized Buddhist organization in imperial times, as discussed in Chap. xii.

In addition to the Buddhist associations, there were institutes and schools set up in various parts of the country during the late 1920's and early 1930's. These provided centers for the study of Buddhist theology and, more important, for the training of new leaders for the revitalized ancient religion. Although students in these institutions were relatively few, this was nonetheless a gain, in view of

TABLE 20

Membership in Buddhist Societies in Hunan Province, 1933

NUMBER OF MEMBERS	NUMBER OF SOCIETIES
10–50	6
51–100	7
101–200	5
201–500	2
501–1000	3
1001–2000	2
Total	25

Source: *Hunan nien-chien* (1933), pp. 837–856.

the fact that the traditional law had strictly prohibited proselytism and the teaching of many students by one religious teacher.

But the Buddhist associations were voluntary organizations of a small number of monks and devotees. They did not form a hierarchical system, with the numerous Buddhist temples of the land as component units maintaining constant contact with the worshiping laymen. Neither were the associations well supported financially and spiritually by any stable social group; their enduring existence was thus rendered questionable. This was seen in Hunan province, where the number of Buddhist societies dwindled rapidly as soon as T'ang Sheng-chih was forced to retire from the governorship, thus depriving the organizations of their social leadership and financial support.

The shortage of competent intellectual leadership with modern educational background was another vital weakness in the Buddhist movement. To be sure, the level of traditional scholarship of many of the monks and lay leaders was respectable, and some of them were indeed of rare talent. Hsiung Shih-li, for example, who wrote prolifically on Buddhist theology and edited a dictionary of Buddhism, had been a humble tailor. But the modern world was one dominated by science, and the lack of scientific training seriously affected the ability of modern Buddhist leaders to interpret Buddhist theology and to shape the Buddhist movement in the light of vital contemporary problems. T'ai-hsü talked much of developing Buddhism in harmony with scientific knowledge, and yet his speeches and writings betrayed only narrow contact with basic scientific concepts. One strong point of the Buddhist movement was its large volume of current literature, including some very informative periodicals such as the *Hai ch'ao yin* (Sound of the Sea Tide) *Monthly*. The Confucian religious movement had nothing comparable to this as a means of propaganda. But modern Buddhist literature again showed its weakness in the lack of adequate appreciation of science and the new technological environment which had come increasingly to dominate Chinese social trends. This weakness, more than anything else, prevented the Buddhist movement from meeting the challenge of the times, from justifying the significance of an ancient religion in contemporary life, from capturing the devotion of the intellectual class who retained the leadership of Chinese society.

Finally, the movement lacked sufficient time to foster a new leadership, to adapt itself to a new social setting, and to develop its full strength. Rising to popularity in the 1920's after the contending voices about the Confucian religion had died down, the Buddhist movement had hardly a decade to consolidate its new-gained strength before the Japanese total invasion started in 1937. The chaos and destruction of war all but ended the active existence of the movement. The post-World War II period, which might have provided an opportunity for the revival of the movement, was soon ended in 1949 with the accession to power of the Communists, who have no more tolerance for independent organized religious movements than had the imperial authorities before the Republic. Thus, another of China's modern religious movements passed into history.

Sectarian Movements

The Confucian religious movement was mainly among the scholars, and the modern Buddhist movement was largely confined to Buddhist monks and devotees plus a number of middle-class laymen who regularly frequented the Buddhist convents. Neither movement touched the intimate life of the vast masses of common people, particularly the laborers and peasants. But in an age filled with an urgent need for mass salvation, the populace was not to be left without some form of organized religious movement that would invoke the power of the supernatural on their behalf at a time when the abilities of mortal men seemed to be of little avail in overcoming an endless chain of misfortunes. The sectarian societies were familiar to many of the common people, frequently as a last resort in the face of hopeless circumstances. In the modern period sectarian movements thrived in every part of the country, often developing great social and political strength, as indicated in the previous chapters.

The story of contemporary sectarian movements is still a little-known subject, but they show remarkable vitality among the common people. There is only negligible information on their membership, but, judging from the huge numbers of people involved in the modern rebellions raised by the sectarian societies, we can safely conclude that their following far surpassed those of the Buddhist movement and the movement to transform Confucianism into a religion. Sectarian theological appeals were effective among the common people, for they were based on religious premises familiar to them: the supernatural powers of the gods and spirits, and the magical formulas that could bring desired benefits to mortal man. Their collective cause always bore directly upon the deliverance from spiritual and material suffering. The logic was simple, the appeal direct, all without the obstacle of sophistication. For a population that remained devoted to the ancient pantheon of gods and spirits, the advocacy of a new god or a new magic and a new promise of deliverance could easily set afoot a mass sectarian movement. It was, therefore, no historical accident to see a steady succession of large and small sectarian movements in all parts of the country throughout the modern period, and to see the Communist rulers at the present time having to wrestle with them continually (see chap. ix).

So long as the people continued to believe in the superhuman power of a variety of gods and spirits and in magical procedures to enlist their assistance, sectarian movements would continue to rise in times of widespread suffering and mass crisis. The strong organizational pattern and techniques developed in the long struggle against the state gave the sectarian movements a ready weapon for gathering an integrated mass following. Hence the sectarian movements affected the intimate life of a larger number of people than perhaps any other type of religious movement in modern China.

COUNTERCURRENTS OF SECULARIZING INFLUENCES

While nationwide insecurity and anxiety gave birth to a variety of religious movements that involved a considerable proportion of the population in all social classes, these were not of controlling importance to the social and political trends of the time, as they were in the period of the Taiping rebellion and in other historical situations. In the twentieth century, new counterinfluences were at work in China, as elsewhere in the modern world, to turn an age of belief and piety into one of skepticism and atheistic assertions. Dominant social and political movements in the modern period were no longer launched in the name of the gods and with strength borrowed from magic; instead, they rallied their following around the cause of man and developed their strength through secular organizational techniques. The Boxer rebellion was the last religious movement to cause a major political upheaval. Even the Red Spear societies [12] in the 1920's, which helped to bring ruin to a few local warlords in north China, merely took their place with similar movements among the rear guard of a rapidly retreating age. Controlling the trends of the time were the revolution that ushered in the Republic, the Renaissance movement, the Second Revolution of the Kuomintang (Nationalist party), and the Communist movement. Religious movements were forced to take a secondary role to the revolutionary movements in the collective attempt to create a new social order.

The Impact of Science and the Antireligion Movement

Among the leading influences that reduced the power of religion in present-day China, as in the Western world, was the impact of science, founded on skepticism and empirical knowledge, as against religion, founded on faith and nonempirical vision. After a half-century of collective attempt to decipher the secret of Western power and superiority, the Chinese intellectuals at the close of World War I concluded that science and democracy were the twin keys to Western civilization. On these two factors rested the whole theme of the epoch-making Chinese Renaissance movement, which gave a new orientation to the development of the social order in China.[13]

The story of the impact of science on religion in the minds of the intellectuals is familiar to students of modern Chinese history. The movement to make a state religion out of Confucianism failed to develop any vitality, but its insistence that every modern civilized nation must have a state religion (a misconception about the modern Western world gained mainly from the Christian missionaries) gave rise to a question which quickly became a heated issue in the years following World War I: Does China need a state religion to become a modern nation? Both Western and Chinese thinkers contributed to the polemics that affected the attitude of the educated younger generation.

Bertrand Russell, invited by the Young China Association to deliver a series of public lectures in Peking and Nanking, told his Chinese audience that "White men have gone to China with three motives: to fight, to make money, and to convert the Chinese to our religion," [14] and that religion stultified social and individual development and stood as a barrier to the progress of scientific truth. His ideas gave stimulation to nationalism and science as motivations against religion in general and against the Christian religion in particular. French professors such as M. Granet, M. Barbusse, and M. Bougle, who were greatly respected by Chinese students in France, were invited to express their views; they unanimously declared religion to be a product of primitive ignorance and incompatible with science, which was based on reason and objectivity.[15] The writings of Western scientists, such as Huxley, Darwin, Spencer, James, Pearson, and Dewey were widely quoted to glorify science and devaluate religion as an outmoded foundation for modern life.

The overwhelming majority of modern educated Chinese intellectuals embraced this view with fervor and conviction. Typical were the utterances of the eminent educator, Ts'ai Yüan-p'ei, who belittled religion as a relic of man's primitive ignorance of the physical laws of the universe, which led to the belief in Heaven and Hell, in the Creation myth, and in miracles and other superstitions. Astronomy, biology and its theory of evolution, and other physical sciences dismissed the age-old myths about life and the universe which underlay religion. Hu Shih, Ting Wen-chiang, and other intellectuals of the day not merely elaborated on the natural and social world as a causal mechanism without the direction of any immanent anthropomorphic god but advocated the cultivation of the "greater self," guided by scientific knowledge, to replace religious faith as the integrating force for the nation and society. Theories of the psychic and the unknowable, and the minimizing of the scientific method as only one of the roads to knowledge—ideas propounded by Kant and Bergson and introduced by Carsun Chang—were cast aside as resurrecting the metaphysics already dead in Europe.

For almost a decade after 1920, this theme of the omnipotence of science flooded the young Chinese intellectual world with numerous books and articles in newspapers and periodicals, with eloquent speeches and arguments in discussion groups. For a time, it seemed that an age of reason had dawned in a world long locked in darkness under the shadows of the gods and spirits. Not a murmur was heard from the proponents of Confucian religion, and the Buddhist and sectarian movements appeared to be small eddies on the fringe of a raging current. The theme of science had conquered the minds of a young intellectual generation, which was soon to chart the course for a troubled nation. Some of that generation went into responsible government positions, and others, the majority, became writers and teachers. From these vantage points they spread the scientific orientation of life to an ever-increasing number of Chinese through the modern educational system, which was undergoing rapid expansion.

One of the notable results of this intellectual current was the almost complete disappearance of mythological themes from modern Chinese literature. The "new literature," centered on romantic love and scenes of social conflict between the old and the new, was read chiefly by the modern intellectuals. The rich store of mythological stories retained their popularity with the common people and, to a lesser extent, even with the young intellectuals. Mythological literature had been a dominant source of religious information for the Chinese people in the past, so that the purging of supernatural notions from the "new literature" was an important secularizing influence for the young generation educated in modern schools.

The new-found enthusiasm for science, together with the rising tide of nationalism, was the basis for the antireligion movement of 1922, which had Christianity as its first target. When a conference of the World Student Christian Federation was held on the campus of Tsinghua College in Peking, non-Christian scholars and students throughout the nation raised vociferous objections to associating religion with an educational institution. The Great Federation of Anti-Religionists was organized to stir up public protest against the conference and against religion in general. Though it died down within a year, the movement brought the religious issue to the attention of the nation and prepared the way for further antireligious activities.

The Renaissance movement, which glorified science, was soon merged into the broader current of the Second Revolution of the mid-1920's. "Down with superstition" took its place alongside "Down with imperialism" and "Down with warlords" as battle cries of the historic event. As the Nationalist expedition swept northward, its path was strewn with wrecked temples, particularly in and around the southern cities. The Ch'eng-huang miao (city god temple) in the county seat of Pao-shan in the vicinity of Shanghai was thus wrecked by a mob under the leadership of young left-wing Nationalists in 1927. The sacred objects in the main hall of the temple were broken, and the city god idol was decapitated. The local people found the head in a gutter and replaced it on the idol when the temple was restored.

When the Nationalists were installed in Nanking, one of their first measures was to decree the separation of religion from education. Though aimed solely at the Christian missionary schools, the measure followed the basic theme of the antireligious movement of 1922, and strengthened the trend toward secularization. This trend affected not only Christianity and its attempt to propagate through the educational system, but also the classic religious beliefs in Heaven and fate. These ancient concepts of predeterminism were discouraged and despised by the revolutionaries as fetters to man's ambition and confidence in changing the status quo of society, in developing new frontiers for a hard-pressed people. Among the modern educated young generation, there was no doubt that the belief in Heaven and fate was seriously weakened.

The trend against the belief in fate, in magic, and in the supernatural found its expression in many formal decrees of the Nationalist government, which was now staffed by many intellectuals who had once filled the ranks of the Renaissance and the anti-religion movements. In 1929, for example, there was the promulgation of the "Procedure for the Abolition of the Occupations of Divination, Astrology, Physiognomy and Palmistry, Magic and Geomancy." This was followed in 1930 by the decree ordering those who sold "superstitious merchandise" (incense, candles, and other religious articles) to change their occupation within a limited time. But, like so much social legislation of the Nationalist regime, this measure was never effectively enforced. Once or twice in the large southern cities, the police received orders to prosecute the "vendors of superstition," and these familiar figures were temporarily missing from the street corners and market places. But a few months later, they emerged from their homes, occupied their stalls, and resumed their practice, unruffled by the police, many of whom had been bribed by the vendors. Nevertheless, such ripples were signs that times were different, and that new beliefs had been introduced into the minds of those who had come into political power.

The Conversion of Temples to Secular Uses

The impact of science and the antireligious movement were products of the cities, and were felt particularly in the urban centers in south and central China. The inland rural districts, especially in north and west China, remained largely unaffected in the pre-Communist period. But another blow was struck at the foundation of religion in urban as well as rural areas throughout the country:

the increasing conversion of temples to secular uses and the confiscation of temple property by the government and local community leaders.

The process did not start with the Republic, but was hastened by it. There were obvious local variations in the number of temples thus converted, but few communities escaped entirely. Although some new temples were built and some old ones were repaired during the modern period before the Communists assumed power, probably far more fell to the process of conversion. There is no statistical information on the matter, but one encountered a converted temple far more often than he did a newly built or recently renovated one.

Because a large proportion of temples were community property, it was not unusual in the traditional days to see the occasional conversion of temples and their property to nonreligious uses. But conversion on a large scale as a national phenomenon was unique with the modern period, except during occasional historic crises of drastic religious persecution. Soon after the debacle of the Boxer rebellion, the tottering Ch'ing government instituted political reforms to save itself, and among its new measures was the order to convert temples and their property to establish modern schools. The order affected a large number of temples in Wang-tu county of Hopei province, as already mentioned. In the early years of the Republic, a proposal was made in parliament to confiscate the property of all temples for education and public welfare, but the idea met opposition and failed to muster a majority vote.

But from then on, politicians never took their eyes from temple property as an available source of funds either for genuine public enterprises or for lining their own pockets. In the embryonic years of the Nationalist regime (1922–1924), the income properties of numerous temples in Canton were confiscated to relieve the government's financial stringency, and similar action was taken by warlords and local authorities in many parts of China during the decade of the 1920's.[16] Even the local gentry and community agencies availed themselves of temple properties for public education and local charities until 1931, when the Nationalist government had to set up formal regulations to govern such action, giving the temple priests (where there were any) nominal representation in the councils that decided on the disposal of the temple property.[17]

While there is no nationwide statistical data on the subject, available local information shows that the picture varied greatly in different sections of the country. In Pao-shan county of Kiangsu province, for example, only 10 out of a total of 65 major temples were converted to nonreligious uses during the Republic up to the year 1931; five were used for schoolrooms, four as local police stations, and one as a home for orphans and widows.[18] But in north China the conversion of temples seems to have been more widespread. There was the case of Wang-tu county, already presented.

There is much more detailed local information available on the temples of Ting county of Hopei. In 1882, 62 villages in the county had 435 temples, but by 1928, 327, or 75 percent of the total, had been discontinued as temples. Table 21 shows the number of temples discontinued between 1882 and 1928. In most of the

TABLE 21

Conversion of Temples to Nonreligious Uses in Ting County, Hopei Province

Years	NUMBER OF TEMPLES CONVERTED	Years	NUMBER OF TEMPLES CONVERTED
1882	1	1910	10
1889	1	1911	6
1899	1	1912	4
1900	27	1913	2
1902	1	1914	200
1904	6	1915	45
1905	5	1916	1
1906	1	1917	5
1907	1	1926	1
1908	5	1928	1
1909	3	Total	327

Source: Li Ching-han, *Ting hsien she-hui k̮ai-k̮'uang tiao-ch'a* (Social Survey of Ting County) (Peking, 1928), p. 423. No data are available for the years omitted.

46 years, the annual discontinuation of a small number of temples was largely a consequence of the normal rise and fall of individual cults. But in three of the years, 1900, 1914 and 1915, large numbers were converted into schools, especially in 1914, when 200 were converted under the zealous promotion of modern education by the magistrate Sun Fa-hsü. In a sample investigation of 132 discontinued temples, there was the following distribution of their uses: 57 as schools, 47 sold into private ownership, 8 as night watchmen's stations, 8 for public use by the villagers, 3 as offices for village government, 2 for storage of public articles, 2 rented out to obtain village income, 2 as village agricultural experimental stations, 1 as a public tree nursery, 1 as an office for the Mass Education Association, and 1 as a residence for a Taoist priest.[19]

Ting county is an inland rural district lying beyond the storm centers of the antireligious movement of the 1920's, and the account of the discontinuation of temples in Table 21 does not reflect the direct impact of this movement. But Ting county was not spared in the national tendency to convert temples into schools and offices for other public functions while a new social and political order was being formulated.

The effect on religion of large-scale conversion of temples and confiscation of temple properties is obvious. Besides the decrease in centers of public worship, there was the destruction of the economic foundation of those temples which had escaped conversion but had had their properties confiscated. The average temple properties were already inadequate; the confiscation of any part of a temple's property made it exceedingly difficult for the remainder to continue to support the priests and to maintain minimum religious functions. In Hunan province during the first twenty years of the Republic, half the temples became schoolrooms and many others were converted into private residences, causing a marked decrease in the number of priests.[20]

The above accounts did not include the billeting of soldiers in temples in practically every region throughout the Republican period of civil wars. When a band of soldiers came into a community, the temples were the most readily available billeting places unless the homes of local residents were to be occupied. And shortly

after one band left, another moved in, at a time when troop movements of warlords had become routine. The occupancy of temples
by soldiers not only excluded public worship but brought wanton
destruction of temple property, often beyond repair, as furniture
and at times even structural timbers were broken up for firewood.
The eight years of Japanese invasion reduced large numbers of
temples to ruins.[21]

SECULARIZATION OF THE ETHICOPOLITICAL ORDER

In the modern age, when many major aspects of Chinese culture
seemed to disintegrate under the impact of Western influences,
one characteristic feature of traditional Chinese society that survived the revolutionary changes was the sociopolitical supremacy
of the intellectual class in the power structure. Once the challenge
of science and the operation of other secularizing influences had
weakened religious concepts among the young intellectuals, what
was happening to the religious element in the political institution
with which they had maintained intimate connection? And what
was happening to the ethicopolitical cults that once studded the
land as instrumental factors in the control of moral conduct?

One basic change was the shift from the divine justification of
power in the name of the Mandate of Heaven to the secular justification of power in the name of the rights of man. Although the
Chinese Republic never succeeded in institutionalizing the Western
democratic concept of man's rights, the theory of political power
did become secularized. Throughout the Republican period the
majestic Altar of Heaven stood empty and silent, serving only
as the reminder of a past when it was the very ground where
mighty monarchs sought communion with and sanction of the
supreme power of the universe. The young intellectuals might not
have been as completely free in their inner thoughts from the influence of the supernatural concepts of Heaven and fate as they
claimed in their public pronouncements, but they consistently rejected any return to the Mandate of Heaven as the final justification of political power.

The concept of Heaven and fate as the basis of political power was by no means dead in the minds of the common people. Throughout the Republican period, the impending emergence of a "true Son of Heaven" remained as the undertone of many superstitious rumors and sectarian movements with political designs. But it was the intellectual class and not the common people who were in the political saddle, and the political concept of Heaven failed to develop real potency in spite of its survival in the popular mind. Many sectarian movements of a political nature continued to use supernatural sanction of power as an instrument to collect a popular following, but these movements lacked the necessary educated leadership to achieve success. When those in power ceased to use the supernatural factor to consolidate their political system, its cultic symbols and rituals no longer operated to sustain it in the popular mind. As a religious idea cannot live long without the operation of its cultic symbols and rituals, it is highly questionable whether the concept of the Mandate of Heaven can continue to fire hope and enthusiasm in the popular mind of the next generation.

In the religious aspect of the Chinese political institution, next to the concept of the Mandate of Heaven came the complex body of ethicopolitical cults. We have mentioned previously that these cults fell into two groups, the official and the popular cults. Under the Republic, the official cults, many of which depended upon official sacrifice and maintenance, deteriorated rapidly or were discontinued altogether, while many popular cults continued to enjoy extensive influence.

The cultic veneration of men of exemplary deeds was such a deep-seated element in the Chinese culture that it retreated only slowly. Even the young generation educated in the modern agnostic atmosphere was not completely free from its influence. Furthermore, the Republican governments were manned by a mixture of traditional-minded officials and modern-educated scholars. It was inevitable that the classical tradition of ethicopolitical cults would continue to be regarded by many as an instrument of government. Among the most important official cults was that of Confucius. In 1914 the shrewd renegade president Yüan Shih-k'ai saw the times as opportune to perform an exceedingly impressive sacrifice to Confucius and to order the governors of all provinces to do likewise, obviously as a means to win moral and political respect for his government as well as to resuscitate the Confucian orthodoxy. But after Yüan passed from the picture, sacrifice to Confucius as a grand official occasion was generally discontinued. It survived on into the late 1920's largely in classical schoolrooms and in community celebrations under the unofficial leadership of the Confucian local gentry. The Nationalist government in 1928 did not see fit to reinstate the official sacrifice, but merely ordered all schools in the country to observe the birthday of Confucius with a memorial service. After that, one of the most important cults of traditional China passed into history.

A similar rear guard action was fought to retain the cults of other national and local heroes. It was the Confucian-minded Yüan Shih-k'ai in 1914 who ordered the grouping of Kuan Yü and Yo Fei in the same temple and instructed his officials to pay sacrifice to these two military heroes as a means of stimulating a military spirit in the new Republic. But the official sacrifice did not survive the resignation and death of Yüan in 1916, so that the cult of these two heroes depended upon unofficial popular support for its continued existence.

In later years, provincial authorities in different parts of the country occasionally made attempts to revive the ethicopolitical cults on an official basis. In 1926, for example, the provincial government of Kiangsu ordered local officials in all its counties to perform sacrifice at government expense in four temples, the Sanctuary for the Adoration of the Virtuous, the Hall of Tribute to the Virtuous, the Sanctuary for the Loyal and the Righteous, and the Sanctuary of Chastity and Filial Piety. The decree had a familiar echo:

. . . Our country has always . . . emphasized the ritual of sacrifice . . . Glorification of the virtuous and paying tribute to those who have rendered distinguished public service will stimulate benevolence and morality . . . Since the establishment of the Republic . . . the sacrifices to deceased local men of merit have stopped. Now there is a general moral deterioration and a mass scramble for materialistic gain entirely unbridled by any sense of shame . . . In the local registry of sacrifice we have pillars of officialdom, renowned military leaders, guardians of the

Confucian doctrine, learned men of genius, people of unusual observance of filial piety and chastity, all of high reputation in their generation and respected in the territory . . . Local officials should go to their temples in the spring and autumn to offer sacrifice, so as to move the gods above and to benefit the morality of men. The sacrificial expenses should be included in the local budget. . . .[22]

Soon after this, in 1928, the newly founded Nationalist government ordered the maintenance of temples dedicated to sages and worthy men of the past. Temples of distinguished followers of Buddhism, Taoism, and Mohammedanism as well as Christian churches were permitted to function. But temples of legendary deities and animistic spirits were to be suppressed. The purpose of the decree was to preserve the cults of exemplary historical figures so as to strengthen the moral foundation of the social order, and at the same time to stamp out superstition among the people.

But these and similar efforts by many provincial authorities in the late 1920's and early 1930's represented the epilogue of a long tradition that had already performed its duty in a culture no longer adaptable to modern needs or capable of meeting the challenge from new moral and material influences. The once colorful sacrificial rituals failed to impress the young generation as relevant to the rapidly shifting social, economic, and political situation. The central and local government decrees resulted in spotty restoration of official sacrifices for a few years and then were ignored, together with so many other orders and regulations issued as expedients in an eventful time. It is a notable fact that, in the Republican period, great men like Sun Yat-sen were no longer deified.

The disappearance of the official cults as a part of the political institution was an inevitable trend. In Ch'uan-sha county of Kiangsu province, the gazetteer of 1879 listed 31 (45.5 per cent) of 68 major temples as in the official category, but the gazetteer of 1936 showed only 9 (8.8 per cent) of 67 major temples still in the official status,[23] and it is highly questionable whether those remaining continued to be visited for sacrifice by the local officials. While there is no comparable information available for other localities, general observation bore out the universality of this trend. By the mid-1930's, official altars dedicated to wind, rain, mountains, rivers, and other elements of nature had totally disappeared from the local districts, many becoming agricultural fields or sites for private and public buildings. Temples devoted to personalities and depending on official maintenance were everywhere abandoned to the corrosion of weather or wanton destruction by local people and passing troops. With the passing of the generation of Confucian-trained scholars who participated in the Republican regimes, probably few Chinese officials will retain any intimate understanding of the concept of "guidance by the way of the gods" and be able to compose even unenforced decrees in its spirit.

But the function of religious sanction in the maintenance of general morality had not altogether crumbled with the abandonment of official sacrifice to the ethicopolitical cults, for the unofficial popular cults still operated extensively among the common people privately and under spontaneous community leadership. Gods and spirits that had unmistakable connection with the moral and political order, such as the city god or the spirit of the Eastern Peak or T'ai-shan, still flourished, and birthdays of local patron deities were still celebrated with colorful pageantry and fanfare in the rural towns and villages. The Nationalist government order of 1928 suppressing such temples was never enforced. The remark by Confucius that, when a ritual is lost (among the ruling class) one may rediscover it in the countryside, seemed applicable.

It is true that the dominant motivation in the continuation of worship of these popular cults was the belief in the magical power of the gods and spirits. But, as pointed out, this magical potency had the derivative effect of enforcing the moral standards that were popularly believed to have been sanctioned by the gods. The magical and the ethical aspects of these cults were inseparably intertwined. As long as the traditional moral system continued to be effective among the common people, especially in the rural areas, religion retained its role in helping to avert the collapse of the moral order at a time when there was a high degree of instability in government and law, and when foreign influences had shaken the foundation of the traditional ethical system among the moddern educated ruling class in the major urban centers.

On the other hand, many of the new ethical ideas that were introduced into the minds of the modern educated generation were strange to the native gods who knew only the traditional moral rules, and there was little likelihood that the old ethicopolitical cults could help in the devolpment of the new moral order. One way in which religion might have played a role in the new situation would have been the invention of new cults by the young intellectuals who were familiar with the new ethical concepts, but they were deeply affected by the notion of the omnipotency of science and retained little faith in religion. The few who were interested in spiritual matters were drawn into the Christian faith, which was intimately related to the new ethical ideas that were having a strong impact on modern China. The modern educated generation abandoned the traditional gods not only because of their disbelief in magic and miracles but also because they increasingly refuted the ethical system that the gods symbolized. Hence the ineffectiveness of the Kiangsu government decree that tried to resuscitate the Confucian ethical system by resurrecting its patron gods. Meanwhile, we are not underestimating the contemporary agnostic influence.

In the urban centers that saw drastic social changes, religion was losing its hold not only on the ethicopolitical order but also on all other major social institutions. Ancestor worship was losing its hold on the intellectuals. The ignoring of ancestral sacrifice, a serious social and ethical offense a generation earlier, was far from being uncommon among young students and scholars. Among them, the ideal of the traditional family was being replaced by the small conjugal family which stressed neither the consolidation of extensive consanguinary ties nor the perpetuation of the lineage. While ancestor worship was a vital factor in the solidarity of the traditional consanguinary family, it performed little function for the operation of the small conjugal family, which was becoming increasingly common in the urban centers. It is in the rural areas, where the traditional family has remained the basic unit of social life, that the ancestor cult has retained its vitality.

An increasing proportion of social and economic organizations were transformed into purely secular bodies by abandoning their patron deities and cultic rituals as an integrating influence for the group. The transformation of the commercial guilds into chambers of commerce and business associations, and the craft guilds into labor unions since the 1920's are prominent examples. The image of the patron gods no longer adorned the halls of these new organizations, and religious rituals no longer guided the procedure of their meetings. Toward the mid-1930's, the impressive religious processions of the craft guilds in celebration of the patron deities' birthdays were increasingly absent from the larger towns and cities.

As the towns and cities underwent modernization, the widening and paving of streets meant the tearing down of the wayside shrines and old arches that had a sacred connotation for the local community. While even urban neighborhoods still held their temple fairs as major community events, and private homes continued to observe religious holidays, city-wide and nationwide holidays were no longer religious occasions but were mass activities in commemoration of historic events connected mainly with the modern revolutions. The modern official calendar of Chinese holidays was almost a summary of contemporary politics intimately related to the young agnostic intellectuals and their social and political struggle. All these tended to strip the larger towns and cities, especially in the south, of the sacred atmosphere that once characterized their physical appearance and their community life.

XIV

COMMUNISM AS A NEW FAITH

IT WAS STATED IN THE PREFACE that this book is concerned primarily with theistic religion in Chinese society. But the recent decades of social and political revolution have reduced the role of theistic religion and elevated nontheistic faiths to a dominant position in the life of the nation. Hence the need for a brief treatment of the nontheistic faith of Communism and its relation to theistic religion under its dominance.

DECLINE OF THEISTIC RELIGION AND
THE SEARCH FOR A NATIONAL DEVOTION

The previous chapter revealed the lack of vitality of religious movements which arose in response to a century of growing distress both in personal lives and in China's national status. The movement to make Confucianism a religion failed to rejuvenate the outmoded Confucian ideology or to shore up the eroded foundation of the traditional sociopolitical structure built on its principles. Neither the Buddhist movement nor the many sectarian movements of heavy Taoist tint achieved a leading social or political position, as they proved unable to meet the challenge of materialistic rationalism. As the elite of Chinese society turned away from theistic religion, an increasing number of temples were emptied of their gods and were diverted to secular uses in conformity with the materialistic and rationalistic outlook of the age. Theistic cults evoked only feeble response from groups and communities where Western influences had struck root and had made them nerve centers of modern social change. The collapse of the traditional sociopolitical order, together with its theistic symbols and guiding doctrine, recalls such historical situations as the period of disunion following the disintegration of the Han order.

But the silencing of the gods was only part of an ongoing process of social transformation marked by the accelerating disintegration of the traditional order of life during the entire course of the Republic. Politically the succession of Republican regimes was characterized by moral and administrative failure of the ruling elite. The interminable civil wars, which sapped the strength and spirit of the nation, were succeeded by eight years of disastrous Japanese occupation of the richest parts of the country, ending in disintegration of the Nationalist government and the nation's economy. On the social scene, the proliferation of popular movements presented an entire spectrum of social and political hues. These movements, on the one hand, expressed the vitality of a people feverishly searching in every direction for a path to national salvation but, on the other hand, acted as a divisive influence diverting the nation's energy from its central tasks.

With the wide range of unstable and contradictory popular movements vying for his attention, the educated individual became bewildered and desperate, as he could neither drift with the currents nor retreat to the discredited and disorganized traditional pattern of life. His life and the world around him no longer had a consistent system of meanings for him. All this was epitomized in such widely read literary works of the 1920's and 1930's as Lu Hsun's *P'ang huang* (Bewilderment) and Pa Chin's *Huan mieh* (Illusion). The great War of Resistance against the Japanese invasion in the late 1930's shocked the people out of their bewilderment and gave them a national purpose, and for several years they found a common center of devotion and unity: to achieve national victory. But, as the war dragged on with major military setbacks, political and economic difficulties rekindled internal strife and led to the moral and administrative collapse of the government. Individuals were once more thrown into bewilderment and despair. As to the unreflective common men, they could neither rely on the disorganized traditional institutional system nor drift with the unstable new social and political structure, and their life was completely shattered by the destructive war. They sank to new depths of misery as war fortunes piled up for the few. And the "victory" over the Japanese invasion, when it did come, was but a hollow fulfillment of the nation's aspiration, as the great battle between the Nationalist and the Communist forces was soon to follow.

Clearly, both the nation and the individual were in a state of disorganization, and both craved consciously and unconsciously the emergence of a supreme concern which could transcend divergent interests and claims, command undivided national dedication, and at the same time provide a centered act in which the individual could reintegrate the emotional and rational aspects of his personality toward a central goal. Such a supreme concern for the national community and such a centered act for the individual is, as Paul Tillich has said, a faith.[1]

But such a new faith could no longer be developed in the context of traditional theistic religion as the guiding force for both the individual and the nation. The gods could no longer move the people into effective action in the face of mass sufferings—natural calamities, wars, misgovernment, poverty and disease, family disorganization—and for the intellectual elite, continued national humiliation, value conflicts, unemployment, insecure social status, emotional anxieties. Any revival of theistic symbols in the development of a new faith faced a twofold difficulty. First, materialistic rationalism was, in the minds of the intellectual elite, incompatible with theistic symbolism, which inevitably involved miracles and magic. The rationalistic phase of the Confucian tradition reinforced this influence. At a time when materialistic progress was the common aspiration of the people, it was rational efforts and not theistic symbols or supernatural miracles that could best answer the purpose.

Secondly, many of the values long represented by theistic symbols had been depreciated by the changing requirements of an emerging social order. Ancestor worship, which symbolized the values of kinship relations and conservatism, was no longer compatible with the changing family pattern and the modern spirit of progress. Even the universal values of *hsiao, ti, chung,* and *hsin* (filial piety, brotherliness, loyalty, and fidelity) were no longer applicable to modern situations without reinterpretation of their traditional meanings as symbolized by the theistic ethicopolitical cults. The entire moral outlook of the *tao t'ung* (Confucian fundamentalism) was collapsing, together with the many theistic symbols that undergirded it. This situation is best generalized by Paul Tillich's statement:

The relation of man to the ultimate undergoes changes. Contents of ultimate concern vanish or are replaced by others. A divine figure ceases to create reply, it ceases to be a common symbol and loses its power to move for action. Symbols which for a certain period, or in a certain place, expressed truth of faith of the past. They have lost their truth, and it is an open question whether dead symbols can be revived. Probably not for those to whom they have died! [2]

As the gods, the symbols of old faiths, declined, Chinese society searched hard for a new faith which would be in harmony with the spirit of materialistic rationalism and the "power to move for action." The whole series of social and political movements in the past century were expressions of this search. Although many of the leaders of popular movements were unaware or only partly aware of the need for a new faith, Sun Yat-sen was fully conscious of the need when he stated in his *San-min chu-i* (Three People's Principles) that China was in urgent need of an ideology, for, said he, ideology would inspire faith, and faith would generate strength—collective strength that was so essential in the national crisis. And a large number of people did find a new faith in his Three People's Principles, as witnessed by its ability to motivate the Republican Revolution and the Second Revolution. But moral and administrative failures and the disintegrating effects of the Japanese invasion brought ruin to the government founded theoretically on that faith. Now another nontheistic faith, Communism, has emerged to replace Sun's ideology as the answer to the long search.

COMMUNISM AS A NONTHEISTIC FAITH

Many have long identified Communism as a nontheistic faith with distinctly religious qualities.[3] The retrospection of many Communists and former Communists, Chinese and Western, has clearly demonstrated the religious quality of the experience of conversion to that ideology, an experience of ecstatic enlightenment in which the once incomprehensible chaotic world suddenly falls into an orderly pattern, explaining everything that has happened before and things that shall happen in the future, delineating all that is goodness and justice from what is evil and oppression, revealing mankind's final destiny, and demanding complete devotion from all men. Communism thus has the quality of an "ultimate concern," to use Tillich's term, which transcends all other claims, whether they be rival ideologies, competing definitions of justice, conflicting philosophies of truth, or goals of success, security, and happiness of the individual or the group.

The ultimacy of this ideological concern is proclaimed in the name of two leading aspirations of the Chinese nation: materialistic progress and nationalism, which have for a century stirred the emotions of the Chinese people and moved them time and again into revolutionary action. From the T'ung Chih reform in the 1860's to the success of the Communist revolution in the 1950's, the political weakness of the nation and the material backwardness of its people have been consistently identified as the main sources of China's inferiority in the modern world. Consequently, the values of materialistic progress and nationalism have been deeply internalized into the emotional "need disposition" of the people, especially those who grew up with the Republic, as the only means to a dignified position for the nation and happiness for the individual, who keenly felt the nation's inferiority and defeats. The emotional driving power of these two aspirations was reinforced by their harmony with the supreme emphasis on science and the national state, the dominant spirit of the age. Thus these values needed no rationalization or defense, as did the theistic faiths, in order to gain acceptance by the modern mind. Human rights as expressed in democracy have also been among the nation's aspirations in the past century. But democracy in the Western sense has never sunk genuine roots among most of the people, including the intellectual elite, mainly because of the inertia of the authoritarian character of the traditional social institutions, and the wide latitude of possible interpretations of the term democracy as its shifting definitions reduced its strength as a coherent force capable of moving for mass action.

For a century, almost all major reforms, revolutions, and popular movements made the claim that they were trying to bring about a strong nation and encourage materialistic progress. The Communist movement makes the same claim but accompanies it with ideological fervor and ruthlessly single-minded and effective action. The supreme quest for national strength and materialistic progress would demand that "all other concerns, economic well-being, health and life, family, aesthetic and cognitive truth, justice and humanity, be sacrificed." [4] This total and unconditional demand, which makes the Communist ideology a faith and an effective integrative force for a nation in social transition, is painfully expressed in the unending persecution and liquidation of all contention, whether made by the Nationalist government, by the merchants in the "Five-Anti Movement," or by the "rightist" intellectuals in the "Hundred Flowers" persecution. The traditional concept of ideological tolerance, *i-t'u t'ung-kuei* (divergent roads to a common end) is now regarded as a camouflage for reactionism.

For the strength of the state and for national economic advancement, the Communist ideology demands from the individual unconditional surrender of all his personal concerns, even betrayal of members of his family should any of them be involved in "reactionary" activities.[5] Above all, one must surrender one's inner self without reservation to the supreme cause, as demanded by the "Dedication of Heart" movement in the wake of the "Hundred Flowers" persecution. A "rightist" caught in that persecution had to divest himself of the entire past self without reservation before being permitted to start life anew. Among these "rightists" was Feng Yu-lan, the eminent author of the *History of Chinese Philosophy*, often quoted in previous chapters of this work. The Communists accused Feng of aspiring to be the "tutor of emperors" (*ti huang shih*). He wrote, in a self-confession statement typical of Communist China:

To travel the road of socialism, one must accept Marxism as the guiding ideology. To expound and disseminate Marxism is the sole function of one devoted to philosophy. I thought that I was studying Marxism and even wished to "develop" it. But what I did exactly tended to sabotage Marxism. . . . During the campaign of resistance to the Japanese aggression I had worked out a new reactionary idealist system. I styled it as "new rationalism" and claimed that it was the successor to orthodox Chinese feudalist philosophy, which was hostile to Marxism. . . . After the liberation I made only some superficial criticisms of the system, which fundamentally remained intact in my mind. I tried to camouflage it with the smattering of Marxism I had learned. In actuality I concealed the weapon, waiting for the ripe moment to strike. . . .

The individualist craving for fame and wealth is incompatible with socialism. However, I had a remarkable individualist craving for fame and wealth. . . . I had harbored a lot of reactionary idealist ideas and was under their influence. This was a crime I committed against the Party and the people. But I was not ashamed of my past after the liberation, and on the contrary, I made capital out of it by exploiting it to bargain with the Party. I thought I was a figure representative of the nation and should be taken seriously by the Party. . . . During the early post-liberation period I showed some repentance, but in a while I was my old self once more and even attempted to sabotage Marxism with revisionism while demanding the Party take me seriously. My individualism was appallingly serious. In my eagerness to make a name I would even prefer notoriety to obscurity. . . .

I thank the Party for launching the all-people's self-remolding movement. Through the Party's enlightenment and the comrades' help I realized that the fatherland has entered into socialism and that my ideology has run counter to socialism. . . . It is nine years since liberation . . . despite the lapse of nine years I have not laid down my arms and surrendered to the people. . . . The Party has elevated my awareness. I am determined to . . . lay down my arms and surrender, and be once more a "common soldier" in the ranks of Marxist-Leninist philosophers under the banner of the Party and Marxism.[6]

Forsaking one's past self for a new self, when sincerely executed, is paralleled only by such experience of religious conversion as taking refuge in Buddhism, so familiar to the Chinese, when the individual tormented by frustration suddenly woke to the error, futility, and sinfulness of all that was part of his past self; when, the more he condemned his former self, the more he was assured of a new self to gain salvation. Confessional documents from Communist China show that such self-condemnation has little to do with a person's dignity or emotional security, should he be a true convert, for the old self is now separated from the new self, and the latter must reconstruct its dignity and integrity through performance in the new light. No sociopolitical movements based on other forms of idealism in modern China demanded the same complete break with the past as the price of admittance to its ranks. Even in insincere confessions, the overt, ideologically correct act of self-condemnation would have the effect of accentuating the consciousness of the complete dominance of the new faith, which threatens disaster to those refusing to surrender all, including one's inner self, to its command.

The unconditional nature of such a command is based on the believer's absolute certainty that the Communist ideology is the only guidance to man's inevitable destiny, the only infallible road to national strength and economic improvement. This absolute certitude is proclaimed in the name of the power of "the people," whose importance transcends any individual, his thought, his judgment, his interests, his existence. The individual's sole function, as stated above by Feng, is to expound and disseminate or enact Marxism and to surrender completely to this task his energy and his thought. His virtue lies in obedience, and his sin in deviation. Those who responded seriously to the "Hundred Flowers" call for ideological contention in 1958 found out too late that a faith, theistic or secular, admits no question or doubt about the soundness of its concrete content.

And yet this absolute certitude of the Communist ideology, like that of a religious doctrine, is based mainly not on empirical evidence, but on a promise of fulfillment for the intangible future, "for posterity" (*wei liao hou-tai*) [7] or for the "distant horizon," which performs a parallel function to "life after death." [8] The most acute suffering and ordeal under Communist rule cannot be regarded as empirical evidence of the fallacy of the ideology, but must be borne as the price of the intangible idealistic future. The nonempirical nature of the Messianic promise, incapable of proof by reality, facilitates the maintenance of the ideological certitude and enhances its idealistic appeal for men who experience profound frustration from reality. This absolute certitude based on a Messianic promise is closely related to the development of Communist fanaticism, which helped carry the revolution to its victory in China, for the state of fanaticism is a psychological mechanism for the suppression of doubt and a dogged refusal to consider any realistic evidence or logical argument against one's faith.

THEISTIC RELIGIONS UNDER THE COMMUNIST FAITH

Since the installation of the Communist ideology as the supreme faith of the nation, and in spite of the radical reorganization of Chinese society, parts of the traditional institutional structure and values have lingered on, and the theistic symbols and beliefs of those parts continue to operate in the people's life, so that both diffused and institutional religions have maintained their tenuous existence. Thus, Chinese society under Communist rule embodies the dominance of a nontheistic political faith coexisting with theistic religions of both the diffused and the institutonal types.

Communist Policy Toward Theistic Religions

The position of Communism toward theistic religion is that of faith encountering faith.[9] Since faith embodies ultimacy, the relation between faiths implies mutual exclusion. Between mutually exclusive bodies, there may be either mutual tolerance or conflict. The latter applies to the relation between Communism and theistic religion because of the nature of the Communist faith and its interpretation of religion. The absolute certitude of its own historical destiny and the centralist nature of its organization ("democratic centralism," "democratic dictatorship") prevent any genuine tolerance of theistic religions. Hence, theistic religion is viewed in the Marxist-Leninist light as a product of ignorance and of nature, which has been used as an "opiate on the people" by the exploiting class. With cultural liberation of the people by modern science and political liberation of them by the revolution, such a product of ignorance and class exploitation is destined to become an historical relic. The eventual elimination of theistic religion has been consistently propounded in all Communist literature in China, from the early writings of Chen Tu-hsiu,[10] a founder of the Chinese Communist party, to current pamphlets and articles by lesser Communist writers.

Though the Communists believe that theistic religion must be abolished eventually, practical considerations prevent immediate, forcible elimination of it. Theistic religion in China is permitted a restricted existence, which in some ways could even contribute toward the Communist transformation of the traditional society. The Communists hope that theism will eventually pass out of existence, since the younger generation will grow up under the new social order. But any religion attempting to raise the banner of resistance or obstruction against the Communist faith would be violently suppressed.

In the first ten years of the Communist rule, there was little serious difficulty in China proper in executing this policy of permitting continued restricted existence for theistic religion under the condition of political submission. The traditionally weak institutional religion could offer little effective organized resistance to Communist pressure, a situation substantially different from Communist countries where there are large and strongly organized churches. The only organized religion by which the Communists feel threatened is Christianity, particularly the Catholic Church, because of its long association with Western powers, but the numerical size of the Christian group is not so large as to present difficulties to the Communists. Posing some difficulties are institutional religions in the borderlands, such as Islam in Hsinkiang and Lamaism in Inner Mongolia and Tibet, but these are culturally beyond the confines of Chinese society. As to the pervasive influence of diffused religion, in which worship is conducted on a personal or a decentralized small group basis, it would be difficult to eliminate it before completely eliminating the social institutions into which such religion has been diffused. So long as the traditional institutional groups are under Communist control, their diffused religious elements would not pose any danger for the Communist power.

The subordinate relation of theistic religion to the Communist faith may be considered in two aspects, one concerning theistic beliefs and the other, religious organizations.

Communist Treatment of Theistic Beliefs

The broad policy of nonviolent elimination of theistic beliefs, so long as this does not obstruct operation of the Communist power, is clearly stated by the Communist leadership. Mao Tse-tung, in his report on the investigation of the peasant movement in Hunan province in the 1920's, expressed the opinion that superstition cannot be suppressed by force and that it will disappear when men are liberated from sufferings by the success of the new social order. In line with this view, the Ministry of Interior of the Communist central government issued a policy statement in 1952: "The long feudalistic rule has given the people their superstitious ideas, which cannot be dismissed merely by government decrees. . . . The masses themselves must take the initiative in reform." [11] The same view led to the formulation of Article 88 of the Constitution of the People's Republic: "Citizens of the People's Republic of China have the freedom of religious belief." This freedom is granted under the condition that the religious belief does not obstruct political programs and laws of the Communist government. Within these limits, which are often stretched in interpretation, the people may continue their worship. Thus, even after the Communists assumed power, religious worship in the theistic sense, burning incense sticks and praying in the temples or going to churches, has continued to be an activity of appreciable importance.

But the policy of tolerance with political subordination does not mean relaxation of the Communists' long-term plan of nonviolent elimination of theistic religion. The most vital measure in this direction is the atheist education in an educational system which has come to include a total school population of close to 100 million in 1959. Especially important are the 30 million primary school children.[12] Beyond the classrooms, in numerous meetings and discussion groups, elementary scientific ideas are introduced to dismiss age-old myths. A significant measure is the attempt to stop further transmission of religious ideas through traditional mythological literature and dramas. Mythological fiction and their versions in serial pictures are often confiscated from bookstores and sidewalk bookstands and destroyed. Since 1951, there has been a persistent effort to purge supernatural notions from traditional drama by rewriting it. The popular old play "Romance on the Milky Way," which pictures happy marriages as preordained by the twin deities of the Cow Boy and Weaving Girl stars in the Milky Way, now contains these revised lines at the point where wedding arrangements are being discussed: "We must pick an auspicious day," says the prospective groom, but his sister-in-law corrects him, "You are still a little superstitious. No day is as good as today." [13] In the endeavor to censor plays, the Communists try to distinguish between two types of traditional dramas containing supernatural ideas. One type contains mythological stories symbolizing acceptable moral values, and these are permitted to appear on the stage. The other type contains stories of supernatural miracles with few moral values acceptable to the Communist ideology, and these are ordered suppressed or drastically revised.[14]

Other measures are taken to reduce supernatural influence. A special tax is imposed on "superstitious commodities" such as incense sticks, candles, and paper articles to be burned to the dead, with the obvious purpose of using financial pressure to reduce religious rites. "Anti-superstition exhibitions" are occasionally held. At times, group action is taken to uproot supernatural ideas from certain aspects of life which may affect the Communist political or economic programs. In Kwangtung province in the south, there had long been the folk belief among peasants that the work of repairing river dikes should be restricted to men, for participation by women might cause collapse of the dikes. This was apparently part of the religious sanction of male dominance in the economic structure of traditional society. But the practice kept women from entering fully into the agricultural labor force, thus obstructing the Communist policy of full mobilization of labor. So the Communists in that province mobilized large numbers of women in 1952 to build and repair dikes and, at the completion of the work, staged propaganda meetings to demonstrate the fallacy of the superstition.

Pursuing the policy of nonviolent, gradual elimination of superstition, the Communist leaders sometimes take action directed specifically at local incidents involving supernatural motivation. One instance occurred in Ocheng hsien in Hupeh province, where there was a Ma Hsien Ku (Goddess Ma) temple at the side of which stood the alleged tomb of the deity. Peasants nearby came to burn incense sticks and to seek holy water for family members who were sick. In the spring of 1957, an epidemic swept through the area. There was a rumor that "the other world is drafting new recruits for its armed forces, and those on the call-up list will not survive." The usually deserted tomb of the goddess was crowded with people burning incense and candles. During the busy farm season, three to four hundred persons visited the place daily, and the peak was six hundred persons a day. The local Party leaders were afraid that the large number of people collected daily at the tomb might affect agricultural production, and so they started to dig up the tombstone and told the crowd to disperse. But the crowd was enraged by the leaders' action and threatened to attack them. The leaders suspected there might be "bad elements" behind the incident, and had the local police try again to urge the crowd to go home by explanations and threat. But the people only ridiculed the police. Then the Party leaders investigated the case, found the real cause, and took the following action:

In the spring of this year, measles, meningitis, and influenza attacked the area, and the public health departments there were incompetent in coping with the situation. Many peasants whose family members were sick found no way to turn, and, since the old superstitious ideology was not completely removed, they had no choice but to ask the goddess for holy water. With this knowledge in mind, the Guidance Team immediately organized a medical team. On the one hand, the people were told the scientific reasons for the outbreak of epidemics, and, on the other hand, the sick ones were given treatment. For those unable to pay for their medical treatment, either the agricultural producers' coöperatives advanced the payments on their behalf or they were given treatment free. On the first day after the medical team arrived, over one hundred people were still seen burning incense sticks. On the second day, there were only sixty; cn the third day, thirteen; and on the fourth day, there was no more burning of incense sticks at the Hsien Ku tomb.[15]

But these cases of nonviolent treatment of religious worship or superstition constituted only part of a mixed picture. The "freedom of religious belief" in the Communist Constitution is counteracted by "antireligion freedom." The latter includes not only freedom of disbelief but also antireligious demonstrations and similar actions which have often damaged religious property and affected the personal well-being of the believers. Riotous action by antireligious mobs has been characteristic of the times from the days of the Northern Expedition in the 1920's to the present. Mob emotions ran high under the Communists' victorious revolutionary power. Mobs even invaded some ancestral temples in the southern villages which had been spared in the pre-Communist antireligious movement. In 1951, the writer visited an ancestral temple in a village in Kwangtung province and saw only an empty building left after a Peasants' Association mob had completely stripped it of honorific and religious objects and burned them in order to "sever the present generation from the roots of feudalism."

Often Communist local officials exploited religious properties in the name of antireligious freedom. An outstanding case was the destruction of the invaluable bronze Taoist images in Wutangshan, the mecca of Chinese Taoism. On this scenic mountain were eight palaces; thirty-two temples; twelve shrines; a "golden palace," the largest existing bronze structure in China; and thousands of bronze Taoist images, many of which were unsurpassed works of art. In 1955 and again in 1956, county officials broke up hundreds of "scattered, damaged, or duplicate" bronze images and sold them as scrap metal to help provide funds for the county budget. Over 50,000 catties (about 65,000 pounds) of bronze were collected. In the 1956 campaign it took forty-eight days to destroy the images, one of which weighed over 3000 catties or nearly two tons, and a large number of which had been preserved in good condition. Leading Taoist priests, some even with limited political status, could only watch the heart-rending destruction helplessly. Afterwards, as news of the wanton destruction reached the provincial authorities, several of the county officials responsible were given demerits as punishment, which seemed to be an insignificant gesture to placate the rising popular protest.[16] Although the Wutangshan case was brought to public attention because of its prominence as a national religious center, the destruction or selling of the properties and sacred objects of innumerable obscure temples in villages and towns remained unnoticed or unrecorded.

Although antireligious riots and destruction of temple property and images were partly inspired by the anti-supernatural attitude which characterized the Communist ideology, they were nevertheless scattered local occurrences without organized direction from the central Communist authorities. Furthermore, such actions were largely restricted to the destruction of religious properties without direct harm to believers. But when religious beliefs formed an active part of a "reactionary" social system, such beliefs became the object of drastic and systematic elimination in order to overthrow the social system which the religious beliefs supported. In such cases, professional practitioners of these beliefs would face persecution.

Because of the relative weakness of organized religion in Chinese society, these cases of persecution did not occur often in China proper. But in the non-Chinese border provinces such as Hsinkiang, Tsinghai, and Kansu, the entire system of religious beliefs which gave powerful sanction to the local social structure, especially its ruling class, came under revolutionary attack, and many priests of Islam and Lamaism (a branch of Buddhism) found themselves the objects of "struggle" by the masses. Many such priests were hauled up to platforms to face howling mobs while listening to accusations of their past harsh treatment of the people and cheating the ignorant masses with their false magic. In Minho county of Tsinghai province, for example, a mass meeting was organized in 1958, at which a Lamaist priest in full religious robes was put on the platform to demonstrate the magic of calling down the gods by shaking his head. After he shook his head vigorously for a while, people in the audience asked him: "Have the gods come yet?" He replied in a crestfallen manner, "No, there are no gods." [17] This incident occurred in a place where the establishment of a new commune faced expected resistance from the local ruling class, the large herd owners in the nomadic economy, and from its supporting priesthood. To displace the ruling class and to take over its wealth and power, it was necessary to dismantle its magical prop. The violent struggle against supernatural beliefs was thus guided by political requirements, and atheistic considerations were of only secondary importance.

Religious Organizations and Priesthood under Communist Rule

As the Communist faith admits of a degree of transitional tolerance of theistic beliefs under the condition of political subordination, the same broad policy also holds for Communist treatment of religious organizations. But, while certain politically neutral religious beliefs can theoretically continue to have a measure of independent existence in the mind of the believer, the religious organizations must structurally become a part of the Communist sociopolitical organizational system and accept strict control from the Communist authorities. For the Communists, religious organizations, like any other social groups, constitute an integral part of society and its system of political authority, and there can be no organizational separation of religion and the state. "Although the [Catholic] Church is an organization glorifying our Lord and saving our souls, it is an organized social body, and as such it is inseparable from society."[18] Although this view was expressed by a Catholic about the Catholic Church, it applies to religious organizations of all other faiths, as shown by actual Communist treatment of them.

This is in sharp contrast to the traditional Buddhist view that Buddhist monks and their monastic orders should not be subjected to government control because they have withdrawn from the secular world, and therefore are no longer a part of it. But the Buddhist view never prevailed, and organizational autonomy of religious bodies in the Western sense never existed under the traditional government, and certainly does not under the contemporary Communist rule. For dealing with religious matters, including control of religious organizations, there is the Bureau of Religious Affairs of the State Council in the Communist central government, and the Religious Affairs Department in the provincial and municipal governments,[19] corresponding closely to the central and local agencies in the imperial government for control of the Buddhists and Taoists (see chap. viii). Through these government agencies, religious activities and organizations are controlled and directed so that they function as a part of the Communist sociopolitical order.

In the sense of negative control, activities of all religious groups are under the careful surveillance of the police system. But for more positive control and active motivation of organized religious activities, there is the need for a system of popular religious organizations which, under the centralized direction of the government agencies concerned with religious functions, will work among established religious groups such as those associated with temples and churches as well as among the religiously oriented population at large.

Important among such popular religious organizations are the China Buddhist Association and the China Taoist Association, both set up in 1953 under the direction of the Bureau of Religious Affairs of the State Council in Peking.[20] The Taoist body is regarded as the first national Taoist organization of any extensive representative character in the entire history of that faith, which has always been divided by territorial and denominational differences. Among leading Taoists who attended the founding conference were some from widely separated and secluded locations as Hua Shan, Sung Shan, and T'ai Shan. Although Buddhists have had national associations in the past, it is possible that the present one is reaching more Buddhist centers and groups throughout the country than did its pre-Communist predecessors. Other national organizations of the same type are the Chinese Catholic Patriotic Association and the National Committee for Self-Administration of the Protestant Churches.

The Communist motive for investing financial and human resources in organizing such bodies and for bringing national organizational unity to the traditionally divided Taoist faith is obviously not to facilitate development of theistic religious worship. The aim is to build an organizational apparatus for more effective national control of the religious population and for making them accept the "guidance of the Party and the Government," abide by Communist law and policies, and participate in the "socialist construction and various patriotic movements of the motherland."[21] These objectives are found as stereotypes in the constitutions and declarations of all Communist national religious organizations and a large number of their local branches.

The negative control function of these religious organizations, that is, to prevent political deviation and resistance regarding the Communist authority and policies, is strategically important at a time when the Communist power is trying to consolidate its drastically unconventional social and political system. The constant threat from secret religious societies makes the Buddhist and Taoist organizations important in this respect. The same applies to organizations of Christianity, which is historically linked to the Western powers, against which the Communists are waging an "anti-imperialist struggle." Thus, the Chinese Catholic Patriotic Association and its local branches have been instrumental in severing the ties of the Chinese Catholics with the Vatican, whose uncompromising anti-Communist stand has aroused a persistent fear among the Communists. (This is reminiscent of the persecution of the Christian church in the Ch'ing period as a result of the imperial government's rejection of papal authority over Chinese Christians.) The vigorous policy of independence, self-determination, and self-administration for the Christian churches as a means of purging them of their ties with Western political influences would be difficult to execute without the organizational channels set up within these religious bodies.

The organizational effectiveness of the Communist policy is based on the fact that, in a differentiated society, collective control and communication of information tend to be concentrated among members of the same occupational or social group, partly because of their frequent contacts and their similarity of interests. Hence, members of a religious group would know far more about their own political attitudes and activities than would outsiders, and collective control based on the members' knowledge of each other and on the group's specific interest would be more compelling than purely arbitrary control imposed from without.

Treating the religious population and their organizations as an integral part of society, the Communists demanded not only that they refrain from political deviation and resistance but also that they participate in all phases of social and political efforts on the same basis as the secular population. To attain the latter objective, conferences and study groups have been held for representatives of various faiths throughout the country. In 1959, for instance, 182 Buddhist representatives were gathered in Wuchang, Hupeh, from five provinces and one autonomous region in central and south China, and were given over two months of intensive indoctrination on the Communist ideology and government policies so as to prepare them for active participation in the Communist programs. At the conclusion of the session, the group issued a statement of determination "to remold ourselves in the matter of political stand, . . . to participate in labor on the production front, to love the country and abide by the law, to . . . lean to the Party and the Government, and to untiringly contribute all our forces to the struggle for the socialist cause." [22]

A similar instance is the Representative Conference of the Kiangsu Catholic Patriotic Association held in 1959 in Nanking. Some 70 priests and laymen from all parts of the province were called to the city to study documents of Communist domestic and international policies and to learn the Party line on socialist construction, the "big leap forward" movement, and the people's communes. They were taken to visit industrial and agricultural exhibitions and various new industrial plants as demonstrations of progress made under the Communist policies and organization. At the end, they expressed "their determination to strengthen their self-reform, accept leadership of the Communist party with resolution, and take the socialist road." [23] While these declarations were probably written under Communist tutorship and the "determinations" expressed in them apparently lacked sincerity, nonetheless such conferences and study sessions had informative or educational value for the religious population whom the Communists are trying to turn into active participants in the socialist cause.

Under the vigorous drive for participation in the socialist transformation of Chinese society, it is inevitable that the vast majority of the priests of any of the religions will eventually not be permitted to live exclusively by rendering religious services, which the Communists regard as nonproductive. Economic progress must be the supreme concern of a Communist nation, and religious worship must not affect the feverish drive for production quotas in all sectors of the nation's economy. It would be contrary to the central purpose of the Communist ideology to permit priests to utter prayers for a living, existing on the labor of others. Since collectivization of the land, temple land that used to yield rent for support of temple priests has now become part of the commune property, and the priests consequently have lost the economic sustenance which once enabled them to live an exclusively religious life without productive labor.

Generally speaking, temple priests in various provinces have been pressed into agricultural production on the same basis as secular peasants.[24] Buddhist and Taoist priests in Mount Nan-yo, a famous religious center in Hunan province, were organized into a commune and, like other communes, had to engage in "production emulation" campaigns.[25] The priests can still practice their religion in their leisure time, but many have returned to secular life as a result of either local antireligious pressure or the new circumstances which no longer grant priesthood any privilege or advantage.

Actually, in the rural areas of north China, it was a general practice in pre-Communist days for Buddhist or Taoist priests to farm a small plot of land belonging either to the temple or to the priest or rented from landlords, and they would perform religious services in private homes or on community occasions to earn additional income. In such cases the Communist action did not introduce any drastic alteration in their lives. It is the priests in the large cities, especially in south China, who formerly lived entirely on land rent or on religious services, who have been most seriously affected. In a few important temples or convents, however, priests have been permitted to continue their exclusively religious life, drawing financial support both from payments by worshipers visiting the temples and from part-time agricultural production.

The pre-Communist trend of converting temples and other religious premises to secular uses has been accelerated. An important development under the Communist rule has been the vast increase of public organizations and group activities as a part of the revolutionary process. These activities need buildings, and the temples and even some Christian churches stand as the most readily available sites for schools, "cultural palaces," Peasants' Association headquarters, village and town coöperative stores, and even temporary jails for victims of the many persecution campaigns. If Sun Fa-hsü, the magistrate of Ting county of Hopei province, could transform 75 per cent of the county's temples into schools in a single year in the early part of the century when conservatism was strong (see chap. xii), the Communists can certainly improve on his record with their absolute power, their effective organizational and propaganda techniques, and their atheistic enthusiasm.

A seemingly contradictory Communist action has been the vigorous renovation and repair of famous temples in various parts of China. The great temples in Peking, Hangchow, and many other places have not seen such refurbishing work for half a century. The monastery of Six Banyan Trees in Canton, a landmark of Chinese Buddhism dating back to the Tang dynasty, was thoroughly renovated in 1955.[26] And the Hsüan-wu temple in Fo-shan in the neighborhood of Canton (see chap. vii) underwent major repairs and redecoration in 1956, with huge sums of money expended on a complete renewal of its main hall, including the weapons and the official seal for the use of the Hsüan-wu god.[27]

One likely motive for preserving the art and architecture of the great temple buildings is that they are symbols of the renewed pride in Chinese culture and stimulants to nationalistic sentiments. Another possible ground is to win support from the religious population and from the older common people, who still retain much of their traditional religious beliefs. But it should be kept in mind that the restoration work is limited to large, well-known temples in each locality, while innumerable humble ones are left to deteriorate or are converted to nonreligious uses. The wholesale impressing of priests into secular production work and the conversion of most temples into secular quarters would seriously reduce the already weak foundation of traditional institutional religion, an effect not canceled by the restoration of large temples.

SUPPRESSION OF RELIGIOUS SOCIETIES

We recall that sectarian societies were the dreaded enemies of the imperial government from the Ming dynasty on. Even under the Republic, the warlords and provincial authorities were at odds with them, and the Nationalist government more than once took suppressive action against some of the suspected sectarian organizations. This ancient tradition of antagonism to politically insubordinate religious societies has remained with the Communsts.

A year after they took power, in 1950, the Communists began accusing the religious societies of being a major system of counterrevolutionary organizations. The names of the accused groups are familiar to those acquainted with the story of popular religious movements since the eighteenth century: Pai-yang Chiao (White Sun religion), Lung Hua Hui (Dragon Flower association), Chiu-kung Tao (Nine Mansions sect), Sheng Hsien Tao (Sages sect), Red Spear association, Big Sword association, I-kuan Tao (Unity sect), and so on. These familiar organizations have re-emerged to play their traditional role of offering resistance to a government of absolute power. Only the specific crimes they are accused of are new: being the underground for Chiang Kai-shek and the United States. The Communists have spared no effort in their attempts to suppress the sects.[28]

During the land reform of 1951–52, many landlords were executed under the charge of organizing superstitious societies and spreading rumors to delude the public.[29] In the fall of 1952, the chief of security police, Lo Jui-ch'ing, announced the liquidation of leaders of many religious societies as a great accomplishment of the new regime.[30] But obviously the accomplishment was far from a complete victory, for three years later, despite the announced liquidation of over 40,000 members, traditional religious societies were found very much occupied with their "counterrevolutionary" role in practically every part of the country. Reports of their activities came in from the provinces of Shensi, Kansu, Hunan, Hupeh, Hopei, Shantung, Szechwan, Kweichow, Kwangtung, Kwangsi and Chekiang. Shensi province, where the Communists had en-

joyed power for over two decades, longer than in any other province, was found to be far more infested with sectarian activities than
were other territories.[31]

Long adapted to underground resistance, the sectarians have
carried on their activities under a variety of camouflage. They often
change their society labels to divert attention. The I-kuan Tao (see
chap. ix) took on the name of Chung Tao (Middle sect) in some
localities in Shensi province. Many of its members traveled great
distances disguised as itinerant merchants. From inland Shensi to
coastal Hopei, the construction of underground chambers and extensive systems of communication tunnels has become widespread.
Some of the subterranean chambers are large enough to accommodate over 30 people, and the tunnels long enough to connect
strategic places throughout entire villages. In 1955, the Communist
police uncovered 102 subterranean hiding places in Shensi alone,
arresting 434 sectarian leaders.[32] In Tung-kuang county of Hopei
province, several long-hunted sectarian leaders were found to have
taken refuge in tunnels for over four years.[33]

By these and many other devious means, the sectarians bored into
all branches of government-approved local organizations. Before the
establishment of people's communes, they aimed especially at controlling mutual-aid teams and agricultural producers' coöperatives.
Many of these organizations were discovered to be branch units of
sectarian systems. Under the protection of these legitimate organizations, the sectarians spread rumors and sabotaged Communist programs, for example, by advising people to store up grain as an act
of religious piety, in order to prevent the fulfillment of the state
quota of grain collection. Their claim of age-old miracles, such as the
potency of a new magical formula or the healing power of a magical
water, drew large followings, especially among the peasants.

All these magical practices were familiar to the imperial officials
who for centuries combated the sectarian systems. It is probably
incorrect to assume that the Communists, although they have recently won success by their mastery of underground techniques, possess fully effective countermeasures against the underground sectarian societies. While the Communists can infiltrate into any of the
known societies at will, they may not be able to penetrate into every

one of the numerous isolated small units in a highly decentralized organizational system. Furthermore, as one society is suppressed, others continue to rise spontaneously. The root of the matter lies in the popular belief in the gods and their magic to bring deliverance from suffering, and in the popular tradition of organizing religious groups to offer resistance to an oppressive ruling power against which the individual seems helpless.

PROSPECTS

The decline of theistic religion in recent decades, whether spontaneous or induced, has the sociological significance of stripping the traditional social order of its sacred character or awe-inspiring quality. This facilitates the process of replacement of the old social order by the new. In this light, the decline of theistic religion is part of the larger process of the transition of the traditional Chinese society to a different pattern.

As theistic religion declined, popular movements of secular faiths arose to fill the vacated function of providing integrative forces for society as well as for the individual personality, climaxing in domination by the Communist ideology which, despite its non-theistic nature, has all the qualities of a vigorous new faith. This new faith commands dynamic power for mass action by holding forth the promise of fulfillment of popular aspirations for national political strength and materialistic progress; it gains broad acceptance among the new generation by its advocacy of materialistic rationalism; it generates courage and fanaticism among its followers by its absolute certitude that the Communist ideology is the only road to fulfillment of the nation's aspirations.

Under the demand for unconditional submission to the new faith, theistic religious organizations continue to exist on a limited and precarious level. But theistic beliefs remain a strong influence among the people in spite of persistent interference and systematic control from the new faith. Thus, the current picture is one of both a new nontheistic faith and the old theistic traditions. Since both secular faiths and theistic traditions are expressions of man's struggle with the problems of social existence, this mixed picture fully reflects the state of transition of Chinese society. What are the possible developments from this transitory situation?

We have seen in the foregoing chapters that traditional Chinese religious life was mostly diffused in the secular social institutions, and that, as old institutions crumbled under the impact of new social pressures, their theistic symbols also waned or died. Continued consolidation of the Communist system would cause further decay of the traditional institutions which, in turn, would bring progressive weakening or even elimination of the old religious elements diffused in them. Even in the pre-Communist decades, modern urban nuclear families no longer regarded ancestor worship as the centered act of the kinship group; labor unions and chambers of commerce, which replaced the traditional guilds, neither retained their trade patron gods nor installed new ones; the central and local governments no longer expressed their operating values and even their own existence in terms of theistic symbols, although the untutored populace still believed in the preordained course of Heaven and its subsidiary deities. The intensification of the same trend during the first ten years of Communist rule makes it unlikely that the old myths and theistic cults will be revived as operating symbols for the major institutions. Any such revival would have to combat systematic Communist efforts to teach the view that "religion . . . has to run through the process of growth, development and extinction; it must eventually go on the path of extinction." [34]

But will theistic religion "eventually go on the path of extinction," and will new theistic symbols rise to replace the fallen gods? This will depend on the adequacy and enduring quality of secular faiths, including Communism, as the new stabilizing foundations for social institutions. There is no common agreement on an answer to this problem. Proponents of humanist faiths in the West, having rejected sacramental myths and cults, would maintain an affirmative view. Accordingly, the secular faith of Communism would embody the ultimate concern for both society and the individual for a long period of time, during which theistic beliefs, rituals, and organizations would be eliminated in the course of group and personal adjustment to the atheistic requirements of the Communist system. But other observers doubt the permanence of the current

humanist movement as an effort to develop a new faith for life in
the turbulent age of revolutions. Speaking of believers in humanist
faiths and "independent morals," Paul Tillich maintains that their

moral strength was and is greater than in members of a religiously active
community. But this is a transitory stage. There is still faith in these
men, ultimate concern about human dignity and personal fulfillment.
There is religious substance in them, which, however, can be wasted in
the next generation if the faith is not renewed. This is possible only in
the community of faith under the continuous impact of its mythical and
cultic symbols. . . . Cult and myth keep faith alive.[35]

Thus, the humanitarian values of the first-generation Communists
are inherited from conventional faiths and would be difficult to
transmit to later generations for lack of mythical and cultic vehicles. The new generation, nurtured in a completely demythologized
doctrine, may enjoy a sense of fulfillment in economic security
and national power, should the Communist program succeed, but
they will be anemic in moral integrative values, which up till now
have been conveyed by the awe and fascination of myths and cults.

It would be difficult to evaluate the two opposing views as a basis
for interpreting the durability of the Communist faith and the
fate of theistic religion under its dominance. The unprecedented
situation of China's being ruled by a completely demythologized
faith leaves us with no historical case for comparison. Confucianism,
despite its rationalistic qualities, may be regarded only as a partially
secular faith, for, although it set up no supernatural premise for its
system of values, its theoretical system as a whole drew confidence
from supernatural notions of Heaven and fate, and as a practiced
tradition it developed many associated myths and cults which
helped undergird its values. Buddhism and Taoism both originated
as nontheistic philosophies but both developed into theistic religions
when they came to be concerned with the life of the masses. Therefore, none of these great historical faiths can supply us with relevant
examples.

Considering the modern secular rationalistic trend in China, the
materialistic premise of the Communist ideology would preclude
the development of a mythological content of its own, similar to

that in Buddhism and Taoism. On the other hand, Communism's probable inability to cope with all social and personal crises that may arise in the future would compel the people, when subjected to extreme distress, to continue to reach beyond the finitude of empirical experience and rational thought for relief. Should this be the case, even if the Communist ideology were to endure as a sociopolitical doctrine, it would have to develop permanent tolerance of theistic religion so that theism could perform the moral integrative function of stabilizing the new social order. The gods might then emerge from their eclipse to play a familiar role under the dominance of a disbelieving political orthodoxy, a situation reminiscent of the long and often stormy co-existence of theistic religion and Confucianism, whose excessively earthly quality invited the development of theistic faiths.

NOTES

Chapter I

[1] Y. C. Yang, *China's Religious Heritage* (New York, 1953), pp. 42–43, and W. T. Chan, *Religious Trends in Modern China* (New York, 1953), pp. 14 and 246.

[2] *China,* ed. by H. F. MacNair (Berkeley and Los Angeles, 1951), pp. 18–21.

[3] Liang Ch'i-ch'ao, "Chung-kuo li-shih yen-chiu fa" (Methodology for the Study of Chinese History) in his *Yin-ping shih ch'uan-chi* (The Complete Collected Works of the Ice-Sipping Studio) (Shanghai, 1929), chüan 23, pp. 138–141. Also see his two articles, "Lun Chi-na tsung-chiao kai-ke" (On the Reform of Chinese Religion) and "K'ung Tzu chiao-i shih-chi Pi-yi yü chin-jih kuo-min che ho-tsai, yü ch'ang-ming-chih ch'ih-tao ho-yu" (How Does the Doctrine of Confucius Actually Benefit the Present-Day Citizens, and What Is the Way to Broaden Its Light?), both printed in the same collection, chüan 21. In the present volume, unless a specific translator is indicated in the reference note, the translation from Chinese sources is the author's own.

[4] Hu Shih, *The Chinese Renaissance* (Chicago, 1934), p. 78.

[5] Hu Shih, "Ming Chiao" (The Doctrine of Names) in *Hu Shih wen ts'un* (Shanghai, 1928), vol. 1, p. 91.

[6] Ch'ien Tuan-sheng, *The Government and Politics in China* (Cambridge, Mass., 1950), p. 15.

[7] Li Ching-han, *Ting hsien she-hui kai-k'uang tiao-ch'a* (A Social Survey of Ting County) (Peking, 1932), pp. 424–426.

[8] Willem A. Grootaers, with Li Shih-yü and Chang Chih-wen, *Temples and History of Wanchuan* (Chahar), Monumenta Serica (Peking, 1948), vol. XIII.

[9] *Wang-tu hsien hsiang-t'u t'u-shuo* (Illustrated Gazetteer of Wang-tu County) (1905 edition).

[10] *Sang-yuan wei chih* (Gazetteer of the Mulberry Garden Dike Village) (1932), chüan 14, pp. 3–10.

[11] L. Newton Hayes, "Gods of the Chinese," *Royal Asiatic Society, North China Branch* (1924), vol. 55, pp. 97, 103, quoted in Clarence B. Day, *Chinese Peasant Cults* (Shanghai, 1940), p. 13.

[12] *Ch'ang-chiang jih-pao* (Hankow, March 18, 1953), p. 3.

[13] C. A. S. Williams, *Outlines of Chinese Symbolism and Art Motives* (Shanghai, 1932); J. LeRoy Davidson, *The Lotus Sutra in Chinese Art* (New York, 1954).

14 The Tatung cave temples, which René Grousset compared in grandeur to France's Chartres and Rheims, were cut from sandstone caves and hillsides by the T'o-pa people of the Northern Wei dynasty between A.D. 460 and 494, and additions and restorations were later undertaken by the Khitan people of the Liao dynasty. See Suiichi Mizuno, "Archeological Survey of the Yün-kang Grottoes," *Archives of the Chinese Art Society of America*, 1950, vol. IV, pp. 39–60; T. Sekino and T. Takejuma, *Ryo-kin-jidai no Kenchiku to sano Butsuzo* (Buddhist Architecture and Sculpture of the Liao and Chin Dynasties) (Tokyo, 1934), vol. I, pls. 50–55; L. Carrington Goodrich, *A Short History of the Chinese People* (New York, 1943), p. 100.

15 J. J. M. DeGroot, *Sectarianism and Religious Persecution in China* (Amsterdam, 1903).

16 See, for example, the mainland press summary on "reactionary" minority religious leaders in Tsinghai and Kansu, *Survey of China Mainland Press* (American Consulate General, Hong Kong, February, 1959), no. 549.

17 W. T. Chan, *Religious Trends in Modern China*, pp. 144 and 240.

18 E. R. Hughes and K. Hughes, *Religion in China* (London, 1950), p. 9.

19 Hu Shih, *Chung-kuo chang-hui hsiao-shuo k'ao-cheng* (A Study of Chinese Fiction Written in Chapters) (Dairen, Manchuria, 1943), pp. 315–379.

20 See John Ross, *The Original Religion of China* (Edinburgh, 1909), and H. G. Creel, *Sinicism* (Chicago, 1929).

21 Willem A. Grootaers, Li Shih-yü, and Chang Chih-wen, *Temples and History of Wanchuan* (Chahar), Monumenta Serica (Peking, 1948), vol. XIII, pp. 314–315.

22 J. Milton Yinger, *Religion, Society and the Individual* (New York, 1957), chap. 1.

CHAPTER II

1 A spirit tablet was made of wood, about 4 inches wide, 8 or 9 inches high, and 1 inch thick, standing on a wooden pedestal. On the front was written the name of the deceased, his or her family status, and official government ranks and titles, if any. On the back was written the hour, day, month, and year of the birth and death of the deceased.

2 *Lieh tzu*, chüan 7, p. 2, quoted in Feng Yu-lan, *Chung-kuo chieh-hsüeh shih*, 1933 (Shanghai, Commercial Press edition), vol. 1, p. 418, tr. by Derk Bodde, *A History of Chinese Philosophy* (Princeton, N.J., 1952), vol. 1, p. 345.

3 See, for example, the description in Francis L. K. Hsü, *Under the Ancestors' Shadow* (London, 1949), pp. 158–160.

4 See, for example, Bronislaw Malinowski, *Magic, Science and Religion* (New York, 1954), pp. 41–43. Also, Emile Durkheim, *The Elementary Forms of the Religious Life*, tr. by Joseph Swain (New York, 1926), p. 33.

5 *Li Chi*, chüan 8, p. 6, quoted in Feng Yu-lan, *op. cit.*, vol. 1, p. 353.

6 *Yüeh-p'u li chih*, ed. by Chen Ying-k'ang (1933), chüan 4, p. 3.

7 *Lun yü*, book 1, chap. 9.

8 Feng Yu-lan, *op. cit.*, p. 345.

9 *Ibid.*, p. 349.

[10] Chiang Yung, *Li Chi hsün i che yen* (Selected Annotations of the Book of Rites) (1873), chüan 2, p. 31.

[11] *Hsün Tzu,* quoted in Feng Yu-lan, *op. cit.,* p. 351.

[12] *Ibid.,* p. 352.

[13] *Ibid.*

[14] Robert H. Lowie, *Primitive Religion* (London, 1936), pp. 3–14.

[15] William James, *Varieties of Religious Experience* (London, 1902), pp. 386–388.

[16] *Ta-ch'ing lü li ch'eng-hsiu t'ung-ts'uan chih-ch'eng* (New Complete Edition of Laws and Regulations of the Ch'ing Government) (Shanghai, 1900), chüan 17, p. 19.

[17] Quoted in Feng Yu-lan, *op. cit.,* p. 356.

[18] *Hun-yin fa chiang-hua* (Talks on the Marriage Law) (Shanghai, 1952), p. 48.

[19] C. K. Yang, *The Chinese Family in the Communist Revolution* (Cambridge, Mass., 1959), chap. II.

CHAPTER III

[1] Joachim Wach, *Sociology of Religion* (Chicago, 1944), p. 256; also H. T. Fei, *Peasant Life in China* (London, 1940), chaps. 3–6.

[2] See, for example, J. S. M. Ward and W. G. Sterling, *The Hung Society* (London, 1925).

[3] Hirayama Amane, *Chung-kuo mi-mi she-hui shih* (A History of Chinese Secret Societies) (Shanghai, 1912), pp. 36–48.

[4] Feng Yu-lan, *History of Chinese Philosophy* (Princeton, N.J., 1952), tr. by Derk Bodde, vol. I, p. 352.

[5] See the definition of the word *wen* in *T'zu-yuan* (Commercial Press, Shanghai, 1949 edition), p. 668.

[6] *Ta-ch'ing lü li ch'eng-hsiu t'ung-ts'uan chih-ch'eng,* chüan 16, pp. 4–5, section on sacrifices.

[7] For example, *Ch'ing-ch'ao hsü wen-hsien t'ung-k'ao* (Classified Collection of Official Documents of the Ch'ing Dynasty, Late Edition) (Shanghai, 1935), chüan 158.

[8] *Fo-shan chung-i-hsiang chih* (1923), chüan 8, p. 12.

[9] Willem A. Grootaers, Li Shih-yü, and Chang Chih-wen, *Temples and History of Wanchuan* (Chahar), Monumenta Serica (Peking, 1948), vol. XIII, p. 298.

[10] *Ch'uan-sha t'ing chih* (1880), chüan 5, p. 2.

[11] Bronislaw Malinowski, *Magic, Science and Religion* (New York, 1954), pp. 24–36.

[12] *Ch'ing-ch'ao hsü wen-hsien t'ung-k'ao,* chüan 158, p. 9128.

[13] *Sang-yuan wei chih* (Gazetteer of the Mulberry Garden Dike Village) (1932), chüan 14, pp. 1–8.

[14] Bronislaw Malinowski, *Magic, Science and Religion* (New York, 1954), pp. 24–36; also Joachim Wach, *Sociology of Religion* (Chicago, 1944), pp. 220 ff.

15 John S. Burgess, *The Guilds of Peking* (New York, 1928), p. 176.

16 For a description of patron deities in different occupations, see Clarence B. Day, *Chinese Peasant Cults* (Shanghai, 1940), pp. 108–113, 213; Burgess, *The Guilds of Peking* (New York, 1928); pp. 172–182, 188–189; and John Shryock, *The Temples of Anking and Their Cults* (Paris, 1931), p. 162.

17 Ch'ü Tui-chi, *Chung-kuo she-hui shih-liao ts'ung-ch'ao* (Source Book on Chinese Social History) (Shanghai, 1937), p. 505.

18 Compare the versions in *Pao-shan hsien chih* (1921), chüan 5, p. 3, and *Fo-shan chung-i hsiang-chih* (1923), chüan 8, pp. 11–12.

19 Burgess, *The Guilds of Peking,* pp. 182–187.

20 *Ibid.,* pp. 181–182.

21 *Ibid.,* pp. 183–184.

22 See *Ch'uan-sha hsien chih* (1936 edition), chüan 12, p. 7; see also Appendix 1 at the end of this volume.

23 Clarence B. Day, "Shanghai Invites the God of Wealth," *China Journal* (June, 1928), pp. 289–294.

24 Clarence B. Day, *Chinese Peasant Cults,* p. 20.

25 Vasilii M. Alexseev, *The Chinese Gods of Wealth* (Hertford, 1928), p. 4.

26 R. H. Tawney, *Religion and the Rise of Capitalism* (New York, 1953), pp. 39–54.

27 Max Weber, *The Religion of China: Confucianism and Taoism,* tr. and ed. by Hans H. Gerth (Glencoe, Ill., 1951), pp. 247–248, 237.

Chapter IV

1 C. K. Yang, *A North China Rural Market Economy* (Institute of Pacific Relations, New York, 1944).

2 Sidney D. Gamble, *Ting Hsien, A North China Rural Community* (New York, 1954), pp. 412–413. For the worship of tree spirits as a universal trait, see James George Frazer, *The Golden Bough* (New York, 1922), pp. 126–138.

3 Gamble, *Ting Hsien,* pp. 411–412. See also Li Ching-han, *Ting-hsien she-hui kai-k'uang tiao-ch'a* (A Social Survey of Ting-hsien) (Peiping, 1933), pp. 436–443.

4 See, for example, John Shryock, *The Temples of Anking and Their Cults* (Paris, 1931), p. 32.

5 Gamble, *Ting Hsien,* p. 414.

6 *Ibid.,* pp. 4–5.

7 Clarence B. Day, *Chinese Peasant Cults,* chap. 3.

8 See, for example, Li Ching-han, *Ting-hsien she-hui kai-k'uang tiao-ch'a,* pp. 431–432.

9 Francis L. K. Hsü, *Religion, Science and Human Crises* (London, 1952), chaps. 2–5.

10 For English sources see, for example, Wolfram Eberhard, *Chinese Festivals* (New York, 1952). Chinese sources on festivals are inexhaustibly rich, as there are the large variety of *feng-su chi* or records of customs and tradition, either in the form of independent works or as parts of local gazetteers.

[11] Bronislaw Malinowski, *Magic, Science and Religion* (New York, 1954), p. 65.

[12] Ch'ü Tui-chi, *Chung-kuo she-hui shih-liao ts'ung-ch'ao* (Source Book on Chinese Social History) (Shanghai, 1937), p. 498.

[13] *Ibid.*, pp. 482–498.

[14] *Fo-shan chung-i-hsiang chih* (Gazetteer of Fo-shan, the Home of the Loyal and the Righteous) (1923 edition), chüan 8, pp. 19–22.

[15] *Wang-tu hsien chih* (Gazetteer of Wang-tu County) (1905 edition), chüan 2, p. 92.

[16] *Wang-tu hsien chih* (1934 edition), chüan 2, pp. 42–55.

[17] *Ch'ing-ho hsien chih* (Gazetteer of Ch'ing-ho County) (1934 edition), chüan 2, p. 66.

[18] *Wang-tu hsien chih* (1934 edition), chüan 2, p. 50.

[19] Clarence B. Day, *Chinese Peasant Cults,* chap. 3. Also see *Ch'uan-sha hsien chih* (1936 edition), chüan 2.

[20] See, for example, the list of names of temples in *Pao-shan hsien chih* (Gazetteer of Pao-shan County, Kiangsu Province) (1921 edition), chüan 3, pp. 17–20; chüan 5, pp. 8–23.

[21] *Wang-tu hsien hsiang-t'u t'u shuo* (Illustrated Gazetteer of Wang-tu County) (1905), pp. 59–60.

CHAPTER V

[1] See, for example, the extensive survey of this question by Joachim Wach in his *Sociology of Religion* (Chicago, 1944), chap. VII; also Ernst Cassirer, *The Myth of the State* (New York, 1955), chap. VII, and Henry Sumner Maine, *Ancient Law* (New York, 1864), pp. xv–xvi.

[2] Joachim Wach, *Sociology of Religion,* chap. VII.

[3] Fu Ch'in-chia, *Chung-kuo tao-chiao shih* (History of Taoist Religion in China) (Shanghai, 1937), chaps. 1–8; Wang Chih-hsin, *Chung-kuo tsung chiao szu-hsiang shih* (History of Chinese Religious Thought) (Shanghai, 1930), chaps. 1–6; and Hu Shih's periodization in his "Religion and Philoso-phy in Chinese History," in *Symposium on Chinese Culture,* ed. by Sophia H. Chen Zen (Shanghai, 1931), p. 32.

[4] Fu Ch'in-chia, *Chung-kuo tao-chiao shih,* p. 45.

[5] *Ibid.*

[6] Marcel Granet, *La Religion des Chinois* (Paris, 1922), pp. 1–35, 102–139.

[7] Herlee C. Creel, "Shih T'ien" (The Meaning of T'ien), *Yenching Journal* (1935), no. 18, p. 71. See also Kuo Mo-jo, *Hsien-ch'in t'ien-tao kuan-nien ti chin-chan* (The Development of the Concept of Heaven in the Pre-Ch'in Period) (Shanghai, 1930), p. 14.

[8] Hsü Ti-shan, "Tao-chia szu-hsiang yü tao-chiao" (Taoist Thought and the Taoist Religion), *Yenching Journal* (1927), no. 2.

[9] Liang Ch'i-ch'ao, "Yin-yang wu-hsing shuo chih lai-li" (Origin of the Theory of Yin-yang and the Five Elements); Ku Chieh-kang, "Wu-te tsung-shih shuo hsia ti cheng-chih ho li-shih" (Politics and History under the

Cyclical Theory of the Five Virtues); both articles in *Ku-shih pien* (Critical Studies of Ancient History), ed. by Ku Chieh-kang (Shanghai, 1935), vol. V, pp. 343–353 and 404–597.

[10] C. K. Yang, "Functional Relationship between Confucian Thought and Religion," in *Chinese Thought and Institutions,* ed. by John K. Fairbank (Chicago, 1957), pp. 269–290.

[11] Jacob Burckhardt, *Reflections on History* (London, 1943), p. 43.

[12] See the vivid reconstruction of the social and political conditions of this period in Etienne Balazs, "La crise sociale et la philosophie à la fin des Han," *T'oung Pao* (1949), vol. XXIX, pp. 83–131; also, Liu Shao-hsien, "Tung Han ching-chi chuang-k'uang" (Economic Conditions in Eastern Han), in *Chin-ta wen-hsüeh-yuan chi-k'an* (Liberal Arts College Quarterly of Chinling University) (1936), vol. I, no. 2.

[13] The "chu ti chi" (Emperors' Records) section of the *Hou han shu* (History of the Later Han) listed thirty-one peasant rebellions in the period 109–183.

[14] P'eng Tsu-shen, *Han-mo huang-chin chi luan ti she-hui ken-yuan* (Social Roots of the Yellow Turban Rebellion at the End of Han) (Shanghai, 1934), pp. 41–85. Also Howard S. Levy, "Yellow Turban Religion and Rebellion at the End of Han," *Journal of the American Oriental Society* (1956), vol. LXXVI, pp. 214–227.

[15] Max Weber, *The Religion of China,* tr. by Hans H. Gerth (Glencoe, Ill., 1951), p. 193.

[16] *Shih lao chih* (Records of Buddhism and Taoism), chüan 8, p. 28.

[17] Teng Yün-t'e, *Chung-kuo chiu fang shih* (History of Famine Relief in China) (Peking, 1958), pp. 8–12.

[18] Han Yü, "Chien ying fo ku piao" (Memorial against Welcoming the Bone of Buddha), in *Ku wen p'ing chu* (Annotated Ancient Prose) (Shanghai, 1921), chüan 6, pp. 16–17.

[19] Ch'ien Mu, *Kuo-shih ta-kang* (Outline of Chinese History) (Shanghai, 1934), vol. I, p. 260.

[20] Paul Tillich, *The Interpretation of History,* tr. by N. A. Rasetzki and Elso L. Talmey (New York, 1936), pp. 77–107.

[21] *Kuang hung ming chih,* quoted in Ch'ien Mu, *Kuo-shih ta-kang,* pp. 260–261.

[22] For the Emperor Yang's patronage of Buddhism, see Arthur F. Wright, "The Formation of Sui Ideology," in *Chinese Thought and Institutions,* ed. by John K. Fairbank (Chicago, 1957), pp. 71–105.

[23] Both quoted in Ch'ien Mu, *Kuo-shih ta-kang,* p. 264.

[24] Hu Shih, "Ch'an Buddhism in China," *Philosophy East and West* (April, 1953), vol. III, p. 17.

[25] See also Kenneth Ch'en, "On Some Factors Responsible for the Anti-Buddhist Persecution under the Pei Ch'ao," in *Harvard Journal of Asiatic Studies* (June, 1954), vol. XVII, nos. 1 and 2, pp. 261–274.

[26] E. R. Hughes and K. Hughes, *Religion in China* (London, 1950), chap. V.

[27] Liang Ch'i-ch'ao, "Nan-hai hsien-sheng chuan" (A Biography of [Kang] Nan-hai), in *Yin-ping-shih wen-shih* (Shanghai, 1924), vol. 3, pp. 50–59.

CHAPTER VI

[1] E. R. Hughes and K. Hughes, *Religion in China* (London, 1950), p. 92.

[2] *Ch'ing-ch'ao hsü wen-hsien t'ung-k'ao,* chüan 147–149, pp. 9071–9088.

[3] *Ibid.,* chüan 147, p. 9076.

[4] *Ibid.,* chüan 148, p. 9079.

[5] Li Chien-nung, *Chung-kuo chin-pai-nien cheng-chih shih* (History of Chinese Politics in the Recent Century) (Shanghai, 1947), pp. 426–451.

[6] See, for example, Clarence B. Day, *Chinese Peasant Cults,* p. 75, and E. R. Hughes and K. Hughes, *Religion in China,* pp. 90–93.

[7] *Tso chuan* (The Seventh Year of Duke Ch'ao), quoted in *Ma-ch'eng hsien chih* (1881 edition), chüan 8, p. 1.

[8] Ernst Cassirer, *The Myth of the State* (New York, 1955), chap. VII; Robert W. Williamson, *Religion and Social Organization in Central Polynesia* (Cambridge, England, 1937), chap. XI.

[9] For a discourse on the nature of the sagelike wisdom and the proper qualities of the ruler, see the translation of a passage on the Doctrine of the Mean in *Chung Yung,* tr. by E. R. Hughes in *The Great Learning and the Mean-in-Action* (London, 1942).

[10] *Ch'ing-ch'ao hsü wen-hsien t'ung-k'ao,* chüan 156, p. 9117.

[11] Ku Chieh-kang, "Wu-te chung-shih shuo hsia chih cheng-chih ho li-shih" (Politics and History under the Cyclical Theory of the Five Virtues), *Ku shih pien* (Critical Studies of Ancient History), ed. by Ku Chieh-kang (Shanghai, 1935), pp. 404–616.

[12] See, for example, Henri Doré, *Researches into Chinese Superstitions* (Shanghai, 1911–1934); and in Chinese, Jung Shao-tsu, *Mi-hsin yü ch'uan-shuo* (Superstitions and Lore) (Canton, 1929).

[13] Franz Michael, "State and Society in Nineteenth-Century China," in *World Politics* (April, 1955), vol. VII, no. 3, p. 420.

[14] C. K. Yang, *A Chinese Village in Early Communist Transition* (Cambridge, Mass., 1959), p. 255.

[15] See, for example, Wolfram Eberhard, "The Function of Astronomy and Astronomers in China during the Han Period," in *Chinese Thought and Institutions,* ed. by John K. Fairbank (Chicago, 1957), pp. 33–70.

[16] *Ch'ing-ch'ao hsü wen-hsien t'ung-k'ao,* chüan 150, p. 9092.

[17] *Ch'uan-sha t'ing chih* (1879 edition), chüan 14, p. 16.

[18] *Ibid.,* chüan 14, p. 1.

[19] *Chung Yung,* tr. by James Legge, chap. 24.

CHAPTER VII

[1] *Fo-shan chung-i-hsiang chih* (Gazetteer of Fo-shan, the Home of the Loyal and the Righteous) (1923 edition), chüan 8, p. 13.

[2] *Ta-ch'ing lü-li cheng-hsiu t'ung-ts'uan chih-ch'eng* (Revised Compilation of Laws and Regulations of the Ch'ing Dynasty) (Shanghai, 1908), chüan 16, p. 5.

[3] Feng, *History of Chinese Philosophy*, tr. by Derk Bodde, vol. 1, pp. 353–354.

[4] See the preamble to the sacrificial canon for the gods of earth and grain in *Ch'ing-ch'ao hsü wen-hsien t'ung-k'ao*, chüan 153, p. 9105.

[5] Sidney D. Gamble, *Ting Hsien*, p. 401.

[6] Yü Mu-jen, "T'an Ssu-t'ung ti tsung-chiao kuan" (The Religious Views of T'an Ssu-t'ung), in *Wen She Monthly* (February, 1928), vol. 3, no. 5, p. 24.

[7] Clarence B. Day, *Chinese Peasant Cults*, chaps. 8 and 9. The six boards were: personnel, justice, finance, public works, rites, and military affairs.

[8] The mythological background of this god was well told in Willem A. Grootaers' "The Hagiography of the Chinese God Chen-wu," in *Folklore Studies* (1952), vol. XI, no. 2; and in Hsü Tao-ling, "Hsüan-wu ti shih-yuan yü tui-pien" (The Origin and Evolution of Hsüan Wu), in *Shih-hsüeh chi-k'an* (Historical Quarterly) (December, 1947), no. 5.

[9] *Wang-tu hsien chih* (Gazetteer of Wang-tu County) (1934 edition), chüan 2, pp. 46–47.

[10] *Fo-shan chung-i-hsiang chih*, chüan 8, pp. 1–34.

[11] *Ibid.*, chüan 8, p. 20.

[12] *Ibid.*, chüan 8, p. 32.

[13] *Ibid.*

[14] *Wang-tu hsien chih* (1934 edition), chüan 2, p. 42.

[15] Lewis Hodous, *Folkways in China* (London, 1929), pp. 114 ff.

[16] *Ch'ing-ch'ao hsü wen-hsien t'ung-k'ao*, chüan 154, p. 9111.

[17] See, for example, the quotation of this statement in a memorial to the throne on the need of bestowing an honorific title upon a river god. *Ibid.*, chüan 158, p. 9128.

[18] See, for example, Florence Ayscough, "The Chinese Cult of Ch'eng Huang Lao Yeh," in *Royal Asiatic Society, North China Branch* (1924), vol. 55, p. 136; and E. T. C. Werner, *Dictionary of Chinese Mythology* (Shanghai, 1932), p. 49.

[19] Clarence B. Day, *Chinese Peasant Cults* (Shanghai, 1940), p. 121.

[20] *Wang-tu hsien chih* (1934 edition), chüan 2, pp. 47–48.

[21] Francis L. K. Hsü, *Under the Ancestors' Shadow* (London, 1949), p. 150.

[22] John Shryock, *The Temples of Anking and Their Cults* (Paris, 1931), p. 45.

[23] See R. F. Johnston, "The Cult of Military Heroes in China," in *New China Review* (February, 1921), vol. VIII, no. 1, pp. 49 ff.

[24] *Fo-shan chung-i-hsiang chih*, chüan 8, p. 20.

[25] *Ch'ing-ch'ao hsü wen-hsien t'ung-k'ao*, chüan 157, p. 9119.

[26] *Ibid.*

[27] *Fo-shan chung-i-hsiang chih*, chüan 8, pp. 20–23.

[28] *Ch'ing-ch'ao hsü wen-hsien t'ung-k'ao*, chüan 158, pp. 9127–9128.

[29] *Wang-tu hsien chih* (1934 edition), chüan 2, pp. 59–60.

[30] *Ch'uan-sha hsien chih* (1936 edition), chüan 12, pp. 5–6.

[31] *Ch'ing-ch'ao hsü wen-hsien t'ung-k'ao*, chüan 158, pp. 9129–9130.

[32] *Lo-ting hsien chih* (1881 edition), chüan 4, pp. 11–12.

[33] *Ch'ing-ho hsien chih* (1936 edition), chüan 2, pp. 28–29.

[34] *Fo-shan chung-i-hsiang chih,* chüan 8, Tz'u-ssu (Sanctuaries and Sacrifices), sec. 2, p. 11.

[35] *Wang-tu hsien chih* (1934 edition), chüan 2, pp. 47–48.

[36] Max Weber, *Religion of China,* p. 173.

[37] Feng, *History of Chinese Philosophy,* tr. by Derk Bodde, vol. 1, p. 350.

CHAPTER VIII

[1] *Ch'ing-ch'ao hsü wen-hsien t'ung-k'ao,* chüan 158, p. 9128.

[2] *Pao-shan hsien hsü-chih* (1921 edition), chüan 3, p. 19.

[3] *Ibid.*

[4] E. H. Parker, *Studies in Chinese Religion* (New York, 1910), p. 8.

[5] *Ta-ch'ing lü li cheng-hsiu t'ung-ts'uan chih-ch'eng* (Revised Complete Edition of Fundamental and Supplementary Laws of the Ch'ing Dynasty) (Shanghai, 1908), chüan 23, p. 10.

[6] *Ch'ing-ch'ao hsü wen-hsien t'ung-k'ao,* chüan 147, p. 9076, and chüan 148, p. 9079.

[7] *Ta-ch'ing lü li,* chüan 20, p. 7.

[8] *Ibid.,* chüan 17, p. 20.

[9] J. J. M. De Groot, *Sectarianism and Religious Persecution in China* (Amsterdam, 1903), pp. 157, 523, 540.

[10] *Ta-ch'ing lü li,* chüan 8, pp. 12–18.

[11] *Ta-ch'ing hui-tien shih-li* (Collected Institutes and Rules of the Ch'ing Dynasty, with Illustrated Cases) (Shanghai, 1909), chüan 390, p. 4.

[12] *Ta-ch'ing lü li,* chüan 8, p. 13.

[13] *Ibid.,* chüan 8, p. 15.

[14] *Ch'in-ting ta-ch'ing hui-tien* (Imperial Approved Collected Institutes of the Ch'ing Dynasty) (Shanghai, 1900), chüan 55, p. 20; hereafter cited as *Ta-ch'ing hui-tien.*

[15] *Ibid.*

[16] *Ibid.*

[17] *Ibid.*

[18] Fu Ch'in-chia, *Chung-kuo tao-chiao shih* (History of Taoist Religion in China) (Shanghai, 1937), p. 88.

[19] *Ta-ch'ing hui-tien,* chüan 36, p. 3.

[20] See the Chinese text in J. J. M. De Groot, *Religious Persecution,* p. 417.

[21] J. J. M. De Groot, *The Religion of the Chinese* (New York, 1910), chap. 11.

[22] De Groot, *Religious Persecution,* p. 417.

[23] *Ibid.,* pp. 216–217, 242.

[24] *Ibid.,* p. 531.

[25] *Ibid.,* pp. 244–248. The English translation by De Groot has been considerably altered by the present writer on the basis of the original Chinese text.

[26] *Erh-shih-wu shih* (Twenty-five Dynastic Histories) (Shanghai, 1934), reproduced edition, vol. 6 (Sung History), chüan 18, p. 50.

27 De Groot, *Religious Persecution,* pp. 108–109.

28 *Erh-shih-wu shih,* vol. 3 (Wei History), chüan 114, p. 297.

29 *Ibid.,* vol. 4 (Old T'ang History), chüan 79, p. 282.

30 Quoted in Ch'ien Mu, *Kuo-shih ta kang* (Outline of Chinese History) (Shanghai, 1930), vol. 1, p. 270.

31 *Erh-shih-wu shih,* vol. 4 (T'ang History), chüan 18, pp. 3–6.

32 Fan Chung-yen, *Fan Wen-cheng-kung wen-chih* (Collected Works of Fan Chung-yen) (Shanghai, 1910), chüan 8, pp. 8–9.

33 Karl A. Wittfogel and Feng Chia-sheng, "History of Chinese Society, Liao," *Transactions of the American Philosophical Society* (1946), vol. 36, n. s., 291–310.

34 *Ta-ch'ing lü li,* chüan 8, p. 16.

35 *Ibid.,* chüan 8, p. 15.

36 *Ibid.,* p. 19.

37 *Ta-ch'ing hui-tien,* chüan 36, p. 3.

38 *Sheng Hsün* (Imperial Instructions), chüan 78, pp. 10–13, quoted in De Groot, *Religious Persecution,* p. 528.

39 De Groot, *Religious Persecution,* p. 171.

40 See the interpretation of this quotation in Ch'en Huan, *Nan-Sung ch'u ho-pei hsin-tao-chiao k'ao* (A Research on the New Taoist Religion in Hopei During the Early Southern Sung Period) (Peking, 1941), p. 43.

41 *Ta-ch'ing lü li,* chüan 16, p. 8.

42 *Ibid.,* chüan 23, p. 10.

43 *Ta-ch'ing hui-tien,* chüan 55, p. 18.

44 *Ta-ch'ing lü li,* chüan 23, p. 6.

45 *Ch'in-ting p'ing-ting chiao-fei chih-lüeh* (Imperial Approved Abbreviated Account of Pacification of Religious Rebels) (1817), chüan 26, p. 6.

46 Sheng Hsün, chüan 78, quoted in De Groot, *Religious Persecution,* pp. 19–23.

47 See, for example, the order affecting the reconstruction of destroyed temples in the town of Lo-tien in Kiangsu province, *Lo-tien chen chih* (Gazetteer of Lo-tien Town) (1899 edition), chüan 1, p. 23.

48 *Erh-shih-wu shih,* vol. 5 (Chou History in the Old Histories of the Five Dynasties), chüan 104, p. 153.

49 *Ibid.*

50 *Ta-ch'ing hui-tien,* quoted in De Groot, *Religious Persecution,* pp. 104, 113.

51 This issue was being discussed as late as 1956; see the *Hua-chiao jih-pao* (Overseas Chinese Daily) (Hong Kong, February 29, 1956), p. 4.

52 De Groot, *Religious Persecution,* p. 524.

53 *Hunan nien-chien* (Hunan Yearbook) (1933), p. 837.

54 W. T. Chan, *Religious Trends in Modern China* (New York, 1953), p. 68.

55 Li Shih-yü, *Hsien-tsai Hua-pei mi-mi tsung-chiao* (Contemporary Secret Religions in North China) (Chengtu, Szechwan, 1948), Studia Serica, series B, no. 4, pp. 10–31.

56 See the editor's note, *Shih Huo* (Food and Money) *Bi-monthly* (September, 1935), vol. 1, no. 9, p. 53.

[57] Kenneth Ch'en, "On Some Factors Responsible for the Anti-Buddhist Persecution under the Pei Ch'ao," *Journal of Asiatic Studies* (June, 1954), vol. 17, nos. 1 and 2, pp. 261–274.

CHAPTER IX

[1] Max Weber, "Religious Rejections of the World and Their Directions," in *From Max Weber,* tr. by H. H. Gerth and C. Wright Mills (Galaxy Book edition, New York, 1958), pp. 323–362; Joachim Wach, *Sociology of Religion* (Chicago, 1944), p. 391.

[2] Nieh Ch'ung-ch'ih, *Erh-ch'ien nien lai mi-hsin chih-t'uan chih pien-luan* (Rebellions by Superstitious Organizations in Two Thousand Years). Also Ch'en Huan, *New Taoist Societies,* pp. 29 and 43 ff. (Publication place and date for both books unspecified.)

[3] Yano Jinichi, tr. into Chinese by Yang T'eh-fu, "Kuan-yü pai-nien-chiao chi luan" (On the Rebellion by the White Lotus Sect), in *Jen Wen Monthly* (February and March, 1935), vol. 6, nos. 1 and 2.

[4] *Ch'in-ting p'ing-ting chiao-fei chih-lüeh* (1817), chüan 26, p. 24.

[5] Sheng Hsün (Imperial Instructions), chüan 46–50, quoted in J. J. M. De Groot, *Sectarianism and Religious Persecution in China* (Amsterdam, 1903), pp. 487–550.

[6] Li Shih-yü, *Hsien-tsai Hua-pei mi-mi tsung-chiao* (Contemporary Secret Religions in North China) (Chengtu, Szechwan, 1948), Studia Serica, series B, no. 4, p. 166.

[7] *Survey of China Mainland Press* (American Consulate General, Hong Kong, 1955), no. 96, p. 3; also *Jen-min jih-pao* (People's Daily) (Peking, July 2, 1955), p. 3; (June 23, 1956), p. 1, with a statement by Lo Jui-ch'ing, Minister of Public Security in the Communist Central Government.

[8] Li Shih-yü, *op. cit.,* p. 37.

[9] Teng Yün-t'e, *Chung-kuo chiu fang shih* (History of Famine Relief in China) (Peking, 1958), pp. 58–133.

[10] De Groot, *op. cit.,* p. 518.

[11] Yü Mu-jen, "Taiping t'ien-kuo tsung-chiao-hua ti chun-shih yü cheng-chih" (Religionized Military and Political Systems Under the Taiping Heavenly Kingdom), *Wen She Monthly* (December, 1927), vol. 3, no. 2, pp. 38–40.

[12] *Ibid.,* p. 38.

[13] *Ibid.*

[14] *Ibid.*

[15] De Groot, *op. cit.,* p. 515.

[16] Li Shih-yü, *op. cit.,* p. 36.

[17] *Ibid.,* p. 15.

[18] Hu Shih, "Shuo Ju" (On Confucians), *Academica Sinica Bulletin* (1934), vol. IV, no. 3, pp. 233–284.

[19] Wang Chih-hsin, *Chung-kuo tsung-chiao ssu-hsiang shih ta-kang* (Outline History of Chinese Religious Thought) (Shanghai, 1930), pp. 79–83.

[20] *Erh-shih-wu shih* (Twenty-five Dynastic Histories) (Shanghai, 1934), vol. 9 (History of Ming Dynasty), pp. 302–303.

21 Yano Jinichi, "On the Rebellion by the White Lotus Sect" (cited in note 3).

22 Yü Mu-jen, *op. cit.*

23 *Ibid.*, pp. 32–33.

24 *Ibid.*, pp. 14–15.

25 Max Weber, *The Religion of China*, p. 230.

26 "Instruction to Kill the Evil Spirits, Save Mankind, and Protect the People in the Name of Heaven," quoted in "Lun hsin-hsing shih-min teng-chi tsai Taiping T'ien-kuo ke-ming chung ti tso-yung" (The Function of Newly Developed Classes of Citizens in the Taiping Revolution), by Kuo I-seng, *Li-shih yen-chiu* (Study of History), (March, 1956), no. 3, p. 11.

27 See, for example, De Groot, *op. cit.*, pp. 447–448, 451.

28 *Ibid.*, p. 228.

29 Yü Mu-jen, *op. cit.*, pp. 32–35.

CHAPTER X

1 See the excellent summary and interpretation in chap. v of E. R. and K. Hughes, *Religion in China* (London, 1950).

2 How the outlook of life of a great contemporary Confucian, K'ang Yu-wei, was colored by the Buddhist spirit of compassion is explained in Liang Ch'i-ch'ao's article, "K'ang nan-hai hsien-sheng chuan" (A Biography of K'ang Yu-wei), in *Yin-ping shih wen-chih* (Collected Works of the Ice-Sipping Studio) (Shanghai, 1924 edition), vol. 3, p. 70.

3 W. T. Chan, *Religious Trends in Modern China* (New York, 1953), p. 241; C. K. Yang, "Functional Relationship between Confucian Thought and Religion," in *Chinese Thought and Institutions,* ed. by J. K. Fairbank (Chicago, 1957), pp. 269–290.

4 Max Weber, *From Max Weber,* tr. and ed. by H. H. Gerth and C. Wright Mills (London, 1947), pp. 350 ff.

5 *Lun yü*, Book VII, chap. 20. The present translation of *kuai-li luan-shen* differs from most of the Chinese commentaries on which James Legge based his translation: "The subjects on which the Master did not talk were—extraordinary things, feats of strength, disorder, spiritual being." This is contradictory to the fact that Confucius did talk often of disorder and referred frequently to spiritual beings. Hence the adoption of the present version. In other places in this work, translations of statements in *Lun yü, Chung yung,* and *Meng tzu* are Legge's.

6 *Lun yü*, Book XI, chap. 11.

7 *Ibid.*, Book VI, chap. 20.

8 H. G. Creel, "Was Confucius Agnostic?" in *T'oung Pao* (1932), vol. XXIX, pp. 55–59.

9 See the numerous miracle stories in *Tso Chuan.*

10 "What I Believe: Autobiography," *Forum* (January–February, 1931), vol. 85, p. 42.

11 See, for example, the reprints of some of the leading articles in *Ku-shih pien* (Critical Studies of Ancient History), ed. by Ku Chieh-kang (Peking,

1935), vol. V, pp. 343–753; also see H. G. Creel, "Shih T'ien" (The Meaning of T'ien), *Yenching Journal* (1935), no. 18, pp. 59–71; Wen I-to, "T'ien-wen shih t'ien" (The Meaning of T'ien in *T'ien-wen*), *Tsing-hua Journal* (1934), vol. 9, pp. 873–895.

[12] Ch'ien Ta-hsin, *Shih-chia chai yang-hsin lu* (Notes on Nourishing the New in the Ten-Carriage Studio) (1840), chüan 3, p. 18.

[13] Ma Hsü-lun, "Shuo ming" (The Meaning of Fate), in *Hsüeh lin* (July, 1941), no. 9, pp. 15–34; Fu Ssu-nien, *Hsing ming ku-hsun pien-cheng* (A Critical Study on the Ancient Teachings on Human Nature and Fate). A summary of the latter work appears in Chan, *Religious Trends in Modern China*, pp. 27–29.

[14] *Lun yü*, Book XII, chap. 5.

[15] *Ibid.*, Book XIII, chap. 38.

[16] *Works of Mencius* (Hong Kong, 1948), tr. by James Legge, Book I, chap. 16.

[17] *Ibid.*, Book II, chap. 13.

[18] *Lun yü*, Book XX, chap. 3, and Book XVI, chap. 8.

[19] *Ibid.*, Book II, chap. 4.

[20] *The Doctrine of the Mean* (Hong Kong, 1948), tr. by James Legge, chap. 24.

[21] *Academica Sinica Bulletin* (1928), vol. 1, no. 1.

[22] Jung Shao-tsu, "Chan-pu ti yüan-liu" (Origin of Divination), *Academica Sinica Bulletin* (1928), vol. 1, no. 1, pp. 8–16, and Hsü Ti-shan, "Tao-chia ssu-hsiang yü tao-chiao" (Taoist Thought and Taoist Religion), in *Yenching Journal* (December, 1927), no. 2, pp. 249–283.

[23] *Lun yü*, Book VII, chap. 16.

[24] Liang Ch'i-ch'ao, "Yin-yang wu-hsing shuo chih lai-li" (Origin of the Theory of Yin-yang and the Five Elements), in *Ku-shih Pien*, ed. by Ku Chieh-kang, vol. V, pp. 353–359.

[25] *Ibid.*

[26] Ku Chieh-kang, "Wu-te chung-shih shuo hsia chih cheng-chih ho li-shih" (Politics and History under the Cyclical Theory of the Five Virtues), *Ku-shih Pien*, vol. V, pp. 404–617, 463, 585.

[27] Hsü Wen-shan, "Ju-chia ho wu-hsing ti kuan-hsi" (Relation between Confucianism and the Five Elements), *Ku-shih Pien*, vol. V, pp. 669–703.

[28] *Hsün Tzu*, vol. XIII, pp. 24–26, in Feng Yu-lan, *History of Chinese Philosophy*, tr. by Derk Bodde, vol. 1, p. 351.

[29] See E. R. and K. Hughes, *Religion in China*, pp. 56–58.

[30] Wu Ching-tzu, *Ju-lin wai-shih* (Shanghai, 1934), vol. 1, pp. 1–6.

[31] *Lo-tien chen chih* (Gazetteer of Lo-tien Town in Pao-shan County) (1889), chüan 8, p. 28.

[32] *Fo-shan chung-i-hsiang chih*, chüan 8, pp. 22–23.

[33] Hsü Ti-shan, *Fu-chi mi-hsin ti yen-chiu* (A Study of the Superstition of Coscinomancy) (Chungking, 1940), pp. 35–50.

[34] Hsü K'o, *Ch'ing pai lei-ch'ao* (Classified Miscellaneous Information of the Ch'ing Period) (Shanghai, 1928), chüan 73, p. 116.

[35] Hsü Ti-shan, *op. cit.*, p. 36.

[36] *Ibid.*

[37] Jung Shao-tsu, "Chan pu ti yüan-liu" (Origin of Divination), *Academica Sinica Bulletin* (1928), vol. 1, no. 1, p. 75.

[38] Li Shih-yü, *Hsien-tsai hua-pei mi-mi tsung-chiao* (Contemporary Secret Religions in North China) (Chengtu, 1948), pp. 63–66.

[39] *Lo-ting hsien chih* (1935 edition), chüan 2, pp. 1–2.

[40] *Yün-yang chang-shih tsung-p'u* (Genealogy of the Chang Family of the Yün-yang District) (1887), chüan 1, p. 6.

[41] *Chiang-yin kao-shih tsung-p'u* (Genealogy of the Kao Family of the Chiang-yin District) (1881), chüan 1, p. 2.

[42] *Wan t'ung-i wu-shih chia-ch'eng* (Genealogy of the Wu Family of the T'ung District in Anhui Province) (1868), chüan 1.

[43] Lü Fu-ch'en, *K'o-ch'ang i-wen lu* (published in the 1870's), chüan 8, p. 16.

[44] Wu Ching-tzu, *Ju-lin wai-shih,* vol. 1, pp. 35–36.

[45] *Sui-ning hsien chih* (Gazetteer of Sui-ning County, Szechwan Province) (1929 edition), chüan 1, pp. 39–40.

[46] W. T. Chan, *Religious Trends in Modern China,* pp. 258 ff.

[47] E. R. and K. Hughes, *Religion in China,* pp. 56–57.

[48] Wang Chao-hsiang, "Chung-kuo mi-mi hui-she ti tsung-chiao" (Religion in Chinese Secret Societies), in *Wen She Monthly* (January, 1927), vol. 2, no. 3, pp. 42 ff.

[49] Yü Mu-jen, "T'an Ssu-t'ung ti tsung-chiao kuan" (Religious Views of T'an Ssu-t'ung), in *Wen She Monthly* (February, 1928), vol. 3, no. 5, p. 24.

CHAPTER XI

[1] This is the general self-justification among Taoist and Buddhist groups. Religious societies, even those with political involvements, made the same claim, as seen in statements by the leaders of the modern Unity sect (I-kuan Tao). See chap. viii on political control of religion.

[2] Fu Ch'in-chia, *Chung-kuo tao-chiao shih* (History of Taoist Religion in China) (Shanghai, 1937), pp. 145–148.

[3] Hsü k'o, *Ch'ing pai lei ch'ao* (Classified Miscellaneous Information of the Ch'ing Dynasty) (Shanghai, 1928), chüan 75, pp. 30–40.

[4] Robert H. Lowie, *Primitive Religion* (New York, 1924), p. 30.

[5] *Lo-tien chen chih* (Gazetteer of Lo-tien Town in Pao-shan County) (1899 edition), chüan 8, p. 27.

[6] *Pao-shan hsien chih* (1879 edition), chüan 14, p. 13.

[7] Chi Hsiao-lan, *Yüeh-wei ts'ao-t'ang pi-chih* (1890 edition), chüan 1, p. 1.

[8] *Ibid.,* p. 2.

[9] *Pao-shan hsien chih* (1879 edition), chüan 2, p. 12.

[10] *Pao-p'u tzu,* Nei Pien section, chüan 6, pp. 5–6.

[11] T'an Ssu-t'ung, *Jen hsüeh* (Study of Benevolence), quoted in Yü Mu-jen, "T'an Ssu-t'ung ti tsung-chiao kuan" (Religious Views of T'an Ssu-t'ung), in *Wen She Monthly* (February, 1928), vol. 3, no. 5, pp. 13–14.

[12] *Hunan nien-chien* (Hunan Yearbook) (1933), p. 824.

[13] E. H. Parker, *Studies in Chinese Religion* (New York, 1910), p. 9.

[14] *Wang-tu hsien chih* (1934 edition), chüan 2, p. 63.

[15] Chi Hsiao-lan, *Yüeh-wei ts'ao-t'ang pi-chi,* chüan 14, p. 85.

CHAPTER XII

[1] Joachim Wach, *Sociology of Religion* (Chicago, 1944), chaps. IV and V.

[2] See his *Elementary Forms of the Religious Life,* tr. by Joseph W. Swain (London, 1915), and his *Professional Ethics and Civic Morals* (London, 1957), chaps. i–iii, vi, and xii–xvii.

[3] Fu Ch'in-chia, *Chung-kuo tao-chiao shih* (History of Taoist Religion in China) (Shanghai, 1937), chap. v; Ch'ü T'ui-chih, "Shih Wu" (Ancient Witchcraft), *Yenching Journal* (June, 1930), no. 7, pp. 1327–1347.

[4] *Chan-k'ai fan-wu-shen ti tou-tseng* (Develop the Struggle against the Witch Doctors), edited and published by the Shen-Kan-Ning Pien-Ch'ü Pan-Kung-t'ing (Executive Office of the Border District of Shensi, Kansu, Ningsia) (1944).

[5] Karl A. Wittfogel and Feng Chia-sheng, *History of Chinese Society, Liao,* transactions of the American Philosophical Society (1946), vol. 36, pp. 291 ff.

[6] See the description of the qualifications of Buddhist and Taoist priesthood in *Hunan nien-chien* (Hunan Yearbook) (1933), p. 854.

[7] For sources of the estimates, see W. T. Chan, *Religious Trends in Modern China* (New York, 1953), p. 80.

[8] *Hunan nien-chien* (1933), p. 837.

[9] Ta Sheng, "Shih-wu nien lai chiao-nan chih hui-ku" (A Retrospection of Religious Calamities in the Past Fifteen Years), *Hai ch'ao yin* (Sound of the Sea Tide) *Monthly* (January, 1931), vol. 16, no. 1, pp. 99–102.

[10] *Wang-tu hsien hsiang-t'u t'u shuo* (Illustrated Gazetteer of Wang-tu County) (1905 edition), p. 4.

[11] Sidney D. Gamble, *Ting Hsien* (New York, 1954), pp. 400–401.

[12] Willem A. Grootaers, Li Shih-yü, and Chang Chih-wen, *Temples and History of Wanchuan* (Chahar), Monumenta Serica (Peking, 1948), vol. XIII, pp. 209–316.

[13] *Ch'uan-sha hsien chih* (Gazetteer of Ch'uan-sha County) (1936 edition), chüan 3, p. 13.

[14] Grootaers, Li, and Chang, *op. cit.,* p. 307.

[15] Hsü K'o, *Ch'ing pai lei ch'ao* (Classified Miscellaneous Information of the Ch'ing Dynasty) (Shanghai, 1928), chüan 75, p. 55.

[16] *Hunan nien-chien* (1933), p. 848.

[17] *Ibid.,* pp. 837–856.

[18] W. T. Chan, *op. cit.,* pp. 151–152.

[19] *Wang-tu hsien hsiang-t'u t'u shuo* (1905 edition), p. 4.

[20] *Hunan nien-chien* (1933), p. 437.

[21] Li Ching-han, *Ting hsien she-hui kai-k'uang tiao-cha* (A Social Survey of Ting County) (Peking, 1932), p. 437.

[22] Grootaers, Li, and Chang, *op. cit.,* pp. 314 ff.

23 *Ch'uan-sha hsien chih* (1936 edition), chüan 12, p. 8.

24 Li Shih-yü, "Wanchuan Ti Huang-t'ien Tao" (The Yellow Heaven Sect in Wanchuan), in *Wen-tsao yüeh-k'an* (Nanking, 1948), vol. I, no. 4.

25 *Wang-tu hsien chih* (1905 edition), chüan 2, pp. 48 and 55.

26 Gamble, *op. cit.*, p. 401.

27 Grootaers, Li, and Chang, *op. cit.*, p. 316.

28 "Nei-cheng-pu ssu-miao teng-chih t'iao-li" (Ministry of Interior Regulations on the Registration of Temples and Convents), *Hai ch'ao yin* (Sound of the Sea Tide) *Monthly* (November, 1931), vol. 16, no. 11, p. 4.

29 W. T. Chan, *op. cit.*, p. 68.

30 Max Weber, *From Max Weber* (London, 1947), tr. by H. H. Gerth and C. Wright Mills, pp. 303–305.

31 See Jacques Gernet, *Les Aspects Économiques du Bouddisme dans la société du Vᵉ au Xᵉ siècle* (Saigon, 1956), pp. 245–269.

32 Ch'ien Mu, *Kuo-shih ta-kang* (Outline of Chinese History) (Shanghai, 1930), vol. 1, pp. 269–270.

33 W. T. Chan, *op. cit.*, p. 81.

34 See, for example, E. H. Parker, *Studies in Chinese Religion* (New York, 1910), p. 4.

35 *Pi-ling Kang-hsiang t'an-shi tsung-p'u* (Genealogy of the T'an Clan in Kang-hsiang Village of Pi-ling District) (1883), p. 2.

36 Fu Ch'in-chia, *op. cit.*, pp. 83–87; Ch'en Huan, *Nan-sung ch'u ho-pei hsin tao-chiao k'ao* (Research on the New Taoist Religion in Hopei during the Early Southern Sung Period) (Peking, 1941), p. 35.

37 *Ch'uan-sha hsien chih* (1936 edition), chüan 11, pp. 12–19.

38 *Yüeh-p'u li chih* (1933 edition), chüan 10, pp. 1–3.

39 *Hunan nien-chien* (1933), pp. 875–876.

40 See Y. C. Yang, *China's Religious Heritage,* p. 36; also Max Weber, *op. cit.*, p. 352.

41 R. H. Tawney, *Religion and the Rise of Capitalism* (Mentor Book edition, New York, 1953), pp. 16–17; see also Joachim Wach, *op. cit.*, p. 53.

42 See Grootaers, Li, and Chang, *op. cit.*

CHAPTER XIII

1 *Ch'uan-sha t'ing chih* (1879 edition), chüan 5, pp. 1–17.

2 *Lo-tien chen chih* (1899 edition), chüan 1, pp. 23–28.

3 *Wang-tu hsien chih* (1934 edition), chüan 3, p. 32.

4 *Ch'uan-sha hsien chih* (1936 edition), chüan 12, p. 4; *Pao-shan hsien hsü-chih* (1921 edition), chüan 5, p. 20.

5 J. S. Burgess, *The Guilds of Peking* (New York, 1928), p. 61.

6 *Lo-tien chen chih* (1899), chüan 8, p. 28.

7 Sydney Gamble, *Ting hsien* (New York, 1954), p. 412.

8 Ch'en Shou-i, *San-pai nien ch'ien ti li K'ung-chiao lun* (A Discourse on the Establishment of a Confucian Religion Three Hundred Years Ago), *Academica Sinica Bulletin* (1936), vol. 9, no. 6, pp. 133–162.

[9] *Min-kuo ching-shih wen-pien* (Collected Essays on Public Affairs in the Chinese Republic) (Shanghai, 1924), vol. 39, p. 62.

[10] See the analysis in Chu Yu-yü's article, "Chin-jih wo-kuo chung-chiao chih hsin ts'u-shih" (New Religious Trends in Our Country), *Wen She Monthly* (May, 1927), vol. 2, no. 7, pp. 37–52.

[11] *Hunan nien-chien* (1933), pp. 837–856.

[12] Wang Chiao-wo, "Hung-ch'iang hui ti tsung-chiao kuan chi ch'i hsin-yang ti ch'eng-shih" (The Red Spear Society's Religious Views and Its Forms of Worship), *Wen She Monthly* (June, 1928), vol. III, no. 8.

[13] Many descriptive and analytic accounts of the impact of science and the antireligion movement have been rendered in English. For brevity, see Hu Shih, champion of the Renaissance cause, "Religion in Chinese Life," in the *Chinese Renaissance* (Chicago, 1934), chap. V; Chiang Wen-han, *The Chinese Student Movement* (New York, 1948), chap. II; C. S. Shang, "The Antireligious Movement," in the *Chinese Recorder* (August 23, 1923), vol. IV, no. 8, p. 460.

[14] Bertrand Russell, *The Problem of China* (New York, 1922), pp. 198 ff.

[15] *Ibid.*, pp. 148–154.

[16] Ta Sheng, "Shih-wu nien lai chiao-nan chih hui-ku" (A Retrospection of Religious Calamities in the Past Fifteen Years), in *Hai ch'ao yin Monthly*, vol. 16, no. 1 (January, 1935), pp. 99 ff.

[17] *Chung-hua min-kuo fa-kuei ta-ch'uan* (Complete Edition of Laws and Regulations of the Chinese Republic) (Shanghai, 1936), vol. 1, p. 802.

[18] *Pao-shan hsien hsü-chih* (1931 edition), chüan 5, pp. 6–22.

[19] Li Ching-han, *Ting-hsien she-hui kai-k'uang tiao-ch'a*, pp. 423–436.

[20] *Hunan nien-chien* (1933), p. 835.

[21] The destruction of temples in the early part of the War of Resistance is told in "Wartime Correspondence" among Buddhists in *Hai ch'ao yin Monthly* (October, 1938), vol. 19, no. 10, pp. 53–60.

[22] Quoted in the *Ch'uan-sha hsien chih* (1936 edition), chüan 12, p. 6.

[23] *Ch'uan-sha t'ing chih* (1879 edition), chüan 5, pp. 1–17; *Ch'uan-sha hsien chih* (1936 edition), chüan 12, pp. 1–26; chüan 13, pp. 1–10.

CHAPTER XIV

[1] Paul Tillich, *Dynamics of Faith* (New York, 1957), pp. 1–30. The following discussion of faith draws heavily from this and other works of Tillich.

[2] *Ibid.*, p. 96.

[3] Paul Tillich, *The Shaking of the Foundations* (New York, 1948), pp. 98 ff.; *Dynamics of Faith*, pp. 67, 69, 122; and J. Milton Yinger, *Religion, Society and the Individual* (New York, 1957), pp. 120–121.

[4] Paul Tillich, *Dynamics of Faith*, p. 1.

[5] C. K. Yang, *The Chinese Family in the Communist Revolution* (Cambridge, Mass., 1959), chap. IX.

[6] *Extracts from China Mainland Magazines* (American Consulate General, Hong Kong, September 8, 1958), no. 141, pp. 1–8.

[7] Erich Fromm, *Psychoanalysis and Religion* (New Haven, 1958), p. 36.

[8] Chou Ching-wen, *Feng-pao shih-nien* (Stormy Decade) (Hong Kong, 1959), p. 543.

[9] Paul Tillich, *Dynamics of Faith*, pp. 122 ff.

[10] *Chiao-yü p'ing-lun* (Educational Review) (October, 1924), pp. 471–472.

[11] *Jen-min jih-pao* (People's Daily) (Peking, October 21, 1952), p. 3.

[12] *Survey of China Mainland Press* (American Consulate General, Hong Kong, February 11, 1960), no. 2194, p. 8.

[13] *Jen-min chou-k'an* (People's Weekly) (Peking, 1951), no. 48, p. 21.

[14] Ma Shao-po, "Yen-shu tui-tai cheng-li shen-hua chü ti kung-tso" (Treat Seriously the Work on Revision of Mythological Dramas), *Jen-min chou-ka'n* (December, 1951), no. 48, p. 26.

[15] *Survey of China Mainland Press* (May 23, 1957), no. 1536, p. 21.

[16] *Ibid.* (April 26, 1957), no. 1517, p. 10.

[17] *Ibid.* (October 23, 1958), no. 549, p. 18.

[18] Ch'en Ch'i-pin, "Report on Condition and Task of Catholic Anti-Imperialist, Patriotic Campaign in Heilungkiang," *Current Background* (American Consulate General, Hong Kong, January 15, 1960), no. 610, p. 12.

[19] *Survey of China Mainland Press* (October 1, 1956), no. 1381, p. 10; *Current Background* (January 15, 1960), no. 610, p. 8, and (February 13, 1959), no. 550, p. 8.

[20] *Current Background* (February 13, 1959), no. 550, p. 8; *Survey of China Mainland Press* (April 16, 1957), no. 1517, pp. 7–8.

[21] *Current Background* (February 13, 1959), no. 550, p. 8; (January 15, 1960), no. 610, p. 4; *Survey of China Mainland Press* (March 29, 1957), no. 1500, p. 11.

[22] *Extracts from China Mainland Magazines* (September 8, 1958), no. 141, p. 27.

[23] *Current Background* (January 15, 1960), no. 610, p. 23.

[24] *Extracts from China Mainland Magazines* (September 8, 1958), no. 141, pp. 28–29.

[25] *Current Background* (February 13, 1959), no. 550, pp. 7–8.

[26] *Ta-kung pao* (daily) (Hong Kong, March 1, 1956), p. 5.

[27] *Ibid.* (March 9, 1956), p. 3.

[28] Chang Lin, "Yen-li ts'ü-t'i fan-tung hui-tao-men" (Severely Suppress the Reactionary Sectarian Societies), in *Hsin-hua yüeh-pao* (New China Monthly) (December, 1950), vol. 3, no. 2, p. 314.

[29] Hsiao Ch'ien, *How the Tillers Win Back Their Soil* (Peking, 1951), pp. 74–80.

[30] *Jen-min jih-pao* (Peking, September 29, 1952), p. 2.

[31] *Hua-ch'iao jih-pao* (Chinese Overseas Daily) (Hong Kong, July 20, 1955), p. 4.

[32] *Jen-min jih-pao* (July 29, 1955), p. 3.

[33] *Ibid.* (July 2, 1955), p. 3.

[34] Chang Chih-yi, "Atheists and Theists Can Cooperate Politically and Travel the Road of Socialism," in *Che-hsüeh yen-chiu* (Philosophical Research) (February 15, 1958), issue I, pp. 12–13, in *Current Background* (June 15, 1958), no. 510.

[35] Paul Tillich, *Dynamics of Faith*, p. 120.

BIBLIOGRAPHY

The following are leading items of consulted works, and do not represent an exhaustive bibliography on the subject.

1. Books in Western Languages

Alexseev, Vasilli M., *The Chinese Gods of Wealth* (Hertford, England: S. Austin, 1928).

Almond, Gabriel A., *The Appeals of Communism* (Princeton, N.J.: Princeton University Press, 1954).

Bergson, Henri, *The Two Sources of Morality and Religion,* tr. by R. Ashley Audra and Cloudesley Brereton (New York: Holt, 1949).

Burckhardt, Jacob, *Reflections on History* (London: George Allen & Unwin, 1943).

Burgess, John S., *The Guilds of Peking* (New York: Columbia University Press, 1928).

Cassirer, Ernst, *The Myth of the State* (New Haven: Yale University Press, 1946).

Chan, W. T., *Religious Trends in Modern China* (New York: Columbia University Press, 1953).

Chavannes, Edouard, *Le T'ai Chan* (Paris: Ernest Leroux, 1910).

Chiang Wen-han, *The Chinese Student Movement* (New York: Columbia University Press, 1948).

Ch'ien Tuan-sheng, *The Government and Politics in China* (Cambridge, Mass.: Harvard University Press, 1950).

Clennel, W. J., *The Historical Development of Religion in China* (London: T. Fisher Unwin, 1926).

Creel, H. G., *The Birth of China* (London: P. Owen, 1958).

———, *Sinicism* (Chicago: Open Court, 1929).

Davidson, LeRoy, *The Lotus Sutra in Chinese Art* (New Haven: Yale University Press, 1954).

DeGroot, J. J. M., *The Religion of the Chinese* (New York: Macmillan, 1910).

———, *Sectarianism and Religious Persecution in China* (Amsterdam: Johannes Müller, 1903).

Doré, Father Henri, *Researches into Chinese Superstitions,* tr. by M. Kennelly (Shanghai: T'usewei Press, 1914–1938), 11 vols.

Dunlap, Knight, *Religion: Its Functions in Human Life* (New York: McGraw-Hill, 1946).

Durkheim, Emile, *The Division of Labor in Society,* tr. by George Simpson (Glencoe, Ill.: Free Press, 1949).

——, *The Elementary Forms of the Religious Life,* tr. by Joseph W. Swain (London: George Allen & Unwin, 1915).

——, *Professional Ethics and Civic Morals,* tr. by Cornelia Brookfield (London: Routledge & Kegan Paul, 1957).

Eberhard, Wolfram, *Chinese Festivals* (New York: Henry Schuman, 1952).

Fairbank, John K., ed., *Chinese Thought and Institutions* (Chicago: University of Chicago Press, 1957).

Fei, Hsiao-t'ung, *Peasant Life in China* (New York: E. P. Dutton, 1939).

Feng, Yu-lan, *History of Chinese Philosophy,* tr. by Derk Bodde (Princeton, N.J.: Princeton University Press, 1952).

Frazer, James George, *The Golden Bough* (London: Macmillan, 1927).

Freud, Sigmund, *Civilization and Its Discontents,* tr. by Joan Rivière (New York: Doubleday Anchor Books, 1958).

Fromm, Erich, *Psychoanalysis and Religion* (New Haven: Yale University Press, 1958).

Gamble, Sidney D., *Peking, A Social Survey* (New York: George H. Doran, 1921).

——, *Ting Hsien, A North China Rural Community* (New York: Institute of Pacific Relations, 1954).

Gernet, Jacques, *Les Aspects Économiques du Bouddisme dans la société du Vᵉ au Xᵉ siècle* (Saigon: École française d'Extrême-Orient, 1956).

Granet, Marcel, *Chinese Civilization,* tr. by Cathleen Innes and Mabel Brailsford (London: Kegan Paul, 1950).

——, *La Pensée Chinoise* (Paris: Albin Michel, 1950).

——, *La Religion des Chinois* (Paris: Presses Universitaires de France, 1922).

Grootaers, Willem A., with Li Shih-yü and Chang Chih-wen, *Temples and History of Wanchuan* (Chahar) (Peking: Catholic University, Monumenta Serica, 1948), Vol. XIII.

Hodous, Lewis, *Buddhism and Buddhists in China* (New York: Macmillan, 1924).

——, *Folkways in China* (London: Arthur Probsthain, 1929).

Hsiao, Ch'ien, *How the Tillers Win Back Their Soil* (Peking: Foreign Languages Press, 1951).

Hsü, Francis L. K., *Religion, Science and Human Crises* (London: Routledge & Kegan Paul, 1952).

———, *Under the Ancestors' Shadow* (New York: Columbia University Press, 1948).

Hu, Shih, *The Chinese Renaissance* (Chicago: University of Chicago Press, 1934).

Hughes, E. R., and K., *Religion in China* (London: Hutchinson's University Library, 1950).

James, William, *The Varieties of Religious Experience* (New York: Longmans, Green, 1902).

Kulp, Daniel H., II, *Country Life in South China* (New York: Columbia University Press, 1925).

Legge, James, tr., *The Chinese Classics* (Oxford: Clarendon Press, 1895), Vols. I–VIII.

Lowie, Robert H., *Primitive Religion* (New York: Boni & Liveright, 1924).

MacNair, H. F., ed., *China* (Berkeley and Los Angeles: University of California Press, 1951).

Maine, Henry Sumner, *Ancient Law* (London: J. Murray, 1874).

Malinowski, Bronislaw, *The Foundations of Faith and Morals* (London: Oxford University Press, 1936).

———, *Magic, Science and Religion* (New York: Doubleday Anchor Books, 1954).

———, *A Scientific Theory of Culture and Other Essays* (Chapel Hill, N.C.: University of North Carolina Press, 1944).

Mannheim, Karl, *Diagnosis of Our Time* (London: Routledge & Kegan Paul, 1950).

Nottingham, Elizabeth K., *Religion and Society* (New York: Random House, 1954).

Otto, Rudolf, *The Idea of the Holy*, tr. by John W. Harvey (London: Oxford University Press, 1923).

Parker, E. H., *Studies in Chinese Religion* (New York: New Century Review, 1910).

Parsons, Talcott, *The Social System* (Glencoe, Ill.: Free Press, 1951).

Radcliffe-Brown, Alfred R., *Religion and Society* (London, 1945).

Radin, Paul, *Primitive Religion* (New York: Viking Press, 1937).

Redfield, Robert, *The Primitive World and Its Transformation* (Ithaca: Cornell University Press, 1953).

Reichelt, K. L., *Truth and Tradition in Chinese Buddhism,* tr. by
Kathrina van Wagenen Bugge (Shanghai: Commercial Press, 1927).

Ross, John, *The Original Religion of China* (Edinburgh: Oliphants,
1909).

Russell, Bertrand, *The Problem of China* (London: George Allen &
Unwin, 1922).

Shryock, J. K., *The Origin and Development of the State Cult of Confucius* (New York: Century, 1932).

———, *The Temples of Anking and Their Cults* (Paris: privately
printed, 1931).

Sickman, Lawrence, and Alexander Soper, *The Art and Architecture of
China* (Baltimore: Penguin Books, 1956).

Soothill, W. E., *The Lotus of the Wonderful Law* (Oxford: Clarendon
Press, 1930).

———, *The Three Religions of China* (London: Oxford University
Press, 1923).

Stanton, W., *The Triad Society* (Hong Kong: Kelly and Walsh, 1900).

Sun, Yat-sen, *San Min Chu I* (The Three People's Principles), tr. by
Frank W. Price (Shanghai: Institute of Pacific Relations, 1927).

Suzuki, D. T., *Mahayana Buddhism* (London: David Marlowe, 1948).

Tawney, Richard H., *Religion and the Rise of Capitalism* (New York:
Harcourt, Brace, 1926).

Tillich, Paul, *Dynamics of Faith* (New York: Harper, 1957).

———, *The Interpretation of History,* tr. by N. A. Rasetzki and Elso
L. Talmey (New York: Charles Scribner's Sons, 1936).

———, *The Shaking of Foundations* (New York: Charles Scribner's
Sons, 1948).

Wach, Joachim, *Sociology of Religion* (Chicago: University of Chicago
Press, 1944).

———, *Types of Religious Experience* (Chicago: University of Chicago
Press, 1951).

Wang, Ch'ung, *Lun Heng,* tr. by Alfred Forke (London, 1907).

Ward, J. S. M., and W. G. Sterling, *The Hung Society* (London: Baker-
ville Press, 1925).

Weber, Max, *From Max Weber: Essays in Sociology,* ed. and tr. by
H. H. Gerth and C. Wright Mills (New York: Oxford University
Press, 1958).

———, *The Protestant Ethic and the Spirit of Capitalism,* tr. by Talcott
Parsons (London: George Allen & Unwin, 1930).

———, *The Religion of China,* tr. and ed. by Hans H. Gerth (Glencoe,
Ill.: Free Press, 1951).

Williams, C. A. S., *Outlines of Chinese Symbolism and Art Motifs* (Shanghai: Kelly and Walsh, 1932).

Williamson, Robert W., *Religion and Social Organization in Central Polynesia* (Cambridge, England: Cambridge University Press, 1937).

Wittfogel, Karl A., and Feng Chia-sheng, *History of Chinese Society, Liao,* transaction of the American Philosophical Society (New York: Macmillan, 1949), Vol. XXXVI.

Wright, Arthur F., *Buddhism. in Chinese History* (Stanford, Calif.: Stanford University Press, 1959).

Yang, C. K., *The Chinese Family in the Communist Revolution* (Cambridge, Mass.: Technology Press and Harvard University Press, 1959).

——, *A Chinese Village in Early Communist Transition* (Cambridge, Mass.: Technology Press and Harvard University Press, 1959).

——, *A North China Rural Market Economy* (New York: Institute of Pacific Relations, 1944).

Yang, Y. C., *China's Religious Heritage* (New York: Abingdon-Cokesbury Press, 1943).

Yinger, J. Milton, *Religion, Society and the Individual* (New York: Macmillan, 1957).

Zen, Sophia H. Chen, ed., *Symposium on Chinese Culture* (Shanghai: Institute of Pacific Relations, 1931).

2. Books in Chinese

Chan-k'ai fan wu-shen ti tou-tseng (Yenan: Shen-kan-ning Pien-ch'ü Pan-kung T'ing, 1944). 展開反巫神的鬥爭，延安，陝甘寧邊區辦公廳

Ch'en, Huan, *Nan-Sung ch'u ho-pei hsin tao-chiao k'ao* (Peking: K'o-hsüeh Ch'u-pan She, 1958). 陳垣，南宋初河北新道教攷，北京，科學出版社

Cheng, Pan-ch'iao, *Cheng Pan-ch'iao ch'üan-chih* (Hong Kong, 1950). 鄭板橋，鄭板橋全集

Chi, Hsiao-lan, *Yüeh-wei ts'ao-t'ang pi-chih* (Peking: Sheng-wen Wang-i Shu-wu, 1890). 紀曉嵐，閱微草堂筆記，北京，盛文望益書屋刊本

Chiang-yin Kao-shih tsung-p'u (1881). 江陰高氏宗譜

Chiang, Yung, *Li Chi hsün-i che yen* (Shanghai: Chung-hua Shu-chü, 1933, reprint). 蔣榮，禮記訓義擇言，上海，中華書局

Ch'ien, Mu, *Kuo shih ta-kang* (Shanghai: Commercial Press, 1930). 錢穆，國史大綱，上海，商務

Ch'ien, Ta-hsin, *Shih-chia chai yang-hsin lu* (Shanghai: Commercial Press, 1935, reprint). 錢大圻，十駕齋養新錄，上海，商務重印

Ch'ing-ch'ao hsü wen-hsien t'ung-k'ao (Shanghai: Commercial Press, 1935). 清朝續文獻通攷,上海,商務

Ch'ing-ho hsien chih (1934). 清河縣誌

Ch'ing-ho hsien chih (1936). 清河縣誌

Chou, Ching-wen, *Feng pao shih nien* (Hong Kong, 1959).
周鯨文·風暴十年

Chu, Lin, *Hung-men chih* (Shanghai, 1930). 朱琳·洪門志

Ch'ü, Tui-chi, *Chung-kuo she-hui shi-liao ch'ung-ch'ao* (Changsha: Commercial Press, 1937). 瞿兌之,中國社會史料叢鈔,長沙,商務

Ch'uan-sha hsien chih (1936). 川沙縣志

Ch'uan-sha t'ing chih (1879). 川沙廳志

Ch'uan-sha t'ing chih (1880). 川沙廳志

Chung-hua Min-kuo fa-kuei ta-ch'uan (Shanghai: Commercial Press, 1936). 中華民國法規大全,上海,商務

Erh-shih-wu shih (Shanghai: Wen-ming Shu-chü, 1934).
二十五史,上海,文明書局

Fan, Chung-yen, *Fan Wen-cheng kung wen-chih* (Shanghai: Commercial Press, 1929). 范仲奄,范文正公文集,上海,商務重印

Fo-shan Chung-i hsiang chih (1923). 佛山忠義鄉志

Fu, Ch'in-chia, *Chung-kuo tao-chiao shih* (Shanghai: Commercial Press, 1937). 傅勤家,中國道教史,上海,商務

Hirayama, Amane, *Chung-kuo mi-mi she-hui shih* (Shanghai: Commercial Press, 1912). 平山周,中國秘密社會史,上海,商務

Hsü, K'o, *Ch'ing pai lei ch'ao* (Shanghai: Commercial Press, 1928).
徐珂,清稗類鈔,上海,商務

Hsü, Sung, ed., *Sung hui yao chih kao* (Peking: Peiping T'u-shu Kuan, 1936). 徐松輯,宋會要輯稿·北京,北平圖書館

Hsü, Ti-shan, *Fu-chi mi-hsin ti yen-chiu* (Chungking: Commercial Press, 1940). 許地山,扶機迷信之研究,重慶,商務

Hu, P'o-an, *Chung-hua ch'uan-kuo feng-su chih* (Shanghai: Tai-ta T'u-shu Kung-ying She, 1936). 胡樸安,中華全國風俗志,上海,
大達圖書供應社

Hu, Shih, *Chung-kuo chang-hui hsiao-shuo k'ao-cheng* (Dairen, Manchuria, 1943). 胡適,中國章回小說考證

——, *Hu Shih wen ts'un* (Shanghai: Ya-tung T'u-shu Kuan, 1933)
胡適文存,上海,亞東圖書館

Hun-yin fa chiang-hua (Peking: T'ung-hsü Tu-wu Ch'u-pan She, 1951). 婚姻法講話,北京,通俗讀物出版社

Hunan nien-chien (Changsha: Secretariat of the Hunan Provincial Govment, 1933). 湖南年鑑,長沙,湖南省政府秘書處

Jung, Shao-tsu, *Mi-hsin yü ch'uan-shuo* (Canton: Institute of History and Philology, Sun Yat-sen University, 1929). 容肇祖，迷信與傳說，廣州，中山大學，歷史語言研究所

Ku, Chieh-kang, *Ku shih pien* (Shanghai: K'ai-ming Shu-chü, 1935) 顧頡剛，古史辨，上海，開明書局

Ku-wen p'ing chu (Canton: Sheng-wen T'ang, 1921, lithograph edition) 古文評註，廣州，盛文堂石印本

Kuo-ch'ao wen lu (Shanghai: Wen-yuan Shan-fang, 1903). 國朝文錄，上海，文淵山房

Kuo, Mo-jo, *Hsien-ch'in t'ien-tao kuan-nien ti chin-chan* (Shanghai: Chung-fa Wen-hua Ch'u-pan Wei-yuan-hui, 1936). 郭若沫，先秦天道觀念的進展，上海，中法文化出版委員會

Li, Chien-nung, *Chung-kuo chin-pai-nien cheng-chih shih* (Shanghai: Commercial Press, 1947). 李劍農，中國近百年政治史，上海，商務

Li, Ching-han, *Ting hsien she-hui kai-k'uang tiao-ch'a* (Peking: Chung-hua P'ing-min Chiao-yü Ch'u-chin Hui, 1932). 李景漢，定縣社會概況調查，北京，中華平民教育促進會

Li, Shih-yü, *Hsien-tsai hua-pei mi-mi tsung-chiao* (Chengtu, 1948). 李世瑜，現在華北秘密宗教

Liang, Ch'i-ch'ao, *Yin-ping shih ch'uan-chi* (Shanghai: Chung-hua Shu-chü, 1929). 梁啟超，飲冰室全集，上海，中華書局

———, *Yin-ping shih wen-chi* (Shanghai: Chung-hua Shu-chü, 1924). 飲冰室文集，上海，中華書局

Lin, P'ing, *Chi-nien-jih shih-liao* (Shanghai, 1948). 林平，紀念日史料

Lo-tien chen chih (1899). 羅店鎮志

Lo-ting hsien chih (1935). 羅定縣志

Lü, Fu-ch'en, *K'o-ch'ang i-wen lu* (1870). 呂徽臣，科場異聞錄

Ma-ch'eng hsien chih (1881). 麻城縣志

Ma-ch'eng hsien chih (1935). 麻城縣志

Min-kuo ching-shih wen pien (Shanghai: Ching-shih Wen She, 1924) 民國經世文編，上海，經世文社

Pao-shan hsien chih (1879). 寶山縣志

Pao-shan hsien chih (1921). 寶山縣志

Pao-shan hsien hsü-chih (1931). 寶山縣續志

Pi-ling kang-hsiang t'an shi tsung-p'u (1883). 毘陵缸巷譚氏宗譜

(Ch'in-ting) P'ing-ting chiao-fei chih-lüeh, written by T'o Tsin and others at the Emperor's command (1816). 欽定平定教匪紀略，托津等奉敕撰

San-chiao ying-chieh tsung-kuan t'ung-shu. 三教應劫總觀通書

San-chiao yuan-liu shou shen ta-ch'uan (written in the Yuan period, 1264–1367, author unknown). 三教源流搜神大全，元閱名撰

Sang-yuan wei chih (1932). 桑園圍志

Sui-ning hsien chih (1929). 遂寧縣志

Szu-shu ku-chin hsün-shih (Fou-hsi-ts'ao T'ang, 1813). 四書古今訓釋，浮溪草堂刊本

(Ch'in-ting) Ta-ch'ing hui-tien (Shanghai, 1900, lithographic reprint) 欽定大清會典，光緒二十六年上海石印版

Ta-ch'ing hui-tien shih-li (Shanghai: Commercial Press, 1909). 大清會典事例，上海，商務

Ta-ch'ing lü-li cheng-hsiu t'ung-ts'uan chih-ch'eng (Shanghai: Wen-yuan Shan-fang, 1908). 大清律例增修統纂集成，上海，文淵山房

Ta-tai li chi (Shanghai: Commercial Press, 1929, as a part of the *Szu-pu ts'ung-k'an* collection). 大戴禮記，上海，商務，四部叢刊之內

Teng, Yün-t'e, *Chung-kuo chiu-fang shih* (Peking, 1958, reprint from Commercial Press, 1936, edition). 鄧雲特，中國救荒史，上海，商務，北京重印

Wan t'ung-i wu-shih chia-ch'eng (1868). 皖桐邑吳氏家乘

Wang, Chih-hsin, *Chung-kuo tsung-chiao ssu-hsiang shih* (Shanghai: Chung-hua Shu-chü, 1930). 王治心，中國宗教思想史，上海，中華書局

Wang-tu hsien chih (1905). 望都縣志

Wang-tu hsien chih (1934). 望都縣志

Wang-tu hsien hsiang-t'u t'u-shuo (1905). 望都縣鄉土圖說

Wu, Ching-tzu, *Ju-lin wai-shih* (Shanghai: Ya-tung T'u-shu Kuan, 1934). 吳敬梓，儒林外史，上海，亞東圖書館

Yüeh-p'u li chih (1933). 月浦里志

Yün-yang chang-shih tsung-p'u (1887). 鄆陽張氏宗譜

3. Papers in Collected Works and Periodicals and Newspapers in Western Languages

Ayscough, Florence, "The Chinese Cult of Ch'eng Huang Lao Yeh," in *Royal Asiatic Society, North China Branch,* Vol. 55 (1924), pp. 136 ff.

Balazs, Etienne, "La crise sociale et la philosophie à la fin des Han," *T'oung Pao,* Vol. 39 (1949), pp. 83–131.

Ch'en, Kenneth, "On Some Factors Responsible for the Anti-Buddhist

Persecution under the Pei Ch'ao," in *Harvard Journal of Asiatic Studies*, Vol. 17 (June, 1954), nos. 1 and 2, pp. 261–274.

Creel, H. G., "Was Confucius Agnostic?" in *T'oung Pao*, Vol. 29 (1932), pp. 55–59.

Current Background, American Consulate General, Hong Kong.

Day, Clarence B., "Shanghai Invites the God of Wealth," *China Journal* (June, 1928), pp. 289–294.

Extracts from China Mainland Magazines, American Consulate General, Hong Kong.

Grootaers, Willem A., "The Hagiography of the Chinese God Chenwu," in *Folklore Studies*, Vol. 11 (1952), no. 2.

Hu Shih, "Ch'an Bhuddism in China," *Philosophy East and West*, Vol. 3 (April, 1953), pp. 17–22.

Johnston, R. F., "The Cult of Military Heroes in China," in *New China Review*, Vol. 8 (February, 1921), no. 1, pp. 49 ff.

Levy, Howard S., "Yellow Turban Religion and Rebellion at the End of Han," *Journal of the American Oriental Society* (1956), issue LXXVI, 1956.

Li, Shih-yü, and Wang, Fu-shih, "Rural Temples Around Hsüan Hua," in *Folklore Studies*, Vol. 10 (1951), no. 1.

Michael, Franz, "State and Society in Nineteenth-century China," in *World Politics*, Vol. 7 (April, 1955), no. 3, pp. 420–428.

Shang, C. S., "The Anti-Religious Movement," in *Chinese Recorder*, Vol. 4 (August 23, 1923), no. 8, p. 460.

Shih, Vincent Y. C., "The Ideology of Taiping Tien Kuo," *Sinologica*, Vol. 3 (1951), no. 1, pp. 1–15.

Suiichi, Mizuno, "Archeological Survey of the Yünkang Grottoes," *Archives of the Chinese Art Society of America* (1950), issue IV, pp. 39–60.

Survey of China Mainland Press, American Consulate General, Hong Kong.

4. Papers in Collected Works and Periodicals and Newspapers in Chinese

"Chan shih t'ung-hsin," in *Hai ch'ao yin Monthly*, Vol. 19 (October, 1938), no. 10, pp. 53–60. 戰時通訊，海潮音月刊

Ch'ang-chiang jih-pao, Hankow. 長江日報

Chang, Tung-sun, "Chung-kuo chieh-hsüeh shih shang fo-chiao ssu-hsiang chih ti-wei," in *Yenching Journal* (1950), no. 38, pp. 147–178. 張東蓀，中國哲學史上佛教思想之地位，燕京學報

Ch'en, Pan, "Ch'ien-wei shu-yüan, shang," in *Academica Sinica Bulletin* (1947), issue XX, pp. 317–335. 陳槃，讖緯溯源上，中央研究院歷史語言研究所集刊

————, "Lun tsao-ch'i ch'ien-wei chi ch'i yü Tsou Yen shu-shuo chih kuan-hsi," *Academica Sinica Bulletin* (1946), issue XI, pp. 159–178. 陳槃，論早期讖緯及其與鄒衍書說之關係，同上

Ch'en, Shou-i, "San-pai nien ch'ien ti li k'ung-chiao lun," *Academica Sinica Bulletin,* Vol. 9 (1936), issue VI, pp. 133–162. 陳受頤，三百年前的立孔教論，中央研究院歷史語言研究所集刊

Ch'ü, T'ui-chih, "Shih wu," *Yenching Journal* (June, 1930), no. 7, pp. 1327–1347. 瞿兌之，釋巫，燕京學報

Chu, Yu-yü, "Chin-jih wo-kuo tsung-chiao chi hsin ts'ü-shih," in *Wen she Monthly,* Vol. 2 (May, 1927), no. 7, pp. 37–52. 朱友漁，今日我國宗教之新趨勢，文社月刊

Creel, H. C., "Shih t'ien," *Yenching Journal* (1935), no. 18, pp. 71–77. 顧立雅，釋天，燕京學報

Feng, Yu-lan, "Ju-chia tui-yü hun sang chi chi li-lun," *Yenching Journal* (1928), no. 3, pp. 343–358. 馮友蘭，儒家對於婚喪祭之理論，燕京學報

Han, Yü, "Chien ying fo ku piao," in *Ku wen p'ing chu* (Shanghai) (1921), chüan 6, pp. 16–17. 韓愈，諫迎佛骨表，古文評註

Hsü, Tao-ling, "Hsüan-wu ti shih-yüan yü tui-pien," in *Shih hsüeh chi-k'an* (1947), no. 5. 許道齡，玄武的始原與蛻變，史學季刊

Hsü, Ti-shan, "Tao-chia ssu-hsiang yü tao-chiao," in *Yenching Journal* (1927), no. 2, pp. 249–283. 許地山，道家思想與道教，燕京學報

Hu, Shih, "Shuo ju," *Academica Sinica Bulletin* (1934), issue III, pp. 233–284. 胡適，說儒，中央研究院歷史語言研究所集刊

Hung, Liang-chi, "Cheng hsieh-chiao su," in *Kuo-ch'ao wen lu* (Shanghai) (1903), chüan 30, pp. 46–47. 洪亮吉，征邪教疏，國朝文錄

Jen-min jih-pao (Peking). 人民日報

Jung, Shao-tsu, "Chan-pu yüan-liu," *Academica Sinica Bulletin,* Vol. 1 (1928), issue I, pp. 8–16. 容肇祖，占卜源流，中央研究院歷史語言研究所集刊

Ku, Chieh-kang, "Wu-te chung-shih shuo hsia chih cheng-chih ho li-shih," *Ku shih pien* (Shanghai), Vol. V (1921), pp. 404–585. 顧頡剛，五德終始說下之政治和歷史，古史辨

Kuo, I-sheng, "Lun hsin-hsing shih-min teng-chi tsai taiping tien-kuo ke-ming chung ti tso-yung," in *Li-shih yen-chiu* (March, 1956), no. 3, pp. 11-20. 郭一生，論新興市民等級在太平天國革命中的作用，歷史研究

Li, shih-yü, "Wanchuan ti huang-t'ien tao," in *Wen-tsao yüeh-k'an*, Vol. 1 (1948), no. 4. 李世瑜，萬全的黃天道，文藻月刊

Liang, Ch'i-ch'ao, "Chung-kuo li-shih yen-chiu fa," in Liang Ch'i-ch'ao, *Yin-ping shih ch'uan-chi* (Shanghai) (1929), chüan 23. 梁啓超，中國歷史研究法，飲冰室全集

———, "K'ang Nan-hai hsien-sheng chüan," in Liang Ch'i-ch'ao, *Yin-ping shih wen-chih* (Shanghai), Vol. 3 (1924). 康南海先生傳，飲冰室文集

———, "K'ung Tzu chiao-i shih-chi pi-i yü chin-jih kuo-min che ho-tsai, yü ch'ang-ming chih ch'ih tao ho-yu?" *Yin-ping shih ch'uan-chi* (Shanghai) (1929), chüan 23. 梁啓超，孔子教義實際裨益於今日國民者何在，與昌明之其道何由？見飲冰室全集

———, "Lun Chi-na tsung-chiao kai-ke," *Yin-ping shih ch'uan-chi* (Shanghai) (1929). 論支那宗教改革，見同書

———, "Yin-yang wu-hsing shuo chih lai-li," in Ku Chieh-kang, *Ku shih pien* (Shanghai), Vol. V (1921), pp. 353-359. 陰陽五行說之來歷，顧頡剛，古史辨

Liu, Chen-ch'ing, "Ma shen miao ti chi shen k'ao," *Peiping ch'en-pao* (July 20, 1932), p. 3. 劉振卿，馬神廟的祭神考，北平晨報

Ma, Hsü-lun, "Shuo ming," in *Hsüeh lin* (1941), no. 9, pp. 15-34. 馬敍倫，說命，學林

Ma, Shao-po, "Yen-shu tui-tai cheng-li shen-hua chü ti kung-tso," *Jen-min chou-k'an* (December, 1951), no. 48, pp. 26-27. 馬少波，嚴肅對待整理神話劇的工作，人民週刊

"Nei-cheng-pu ssu-miao teng-chih t'iao-li," *Hai ch'ao yin Monthly*, Vol. 16 (1935), no. 11, p. 4. 內政部寺廟登記條例

Ta Sheng, "Shih-wu nien lai chiao-nan chih hui-ku," in *Hai ch'ao yin Monthly*, Vol. 16 (1935), no. 1, pp. 99-104. 大醒，十五年來教難之回顧，海潮音月刊

T'ao, Hsi-sheng, "Chou tai ta chu ti hsin-yang ho tsu-chi," in *Tsinghua hsüeh-pao*, Vol. 10 (1935), no. 3, pp. 565-585. 陶希聖，周代大族的信仰和組織，清華學報

Teng, Ssu-yü, "Ch'eng-huang k'ao," in *Historical Annual*, Vol. 2 (1936), no. 2, pp. 249-276. 鄧嗣禹，城隍考，史學年報

Wang, Chao-hsiang, "Chung-kuo mi-mi hui-she ti tsung-chiao," in *Wen she Monthly*, Vol. 2 (1927), no. 3, pp. 42-50. 汪兆翔，中國秘密會社的宗教，文社月刊

Wang, Chiao-wo, "Hung-ch'iang hui ti tsung-chiao kuan chi ch'i hsin-yang ti ch'eng-shih," in *Wen she Monthly*, Vol. 3 (1928), no. 8, pp. 42–46. 王皎我，紅槍會的宗教觀及其信仰的程式，文社月刊

Wen, I-to, "T'ien-wen shih t'ien," *Tsinghua hsüeh-pao*, Vol. 9 (1934), pp. 873–895. 聞一多・天問釋天；清華學報

Yano, Jinichi, "Kuan-yü pai-nien-chiao chih luan," *Jen wen Monthly*, Vol. 6 (1935), nos. 1 and 2. 矢野仁一，關於白蓮教之亂，人民月刊

Yü, Mu-jen, "Taiping tien-kuo tsung-chiao-hua ti chün-shih yü cheng-chih," *Wen she Monthly*, Vol. 2 (December, 1927), no. 2, pp. 38–40. 余牧仁，太平天國宗教化的軍事與政治，文社月刊

———, "T'an Ssu-t'ung ti tsung-chiao kuan," in *Wen she Monthly*, Vol. 3 (February, 1928), no. 5, pp. 24–26. 余牧仁，譚嗣同的宗教觀，文社月刊

Yü, Sun, "Tsao-ch'i tao-chiao chi cheng-chih hsin-nien," *Fu-jen hsüeh-pao* (1942), issue XI, pp. 87–136. 余遜，早期道教之政治信念，輔仁學報

APPENDIX 1

*Functional Classification of Major Temples
in Eight Localities*

	NUMBER OF	
FUNCTIONS	Wang-tu	Ch'ing-ho
I. Integration and well-being of social organizations	48	86
A. Kinship group	20	20
1. Marriage		
Niu-lang miao (god and goddess of happy marriage)		
2. Fertility	19	19
Kuan-yin miao, Ta-shih miao, Pai-i miao (goddess of mercy)		
Nai-nai miao (child-giving goddess)	8	5
Niang-niang miao (child-giving goddess)	11	14
Hua-shen miao, Hua-wang miao, Chang-hsien miao (goddess of flowers)		
Chin-hua miao (goddess of golden flowers)		
Liu shih fu-jen miao (Madame Liu)		
Wei-sheng tien (protector of children against infanticide)		
3. Kinship values	1	1
Chieh-hsiao tz'u (spirits of chaste women and filial children)	1	1
Hsiao-ti tz'u (spirits of filial sons and dutiful brothers)		
Chieh-lieh tz'u (spirits of martyrs for chastity [women])		
B. Local community protection	3	8
Huo-shen miao, Huo-ti miao, Hua-kuang miao (god of fire)	1	
Shui-huo shen miao (gods of fire and flood)		1

Temples

Ch'uan-sha	Pao-shan	Lo-ting	Fo-shan	Sui-ning	Ma-ch'eng	Total
70	93	59	78	71	97	602
26	29	3	31	9	23	161
	1					1
	1					1
24	26	2	30	8	22	150
13	13	1	15	4	11	57
11	11	1	4	4	11	42
						13
			5			30
	1		1			2
			4			4
			1			1
	1					1
2	2	1	1	1	1	10
1		1	1	1	1	7
1	1					2
	1					1
14	26	24	15	12	36	138
		2	11	1	3	18
						1

FUNCTIONS	NUMBER OF	
	Wang-tu	Ch'ing-ho
Hai-shen miao (god of the sea, controller of tidal waves)		
Tu-k'ou miao (god of ferry docks, for safe crossing of rivers)		
Ch'iao-shen miao (god of bridges, protector against falling into rivers)		
Ta-lu miao (god of roads)		
She-chi t'an (god of earth and grain)	1	1
Temples bearing names of local villages and towns	1	6
C. The state	25	58
1. Figures symbolizing civic and political virtues	21	54
a. Civic and political figures	10	2
(1) Historical personalities	7	1
Yang-te tz'u (sanctuary for adoration of the virtuous)	1	
Pao-kung t'zu, Pao-en tz'u (sanctuary for repaying distinguished service of officials and public leaders)		
Ming-huan tz'u (sanctuary for distinguished officials)	1	
Erh-kung tz'u (sanctuary of the Two Lords)		
I-ai tz'u (sanctuary of lingering affection for benevolent officials)		
Hsiang-hsien tz'u (sanctuary for meritorious local personalities)	1	
Sanctuaries dedicated to single individuals of civic or political merit	4	
Sanctuaries dedicated collectively to distinguished officials and civic leaders		1

TEMPLES

Ch'uan-sha	Pao-shan	Lo-ting	Fo-shan	Sui-ning	Ma-ch'eng	Total
1	2					3
	5					5
	1					1
	1					1
1	1	1		1	1	7
12	16	21	4	10	32	102
30	38	32	32	50	38	303
25	34	26	24	43	31	258
15	22	17	9	28	19	122
15	21	14	4	24	18	104
1				1	2	5
	1		1			2
	1					2
	1					1
					1	1
		1		1		3
14	18	13	3	22	14	88
					1	2

FUNCTIONS	Wang-tu	NUMBER OF Ch'ing-ho
(2) Legendary figures	3	1
P'an-ku miao, K'ai-t'ien miao (P'an-ku, creator of Heaven and earth)		
Yao-ti miao (Emperor Yao)	2	
Hsien Ko miao (Empresses Hsien Yuan Shih and Ko T'ien Shih)		
San-huang miao (Emperors Fu Hsi, Shen Nung, Huang Ti)	1	1
San-sheng miao (the three saints, Po-i, Shu-ch'i, Han chen-jen)		
b. Military personalities	11	52
Kuan-ti miao, Wu-ti miao, Wu-sheng miao (Kuan Yü, god of righteousness and war)	5	42
Yo-wang miao (Yo Fei, deity of patriotism)		3
Kuan Yo miao (Kuan Yü and Yo Fei)		1
San-i miao (Kuan-Yü, Liu Pei, Chang Fei, of the Three Kingdoms)	5	5
Hsien-feng miao (Fu Po, the Vanguard General of Han dynasty)		
Chiang-chün miao ("The general" or military leaders in general)		1
Chung-i tz'u (spirits of the loyal and the righteous)	1	
Chung-chieh tz'u (sanctuaries for spirits of officers and men who died defending the community)		
2. Deities of justice	1	1
Pao Kung miao (Pao Kung, the model judge)		
Yü-shen miao (god of prison)		1

TEMPLES

Ch'uan-sha	Pao-shan	Lo-ting	Fo-shan	Sui-ning	Ma-ch'eng	Total
	1	3	5	4	1	18
		2	2			4
	1		1			4
				1		1
						2
		1	2	3	1	7
10	12	9	15	15	12	136
3	8	6	6	7	6	83
2					1	6
1				2		4
						10
				1		1
	4	3	7	4	3	22
1				1	2	5
3			2			5
1	1			1		5
	1					1
						1

FUNCTIONS	NUMBER OF	
	Wang-tu	Ch'ing-ho
Wei T'o miao (Buddhist god of the law)	1	
Ya-shen miao (Hsiao Ts'ao, prime minister of Han dynasty, deified as god of law)		
3. Patrons of the scholar-official class and the literary tradition	3	3
Wen miao, K'ung miao, Sheng miao (Confucius temple)	1	1
Wen-ch'ang miao, Wen-ti miao (patron of literature and literary success)	1	1
K'uei-sheng ko (god of the imperial examinations)	1	1
Tzu-tsu miao (Ts'ang Chieh, creator of writing)		
II. General moral order	26	73
A. Heavenly deities	14	61
Yü-huang miao (The Jade Emperor, ruler of Heaven)	2	8
Lao Tzu miao, Lao-chün miao, T'ai-shang miao, Kan-ying miao, Wan-shou kung (Lao Tzu)		
Chen-wu miao, Hsüan T'an miao, Hsüan Ti miao, Hsüan-wu miao, Shuai Fu miao, Pei Wang miao, Pei Ti miao, T'ai Wei miao, T'ai I miao (collective gods of the Dipper, the Seven Mansions of the Zodiac, rulers of the northern skies)	3	27
San-yuan miao, San-kuan miao, San-sheng miao, San-wang miao, San-chieh miao (The Triad, Heaven, earth, water; at times the Triad refers to the legendary rulers Yao, Shun, Yü who symbolized these three elements, respectively)	5	6

TEMPLES

Ch'uan-sha	Pao-shan	Lo-ting	Fo-shan	Sui-ning	Ma-ch'eng	Total
1						2
				1		1
4	3	6	8	6	7	40
2	1	1	1	1	1	9
1	1	4	3	4	5	20
1	1	1	1	1	1	8
			3			3
20	28	64	117	37	41	406
3	10	11	31	29	25	184
1	2			9	11	33
		4	2	9	7	22
1	2	4	16	2	1	56
1	6	2	13	9	6	48

FUNCTIONS	NUMBER OF	
	Wang-tu	Ch'ing-ho
Fo-yeh miao (Buddha)	1	18
P'ei-sha miao (Bodhisattva)	2	1
Ch'i-shen miao, Ch'i-sheng miao (Seven Stars of the Dipper)	1	1
B. Underworld authorities	12	12
Ch'eng-huang miao (local ruler over spirits of the dead)	1	1
An-ch'a-szu miao (local judge over spirits of the dead)		
T'ai-shan miao, Tung-yo miao, T'ien-ch'i miao (god of Mount T'ai, one of judges in Hell)	2	3
T'u-ti miao (local god of earth, a tutelary god)	1	1
Wu-tao miao (god of five roads [east, west, north, south, central] traveled by the dead)	8	6
I Li t'an (altar for homeless spirits of the dead)		
Ti-chuang miao (Buddha, savior from Hell)		1
III. Economic functions	12	10
A. Agricultural deities	12	10
Hsien-nung t'an (altar of Shen-nung, creator of agriculture)	1	1
Lei-yü-feng-yün t'an (altar of gods of thunder, rain, winds, clouds)	1	1
Feng-shen miao (god of wind)		
Lei-shen miao, Lei-ti miao (god of thunder)		
Yü t'an (god of rain)		
Kan-lu miao (god of sweet dew)		
Lung-shen miao, Lung-wang miao, Wu-lung miao, Wu-lung Sheng-mu miao (Dragon god or Dragon mother goddess)	4	2

TEMPLES

Ch'uan-sha	Pao-shan	Lo-ting	Fo-shan	Sui-ning	Ma-ch'eng	Total
		1				20
						3
						2
17	18	53	86	8	16	222
7	10	1	2	2	1	25
1						1
3	3	1	3	3	10	28
6	3	49	79	1	1	141
						14
	1	1	1	1	1	5
	1	1	1	1	3	8
21	29	18	17	25	11	143
17	17	12	8	24	8	108
1	1	1		1	1	7
1	1	1		1	1	7
	1					1
	1	1	1	1		4
	1			1	1	3
	1					1
2	4	8	1	2	3	26

FUNCTIONS	NUMBER OF Wang-tu	Ch'ing-ho
Ho-shen miao, Ch'uan-chu miao, Shui-fu miao (river god)	1	1
Hung-sheng miao (god of floods)		
Yü-wang miao (Emperor Yü, controller of water and floods)		
Shui-kuan miao (god of sluice gates)		
Ch'ung-wang miao (god of insects)	2	1
Liu-meng Chiang-chün miao (General Liu, the locust eradicator)		
Chü-mang miao (god of trees)		
Sung-mu miao (god of pine trees)		
Pa-la miao (eight deities of agriculture, mainly of insects)	2	3
Ma-wang miao (god of horses, serving as protector of all domesticated animals)	1	1
Hua-kuang miao (god of fire)		
B. Patrons of crafts and trades		
Lu-pan miao, Kung-shu-tzu miao (Lu-pan or Kung-shu-tzu, god of carpentry and construction)		
T'ien-hou miao (goddess of sailing)		
T'an-shen miao (god of rapids, for safe sailing)		
Lü-shi tz'u (spirits of dead members of dyestuff guild)		
C. Commerce and general economic prosperity		
Ts'ai-shen miao (god of wealth)		
IV. Health	3	2
Yo-shih miao (Baishajiaguru, Buddhist deity of healing)	2	1
Yo-wang miao (Emperor Shen-nung, god of herb medicine)		
Hua-t'o miao (Hua-t'o, patron of doctors and health)		
Yen-mu miao (goddess of the eyes)		

TEMPLES

Ch'uan-sha	Pao-shan	Lo-ting	Fo-shan	Sui-ning	Ma-ch'eng	Total
1			1	9	1	14
			5			5
				8		8
	3					3
						3
11	3					14
				1		1
		1				1
						5
					1	3
1	1					2
2	7	4	7			20
1	4					5
1	3	1	6			11
		3				3
			1			1
2	5	2	2	1	3	15
2	5	2	2	1	3	15
2	3	1	8			19
						3
1	2					3
		1	5			6
1			1			2

FUNCTIONS	NUMBER OF Wang-tu	Ch'ing-ho
Tou-mu miao (goddess of smallpox)		
I Li t'an (altar for gods of epidemics and homeless spirits of the dead)	I	
Tou-lao miao (goddess of the Bushel Star, constellation of Sagittarius)		
Wen-shen miao (god of epidemics)		I
V. General public and personal welfare	10	13
A. Pantheons	2	I
Ch'uan-shen miao (temple of all gods)	2	I
Shen-chi t'an (altar of all gods and spirits)		
B. Devil dispellers	I	I
Kuei-ku miao (Kuei-ku Tzu, the devil dispeller)		
San-ch'ing miao (devil driver)	I	I
Erh-lang miao (devil driver)		
Erh-hsien miao (spirits of cedar and willow trees, devil dispellers)		
K'ang Ta-yuan-shuai miao (Generalissimo K'ang)		
C. Blessing deities	7	7
Ta-shih miao, Kuan-yin miao, Pai-i miao, Pai-i Ta-shih miao, Nan-hai miao, Lao-mu miao (goddess of mercy)	7	7
Ch'un-yang tien (Lü Ch'un-yang, Taoist fairy)		
T'an-hsien miao (T'an, Taoist fairy)		
P'u-an miao (P'u-an, Buddhist monk)		
She-jen miao (Liang She-jen, a lay Buddhist)		
Pai-ma Chiang-chün miao (general on a white horse)		
Huang ta-hsien miao, Hu-hsien miao (spirit of fox incarnate)		
Sheng-yo miao (temple of godly music)		

TEMPLES

Ch'uan-sha	Pao-shan	Lo-ting	Fo-shan	Sui-ning	Ma-ch'eng	Total
			1			1
						1
	1		1			2
						1
2	16	4	20	3		68
1	1					5
						3
1	1					2
			12			14
			1			1
			3			5
			1			1
			1			1
			6			6
	5		5	1		25
						14
	3		1	1		5
			1			1
	1					1
			1			1
			1			1
	1					1
			1			1

	NUMBER OF	
FUNCTIONS	Wang-tu	Ch'ing-ho

D. Temples with unspecified gods   4
     Lao miao (old temple)
     Hsin miao (new temple)
     Ta miao (big temple)
     Hsiao miao (small temple)
     Shuang miao (twin temple)
     Sui-t'ang miao (Sui-t'ang temple)   3
     Ts'ao-an miao (thatched roof temple)
     Pai-t'a miao (white pagoda temple)
     Wu-t'ung miao (temple of god lead-
       ing to five directions)
     Wu-fu miao (temple of five pre-
       fectures)
     Chu-sha miao (cinnabar temple)
     Wu-hsien miao (temple of the five
       apparitions)
     T'ung-ch'ing miao (temple of uni-
       versal joy)
     Fei-lai miao (temple that flew here)
     Chiu-sheng miao (temple of nine
       saints)   1
     Ta-wang miao (temple of the great
       king)

VI. Monasteries and nunneries   25   5
     A. Buddhist   25   5
     B. Taoist

                          Total   124   189

Sources: *Wang-tu hsien chih* (Gazetteer of Wang-tu County, Hopei Prov-
    ince), 1934
    Ch'ing-ho hsien chih (Gazetteer of Ch'ing-ho County, Hopei Prov-
    ince), 1924.
    Pao-shan hsien hsü-chih (Gazetteer of Pao-shan County, Kiangsu
    Province, supplemented edition), 1921.
    Ch'uan-sha hsien chih (Gazetteer of Ch'uan-sha County, Kiangsu
    Province), 1936.

TEMPLES

Ch'uan-sha	Pao-shan	Lo-ting	Fo-shan	Sui-ning	Ma-ch'eng	Total
1	10	4	3	2		24
	1	1				2
	2					2
		1				1
	2					2
	1					1
	3					3
	3					3
	1					1
		1				1
1						1
		1				1
				2		2
			1			1
			1			1
						1
			1			1
29	49	24	28	166	222	548
20	48	22	26	146	202	494
9	1	2	2	20	20	54
144	218	170	268	302	371	1,786

Lo-ting hsien chih (Gazetteer of Lo-ting County, Kwangtung Province), 1935.

Fo-shan chung-i hsiang chih (Gazetteer of Fo-shan Subdistrict, Nan-hai County, Kwangtung Province), 1923.

Sui-ning hsien chih (Gazetteer of Sui-ning County, Szechwan Province), 1929.

Ma-ch'eng hsien chih (Gazetteer of Ma-ch'eng County, Hupeh Province), 1935.

APPENDIX 2

*Alphabetical List of Temple Names in Transliteration
and in Chinese from Appendix 1*

An-ch'a-szu miao	按察司廟	Hsien-feng miao	先鋒廟
Chang-hsien miao	張仙廟	Hsien Ko miao	軒葛廟
Chen-wu miao	真武廟	Hsien-nung t'an	先農壇
Ch'eng-huang miao	城皇廟	Hsin miao	新廟
Ch'i-shen miao	七神廟	Hsüan T'an miao	玄壇廟
Ch'i-sheng miao	七聖廟	Hsüan Ti miao	玄帝廟
Chiang-chün miao	將軍廟	Hsüan-wu miao	玄武廟
Ch'iao-shen miao	橋神廟	Hu-hsien miao	狐仙廟
Chieh-hsiao tz'u	節孝祠	Hua-kuang miao	華光廟
Chieh-lieh tz'u	節烈祠	Hua-shen miao	花神廟
Chin-hua miao	金花廟	Hua-t'o miao	華陀廟
Chiu-sheng miao	九聖廟	Hua-wang miao	花王廟
Chü-mang miao	句芒廟	Huang ta-hsien miao	黃大仙廟
Chu-sha miao	硃砂廟	Hung-sheng miao	洪聖廟
Ch'uan-chu miao	川主廟	Huo-shen miao	火神廟
Ch'uan-shen miao	全神廟	Huo-ti miao	火帝廟
Ch'un-yang tien	純陽殿	I-ai tz'u	遺愛祠
Chung-chieh tz'u	忠節祠	I Li t'an	疫厲壇
Chung-i tz'u	忠義祠	I Li t'an	邑厲壇
Ch'ung-wang miao	虫王廟	K'ai-t'ien miao	開天廟
Erh-hsien miao	二仙廟	Kan-lu miao	甘露廟
Erh-kung tz'u	二公祠	Kan-ying miao	感應廟
Erh-lang miao	二郎廟	K'ang ta-yuan-shuai miao	
Fei-lai miao	飛來廟	康大元帥廟	
Feng-shen miao	風神廟	Kuan-ti miao	關帝廟
Fo-yeh miao	佛爺廟	Kuan-yin miao	觀音廟
Hai-shen miao	海神廟	Kuan Yo miao	關岳廟
Ho-shen miao	河神廟	Kuei-ku miao	鬼谷廟
Hsiang-hsien tz'u	鄉賢祠	K'uei-sheng ko	魁星閣
Hsiao miao	小廟	K'ung miao	孔廟
Hsiao-ti tz'u	孝悌祠	Kung-shu tzu miao	公輸子廟

Lao-chün miao	老君廟	San-sheng miao	三聖廟
Lao miao	老廟	San-wang miao	三王廟
Lao-mu miao	姥母廟	San-yuan miao	三元廟
Lao Tzu miao	老子廟	She-chi t'an	社稷壇
Lei-shen miao	雷神廟	She-jen miao	舍人廟
Lei-ti miao	雷帝廟	Shen-chi t'an	神祇壇
Lei-yü-feng-yün t'an	雷雨風雲壇	Sheng miao	聖廟
Liu-meng Chiang-chün miao		Sheng-yo miao	聖樂廟
劉猛將軍廟		Shuai Fu miao	帥府廟
Liu shih fu-jen miao	柳氏夫人廟	Shuang miao	雙廟
Lu-pan miao	魯班廟	Shui-fu miao	水府廟
Lü-shi tz'u	旅食祠	Shui-huo shen miao	水火神廟
Lung-shen miao	龍神廟	Shui-kuan miao	水關廟
Lung-wang miao	龍王廟	Sui-t'ang miao	隨堂廟
Ma-wang miao	馬王廟	Sung-mu miao	松木廟
Mi-t'o miao	彌陀廟	Ta-lu miao	大路廟
Ming-huan tz'u	名宦祠	Ta miao	大廟
Nai-nai miao	奶奶廟	Ta-shih miao	大士廟
Nan-hai miao	南海廟	Ta-wang miao	大王廟
Niang-niang miao	娘娘廟	T'ai I miao	太乙廟
Niu-lang miao	牛郎廟	T'ai-shan miao	泰山廟
Pa-la miao	八蠟廟	T'ai-shang miao	太上廟
Pai-i miao	白衣廟	T'ai Wei miao	太尉廟
Pai-i Ta-shih miao	白衣大士廟	T'an-hsien miao	譚仙廟
Pai-ma Chiang-chün miao		T'an-shen miao	灘神廟
白馬將軍廟		Ti-chuang miao	地藏廟
Pai-t'a miao	白塔廟	T'ien-ch'i miao	天齊廟
P'an-ku miao	盤古廟	T'ien-hou miao	天后廟
Pao-en tz'u	報恩廟	Tou-lao miao	斗姥廟
Pao Kung miao	包公廟	Tou-mu miao	荳母廟
Pao-kung tz'u	報功廟	Ts'ai-shen miao	財神廟
P'ei-sha miao	菩薩廟	Ts'ao-an miao	草庵廟
Pei Ti miao	北帝廟	Tu-k'ou miao	渡口廟
Pei Wang miao	北王廟	T'u-ti miao	土地廟
P'u-an miao	普庵廟	T'ung-ch'ing miao	同慶廟
San-chieh miao	三界廟	Tung-yo miao	東嶽廟
San-ch'ing miao	三清廟	Tzu-tsu miao	字祖廟
San-huang miao	三皇廟	Wan-shou kung	萬壽宮
San-i miao	三義廟	Wei-sheng tien	衛生殿
San-kuan miao	三官廟	Wei T'o miao	韋馱廟

Wen-ch'ang miao	文昌廟	Wu-ti miao	五帝廟
Wen miao	文廟	Wu-t'ung miao	五通廟
Wen-shen miao	瘟神廟	Ya-shen miao	衙神廟
Wen-ti miao	文帝廟	Yang-te tz'u	仰德祠
Wu-fu miao	五府廟	Yao-ti miao	堯帝廟
Wu-hsien miao	五仙廟	Yen-mu miao	眼母廟
Wu-lung miao	五龍廟	Yo-shih miao	藥師廟
Wu-lung sheng-mu miao		Yo-wang miao	藥王廟
五龍聖母廟		Yo-wang miao	岳王廟
Wu miao	武廟	Yü-huang miao	玉皇廟
Wu-sheng miao	武聖廟	Yü-shen miao	獄神廟
Wu-sheng Lao-mu miao		Yü t'an	雩壇
無生老母廟		Yü-wang miao	禹王廟
Wu-tao miao	五道廟		

APPENDIX 3
Terms, Phrases, and Proper Names in
Transliteration and in Chinese

Chang, Carsun 張嘉森

Chang Fei 張飛

Chao Chan-ju 趙展如

Chao Ch'eng 趙城

Chen Hai 鎮海

Chen-hai Lou 鎮海樓

Chi 祭，禝

Chiao 教

Chieh-pai hsiung-ti, chieh-pai tzu-mei 結拜兄弟，結拜姉妹

Chih Ming 智明

Chih-yuan T'ang 濟元堂

Ch'in Chou 欽州

Chin jen-shih i t'ing t'ien-ming 盡人事以聽天命

Ching-chou 荊州

Ch'ing-ho hsien 清河縣

Chu-i 朱衣

Chu Kuei-fang 朱桂芳

Ch'u Min-i 褚民誼

Chü-shih 居士

Ch'ü Yüan 屈原

Ch'uan-chen Chiao 全真教

Ch'un Yang Kuan 純陽觀

Chung-hsing Fu-lieh Ti 中興孚烈帝

Fan Chung-yen 范仲奄

Fang, chu 房，族

Fo chiao 佛教

Fu-yu Hou 孚祐侯

Han Chen-jen 韓真人

Han Chia Chuang 韓家庄

Han Fu-ch'ü 韓復渠

Han Yü 韓愈

Hao-ch'i ch'ang ts'un 浩氣長存

Ho-ho Erh Hsien 和合二仙

Ho Ju-fa 何汝發

Ho-nan Hui 和南會

Hou Ching 侯景

Hsien-t'ien tao 先天道

Hsin-ning hsien 新寧縣

Hsiung Shih-li 熊十力

Hsü Hung-ju 徐鴻儒

Hsü yüan 許願

Hsüan chi 玄機

Hsüeh Fu-ch'eng 薛福成

Hsün Chi 荀濟

Hsün Tzu 荀子

Huan yüan 還願

Huang Chin-jung 黃金榮

Huang T'ien Tao 黃天道

Hukuang 湖廣

Hunan Fo-hua Hui 湖南佛教會

I-hsin T'ien-tao Lung-hua Sheng-chiao Hui 一心天道龍華聖教會

I-kuan Tao 一貫道

I-t'u t'ung-kuei 異途同歸

Jan-teng Fo 燃燈佛

Ju mao hsüeh, ju-mao yin-hsüeh 茹毛血，茹毛飲血

K'ang Yu-wei	康有爲	Sakya Fo, Sakyamuni	
Kao T'ien-hsia I	告天下檄	釋迦佛，釋迦牟尼	
Ke Yün-fei	葛雲飛	San kang	三綱
Ku Kuo Ssu	固國寺	Sang li	喪禮
Kuan Yü	關羽	Shan-yin	山陰
Kuei-i Tao	魁星	Shang hsiang	尚饗
K'uei Hsing	皈依道	Shao-hsing	紹興
Kun Tan Hui	滾單會	Shao Ping Ke	焼餅歌
K'ung-chiao ch'uan-kung		She	社
孔教全功		She li-shih	社理事
Kuo Tsu-shen	郭祖深	Shen-tao Hui	神道會
Lan ho-shang	懶和尚	Sheng jung ssu ai	生榮死哀
Li Men	理門	Sheng tz'u	生祠
Li Te-yü	李德裕	Shih Fo	石佛
Liang Wu Ti	梁武帝	Shu Ch'i	叔齊
Liao	遼	Shuan Shan	蒜山
Liu Pei	劉備	Ssu-chou	泗洲
Lo-tien Chen	羅店鎮	Sui-ning hsien	遂寧縣
Lo-ting hsien	羅定縣	Ta shih	大事
Lu Hsun	魯迅	Ta-t'ung	大同
Lü Tung-pin	呂洞賓	Ta Yü	大禹
Lung Hua Hui	龍華會	T'ai-ch'eng	臺城
Ma-ch'eng hsien	麻城縣	T'ai Hsü	太虛
Ma Chiang	馬江	T'ai-pei	臺北
Ma Kang	馬岡	Taiping Tien-kuo	太平天國
Ma Shih-wei	馬士偉	Tai Shih-lun	戴士倫
Men	門	T'an Ssu-t'ung	譚嗣同
Ming-tsun Chiao	名尊教	T'ang Sheng-chih	唐生智
Ming Wang	明王	Tao-t'ung	道統
Mou-shih tsai jen, ch'eng-shih tsai		T'ien-chu Chiao	天竹教
t'ien 謀事在人，成事在天		T'ien-li Chiao	天理教
Nai-ho ch'iao	奈何橋	T'ien tsai	天災
Nan-hai hsien	南海縣	Ting-hai	定海
Pa Chin	巴金	Ting Wen-chiang	丁文江
Pai-yang chiao	白陽教	Ts'ai Yüan-p'ei	蔡元培
Pao-liang Kung-fei Hui		Ts'ang Chieh	倉頡
保良攻匪會		Ts'ang-chou	倉州
Pien t'ien	變天	Tseng Kuo-fan	曾國藩
Po I	伯夷	Tsung	宗
P'u-t'o Shan	普陀山	Tsung miao	宗教

T'ui Pei T'u	推背圖	Wu-chih	無極
T'ung Shan She	同善社	Wu-sheng lao-mu	無生老母
Wanchuan	萬全	Wutangshan	武當山
Wang Chüeh-i	王覺一	Wu Tsung	武宗
Wang Ning-chih	王凝之	Yang Chu	楊朱
Wang Ts'ung-hui	王寵惠	Yang Hsiu-ch'ing	楊秀清
Wang-tu hsien	望都縣	Yang-sheng sung-ssu	養生送死
Wei	魏	Yu chiao wu lei	有教無類
Wei hsien	濰縣	Yü Yung-liang	余永梁
Wei liao hou-tai	為了後代	Yüan-chün Sheng-mu Miao	
Wen-ch'ang	文昌	元君聖母廟	
Wen T'ien-hsiang	文天祥	Yün Chin	雲錦
Wu	巫	Yung Shou Kung	永壽宮

INDEX

Abbot, 313
Agnosticism, Confucian, 245–247
Agricultural gods: function of, 13; types of, 65–70
Almanac. *See Li shu*
Altar of Heaven, 41–42, 65, 184–185, 371
An (Buddhist nunneries), 309
Analects, 245, 249
Ancestral altar, 41–42
Ancestral temple, 40–43 *passim,* 350–351; rites in, 41–43
Ancestral worship: importance of, 29–31, 53; rites of, 31–53; classical interpretation of, 44–48; agnostic view of, 48–53; and kinship organization, 52–53; relation of, to Buddhism and Taoism, 125; Catholic prohibition of, 203; religious nature of, 253–255; as enforcement factor for Confucian values, 285–286; as diffused religion, 296–297
Animal protection gods, 66
Anthropolatry, 174
Antireligion movement, 363–367; Communist, 391
Apocryphal literature, 139–140, 141–143, 185–186
Apotheosis of distinguished men, 158–173
Apparition: of river gods, 67; of sailing goddess, 73; of Kuan Yü, 160; of Kuan-yin, 242
Apprentice, in search of Taoist magicians, 17–18
Apprenticeship, of priesthood, 308
Art, and religion, 18–19

Astrology, 260–261
Authoritarian government: and heterodox movements, 222–224; and religious rebellions, 224

Big Sword Society, 221, 399
Bridge of Sighs, 32
Brilliant Kings (Ming Wang), 218
Birth, supernatural influence on, 54–55, 135
Birthdays, celebration of gods', 89–91
Black Dragon (god), 141
Board of Rites. *See Li pu*
Bodde, Derk, 4
Boddhisattva, 109
Book of Change. *See I Ching*
Book of History. *See Shu Ching*
Book of Rites. *See Li Chi*
Boxer Rebellion, 220, 221, 241, 363
Boxers' Association, 219
Brotherhoods: suppression of, 206–207; and salvation, 280
Buddha, Lamplighting, 234
Buddha Maitreya, 233, 235, 242; religion of, 215, 218, 230
Buddha (Sakyamuni), 109, 120, 123, 200, 234; in eclectic faiths, 197, 198
Buddhas, 194
Buddhism: Ch'an school of, 5, 125; statistics of cults of, 24–25; rise of, 110–112, 115–123; magical functions of, 117–119; Hinayana sect of, 118; Mahayana sect of, 119, 124, 125; monastic order of, 121–122, 126; persecution of, 121–122, 197, 209; as legalized religion, 187; versus traditional socioeconomic order, 199–204; success of, 216; and salva-

Buddhism (*continued*)
    tion, 230–232; and redemption, 232;
    as institutional religion, 295; mod-
    ern organizations of, 313–314, 358–
    363; number of devotees of, 327;
    schools for teaching, 359; Com-
    munist indoctrination of, 396
Bureau of Religious Affairs (Com-
    munist), 393, 394
Burgess, J. S., 74, 351
Burckhardt, Jacob, 110

Calamities, natural, 66; and religious
    gatherings, 92–94; during period of
    disunion, 116
Calamities, universal, 234–235
Canton: guild processions in, 75–76;
    temple gathering in, 88–90; reli-
    gious symbol of, 100; superstition
    in, 270; Taoists' organization in,
    315; expropriation of temple prop-
    erties in, 326, 368
Catholic church, 387, 393, 395
Catholic Patriotic Association, Chi-
    nese, 394, 395, 396
Celibacy, 60–61, 200
Chan, W. T., 354
Ch'ang-an, 120
Chang, Carsun, 365
Chang Chüeh, 113
Chang Fei, 59
Chang T'ai-yen, 245
Chang Tao-ling, 113
Chang T'ien-shih (Taoist pope), 191,
    314
Changsha (Hunan province), 336,
    359
Chao Chan-ju, 260–261
Chao-ch'eng (Shansi province), 220
Charisma, 131, 270
Charity: and Christian church, 335;
    lack of religious sponsorship in,
    335–337
Charms, 230, 231
Chekiang province, 137, 399
Chen-hai Lou (Canton), 100
Ch'en Shou-i, 356
Ch'en Tu-hsiu, 245, 386

Chen-wu: god of, 23, 184; and com-
    munity integration, 3, 103; legend
    of, 152–154; cult of, 152–155
Cheng ch'i ko (Ballad of the Great
    Spirit), 274
Cheng-chiao (government through
    education), 138
Ch'eng-huang (city god), 12, 31, 182,
    375; temple of, 25, 258, 366; thrash-
    ing of image of, 68, 92, 182; celebra-
    tion of birthday of, 89; cult of,
    156–157; moral function of, 157–158
Cheng Pan-ch'iao, 267–268
Ch'i (ethereal substance), 124, 273
Chi (sacrifice), 39–43
Ch'i-hsi (festival), 95
Chi Hsiao-lan, 277, 291
Chi yin-te (accumulation of merits
    for the other world), 287, 337
Chia-ch'ing (emperor, Ch'ing dy-
    nasty), 141, 181, 193, 227
Chiao, meaning of, 2
Chieh-pai hsiung-ti, or *chieh-pai tzu-
    mei*, 59–60
Ch'ien-han Shu, 253
Ch'ien Lung (emperor, Ch'ing dy-
    nasty), 197, 219
Ch'ien Tuan-sheng, 5
Chih Ming (monk), 235
Chih-yuan T'ang, 336
Chinese society, religious character
    of: Christian missionary view of,
    3–4; Sinologists' view of, 4; Chi-
    nese scholars' view of, 5–6
Ching-chou (Hupeh province), 186
Ch'ing dynasty, 180–216 *passim*, 218;
    and rite of sacrifice to Heaven, 128–
    129; number of officials in, 138;
    effectiveness of laws of, 180–181,
    184; religious rebellions during,
    219–242 *passim*; temple building
    and repair in, 342–348
Ch'ing-ho county (Hopei province),
    8, 10, 101
Ch'ing-ming (festival), 95
Ch'ing-pu county (Kiangsu province),
    261
Ch'ing society, 62–64

Chou I, 18

Chou li, 204

Chou period, 23, 106–107, 140, 193, 248, 256, 303–304

Christian churches, under Communist rule, 395

Christian missionary schools, 366–367

Christianity, 21, 339, 355, 357, 358, 366, 387

Ch'u-chia jen (priest), 202

Chu Hsi, 195, 247

Chu-i (literary god), 270

Chu Lu (Hopei province), 113

Ch'ü Yuan, 96, 337

Ch'üan-chen Chiao (Complete Truth religion), 218

Ch'uan-sha county (Kiangsu province), 8, 10, 102, 103, 141, 163; insect god in, 68; charity donations, 336; temple land and properties in, 317, 318, 319; donations for temple building and repair, 320, 322; temple building and repair, 348–349

Ch'un Ch'iu Fan Lu (Heavy Dews of Spring and Autumn), 253

Ch'un Ch-iu period, 108

Chung-hsing Fu-lieh Ti, 220

Chung Jung, 250–251

Chung Tao (Middle sect), 400

Civilizations, and religion, 104

Clan solidarity, and ancestor worship, 40–43, 46–48

Class differences, in religion, 275–277

Classical religion, 23–25; statistics of cults in, 24–25; in diffused form, 25; and political life, 106–110; as communal religion, 110–112; reassertion of, 123–126; and institutional religion, 301; status of priests, 303–306; limited number of priests in, 306–307

Commercial organizations, cults of, 77–78

Communal cults, 11–12, 110–112; as diffused religion, 297

Communal observances, religious, 86–96 *passim*

Communism: as nontheistic faith, 381–386; and control of religion, 393–396

Communist Party, membership in, 138

Community, religious symbols of, 96–102

Community integration: and agricultural cults, 70; through religious events, 81–82; and temple fairs, 91; and earth and grain cult, 98–99; and cults of deified men, 102–103, 158–177

Condolence gifts, 37

Confucian values: in divination, 262; dominance of, 279; relation of, to kinship system, 280; fused with Buddhism, 282; in mythology, 283–285

Confucianism: agnostic nature of, 4, 5, 19–20; and concept of power and its moral control, 12, 130–133, 137–139; religious aspects of, 17, 26, 27, 244–276; view of ancestor worship, 44–53 *passim;* and religious nature of Chinese society, 104; and classical religion, 107–110; in Han period, 112–114; decline of, in period of disunion, 119; reassertion of, in Sung period, 123–126; cults of, 164–165; against heterodoxy, 192–211 *passim,* 222–224; as political orthodoxy, 193–196; and salvation, 229; ethics of, and religious sects, 230; moral values of, 245; acceptance of religious elements as moral force, 255–257; rationalistic interpretation of, 256; emphasis on human effort, 272–274; orthodoxy, inadequacy of, 354; as modern religious movement, 355–358, 365; fundamentalism, collapse of, 380–381

Confucius, 4, 5, 245–276 *passim,* 337; on sacrifice, 49; in eclectic faiths, 197–198; and prophecy, 233; *Analects* of, 245, 249; and the *I Ching,* 251

Conservatism, and diffused religion, 298–299

Construction trade, cult of, 71–72, 75–76

Convents, number and control of, 187–188

Conversion, 111–112

Corrupt government and religious rebellion, 226

Corvée, 202, 326

Coscinomancy, 259–260

Crafts, gods of, 71–78

Creel, Herlee C., 107, 246

Crisis: and rebellions, 224–229; and prophecy, 233, 235–238 *passim;* and conversion, 238; and divination, 261–262; and institutional religion, 307

Cults: statistics of, 8–11; and political order, 12; and moral order, 12–13; and economic life, 13; functional nature of, 15, 25

Dairen (Liaoning province), 222

Day, Clarence B., 76–77, 90

Dead, fear of the, 33–34

Death anniversary, 39–40

DeGroot, J. J. M., 192, 193, 213, 241, 245, 278

Deified men, temples of, 102–103; cults of, 158–177; in modern period, 353

Democracy, 382

Democratic centralism, 386

Demonology, 118–119, 288

Deviation: moral and political, 111–112, 228, 231; and sectarians, 231–232. *See also I-tuan*

Dewey, John, 364

Diffused religion: defined, 20–21, 294–295; lack of independent ethical values in, 285–286; pervasiveness of, 296–298; and stability of social institutions, 298–299; dependence on secular institutions, 299–300; weakening of, in modern period, 300; and group needs, 302; under Communists, 387

Divination: in early history, 107; and Confucianism, 250–253; in modern period, 259–261; for guidance of the masses, 261; personal, 261–262; psychological function of, 261–265; and institutional religion, 301

Donations: for temple construction and repair, 320–321; sources of, 321–325; sizes of, 323; to community charity, 336

Dowager, Empress, 220

Dragon, incarnation of, 128–129

Dragon boats, 96

Dragon god, 12, 13, 65, 66, 67, 100

Dream of the Red Chamber, and Buddhism, 17, 331

Drought: gods of, 67–68, 70; and religious observance, 92

Durkheim, Emile, 165, 295

Earth, cults of, 150, 155–156

Earth and grain, god of, 65, 96–99

Eastern Tsin dynasty, 115–116

Eclectic nature of Chinese religion, 25, 123–126

Economic crises and religious rebellions, 224–229

Education: Confucian dominance of, 337; lack of religious participation in, 338–339

Eight Diagram sect (Pa-kua Chiao): persecution of, 207; and rebellion, 219, 220, 224, 225, 227, 242, 243

Emperor Ch'ao (Chou period), 235

England, 324

Epidemics, and religious observances, 92–93

Ethical values: Buddhist, 281; Buddhist and Taoist, 281–283; encouragement and deterrence of, 286–289; separation of, from religion, 290–293; modern depreciation of, 380–381

Ethicopolitical cults: number and types of, 147–149; stages of development in, 165–173; psychological elements in, 165–177; versus function, 177–179; as diffused religion, 298; in Republican period, 372–377; weakened by change in moral values, 375–377

Ethicopolitical order, 138–142, 147

Europe, 104, 212, 364–365

Examination system, 265–272, 338

Fa Hsien, 119–120

Fa Hua Ching (Lotus Flower Scripture of the Mysterious Law), 120, 237

Fairs: temple, 82–86; honoring Willow Tree god, 83; in Pei Ch'i village, 83–84, 86; relaxation of moral control during, 84–85; and recreation, 84–86; in Ting county, 86; and community integration, 91

Faith, quest for, 380–381

Faiths, mixing of, 25

Family: status and rites of, 36–38; solidarity and rites of, 39; and religious aspects of life, 53–58

Family-centered life, broadening of, 81, 85–86

Famine and religious movements, 225

Fan Chen, 247

Fan Chung-yen, 201

Fanaticism, religious, 241; Communist, 385

Fang (clan subdivision), 47

Fate: Confucian belief in, 26–27, 247–250, 255–256; in predeterminism, 135–136; in modern period, 257–265; and examination system, 265–272; man's role in, 272–274

Feast of the Souls, 95

Feng shui (geomancy), 34, 248, 263; Confucian belief in, 264; psychology of, 265

Feng Yu-lan, 383–384, 385

Ferry god, 102

Fertility cults, 11

Festivals: communal significance of, 94–96 *passim;* and integration of groups, 95

Feudal state, 106–107

Fiction, as source of information, 23

Filial piety: and ancestor worship, 38, 45–46, 50, 51; and social values, 282, 285, 287; temple to encourage, 373

Fire, god of, 101

Firewood Gatherers' sect, 226

Five Commandments, 281–282

Five constant virtues, 193

Five Elements, 17, 24, 109–110, 135–136, 247, 248, 250–265 *passim*

Five Emperors, 253

Five-Peck-Rice sect, 113

Flood gods, 67–70 *passim*

Fo-chiao hui (Buddhist societies), 359

Fo-shan (Kwangtung province), 9, 11, 12, 258; *she chi* cult in, 98–99; Chen-wu legend in, 153; sanctuary of deified men in, 162; T'ien Hou temple in, 175–176; Communist renovation of Chen-wu temple in, 398

Forbidden City (Peking), 220

Fraternities, 50–60

French invasion (1881–1882), 168

Fu Hsi, 234

Fukien province, Lung Hua sect in, 207

Funeral procession, 37–38

Gamble, Sidney D., 147

Gatherings, religious: for celebration of gods' birthdays, 86–96 *passim;* in community crises, 92–94; and Kuan Yü's apparition, 160; law against, 205–210

Gazetteers, local, 22, 142, 145, 258, 342, 349

General Liu-meng (insect god), 68–69, 182

Gentry, 297

Geomancy, and institutional religion, 301. *See also Feng shui*

Ghost stories, 56–57

Ghosts (*kuei*), 24

Giles, Herbert, 4, 284

Goddess of Mercy, 28

Gods (*shen*), 23–24

Golden Dragon (god), 67
Government: relation of, to religion, 104–106; and control of supernatural forces, 181–182; monopoly of Heaven worship, 182–185
Grand Canal, 181
Granet, Marcel, 106, 364
Grass Cutters' sect, 226
Great Kings, of Red Heaven, of Red Earth, of Red Mankind, 223–224
Grief, in mortuary rites, 34–35
Grootaers, Willem A., 24
Grottoes, in Tatung, 19
Guild gods: and diffused religion, 297; modern decline of, 377
Guilds: religious worship in meetings of, 74–75; organizational integration of, 74–76 *passim*

Honorific titles: function of, 181; granting of, 181–182
Hai ch'ao yin Monthly, 361
Hai shen (sea god), 12
Halls of Three Religions, 197–198
Han dynasty, 106–107, 112–116, 139–140, 248, 253, 256, 257
Han empire, religious integration of, 109–110; disintegration of, 112–121; society in, 113–115
Han Yü, 118, 122, 197, 200
Hangchow (Chekiang province), 88, 102, 313
Hao-ch'i (immense and indomitable spirit), 171
Heaven: supremacy of, 23–24, 106, 123; Confucian concept of, 26–27, 247–250; Will of, 108; Mandate of, 108–110; nature of, 108–110, 139–142; and community integration, 111–112; sacrificial rites to, 128; as sanction for political power, 129–136 *passim*; as unifying influence for empire, 136–137; ethical function of, 139–142; cults of, 150–155; government monopoly of worship of, 183–185; and sectarian movements, 231; as anthropomorphic force, 247–250, 255–256; ordinance of, 250–251

Heaven and Earth: early development of worship of, 108–110; portents of, 185–186; in diffused religion, 207–298; Society of, 221
Heavenly Lamp, 183
Hell, Ten Courts of, 25, 32–33, 155, 156, 158, 288
Heresy, prohibition of, 185–186, 194–196, 204–210
Heroes, temples of, 102–103
Heterodoxy: motivation for, 192–198; persecution of, 192–210; movements of, 222–224
Hinayana Buddhism, 118
Ho Ho Erh Hsien (Twin Genii of Harmony), 77–78
Ho Ju-fa, 350
Ho-nan Hui, 314
Honan province, sectarian movements and rebellions in, 197, 208, 220–221, 225, 226
Hong Kong, 73–74, 210, 261
Hopei province, 399, 400; religious rebellions in, 141, 225
Household gods, 28
Hsien-feng (emperor, Ch'ing dynasty), 128, 141
Hsien-nung (creator of agriculture), 13
Hsien-nung t'an, 65
Hsien T'ien Tao (Prebirth sect), 2, 220, 225
Hsien Tsung (emperor, T'ang dynasty), 118
Hsin Ching (Kiangsu province), 261
Hsinkiang province, 287, 392
Hsiung Shih-li, 358, 360
Hsü, Francis L. K., 92
Hsü, Hung-ju, 220
Hsü, Ti-shan, 261
Hsü yüan, 87
Hsüan chi (the universe as unfathomable mechanism), 279
Hsüan-wu temple, Communist renovation of, 398
Hsüeh, Fu-ch'eng, 168
Hsün, Chih, 122

Hsün Tzu, 45, 48–49, 66–67, 193, 254, 279
Hu, Shih, 23, 178, 245, 247, 256, 365
Hua-kuang (fire god), 91
Hua Shan, 394
Hua-t'o (patron of medicine), 71, 72
Huan yüan, 87
Huang Chin-jung, 350
Huang-chou chu-lou chih, 18
Huang-t'ien Tao (Yellow Heaven doctrine), 215, 230, 235
Hughes, E. R., 22, 124, 128
Hui Tsung (emperor, Sung dynasty), 197
Humanitarian values, 403
Hunan Buddhist Conversion Association (Hunan Fo-hua Hui), 211
Hunan province, 221, 399; Buddhist movement in, 211, 359; religious rebellion in, 226; number of priests in, 308, 311, 312; priests' livelihood in, 318; temple building and repair in, 348; conversion of temples to secular uses in, 370
"Hundred Flowers" persecution, 383–384
Hung Liang-chi, 226
Hung-sheng (flood god), 70
Hung society, 62–64, 207
Huo-shen (fire god), 14
Hupeh province, 226, 399

I Ching (Book of Change), 107, 124, 250–253, 260
I-kuan Tao (Unity sect), 222, 223, 230, 232, 234, 276, 282, 399; and prophecy, 236, 237; and practice of coscinomancy, 263; under Communist rule, 400
I-t'u t'ung-kuei (divergent roads to a common end), 383
I-tuan (heterodoxy), 193, 228
Ideologies, conflict of, 355, 356, 357
Images, Communist wrecking of, 391–392
Incantations, 230, 231

India, 104, 120
Indigenous religion, 23–25
Initiation rites: of fraternities, 59–60; of secret societies, 62–64; vows in, 63
Insect gods, 66, 68–69
Institutional religion: defined, 20, 294–295; and break with the past, 299; types of, 301; functions of, 301–303; and individual needs, 302; weak structural position of, 303; decline of classical priests in, 304–307; number of priests in, 308–309; limited importance of, 328–339
Intellectuals, modern, 363–367
Interaction between Heaven and man, 137, 139–143, 185–186
Islam, 387, 392

Jade Emperor, 28, 150
James, William, 232
Jan Teng Fo (Lamplighting Buddha), 234
Japanese invasion, 379, 380, 381; religious movement during, 222; prophecy of, 237
Jen (benevolence) and Buddhist value, 281
Jen-ho county (Chekiang province), 162
Jen tao (Way of man), 130, 273
Jesuits, 127
Ju-lin wai-shih, 258, 266, 269
Ju mao yin-hsüeh (eating hair and blood), 42–43

Kalpas, 234–236
K'ang Yu-wei, 125, 356, 357
Kansu province, 392, 399
Karma, 120, 125; function of, 151; acculturation of, 152
Ke, Yün-fei, 168–170
Kiangsu province, early Buddhism in, 117; suppression of religious movement in, 208; restoration of sacrificial rites in, 373
Kinship system: and monastic orders, 332; modern vitality of, 351

Kinship values, 51, 56–58
Kitchen god, 28
K'o-chang i-wen lu, 266–267
Kuan (Taoist monasteries), 309
Kuan ssu (official cults), 145
Kuan-ti miao, and community integration, 103. *See also* Kuan Yü
Kuan-yin (Goddess of Mercy), 11, 28; and political struggle, 241
Kuan Yü, 59, 62, 64; as wealth god, 79; ethicopolitical function of cult, 159–161; and ethical values, 262, 286; in Republican period, 373
Kuang-hsiao Ssu, 281
Kuei (ghosts), 24
Kuei-i Tao, 276
K'uei-sheng (literary star god), 270, 288
Kun Tan Hui, 204
Kung-shu Tzu (Lu-pan), 71
Kuo Yü, 106, 254, 303
Kuomintang, 363
Kwangsi province, 221, 227, 399
Kwangtung province, 60–61, 221, 227; religious gatherings in, 90–91; *she chi* cult in, 98–99; local religious tradition in, 137; Communist treatment of superstition in, 389; wrecking of ancestral temple, 391; under Communist rule, 399
Kweichow province, 221, 227, 399

Laity, 309; lack of religious organization of, 327–329
Lamaism, 387, 392
Lamaist priest, Communist persecution of, 392
Land owned by temples, 316–317
Landlords, execution of, 399
Lao Tzu, 114, 279; early worship of, as god, 117; and concept of Heaven, 140, 248; in eclectic faiths, 197–198
Later Chao dynasty, 123
Later Chou period, 209
Legge, James, 4
Li (reason), 124
Li (ritual), 254–255

Li Chi (Book of Rites), 23, 42, 48, 50, 54, 146, 156, 178, 254
Li Men (Reason sect), 276
Li pu (Board of Rites), 187
Li shu (almanac), 17, 136, 341
Li Te-yü, 200
Li Wen-ch'eng (rebel), 141
Liang Ch'i-ch'ao, 5, 6, 245
Liang Wu Ti (Emperor Wu of Liang kingdom), 118, 120, 122
Liao-chai chih-i (Strange Stories from a Chinese Studio), 276, 284
Liao dynasty, 201, 307
Limitless Ultimate, 234
Lin Ch'ing (rebel), 141
Lin Kuang-yün, 259
Liquor in sacrifice, 50
Literary patrons, 270–272
Literati status, supernatural sanction of, 269–272
Literature, religion in, 18
Liu Hai (wealth god), 78–79
Liu Meng Chiang-chün (Fierce General Liu, insect-killing god), 68–69
Liu Pei, 59
Livelihood of priests, 315–319
Lo Jui-ch'ing, 399
Lo-tien town (Kiangsu province), 258, 283; building and repair of temples in, 349; revitalizing of temple in, 352
Lo-ting county (Kwangtung province), 9, 11; Wen-ch'ang cult in, 264; sources of donations for temples in, 322; number and types of temples in, 346; temple building and repair in, 348
Locusts, 68–69
Lord Fu-yu, 168
Lu Hsun, 379
Lu-pan (Kung-shu Tzu), patron of construction trade, 71, 75–76, 350
Lü Tung-pin (literary patron), 270
Lun Heng, 248
Lung Hua sect, 194, 204, 207–208, 399

Ma-ch'eng county (Hupeh province), 9, 10, 130

Ma Hsien Ku (Goddess Ma), 390
Ma Kang, 210, 221
Ma Shih-wei (sectarian leader), 221
Ma Yüan, temple of, 88, 161
Magic: among sectarians, 230, 231, 232; sympathetic, 261, 263; moral function of, 283
Mahayana Buddhism, ethical value of, 281
Maitreya, Buddha. *See* Buddha Maitreya
Man: role of, in shaping fate, 272–274; position of, in universe, 273, 274; perfectibility of, 273–274
Manchu officers, heretic subversion of, 186
Mandate of Heaven: effectiveness of, 127–129, 139; in Confucian concept of power, 130–133; as inspiring confidence, 133–134; acceptance of, by people, 134–136; in modern period, 257–259; and political values, 286; replacement of, 371
Mao Tse-tung, 388
Marriage, supernatural influence in, 54–58
Marxism, 383–384, 385
Masons, trade cult of, 75
Materialistic progress, 382, 383, 401
Memorial arch, in Canton, 270
Mencius, 108, 131, 192, 193, 247, 251–253, 273–274
Messianic promise, 385
Miao-feng Shan, temple fair in, 87–88
Min ssu (popular cults), 145
Ming. *See* Fate
Ming dynasty, 208, 236; rise of, 233; hope for restoration of, 234; temple building and repair in, 242, 343–347, 348
Ming Ti (emperor, Han dynasty), 117
Ming Wang, Big and Little, 218, 233
Miracles, function of, 167, 232; and sectarian leaders, 231; social setting of, 354
Mohammedanism, 21
Mohists, 108

Monasteries: functions of, 14; government control of, 187–188; number of, 188
Monastery of Six Banyan Trees (Canton), Communist renovation of, 398
Monastic orders, 121–122, 222–223; ethical values of, 279–280; obstacles to joining, 330–335
Mongol rule, 123
Mongolia, Inner, 387
Monkey, The, 276
Mountains and rivers, gods of, 155–156
Mourning feast, 37
Moral encouragement and deterrence, 287–289
Moral merits, Taoist record of, 287, 288–289
Moral order, secularization of, 371–377
Moral restrictions, relaxation of, 85, 89
Morale, group, 172
Moralization of power, 137–139
Mortuary rites: functions of, 31–38; and family status, 36–38; classical interpretation of, 44–48
Movements, religious, 218–243; authoritarian government as cause of, 223, 224; heterodox nature of, 222–224; and socioeconomic crises, 224–229; and salvation, 229–232; modern setting for, 354–363
Mulberry Garden Dike village, flood god in, 7, 70
Mythology, 365–366; and ethical values, 283–285; Communist treatment of, 388–389

Nai-nai, 11
Nanching village, temples in, 7; religious life of, 16
Nanking, 75, 364, 366
Nan-p'ing, 264
National devotion, quest for, 378–381
Nationalism, 366, 382, 383, 398, 401; in Sung period, 123

Nationalist government, 260–261, 326, 399; and ethicopolitical cults, 372–375

Neighborhood community, 98–99

Neo-Confucianism and religion, 17, 123–126, 257

Neophyte, 189, 209, 305

New Year, Chinese, celebration of, in shops, 76–77, 94

Niang-niang (fertility goddess), 11

Nine Mansions sect (Chiu-kung Tao), 219, 242, 399

Ning-po (Chekiang province), 168

Niu-lang miao, 54

Occupational groups, religious differences among, 275

Ocheng county (Hupeh province), 389

Official cults, 145–150; nature of, 145–146; number and types, 147–149

Official patronage of Buddhism, 117–119

Official sacrifice, 146, 373

Old maid houses, 60–61

Omei Mountain (Szechwan province), 313

Opium War, 168

Oracle bones, 107, 313

Ordination certificates, 189, 308–309

Orthodoxy, Confucian, 193–196

Pa Chin, 379

Pai-yang chiao, 2

Palmistry, 260–261

Pantheon, 23–24, 25, 298, 362

Pao-chung Ssu, 281

Pao-liang Kung-fei Hui, 227

Pao P'u Tzu, 287–288

Pao-shan county (Kiangsu province), 9, 11, 102, 258, 284, 287, 366; city god in, 181–182; number of priests in temples in, 311; temple building and repair in, 321, 349; number and types of temples in, 344; conversion of temples to secular uses in, 369

Paradise, 230

Parker, H. E., 182

Patrons of trades, 71–76

Pearl River, 100; apparition of Kuan Yü in, 161

Peasants, in Han dynasty, 113

Peking, 186, 364, 366; guild gods in, 71, 74–76, 357

Persecution, religious: against Buddhism, 122; under Communist rule, 222. *See also* Sectarian societies

Phoenix, 253

Physiognomy, 260–261

Pilgrim groups, 87–88

Pien t'ien (changing Heaven), 222

Planchette, 259–260

Political action, related to prophecy, 238–239

Political oppression and religious rebellion, 226

Political power: sanction by Heaven, 19, 129–133, 175–177; moral control of, 137–139; over religion, 210–212, 223; change in concept of, 371

Polytheism, 117–118, 212; and lack of lay organization, 328

Popular cults, 145–150; statistics of, 24–25; nature of, 145–146; number and types of, 147–149; national, 159–161; local, 161–173

Portents, heavenly, 185–186

Prayer slips, 15

Predeterminism: in birth, 54–55; in marriage, 55–56; Confucian belief in, 247, 250, 255–256; notion of, in modern period, 257–261; psychological function of, 261–265; and examination system, 265–268

Priests: of classical religion, 107, 303–306; licensing of, 188–189; privileges of, 189; numerical restriction of, 189–190; conduct of, controlled by government, 190–192; social composition of, 202–203; denial of extralegal status to, 209; number of, 213, 307–312; morality and education of, 290, 338; lack of centralized organization of, 312–315;

social obstacles to, 330–335; under Communist rule, 393–398

Prophecy, function of, 232–239; psychology of, 235–239

Proselytising, law against, 186, 205–206

Protestant churches, National Committee for Self-Administration of, 394

Pseudo-kinship groups, 59–61

P'u-t'o Shan, 350

Rain gods, 92

Rain prayer, 66–67

Rationalism, Confucian, 245–247

Rebellions: political, 218–224, 239–242; religious, 218–227; Taoist, 113–114. *See also* Religious societies; Religious organizations; Sectarian societies

Recreation: in temple fairs, 84–86, 89–91; in festivals, 94–96

Red Spear society, 221, 226, 241, 363, 399

Redemption, 232

Reformation, 212

Religion: defined, 1; Chinese conception of, 2–3; influence of, in social life, 16–26, 59–60; general concept of, 26; disunity in, 214; growth of, 214–216

Religious movements. *See* Movements, religious

Religious organizations: prohibition of, 205–210 *passim;* secrecy of, 213; Communist treatment of, 393–397

Religious societies: and political rebellion, 218–224; and Taoism, 230; material benefits of, 231; and institutional religion, 301; Communist suppression of, 399–401. *See also* Religious organizations; Sects; Sectarian societies

Religious systems, Chinese, 23–27

Renaissance, Chinese, 363, 364, 366

Republican period, 201–202, 341–404 *passim;* religious rebellions in, 207, 221–222; Buddhist movement in,

211, 314; number of clergy in, 213; other religious movements in, 223; relaxation of religious control in, 224; weakening of diffused religion in, 300; temple building and repair in, 342–348

Retribution, 288–289

Revolution, Mencius' theory of, 131

Rightists, 383–384

Rites, 254–255; mortuary, 31–38; Hsün Tzu's interpretation of, 45; fraternity initiation, 59–61. *See also* Sacrifice

River gods, 67–68

Rockets, ritual firing of, 90–91

Romance with ghosts, 56–57

Rural counties, temple building and repair in, 349–350

Russell, Bertrand, 364

Sacred number of five, 253

Sacrifice: and family, 39–40; rites of, 39–43; and clan, 40–43; offerings of, 42; feast of, 43; classical interpretation of, 44–48; early development of, 108; official and popular, 145–150; in *tz'u* (sanctuaries), 165–166; supernatural nature of, 253–255; and stability of social institutions, 299

Sacrificial canon, 145

Sailing, cult of, 72–73

Salvation: religious, 229–232; and magic, 232; in Buddhism and Taoism, 300

San kang (trinity of the universe), 273

San kuan (Three Officials), 100

San-min chu-i (Three People's Principles), 381

San Pao Ching Lü (Three Precious Scriptural Rules), 282

Sanctuary right, absence of, 209–210

Sang li (mortuary rites), 31–39. *See also* Rites; Sacrifice

Sang-yuan Wei, 7, 70

Scholar-official class, 289

Science, impact of, 363–367

Sea god, 102

Second Revolution, 348, 363, 381

Secrecy, of religious organizations, 213, 223, 224

Sectarian societies: Kun Tan Hui, 24; religious elements in, 61–64; Lung Hua Hui, 204, 242, 399; Buddha Maitreya sect, 205; Ming-tsun sect, 205; White Cloud sect, 205, 220, 225; Hung society, 207; White Sun sect, 207, 219; Eight Diagrams sect, 207, 219, 220, 224; Heaven and Earth society, 207, 219, 221; T'ien Li sect, 207, 219, 225, 242; Triads, 207, 221; Boxer association, 219; Nine Mansions sect, 219, 399; T'ien-chu sect, 220; I-hsin T'ien-tao Lung-hua Sheng-chiao Hui, 221; and salvation, 230; Huang T'ien sect, 230; Kuei-i Tao, 276; Li Men, 276; I-kuan Tao, 276, 399; modern movements of, 361–363; Big Sword association, 399; Red Spear association, 399; Sheng-hsien Tao, 399; underground resistance of, against Communism, 400–401

Sects. *See* Sectarian societies

Secularization, 342–351, 363–377

Seven Mansions, 183

Seven-Star Lamp, 183

Sex segregation, 203; relaxation of, 85–86, 89

Shang hsiang, 40

Shang period, 106–107

Shanghai, 342, 350; shops celebrating New Year in, 76–77

Shansi province, religious rebellion in, 220

Shantung province, 399; suppression of religious movement, 208; religious rebellion in, 220–221, 225, 226

Shao-hsing district (Chekiang province), 168

Shao-p'ao, 90–91

Shao Ping Ke (Baked Cake Ballad), 236, 237, 239

She chi (god of earth and grain), 65, 96–99, 107

Shen (gods), 23

Shen-nung (creator of agriculture), 13

Shen-tao Hui, 323

Sheng Hsien Tao (Sages sect), 399

Sheng jung ssu ai, 38

Shensi province, 399, 400

Shih Ching (Book of Songs), 254

Shih-fo (Stone Buddha) village, 234

Shih Hsiang-kung miao, 103

Shih Hu, 123

Shih Tsu (emperor, Wei dynasty), 199

Shows, in temple fairs, 84–85

Shryock, John, 159, 164, 245

Shu Ching (Book of History), 194, 254

Shun, Emperor, 130

Shun T'ien Fu (Hopei province), 128

Shuo Ju, 256

Social values, new, 382

Socialism, 384

Soochow city (Kiangsu province), 208

Sorcerers, 186. *See also* Wu

Sororities, 59–60

Sortilege, 262

Soul, in ancestor worship, 31, 44–45

Spirit tablets, 29, 33, 39, 41–42, 47, 50, 62, 64

Ssu (Buddhist monasteries), 309

Ssuma Kuang, 247

Star gods, 269–272

State: role of religion in, 104–106, 175–177; and agricultural cults, 69–70

Straw Plaiters' sect, 226

Sui dynasty, 121

Sun Yat-sen, 326, 381

Sung dynasty, 123, 197, 246, 256, 307, 394

Supernatural: as factor in religion, 1–3, 26; forces of the, control of, 181–182

Supernatural authorities, 150–151

Superstition, 3, 4, 6, 7, 244; Confucian, 253; movement against, 365–

367; suppression of, 374–375; Communist treatment of, 388–389
Supreme god in Heaven, 28
Szechwan province, 114, 221, 226, 399
Szu-chou, 200

Ta-ch'ing lü li, 180
Ta shih, 220
Ta-tai li chi, 45
T'ai-hsü, 358, 359
T'ai-shan (god Mount T'ai), 155, 375
T'ai Shan (Shantung province), 394
Tai Shih-lun, 264
Taiping rebellion, 105, 128, 133, 141, 182, 198, 209, 221, 224, 225–227 *passim*, 231
T'ai-p'ing tao (Great Peace Taoism), 113–114
T'an Ssu-t'ung, 192, 289
T'ang dynasty, 122, 123, 199, 200, 210, 236
T'ang Sheng-chih, 210, 359, 360
Tantrism, 118
Tao (Way), 2, 194, 279
Tao Kuang (emperor, Ch'ing dynasty), 128, 208, 226
Tao te ching, 114
Taoism, religious, 5; development of, 17, 110–115; statistics of cults in, 24–25; theology, 109; rebellions led by, 113–114; hierarchy of authority, 114; as legalized religion, 187; and sectarian theology, 230; and Taiping rebellion, 231; and redemption, 232; as institutional religion, 295; modern organization of, 315; number of devotees of, 327
Taoist Association, China, 394
Temple of Prayer for the Good Year, 65
Temples: number of, 6–7, 188; social functions of, 7–11; government control of, 187–188; number of priests in, 309–312; donations for construction and renovation of, 315–327; diversion of funds of, 325–326; expropriation of property, 326; building and repair of, in different

periods, 342–353; conversion of, to secular uses, 367–371; Communist refurbishing of, 398
Ten Virtues, 281–282
Theater, in temples, 84–85
Theistic religion: decline of, 378–381; Communist policy toward, 386–393; prospects of, 401–404
Thrashing of gods. *See* Ch'eng-huang
Three basic relations, 193
Ti huang shih (tutor of emperors), 383
Tibet, 216, 387
T'ien. *See* Heaven
T'ien-chu Chiao (Celestial Bamboo sect), 220
T'ien-hou, patron of sailing, 71, 72–73, 147; in Fo-shan district, 175–176
T'ien-kuan (Official of Heaven), 184
T'ien Li Hui (Heavenly Principle sect), 225, 243
T'ien-t'ai Mountain (Shansi province), 313
T'ien tao (Way of Heaven), 130, 273
T'ien tsai (natural calamity), 66
Tillich, Paul, 1, 118, 380, 381, 382, 403
Ting, I-hua, 357
Ting county (Hopei province): temples in, 6–7, 83; number and trade area of temple fairs in, 86; official and popular cults in, 147; number of priests in, 308, 310; priests' livelihood in, 319; new cult in, 353; conversion of temples to secular uses in, 369
Ting-hai district (Chekiang province), 169
Ting Wen-chiang, 365
T'o-pa Wei period, Buddhism in, 217
Trade patrons, 71–76; and diffused religion, 297
Translation of Buddhist literature, 119–120
Tree protection gods, 66
Tree spirit, 353
Triads, 62–64, 221
Tripitaka, 229–230, 338

Ts'ai, Yuan-p'ei, 364
Tsao-shen, 28
Tseng cheng ssu, 191
Tseng hui ssu, 191
Tseng kang ssu, 190
Tseng Kuo-fan, 198, 260
Tseng lu ssu, 190
Tseng Tzu, 45
Tsinghai province, 392
Tsinghua College, 366
Tso Chuan, 303
Tsung, 2
Tsung chiao (religion), 2
Tsung miao, 107
T'u-ti (earth god), 12, 16, 28, 31, 156; celebration of birthday, 90–91; merging with *she chi,* 97–98
T'ui Pei T'u, 235, 237
T'ung Chih (emperor, Ch'ing dynasty), 133
Tung Chung-shu, 108–110, 139–140, 253
Tung-kuang county (Hopei province), 400
T'ung-shan She (Fellowship of Goodness), 275–276
Turkistan, Chinese, 207
Tz'u (sanctuary), 161–177; nature of, 161–162
Tzu-fang (insect god), 68
Tz'u-hsi district (Chekiang province), 170

Ultimate concern, 380, 381, 382
Underworld, 31–33; cults of, 150, 156–158
Urban counties, temple building and repair in, 350–351
Ursa Major (star gods), 183, 270

Values: ultimate, 1, 26–27; Confucian, 26–27, 245, 279–280; in ancestor worship, 45–46; economic, 80; in festivals, 95; ethicopolitical, 147–149, 154–164 *passim,* 160–162, 166–168, 175–177; in divination, 262; in Buddhism, 280–281; in Taoism, 281–283; in mythology, 283–285.

See also Confucianism; Ethical values
Village organization and agricultural cults, 70–71
Voluntary religion, 110–112

Wach, Joachim, 1, 294
Wanchuan county, 7, 68, 215, 310, 313
Wang Ch'i-yuan, 357
Wang Ch'ung (Han), 48, 142, 248, 253, 257
Wang Mang, 131
Wang Ning-chih, 115
Wang Shu-hsün, persecution against, 186
Wang Ts'ung-hui, 289
Wang-tu county (Hopei province), 100, 102; number and types of temples in, 7, 8, 347; Chen-wu temple in, 153; number of priests in, 310; temple land in, 316; uses of temple income in, 325–326; temple building and repair in, 348
Wang Yü-chi'ing, 18
Warring States, 108
Way of man (*Jen tao*), 176–177
Way of the gods (*Shen tao*), 175–177
Wealth acquisition: gods of, 76–78; moral control of, 78–80
Weber, Max, 20, 80, 114, 130, 176, 218, 238
Weeping, ritualistic, 34–36
Wei dynasty, 201
Wei Hsien (Shantung province), 221
Wei liao hou-tai ("for posterity"), 385
Wen-ch'ang (literary god), 164, 184, 264, 270–272, 276
Wen T'ien-hsiang, 274
Wen Wu Kung (Palace for Civil and Military Officers), 163
Werefox, 284–285
West Town, 92
Western Hills, temple fair in, 87–88
Western Paradise, 230
White Lotus sect, rebellion of, 215, 219, 220, 222, 225, 226–227, 230, 233, 234, 241
Widowhood, 56